Open Resources for Community College Algebra (Part I)

Open Resources for Community College Algebra (Part I)

Portland Community College Faculty

August 5, 2019

Project Leads: Ann Cary, Alex Jordan, Ross Kouzes
Technology Engineer: Alex Jordan
Contributing Authors: Ann Cary, Alex Jordan, Ross Kouzes, Scot Leavitt, Cara Lee, Carl Yao, Ralf Youtz
WeBWorK Problem Coding: Chris Hughes, Alex Jordan, Carl Yao
Significant Contributors: Kara Colley, Wendy Lightheart
Cover Image: Ralf Youtz

Edition: 2.0

Website: pcc.edu/ORCCA

Acknowledgements

This book has been made possible through Portland Community College's Strategic Investment Funding, approved by PCC's Budget Planning Advisory Council and the Board of Directors. Without significant funding to provide the authors with the adequate time, an ambitious project such as this one would not be possible.

The technology that makes it possible to create integrated print, HTML eBook, and WeBWorK content is PreTeXt, created by Rob Beezer. David Farmer and the American Institute of Mathematics deserve credit for the PreTeXt HTML eBook layout being feature-rich, yet easy to navigate. A grant from OpenOregon funded the original bridge between WeBWorK and PreTeXt.

This book uses WeBWorK to provide most of its exercises, which may be used for online homework. WeBWorK was created by Mike Gage and Arnie Pizer, and has benefited from over 25 years of contributions from open source developers. In 2013, Chris Hughes, Alex Jordan, and Carl Yao programmed most of the WeBWorK questions in this book with a PCC curriculum development grant.

The javascript library MathJax, created and maintained by David Cervone, Volker Sorge, Christian Lawson-Perfect, and Peter Krautzberger allows math content to render nicely on screen in the HTML eBook. Additionally, MathJax makes web accessible mathematics possible.

The PDF versions are built using the typesetting software LaTeX, created by Donald Knuth and enhanced by Leslie Lamport.

Each of these open technologies, along with many that we use but have not listed here, has been enhanced by many additional contributors over the past 40 years. We are indebted to these contributors for their many contributions. By releasing this book with an open license, we honor their dedication to open software and open education.

To All

HTML, PDF, and print. This book is freely available as an HTML eBook, a PDF for reading on a screen, and a PDF intended for printing. Additionally, a printed and bound copy is available for purchase at low cost. All versions offer the same content and are synchronized such that cross-references match across versions. They can each be found at pcc.edu/orcca.

There are some differences between the HTML eBook, PDF screen version, and PDF-for-print version.

- The HTML eBook offers interactive elements, easier navigation than print, and its content is accessible in ways that a PDF cannot be. It has content (particularly in appendices) that is omitted from the PDF versions for the sake of economy. It requires no more software than a modern web browser with internet access.

- Two PDF versions can be downloaded and then accessed without the internet. One version is intended to be read on a screen with a PDF viewer. This version retains full color, has its text centered on the page, and includes hyperlinking. The other version is intended for printing on two-sided paper and then binding. Most of its color has been converted with care to gray scale. Text is positioned to the left or right of each page in a manner to support two-sided binding. Hyperlinks have been disabled.

- Printed and bound copies are available for purchase online. Up-to-date information about purchasing a copy should be available at pcc.edu/orcca. Contact orcca-group@pcc.edu if you have trouble finding the latest version online. Any royalties generated from these sales support OER development and maintenance at PCC and/or scholarships to PCC students.

Copying Content. The source files for this book are available through pcc.edu/orca, and openly licensed for use. However, it may be more conveneient to copy certain things directly from the HTML eBook.

The graphs and other images that appear in this manual may be copied in various file formats using the HTML eBook version. Below each image are links to .png, .eps, .svg, .pdf, and .tex files for the image.

Mathematical content can be copied from the HTML eBook. To copy math content into *MS Word*, right-click or control-click over the math content, and click to Show Math As MathML Code. Copy the resulting code, and Paste Special into *Word*. In the Paste Special menu, paste it as Unformatted Text. To copy math content into LaTeX source, right-click or control-click over the math content, and click to Show Math As TeX Commands.

Tables can be copied from the HTML eBook version and pasted into applications like *MS Word*. However, mathematical content within tables will not always paste correctly without a little extra effort as described above.

Accessibility. The HTML eBook version is intended to meet or exceed web accessibility standards. If you encounter an accessibility issue, please report it.

- All graphs and images should have meaningful alt text that communicates what a sighted person would see, without necessarily giving away anything that is intended to be deduced from the image.

- All math content is rendered using MathJax. MathJax has a contextual menu that can be accessed in several ways, depending on what operating system and browser you are using. The most common way is to right-click or control-click on some piece of math content.

- In the MathJax contextual menu, you may set options for triggering a zoom effect on math content, and also by what factor the zoom will be. Also in the MathJax contextual menu, you can enable the Explorer, which allows for sophisticated navigation of the math content.

- A screen reader will generally have success verbalizing the math content from MathJax. With certain screen reader and browser combinations, you may need to set some configuration settings in the MathJax contextual menu.

Tablets and Smartphones. PreTeXt documents like this book are "mobile-friendly." When you view the HTML version, the display adapts to whatever screen size or window size you are using. A math teacher will usually recommend that you do not study from the small screen on a phone, but if it's necessary, the HTML eBook gives you that option.

WeBWorK for Online Homework. Most exercises are available in a ready-to-use collection of WeBWorK problem sets. Visit webwork.pcc.edu/webwork2/orcca-demonstration to see a demonstration WeBWorK course where guest login is enabled. Anyone interested in using these problem sets may contact the project leads. The WeBWorK set defintion files and supporting files should be available for download from pcc.edu/orcca.

Odd Answers. The answers to the odd homework exercises at the end of each section are not printed in the PDF versions for economy. Instead, a separate PDF with the odd answers is available through pcc.edu/orcca. Additionally, the odd answers are printed in an appendix in the HTML eBook.

Interactive and Static Examples. Traditionally, a math textbook has examples throughout each section. This textbook uses two types of "example":

Static These are labeled "Example." Static examples may or may not be subdivided into a "statement" followed by a walk-through solution. This is basically what traditional examples from math textbooks do.

Active These are labeled "Checkpoint." In the HTML version, active examples have WeBWorK answer blanks where a reader may try submitting an answer. In the PDF output, active examples are almost indistinguishable from static examples, but there is a WeBWorK icon indicating that a reader could interact more actively using the eBook. Generally, a walk-through solution is provided immediately following the answer blank.

Some readers using the HTML eBook will skip the opportunity to try an active example and go straight to its solution. That is OK. Some readers will try an active example once and then move on to just read the solution. That is also OK. Some readers will tough it out for a period of time and resist reading the solution until they answer the active example themselves.

For readers of the PDF, the expectation is to read the example and its solution just as they would read a static example.

A reader is *not* required to try submitting an answer to an active example before moving on. A reader *is* expected to read the solution to an active example, even if they succeed on their own at finding an answer.

Reading Questions. Each section has a few "reading questions" immediately before the exercises. These may be treated as regular homework questions, but they are intended to be something more. The intention is that reading questions could be used in certain classroom models as a tool to encourage students to do their assigned reading, and as a tool to measure what basic concepts might have been misunderstood by students following the reading.

At some point it will be possible for students to log in to the HTML eBook and record answers to reading questions for an instructor to review. The infrastructure for that feature is not yet in place at the time of printing this edition, but please check pcc.edu/orcca for updates.

Alternative Video Lessons. Most sections open with an alternative video lesson (that is only visible in the HTML eBook). These video play lists are managed through a YouTube account, and it is possible to swap videos out for better ones at any time, provided that does not disrupt courses at PCC. Please contact us if you would like to submit a different video into these video collections.

Pedagogical Decisions

The authors and the greater PCC faculty have taken various stances on certain pedagogical and notational questions that arise in basic algebra instruction. We attempt to catalog these decisions here, although this list is certainly incomplete. If you find something in the book that runs contrary to these decisions, please let us know.

- Basic math is addressed in an appendix. For the course sequence taught at PCC, this content is pre-requisite and not within the scope of this book. However it is quite common for students in the basic algebra sequence to have skills deficiencies in these areas, so we include the basic math appendix. It should be understood that the content there does not attempt to teach basic math from first principles. It is itended to be more of a review.

- Interleaving is our preferred approach, compared to a proficiency-based approach. To us, this means that once the book covers a topic, that topic will be appear in subsequent sections and chapters in indirect ways.

- We round decimal results to four significant digits, or possibly fewer leaving out trailing zeros. We do this to maintain consistency with the most common level of precision that WeBWorK uses to assess decimal answers. We generally *round*, not *truncate*, and we use the $\approx$ symbol. For example, $\pi \approx 3.142$ and Portland's population is ≈ 609500. On rare occasions where it is the better option, we truncate and use an ellipsis. For example, $\pi = 3.141\ldots$.

- We offer *alternative* video lessons associated with each section, found at the top of most sections in the HTML eBook. We hope these videos provide readers with an alternative to whatever is in the reading, but there may be discrepancies here and there between the video content and reading content.

- We believe in opening a topic with some level of application rather than abstract examples, whenever that is possible. From applications and practical questions, we move to motivate more abstract defin-itions and notation. At first this may feel backwards to some instructors, with some easier examples *following* more difficult contextual examples.

- Linear inequalities are not strictly separated from linear equations. The section that teaches how to solve $2x + 3 = 8$ is immediately followed by the section teaching how to solve $2x + 3 < 8$. Our aim is to not treat inequalities as an add-on optional topic, but rather to show how intimately related they are to corresponding equations.

- When issues of "proper formatting" of student work arise, we value that the reader understand *why* such things help the reader to communicate outwardly. We believe that mathematics is about more than understanding a topic, but also about understanding it well enough to communicate results to others. For example we promote progression of equations like

$$1 + 1 + 1 = 2 + 1$$
$$= 3$$

instead of

$$1 + 1 + 1 = 2 + 1 = 3.$$

We want students to understand that the former method makes their work easier for a reader to read. It is not simply a matter of "this is the standard and this is how it's done."

- When solving equations (or systems of linear equations), most examples should come with a check, intended to communicate to students that checking is part of the process. In Chapters 1–4, these checks will be complete simplifications using order of operations one step at a time. The later sections may have more summary checks where steps are skipped or carried out together, or we promote entering expressions into a calculator to check.

- Within a section, any first context-free example of solving some equation (or system) should summarize with some variant of both "the solution is…" and "the solution set is…." Later examples can mix it up, but always offer at least one of these.

- With applications of linear equations (not including linear systems), we limit applications to situations where the setup will be in the form $x + \text{expression-in-}x = C$ and also to certain rate problems where the setup will be in the form $at + bt = C$. There are other classes of application problem (mixing problems, interest problems, …) which can be handled with a system of two equations, and we reserve these until linear systems are covered.

- With simplifications of rational expressions in one variable, we always include domain restrictions that are lost in the simplification. For example, we would write $\frac{x(x+1)}{x+1} = x$, for $x \neq -1$. With *multivariable* rational expressions, we are content to ignore domain restrictions lost during simplification.

Entering WeBWorK Answers

This preface offers some guidance with syntax for WeBWorK answers. WeBWorK answer blanks appear in the active reading examples (called "checkpoints") in the HTML eBook version of the book. If you are using WeBWorK for online homework, then you will also enter answers into WeBWorK answer blanks there.

Basic Arithmetic. The five basic arithmetic operations are: addition, subtraction, multiplication, and raising to a power. The symbols for addition and subtraction are $+$ and $-$, and both of these are directly avialable on most keyboards as + and -.

On paper, multiplication is sometimes written using $\times$ and sometimes written using $\cdot$ (a centered dot). Since these symbols are not available on most keyboards, WeBWorK uses * instead, which is often shift-8 on a full keyboard.

On paper, division is sometimes written using $\div$, sometimes written using a fraction layout like $\frac{4}{2}$, and sometimes written just using a slash, /. The slash is available on most full keyboards, near the question mark. WeBWorK uses / to indicate division.

On paper, raising to a power is written using a two-dimensional layout like 4^2. Since we don't have a way to directly type that with a simple keyboard, calculators and computers use the caret character, ^, as in 4^2. The character is usually shift-6.

Roots and Radicals. On paper, a square root is represented with a radical symbol like $\sqrt{}$. Since a keyboard does not usually have this symbol, WeBWorK and many computer applications use sqrt( ) instead. For example, to enter $\sqrt{17}$, type sqrt(17).

Higher-index radicals are written on paper like $\sqrt[4]{12}$. Again we have no direct way to write this using most keyboards. In *some* WeBWorK problems it is possible to type something like root(4, 12) for the fourth root of twelve. However this is not enabled for all WeBWorK problems.

As an alternative that you may learn about in a later chapter, $\sqrt[4]{12}$ is mathematically equal to $12^{1/4}$, so it can be typed as 12^(1/4). Take note of the parentheses, which very much matter.

Common Hiccups with Grouping Symbols. Suppose you wanted to enter $\frac{x+1}{2}$. You might type x+1/2, but this is not right. The computer will use the order of operations and do your division first, dividing 1 by 2. So the computer will see $x + \frac{1}{2}$. To address this, you would need to use grouping symbols like parentheses, and type something like (x+1)/2.

Suppose you wanted to enter $6^{1/4}$, and you typed 6^1/4. This is not right. The order of operations places a higher priority on exponentiation than division, so it calculates 6^1 first and then divides the result by 4. That is simply not the same as raising 6 to the $\frac{1}{4}$ power. Again the way to address this is to use grouping symbols, like 6^(1/4).

Entering Decimal Answers.   Often you will find a decimal answer with decimal places that go on and on. You are allowed to round, but not by too much. WeBWorK generally looks at how many *significant digits* you use, and generally expects you to use *four or more* correct significant digits.

"Significant digits" and "places past the decimal" are not the same thing. To count significant digits, read the number left to right and look for the first nonzero digit. Then count all the digits to the right including that first one.

The number 102.3 has four significant digits, but only one place past the decimal. This number could be a correct answer to a WeBWorK question. The number 0.0003 has one significant digit and four places past the decimal. This number might cause you trouble if you enter it, because maybe the "real" answer was 0.0003091, and rounding to 0.0003 was too much rounding.

Special Symbols.   There are a handful of special symbols that are easy to write on paper, but it's not clear how to type them. Here are WeBWorK's expectations.

Symbol	Name	How to Type
∞	infinity	infinity or inf
π	pi	pi
$\cup$	union	U
$\mathbb{R}$	the real numbers	R
$\mid$	such that	| (shift-\, where \ is above the enter key)
$\leq$	less than or equal to	<=
$\geq$	greater than or equal to	>=
$\neq$	not equal to	!=

Contents

Part I

Linear Equations and Lines

Chapter 1

Variables, Expressions, and Equations

1.1 Variables and Evaluating Expressions

Algebra helps people solve mathematical problems that are just a bit too complicated to solve in your head. This book is meant to cover basic principles and skills that people need to become successful with algebra. The first things to learn about are *variables, algebraic expressions, equations,* and *inequalities.* In this section, we'll focus on variables and expressions. In the remainder of this chapter, we'll focus on *equations* and *inequalities.*

1.1.1 Introduction to Variables

When we want to represent an unknown or changing numerical quantity, we use a **variable**. For example, if you'd like to discuss the gas mileage of various cars, you could use the symbol "g" as a variable to represent a car's gas mileage. The mileage might be 25 mpg, 30 mpg, or something else. ("mpg" stands for "miles per gallon".) If we agree to use mpg for the units of measure, g might be a place holder for 25, 30, or some other number. Since we are using a variable and not a specific number, we can discuss gas mileage for Honda Civics, Ford Explorers, and all other makes and models at the same time, even though these makes and models have different gas mileages.

When variables stand for actual physical quantities, it's good to use letters that clearly represent those quantities. For example, it's wise to use g to represent gas mileage. This helps the people who might read your work to understand it better.

It is also important to identify what unit of measurement goes along with each variable you use, and clearly tell your reader this. For example, suppose you are working with $g = 25$. A car whose gas mileage is 25 mpg is very different from a car whose gas mileage is 25 kpg (kilometers per gallon). So it would be important to tell readers that g represents gas mileage *in miles per gallon.*

Checkpoint 1.1.2 Identify a variable you might use to represent each quantity. Then identify what units would be most appropriate.

    a. Let [ ] be the age of a student, measured in [   ].

b. Let ☐ be the amount of time passed since a driver left Portland, Oregon, bound for Boise, Idaho, measured in ☐.

c. Let ☐ be the area of a two-bedroom apartment, measured in ☐.

Explanation.

a. The unknown quantity is age, which we generally measure in years. So we could say:

"Let a be the age of a student, measured in years."

b. The amount of time passed is the unknown quantity. Since this is a drive from Portland to Boise, it would make sense to measure this in hours. So we could say:

"Let t be the amount of time passed since a driver left Portland, Oregon, bound for Boise, Idaho, measured in hours."

c. The unknown quantity is area. Apartment area is usually measured in square feet. So we'll say:

"Let A be the area of a two-bedroom apartment, measured in ft^2."

Unless an algebra problem specifies which letter(s) to use, we may *choose* which letter(s) to use for our variable(s). However *without* any context to a problem, x, y, and z are the most common letters used as variables, and you may see these variables (especially x) a lot.

Also note that the units we use are often determined indirectly by other information given in an algebra problem. For example, if we're told that a car has used so many *gallons* of gas after traveling so many *miles*, then this suggests we should measure gas mileage in mpg.

1.1.2 Algebraic Expressions

An **algebraic expression** is any combination of variables and numbers using arithmetic operations. The following are all examples of algebraic expressions:

$$x + 1 \qquad 2\ell + 2w \qquad \frac{\sqrt{x}}{y+1} \qquad nRT$$

Note that this definition of "algebraic expression" does *not* include anything with an equals sign in it.

Example 1.1.3 The expression:

$$\frac{5}{9}(F - 32)$$

can be used to convert a temperature in degrees Fahrenheit to degrees Celsius. To do this, we need a Fahrenheit temperature, F. Then we can **evaluate** the expression. This means replacing its variable(s) (in this case, F) with specific numbers and finding the result as a single, simplified number.

Let's convert the temperature 89 °F to the Celsius scale by evaluating the expression.

$$\frac{5}{9}(F - 32) = \frac{5}{9}(89 - 32) \qquad \text{Review order of operations in A.5.}$$

$$= \frac{5}{9}(57) \qquad \text{Review fraction multiplication in A.2.}$$

$$= \frac{285}{9} \approx 31.67$$

This shows us that 89 °F is equivalent to approximately 31.67 °C.

Warning 1.1.4 Correct Vocabulary. The steps in Example 1.1.3 are not considered "solving" anything. "Solving" is a word you might be tempted to use, because in everyday English you are "finding an answer." In algebra, there is a special meaning for "solving" something, and that will come soon in Section 1.5. When we substitute values in for variables and then compute the result, the technical thing to say is we are "evaluating an expression."

Checkpoint 1.1.5 Try evaluating the temperature expression for yourself.

   a. If a temperature is 50°F, what is that temperature measured in Celsius?

   b. If a temperature is −20°F, what is that temperature measured in Celsius?

Explanation.

a.
$$\frac{5}{9}(F - 32) = \frac{5}{9}(50 - 32)$$
$$= \frac{5}{9}(18)$$
$$= \frac{5}{1}(2)$$
$$= 10$$

So 50°F is equavalent to 10°C.

b.
$$\frac{5}{9}(F - 32) = \frac{5}{9}(-20 - 32)$$
$$= \frac{5}{9}(-52)$$
$$= -\frac{260}{9}$$
$$\approx -28.89$$

So −20°F is equavalent to about −28.89°C.

Example 1.1.6 Allowing Variables to Vary. With the help of technology, it is possible to quickly evaluate expressions as variables vary. In the GeoGebra applet in Figure 1.1.7, you may slide the value of F and see how a computer can quickly calculate the correspoding Celsius temperature.

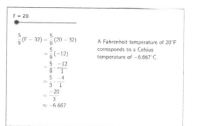

Figure 1.1.7: Allowing Variables to Vary

Example 1.1.8 Target heart rate. According to the American Heart Association, a person's maximum heart rate, in beats per minute (bpm), is given by $220 - a$, where a is their age in years.

   a. Determine the maximum heart rate for someone who is 31 years old.

   b. A person's *target* heart rate for moderate exercise is 50% to 70% of their maximum heart rate. If they want to reach 65% of their maximum heart rate during moderate exercise, we'd use the expression $0.65(220-a)$, where a is their age in years. Determine the target heart rate at this 65% level for someone who is 31 years old.

Explanation. Both parts ask us to evaluate an expression.

a. Since a is defined as age in years, we evaluate this expression by substituting a with 31:

$$220 - a = 220 - 31$$
$$= 189$$

This tells us that the maximum heart rate for someone who is 31 years old is 189 bpm.

b. We again substitute a with 31, but this time using the target heart rate expression:

$$0.65(220 - a) = 0.65(220 - 31)$$
$$= 0.65(189)$$
$$= 122.85$$

This tells us that the target heart rate for someone who is 31 years old undertaking moderate exercise is 122.85 bpm.

Checkpoint 1.1.9 We can use the expression $\frac{p}{100}(220 - a)$ to represent a person's target heart rate when their target rate is $p\%$ of their maximum heart rate, and they are a years old.

Determine the target heart rate at the 53% level for moderate exercise for someone who is 56 years old.

At the 53% level, the target heart rate for moderate exercise for someone who is 56 years old is ⬚ beats per minute.

Explanation. The expression is $\frac{p}{100}(220 - a)$, and we must sustitute in 53 for p and 56 for a.

$$\frac{p}{100}(220 - a) = \frac{53}{100}(220 - 56)$$
$$= \frac{53}{100}(164)$$
$$= \frac{53}{25}(41)$$
$$= 86.92$$

So at the 53% level, the target heart rate for moderate exercise for someone who is 56 years old is 86.92 beats per minute.

Checkpoint 1.1.10 Rising Rents. From January, 2011, to October, 2016, an expression estimating the average rent of a one-bedroom apartment in Portland, Oregon, is given by $10.173x + 974.78$, where x is the number of months since January, 2011.

a. According to this model, what was the average rent of a one-bedroom apartment in Portland in January, 2011?

b. According to this model, what was the average rent of a one-bedroom apartment in Portland in January, 2016?

Explanation.

a. This model uses x as the number of months since January, 2011. So for January, 2011, x is 0:

$$10.173x + 974.48 = 10.173(0) + 974.48$$
$$\approx 974.48$$

According to this model, the average monthly rent for a one-bedroom apartment in Portland, Oregon, in January, 2011, was $974.78.

b. The date we are given is January, 2016, which is 5 years after January, 2011. Recall that x is the number of *months* since January, 2011. So we need to use $x = 5 \cdot 12 = 60$:

$$10.173x + 974.48 = 10.173(60) + 974.48$$
$$\approx 1584.86$$

According to this model, the average monthly rent for a one-bedroom apartment in Portland, Oregon, in January, 2016, was $1584.86.

1.1.3 Evaluating Expressions with Exponents, Absolute Value, and Radicals

Algebraic expressions will often have exponents, absolute value bars, and radicals. This does not change the basic approach to evaluating them.

Example 1.1.11 Tsunami Speed. The speed of a tsunami (in meters per second) can be modeled by $\sqrt{9.8d}$, where d is the depth of the tsunami (in meters). Determine the speed of a tsunami that has a depth of 30 m to four significant digits.

Explanation.   Using $d = 30$, we find:

$$\sqrt{9.8d} = \sqrt{9.8(30)}$$ Review order of operations in A.5.
$$= \sqrt{294}$$ Review square root in A.3.
$$\approx \overbrace{17.14}^{\text{four}}6428\ldots$$

The speed of tsunami with a depth of 30 m is about $17.15\ \frac{m}{s}$.

Up to now, we have been evaluating expressions, but we can evaluate formulas in the same way. A **formula** usually has a single variable that represents the output of an expression. For example, the expression for a person's maximum heart rate in beats per minute, $220 - a$, can be written as the formula, $H = 220 - a$. When we substitute a value for a we are "evaluating" the formula.

Checkpoint 1.1.12 Tent Height. While camping, the height inside a tent when you are d feet from the north side of the tent is given by the formula $h = -2|d - 3| + 6$, where h is in feet.

a. When you are 5 ft from the north side, the height is [   ].

b. When you are 2.5 ft from the north side, the height is [   ].

Explanation.

a. When $d = 5$, we have:

$$h = -2|d - 3| + 6$$
$$= -2|5 - 3| + 6 \quad \text{Review order of operations in A.5.}$$
$$= -2|2| + 6 \quad \quad \text{Review absolute value in A.3.}$$
$$= -2(2) + 6$$
$$= -4 + 6$$
$$= 2$$

So when you are 5 ft from the north side, the height of the tent is 2 ft.

b. When $d = 2.5$, we have:

$$h = -2|d - 3| + 6$$
$$= -2|2.5 - 3| + 6$$
$$= -2|-0.5| + 6$$
$$= -2(0.5) + 6$$
$$= -1 + 6$$
$$= 5$$

So when you are 2.5 ft from the north side, the height of the tent is 5 ft.

Checkpoint 1.1.13 Mortgage Payments. If we borrow L dollars for a home mortgage loan at an annual interest rate r, and intend to pay off the loan after n months, then the amount we should pay each month M, in dollars, is given by the formula

$$M = \frac{rL\left(1 + \frac{r}{12}\right)^n}{12\left(\left(1 + \frac{r}{12}\right)^n - 1\right)}$$

If we borrow \$200,000 at an interest rate of 6% with the intent to pay off the loan in 30 years, what should our monthly payment be? (Using a calculator is appropriate here.)

Explanation. We must use $L = 200000$. Because the interest rate is a percentage, $r = 0.06$ (not 6). The variable n is supposed to be a number of *months*, but we will pay off the loan in 30 *years*. Therefore we take $n = 360$.

$$M = \frac{rL\left(1 + \frac{r}{12}\right)^n}{12\left(\left(1 + \frac{r}{12}\right)^n - 1\right)} = \frac{(0.06)(200000)\left(1 + \frac{0.06}{12}\right)^{360}}{12\left(\left(1 + \frac{0.06}{12}\right)^{360} - 1\right)}$$

$$= \frac{(0.06)(200000)(1 + 0.005)^{360}}{12\left((1 + 0.005)^{360} - 1\right)}$$

$$\approx \frac{(0.06)(200000)(6.022575\ldots)}{12\left(6.022575\ldots - 1\right)}$$

$$\approx \frac{(0.06)(200000)(6.022575\ldots)}{12(5.022575\ldots)}$$

$$\approx \frac{72270.90\ldots}{60.2709\ldots}$$

$$\approx 1199.10$$

Our monthly payment should be \$1,199.10.

Warning 1.1.14 Rounding Too Much. You might have noticed in the explanation to Exercise 1.1.13 that during the computations, many decimal places were recorded at each step. Recording lots of decimal places might be very important in some computations. If you round in the middle of your work, you have changed the numbers a little bit from what they *really* should be. As computations proceed, this little error can become larger and larger, leaving you with a final result that is too far off to be considered correct. So the best practice is to always keep lots of decimal places in all your computations, and then at the very end you may round more if that is appropriate.

1.1.4 Evaluating Expressions with Negative Numbers

When we substitute negative numbers into an expression, it's important to use parentheses around them or else it's easy to forget that a *negative* number is being raised to a power.

Example 1.1.15 Evaluate x^2 if $x = -2$.
  We substitute:

$$x^2 = (-2)^2$$
$$= 4$$

If we don't use parentheses, we would have:

$$x^2 = -2^2 \qquad \text{incorrect!}$$
$$= -4$$

The original expression, x^2, takes x and squares it, so we want to do the same thing to the number -2. But with -2^2, the number -2 is not being squared. Since the exponent has higher priority than the negation in the order of operations, it's just the number 2 that is being squared and then the result is negated. With $(-2)^2$ the number -2 *is* being squared, which is what we want.
  So it is wise to always use some parentheses when substituting in any negative number.

Checkpoint 1.1.16 Evaluate and simplify the following expressions for $x = -5$ and $y = -2$:
  a. $x^3 y^2$ b. $(-2x)^3$ c. $-3x^2 y$

Explanation.   You may review multiplying negative numbers in Section A.1.

a. $x^3 y^2 = (-5)^3(-2)^2$ b. $(-2x)^3 = (-2(-5))^3$ c. $-3x^2 y = -3(-5)^2(-2)$
  $ = (-125)(4)$ $ = (10)^3$ $ = -3(25)(-2)$
  $ = -500$ $ = 1000$ $ = 150$

1.1.5 Reading Questions

1. Describe a situation where it might be better to use a letter other than x, y, or z as a variable.

2. What is the difference between an "algebraic expression" and a "formula," as described in this section? (Other math resources may define these terms differently.)

3. What should you watch out for when substituting a negative number in for a variable?

4. In Figure 1.1.7, when you change the value of F, why do some values of F cause there to be more steps in the calculation than other values of F?

1.1.6 Exercises

1. Identify a variable you might use to represent each quantity. Then identify what units would be most appropriate.

    a. Let ☐ be the depth of a swimming pool, measured in ☐.

    b. Let ☐ be the weight of a dog, measured in ☐.

2. Identify a variable you might use to represent each quantity. Then identify what units would be most appropriate.

    a. Let ☐ be the amount of time a person sleeps each night, measured in ☐.

    b. Let ☐ be the surface area of a patio, measured in ☐.

Evaluating Expressions

3. Evaluate $x - 4$ for $x = -6$.

4. Evaluate $x + 9$ for $x = -4$.

5. Evaluate $2 - x$ for $x = -1$.

6. Evaluate $-5 - x$ for $x = 1$.

7. Evaluate $8x - 10$ for $x = 3$.

8. Evaluate $x - 1$ for $x = 6$.

9. Evaluate $-9p$ for $p = -6$.

10. Evaluate $-4q$ for $q = 7$.

11. Evaluate the expression x^2:

    a. For $x = 6$.

    b. For $x = -7$.

12. Evaluate the expression x^2:

    a. For $x = 3$.

    b. For $x = -2$.

13. Evaluate the expression $-y^2$:

    a. For $y = 5$.

    b. For $y = -4$.

14. Evaluate the expression $-y^2$:

    a. For $y = 3$.

    b. For $y = -5$.

15. Evaluate the expression r^3:

    a. For $r = 2$.

    b. For $r = -3$.

16. Evaluate the expression r^3:

    a. For $r = 5$.

    b. For $r = -5$.

17. a. Evaluate $5x^2$ when $x = 2$.

    b. Evaluate $(5x)^2$ when $x = 2$.

18. a. Evaluate $3x^2$ when $x = 2$.

    b. Evaluate $(3x)^2$ when $x = 2$.

19. Evaluate $-10(t + 7)$ for $t = 5$.

20. Evaluate $-6(x + 5)$ for $x = -3$.

21. Evaluate $\dfrac{9x - 9}{6x}$ for $x = -10$.

22. Evaluate $\dfrac{4y - 2}{6y}$ for $y = 4$.

23. Evaluate $-5c - 2b$ for $c = 4$ and $b = 2$.

24. Evaluate $6A - 3C$ for $A = -8$ and $C = -4$.

25. Evaluate $\dfrac{-6}{C} - \dfrac{7}{A}$ for $C = 5$ and $A = -6$.

26. Evaluate $\dfrac{-5}{m} - \dfrac{7}{b}$ for $m = 2$ and $b = -6$.

27. Evaluate $\dfrac{-4p + 4C - 10}{4p - 3C}$ for $p = -3$ and $C = -1$.

28. Evaluate $\dfrac{-q + 6A + 2}{-8q + 7A}$ for $q = 6$ and $A = -6$.

29. Evaluate $(y + 6)^2 + 8$ for $y = -5$.

30. Evaluate $\frac{1}{6}(r - 2)^2 + 3$ for $r = 8$.

31. Evaluate $-\left(9a^2 + 2a + 2\right)$ for $a = 1$.

32. Evaluate $-\left(c^2 + 8c + 2\right)$ for $c = -6$.

33. Evaluate $(7A)^3$ for $A = -2$.

34. Evaluate $(-5C)^3$ for $C = -5$.

35. Evaluate $(5m)^2$ for $m = 2$.

36. Evaluate $(-8p)^3$ for $p = 8$.

37. Evaluate $\sqrt{q + 4} - 3$ for $q = 21$.

38. Evaluate $\sqrt{y + 8} - 1$ for $y = -4$.

39. Evaluate $-\left(4\sqrt{r - 3} + 7\right)$ for $r = 52$.

40. Evaluate $7 - 4\sqrt{a + 5}$ for $a = 11$.

41. Evaluate $|b - 6| + 2$ for $b = -8$.

42. Evaluate $|A + 2| - 3$ for $A = 4$.

43. Evaluate $-(5|C - 9| + 9)$ for $C = -2$.

44. Evaluate $5 - 5|m - 1|$ for $m = -9$.

45. Evaluate $\dfrac{y_2 - y_1}{x_2 - x_1}$ for $x_1 = 8$, $x_2 = 3$, $y_1 = 8$, and $y_2 = -1$.

46. Evaluate $\dfrac{y_2 - y_1}{x_2 - x_1}$ for $x_1 = 10$, $x_2 = -4$, $y_1 = -5$, and $y_2 = -6$.

47. Evaluate $\sqrt{(x_2 - x_1)^2 + (y_2 - y_1)^2}$ for $x_1 = 4$, $x_2 = 12$, $y_1 = -7$, and $y_2 = -13$.

48. Evaluate $\sqrt{(x_2 - x_1)^2 + (y_2 - y_1)^2}$ for $x_1 = -8$, $x_2 = 0$, $y_1 = -7$, and $y_2 = -1$.

49. Evaluate the algebraic expression $-5a + b$ for $a = \frac{3}{4}$ and $b = \frac{5}{3}$.

50. Evaluate the algebraic expression $-7a + b$ for $a = \frac{4}{9}$ and $b = \frac{9}{2}$.

51. Evaluate each algebraic expression for the given value(s):
$\dfrac{5 + 2|y - x|}{x + 2y}$, for $x = 12$ and $y = 13$:

52. Evaluate each algebraic expression for the given value(s):
$\dfrac{4 + 2|y - x|}{x + 4y}$, for $x = 6$ and $y = -13$:

To convert a temperature measured in degrees Fahrenheit to degrees Celsius, there is a formula:

$$C = \frac{5}{9}(F - 32)$$

where C represents the temperature in degrees Celsius and F represents the temperature in degrees Fahrenheit.

53. If a temperature is $95°F$, what is that temperature measured in Celsius?

54. If a temperature is $113°F$, what is that temperature measured in Celsius?

55. A formula for converting miles into kilometers is

$$K = 1.61M$$

where M is a number of miles, and K is the corresponding number of kilometers. Use the formula to find the number of kilometers that corresponds to six miles.

_____ kilometers corresponds to six miles.

56. A formula for converting pounds into kilograms is

$$K = 0.45P$$

where P is a number of pounds, and K is the corresponding number of kilograms. Use the formula to find the number of kilograms that corresponds to eighteen pounds.

_____ kilograms corresponds to eighteen pounds.

The formula

$$y = \frac{1}{2} a t^2 + v_0 t + y_0$$

gives the vertical position of an object, at time t, thrown with an initial velocity v_0, from an initial position y_0 in a place where the acceleration of gravity is a. The acceleration of gravity on earth is $-9.8 \frac{m}{s^2}$. It is negative, because we consider the upward direction as positive in this situation, and gravity pulls down.

57. What is the height of a baseball thrown with an initial velocity of $v_0 = 60 \frac{m}{s}$, from an initial position of $y_0 = 76$ m, and at time $t = 12$ s?

Twelve seconds after the baseball was thrown, it was ⬚ high in the air.

58. What is the height of a baseball thrown with an initial velocity of $v_0 = 65 \frac{m}{s}$, from an initial position of $y_0 = 58$ m, and at time $t = 4$ s?

Four seconds after the baseball was thrown, it was ⬚ high in the air.

The percentage of births in the U.S. delivered via C-section can be given by the following formula for the years since 1996:

$$p = 0.8(y - 1996) + 21$$

In this formula y is a year after 1996 and p is the percentage of births delivered via C-section for that year.

59. What percentage of births in the U.S. were delivered via C-section in the year 2004?

⬚ of births in the U.S. were delivered via C-section in the year 2004.

60. What percentage of births in the U.S. were delivered via C-section in the year 2006?

⬚ of births in the U.S. were delivered via C-section in the year 2006.

Target heart rate for moderate exercise is 50% to 70% of maximum heart rate. If we want to represent a certain percent of an individual's maximum heart rate, we'd use the formula

$$\text{rate} = p(220 - a)$$

where p is the percent, and a is age in years.

61. Determine the target heart rate at 63% level for someone who is 17 years old. Round your answer to an integer.

The target heart rate at 63% level for someone who is 17 years old is

⬚ beats per minute.

62. Determine the target heart rate at 65% level for someone who is 57 years old. Round your answer to an integer.

The target heart rate at 65% level for someone who is 57 years old is

⬚ beats per minute.

The diagonal length (D) of a rectangle with side lengths L and W is given by:

$$D = \sqrt{L^2 + W^2}$$

63. Determine the diagonal length of rectangles with $L = 24$ ft and $W = 7$ ft.

The diagonal length of rectangles with $L = 24$ ft and $W = 7$ ft is ⬚ .

64. Determine the diagonal length of rectangles with $L = 21$ ft and $W = 20$ ft.

The diagonal length of rectangles with $L = 21$ ft and $W = 20$ ft is ⬚ .

65. The height inside a camping tent when you are d feet from the edge of the tent is given by

$$h = -2|d - 4.2| + 7$$

where h stands for height in feet. Determine the height when you are:

a. 6.7 ft from the edge.

The height inside a camping tent when you are 6.7 ft from the edge of the tent is ⬚ .

b. 3.2 ft from the edge.

The height inside a camping tent when you are 3.2 ft from the edge of the tent is ⬚ .

66. The height inside a camping tent when you are d feet from the edge of the tent is given by

$$h = -1.5|d - 4.6| + 7$$

where h stands for height in feet. Determine the height when you are:

a. 6.2 ft from the edge.

The height inside a camping tent when you are 6.2 ft from the edge of the tent is ⬚ .

b. 2.2 ft from the edge.

The height inside a camping tent when you are 2.2 ft from the edge of the tent is ⬚ .

67. The height inside a camping tent when you are d ft from the edge of the tent is given by:

$$-1.5|d - 4| + 6$$

Determine the height when you are:

(a) 2 ft from the edge

(b) 6.5 ft from the edge

68. The diagonal length of a rectangle with side lengths L and W is given by:

$$\sqrt{L^2 + W^2}$$

Determine the diagonal length of rectangles with:

(a) length 5 cm and width 12 cm

(b) length 4 ft and width 10 ft

1.2 Combining Like Terms

In Section 1.1, we worked with algebraic expressions. Algebraic expressions can be large and complicated, and anything we can do to write the same expression in a simplified form is helpful. The most basic skill for simplfying an algebraic expression is finding parts of the expression that have a certain something in common that allows them to be combined into one. *Combining like terms* is the topic of this section.

1.2.1 Identifying Terms

Definition 1.2.2 In an algebraic expression, the **terms** are quantities being added together.   ◇

Example 1.2.3 List the terms in the expression $2\ell + 2w$.

Explanation.   The expression has two terms that are being added, 2ℓ and $2w$.

If there is any subtraction, we can rewrite the expression using addition to make it easier to see exactly what the terms are and what sign each term has.

Example 1.2.4 List the terms in the expression $-3x^2 + 5x - 4$.

Explanation.   We can rewrite this expression as $-3x^2 + 5x + (-4)$ to see that the terms are $-3x^2$, $5x$, and -4.

   Once you learn to recognize that subtraction represents a negative term, you don't need to rewrite subtraction as addition.

Example 1.2.5 List the terms in the expression $3\,\text{cm} + 2\,\text{cm} - 3\,\text{cm} + 2\,\text{cm}$.

Explanation.   This expression has four terms: $3\,\text{cm}$, $2\,\text{cm}$, $-3\,\text{cm}$, and $2\,\text{cm}$.

Checkpoint 1.2.6 List the terms in the expression $5x - 4x + 10z$.

Explanation.   The terms are $5x$, $-4x$, and $10z$.

1.2.2 Combining Like Terms

In the examples above, you may have wanted to combine terms in some cases. For example, if you have $3\,\text{cm} + 2\,\text{cm}$, it is natural to add those together to get $5\,\text{cm}$. That works because their units (cm) are the same. This idea applies to some other kinds of terms that don't have units. For example, with $2x + 3x$, we have 2 *somethings* and then we have 3 more of the same thing. All together, we have 5 of those things. So $2x + 3x$ is the same as $5x$.

   Terms in an algebraic expression that can be combined like these last examples are called **like terms**.

- Sometimes terms are like terms because they have the same variable, like with $2x + 3x$, which simplfies to $5x$.

- Sometimes terms are like terms because they have the same units, like with $3\,\text{cm} + 2\,\text{cm}$, which simplfies to $5\,\text{cm}$.

- Sometimes terms are like terms because they have something else in common, like with $3\sqrt{7} + 2\sqrt{7}$, which simplfies to $5\sqrt{7}$.

Example 1.2.7 In the expressions below, look for like terms and then simplify where possible by adding or subtracting.

    a. $5\,\text{in} + 20\,\text{in}$

    b. $16\,\text{ft}^2 + 4\,\text{ft}$

    c. $2\,🍎 + 5\,🍎$

    d. $5\,\text{min} + 50\,\text{ft}$

    e. $5\,🐶 - 2\,🐱$

    f. $20\,\text{m} - 6\,\text{m}$

Explanation. We can combine terms with the same units, but we cannot combine units such as minutes and feet, or cats and dogs. We can combine the like terms by adding or subtracting their numerical parts.

    a. $5\,\text{in} + 20\,\text{in} = 25\,\text{in}$

    b. $16\,\text{ft}^2 + 4\,\text{ft}$ cannot be simplified

    c. $2\,🍎 + 5\,🍎 = 7\,🍎$

    d. $5\,\text{min} + 50\,\text{ft}$ cannot be simplified

    e. $5\,🐶 - 2\,🐱$ cannot be simplified

    f. $20\,\text{m} - 6\,\text{m} = 14\,\text{m}$

One of the examples from Example 1.2.7 was $16\,\text{ft}^2 + 4\,\text{ft}$. The units on these two terms may look similar, but they are very different. $16\,\text{ft}^2$ is a measurement of how much area something has. $4\,\text{ft}$ is a measurement of how long something is. Figure 1.2.8 illustrates this.

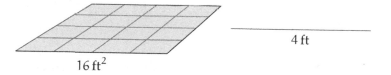

$16\,\text{ft}^2$ $4\,\text{ft}$

Figure 1.2.8: There is no way to add $16\,\text{ft}^2$ to $4\,\text{ft}$.

Checkpoint 1.2.9 Which expressions have like terms that you can combine?

    a. $10x + 3y$ (☐ can   ☐ cannot)   be combined.

    b. $4x - 8x$ (☐ can   ☐ cannot)   be combined.

    c. $9y - 4y$ (☐ can   ☐ cannot)   be combined.

    d. $-6x + 17z$ (☐ can   ☐ cannot)   be combined.

    e. $-3x - 7x$ (☐ can   ☐ cannot)   be combined.

    f. $5t + 8t^2$ (☐ can   ☐ cannot)   be combined.

Explanation. The terms that we can combine have the same variable part, including any exponents.

    a. $10x + 3y$ cannot be combined.

    b. $4x - 8x = -4x$

    c. $9y - 4y = 5y$

    d. $-6x + 17z$ cannot be combined.

    e. $-3x - 7x = -10x$

    f. $5t + 8t^2$ cannot be combined.

Example 1.2.10 Simplify the expression $20x - 16x + 4y$, if possible, by combining like terms.

Explanation. This expression has two like terms, $20x$ and $-16x$, which we can combine.

$$20x - 16x + 4y = 4x + 4y$$

Note that we cannot combine $4x$ and $4y$ because x and y are different.

Example 1.2.11 Simplify the expression $100x + 100x^2$, if possible, by combining like terms.

Explanation.   This expression cannot be simplified because the variable parts are not the same. We cannot add x and x^2 just like we cannot add feet (a measure of length) and square feet (a measure of area).

Example 1.2.12 Simplify the expression $-10r + 2s - 5t$, if possible, by combining like terms.

Explanation.   This expression cannot be simplified because there are not any like terms.

Example 1.2.13 Simplify the expression $y + 5y$, if possible, by combining like terms.

Explanation.   This expression can be thought of as $1y + 5y$. When we have a single y, the numerical part 1 is not usually written. Now we have two like terms, $1y$ and $5y$. We will add those together:

$$y + 5y = 1y + 5y$$
$$= 6y$$

So far we have combined terms with whole numbers and integers, but we can also combine like terms when the numerical parts are decimals or fractions.

Example 1.2.14 Simplify the expression $x - 0.15x$, if possible, by combining like terms.

Explanation.   Note that this expression can be rewritten as $1.00x - 0.15x$, and combined like this:

$$x - 0.15x = 1.00x - 0.15x$$
$$= 0.85x$$

Checkpoint 1.2.15 Simplify each expression, if possible, by combining like terms.
  a. $x + 0.25x$

  b. $\frac{4}{9}x - \frac{7}{10}y + \frac{2}{3}x$

  c. $\frac{5}{6}y - \frac{8}{15}y + \frac{2}{3}x^2$

  d. $4x + 1.5y - 9z$

Explanation.

  a. Rewrite this expression as $1.00x + 0.25x$ and simplify to get $1.25x$.

  b. This expression has two like terms that can be combined: $\frac{4}{9}x$ and $\frac{2}{3}x$. To combine them, we need to add the fractions $\frac{4}{9} + \frac{2}{3}$. (You may find a review of fraction addition in Section A.2.) Here, we have

$$\frac{4}{9} + \frac{2}{3} = \frac{4}{9} + \frac{6}{9}$$
$$= \frac{10}{9}$$

  so $\frac{4}{9}x + \frac{2}{3}x = \frac{10}{9}x$. And together with the third term, the answer is $\frac{10}{9}x - \frac{7}{10}y$.

  c. In this expression we can combine the y terms, but we need to subtract the fractions $\frac{5}{6} - \frac{8}{15}$. (You may find a review of fraction subtraction in Section A.2.) Here, we have

$$\frac{5}{6} - \frac{8}{15} = \frac{25}{30} - \frac{16}{30}$$
$$= \frac{9}{30}$$
$$= \frac{3}{10}$$

so $\frac{5}{6}y - \frac{8}{15}y = \frac{3}{10}y$. And together with the third term, the answer is $\frac{3}{10}y + \frac{2}{3}x^2$.

d. This expression cannot be simplified further because there are not any like terms.

Remark 1.2.16 The Difference Between Terms and Factors. We have learned that terms are quantities that are added, such as $3x$ and $-2x$ in $3x - 2x$. These are different from **factors**, which are parts that are multiplied together. For example, the term $2x$ has two factors: 2 and x (with the multiplication symbol implied between them). The term $2\pi r$ has three factors: 2, π, and r.

1.2.3 Reading Questions

1. What should you be careful with when there is subtraction in an algebraic expression and you are identifying its terms?

2. Describe at least two different ways in which a pair of terms are considered to be "like terms."

3. Describe the difference between "terms" and "factors" in an algebraic expression. Give examples.

1.2.4 Exercises

Review and Warmup

1. Add the following.
   a. $4 + (-6)$
   b. $6 + (-2)$
   c. $9 + (-9)$

2. Add the following.
   a. $4 + (-7)$
   b. $9 + (-3)$
   c. $9 + (-9)$

3. Add the following.
   a. $-9 + 5$
   b. $-4 + 5$
   c. $-2 + 2$

4. Add the following.
   a. $-6 + 5$
   b. $-2 + 8$
   c. $-2 + 2$

5. Subtract the following.
   a. $1 - 9$
   b. $10 - 2$
   c. $6 - 17$

6. Subtract the following.
   a. $1 - 7$
   b. $7 - 1$
   c. $6 - 12$

7. Subtract the following.
   a. $-4 - 5$
   b. $-7 - 5$
   c. $-4 - 4$

8. Subtract the following.
   a. $-3 - 1$
   b. $-7 - 4$
   c. $-9 - 9$

9. Subtract the following.
   a. $-3 - (-6)$
   b. $-8 - (-1)$
   c. $-5 - (-5)$

10. Subtract the following.
    a. $-4 - (-8)$
    b. $-5 - (-1)$
    c. $-5 - (-5)$

Counting, Identifying, and Combining Terms Count the number of terms in each expression.

11. a. $-5t - 9y - 5x - 5x^2$

    b. $5x^2 + 8 - 8s^2$

    c. $3y - 8x$

    d. $4z + 2s^2 + 6y^2 - 7s$

13. a. $-2t + 8.3x - 3.6y + 3y$

    b. $-y^2 - 2s^2 + 4.5x$

    c. $6.6y - 2.1y$

    d. $-4.3x$

12. a. $3t + 5s - 4y + 6t^2$

    b. $-4z^2 - 9y^2$

    c. $3t^2 + 5y^2 + 4y + 7$

    d. $-2y - 6t^2 - y$

14. a. $-t$

    b. $-8.9z - 1.8y + 8.1s$

    c. $-1.8x - 5.3 + 6.2y + 8.4$

    d. $-8.5z - 8.2 + 4.9s + 3.4$

List the terms in each expression.

15. a. $t + 7s^2$

    b. $-8t$

    c. $z + 9z$

    d. $4s^2 - y - 8s + 3$

17. a. $4.5t + 4.9t$

    b. $0.7s^2 + 2.4t - 8.1x$

    c. $7.4t + 5.1y + 5.1s - 5x^2$

    d. $-6.5z$

19. a. $3.2t + 7.7 - 6.3y^2$

    b. $9t + 8.9s + 8.6s + 7.5$

    c. $2.3z^2 + 7t - 1.6s$

    d. $-7.5t^2 - 6.1t^2$

16. a. $-5t - 4x$

    b. $-7x^2 + 5 - 4t - 8y$

    c. $-5y^2 - 8x^2 - 9y^2$

    d. $3t^2 - 5x^2$

18. a. $-7.8t^2 + 0.5t + 1.6x^2$

    b. $-5.5y$

    c. $1.8z + 2y$

    d. $3.4t + 7y + 0.1s - 5.6s$

20. a. $5.2t^2 - 3.2x + 8.6x^2 + 0.1s$

    b. $7.5z + 1.1x^2$

    c. $-5.8t^2 - 3.9z^2$

    d. $5.4z + 5.9y + 9z^2$

Simplify each expression, if possible, by combining like terms.

21. a. $-8t + 2t$

    b. $4z + 7z$

    c. $-5z + 8z$

    d. $9y^2 + 3x^2$

22. a. $4t - 9s$

    b. $5x - z$

    c. $6s - 9s$

    d. $2x + 5x$

23. a. $-4z + 3z$

b. $6x - 9x^2 - 3x$

c. $-7t^2 - 6s + 7t^2$

d. $7z^2 - 7s^2 + 4z$

24. a. $z + 9s$

b. $8x^2 + 9s + 2t^2 - 2t$

c. $9t^2 - 6y - 5z^2 - 9x$

d. $9s - 8s$

25. a. $-8z - 21s^2$

b. $94s^2 + 70s + 51s$

c. $-50z - 51z$

d. $-90y - 70y + 38y + 44$

26. a. $-36z + 14z^2 + 92s^2$

b. $40x^2 + 99x$

c. $-18x^2 + 91y^2 - 70s^2 + 59x^2$

d. $-5t^2 + 46y^2 + 99t^2$

27. a. $2.5z - 3.6z + 4.6z^2$

b. $3.9x^2 - 3.5x + 1.1x + 8.9x$

c. $3.7z^2 - 0.4z^2$

d. $-4.3z + 4.4z$

28. a. $-6.7z^2 + 6t - 8.1t$

b. $5.9y - 7.3t + 2t$

c. $-6.5y^2 - 2.8t^2 - 7.5s^2$

d. $-8.2y^2 + 4.5z^2$

29. a. $6z - \frac{1}{7}z + 4z$

b. $\frac{7}{3}y - \frac{1}{2}y^2$

c. $\frac{3}{7}t^2 - \frac{1}{2}x^2 + \frac{6}{5}x^2 + \frac{2}{7}x$

d. $y + 2y - \frac{5}{8}y + 3y$

30. a. $-\frac{8}{3}z^2 - 7z^2 + 3 + \frac{3}{4}z^2$

b. $-t + 2y + \frac{1}{3}t - \frac{1}{7}x$

c. $-y - 2y$

d. $s + \frac{1}{3} - \frac{4}{9}t$

31. a. $-3z + \frac{2}{3}z + 7z - \frac{2}{5}z$

b. $\frac{8}{5}z - \frac{8}{3}x^2 + \frac{3}{2}z^2$

c. $-x + \frac{7}{2}t - s$

d. $\frac{5}{9}z - 6t$

32. a. $9z^2 + \frac{6}{5}z^2$

b. $\frac{4}{3}t - \frac{4}{3}t$

c. $\frac{3}{2}x + \frac{1}{2}z - \frac{1}{3}y$

d. $\frac{5}{8}s + \frac{3}{4}s + s - \frac{3}{2}s$

1.3 Comparison Symbols and Notation for Intervals

As you know, 8 is larger than 3; that's a specific comparison between two numbers. We can also make a comparison between two less specific numbers, like if we say that average rent in Portland in 2016 is larger than it was in 2009. That makes a comparison using unspecified amounts. In the first half of this section, we will go over the mathematical shorthand notation for making these kinds of comparisons.

In Oregon in 2019, only people who are 18 years old or older can vote in statewide elections.[1] Does that seem like a statement about the number 18? Maybe. But it's also a statement about numbers like 37 and 62: it says that people of these ages may vote as well. So the above is actually a statement about a large collection of numbers, not just 18. In the second half of this section, we will get into the mathematical notation for large collections of numbers like this.

1.3.1 Comparison Symbols

In everyday language you can say something like "8 is larger than 3." In mathematical writing, it's not convenient to write that out in English. Instead the symbol ">" has been adopted, and it's used like this:

$$8 > 3$$

and read out loud as "8 is greater than 3." The symbol ">" is called the **greater-than symbol.**

Checkpoint 1.3.2

    a. Use mathematical notation to write "11.5 is greater than 4.2."

    b. Use mathematical notation to write "age is greater than 20."

Explanation.

    a. $11.5 > 4.2$

    b. We can just write the word age to represent age, and write $age > 20$. Or we could use an abbreviation like a for age, and write $a > 20$. Or, it is common to use x as a generic abbreviation, and we could write $x > 20$.

Remark 1.3.3 At some point in history, someone felt that $>$ was a good symbol for "is greater than." In "$8 > 3$," the tall side of the symbol is with the larger of the two numbers, and the small pointed side is with the smaller of the two numbers.

Another way to remember how the greater-than symbol works is to imagine the symbol as the open mouth of an alligator, or whatever your favorite animal is. And then remind yourself that the alligator is hungry and it wants to eat the larger number.

We have to be careful when negative numbers are part of the comparison. Is -8 larger or smaller than -3? In some sense -8 is larger, because if you owe someone 8 dollars, that's *more* than owing them 3 dollars. But that is not how the $>$ symbol works. This symbol is meant to tell you which number is farther to the right on a number line. And if that's how it goes, then -3 is larger.

---

[1]Some states like Washington allow 17-year-olds to vote in primary elections provided they will be 18 by the general election.

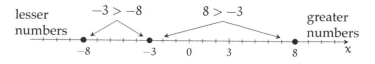

Figure 1.3.4: How the > symbol works.

Checkpoint 1.3.5 Use the > symbol to arrange the following numbers in order from greatest to least. For example, your answer might look like 4 > 3 > 2 > 1 > 0.

$$-7.6 \quad 6 \quad -6 \quad 9.5 \quad 8$$

Explanation. We can order these numbers by placing these numbers on a number line.

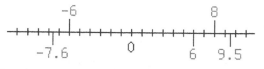

And so we see the answer is $9.5 > 8 > 6 > -6 > -7.6$.

Checkpoint 1.3.6 Use the > symbol to arrange the following numbers in order from greatest to least. For example, your answer might look like 4 > 3 > 2 > 1 > 0.

$$-5.2 \quad \pi \quad \frac{10}{3} \quad 4.6 \quad 8$$

Explanation. We can order these numbers by placing these numbers on a number line. Knowing or computing their decimals helps with this: $\pi \approx 3.141\ldots$ and $\frac{10}{3} \approx 3.333\ldots$.

And so we see the answer is $8 > 4.6 > 3.33333 > 3.14159 > -5.2$.

The greater-than symbol has a close relative, the **greater-than-or-equal-to symbol,** "≥." It means just like it sounds: the first number is either greater than the second number or equal to it. These are all true statements:

$$8 \geq 3 \qquad\qquad 3 \geq -8 \qquad\qquad 3 \geq 3$$

but one of these three statements is false:

$$8 > 3 \qquad\qquad 3 > -8 \qquad\qquad 3 \overset{no}{>} 3$$

Remark 1.3.7 While it may not seem helpful to write $3 \geq 3$ when you could write $3 = 3$, the ≥ symbol is quite useful when specific numbers aren't used on at least one side, like in these examples:

$$\text{(hourly pay rate)} \geq \text{(minimum wage)} \qquad\qquad \text{(age of a voter)} \geq 18$$

Sometimes you want to emphasize that one number is *less than* another number instead of emphasizing which number is greater. To do this, we have symbols that are reversed from > and ≥. The symbol "<" is the **less-than symbol** and it's used like this:

$$3 < 8$$

and read out loud as "3 is less than 8." To help remember which symbol is the "less than" sign and which is the "greater than" sign, notice that you can make a *Less* than sign with your *Left* hand.

Table 1.3.8 gives the complete list of all six comparison symbols. Note that we've only discussed three in this section so far, but you already know the equals symbol and have likely also seen the symbol "$\neq$," which means "not equal to."

Symbol	Means	True	True	False
$=$	equals	$13 = 13$	$\frac{5}{4} = 1.25$	$5 \overset{no}{=} 6$
$>$	is greater than	$13 > 11$	$\pi > 3$	$9 \overset{no}{>} 9$
$\geq$	is greater than or equal to	$13 \geq 11$	$3 \geq 3$	$10.2 \overset{no}{\geq} 11.2$
$<$	is less than	$-3 < 8$	$\frac{1}{2} < \frac{2}{3}$	$2 \overset{no}{<} -2$
$\leq$	is less than or equal to	$-3 \leq 8$	$3 \leq 3$	$\frac{4}{5} \overset{no}{\leq} \frac{3}{5}$
$\neq$	is not equal to	$10 \neq 20$	$\frac{1}{2} \neq 1.2$	$\frac{3}{8} \overset{no}{\neq} 0.375$

Table 1.3.8: Comparison Symbols

1.3.2 Set-Builder and Interval Notation

If you say

$$(\text{age of a voter}) \geq 18$$

and have a particular voter in mind, what is that person's age? *Maybe* they are 18, but maybe they are older. It's helpful to use a variable a to represent age (in years) and then to visualize the possibilities with a number line, as in Figure 1.3.9.

Figure 1.3.9: (age of a voter) ≥ 18

The shaded portion of the number line in Figure 1.3.9 is a mathematical **interval**. For now, that just means a collection of certain numbers. In this case, it's all the numbers 18 and above.

The number line in Figure 1.3.9 is a *graphical* representation of a collection of certain numbers. We have two notations, set-builder notation and interval notation, that we also use to represent such collections of numbers.

Definition 1.3.10 Set-Builder Notation. Set-builder notation attempts to directly tell you the condition that numbers in the interval satisfy. In general, we write set-builder notation like:

$$\{x \mid \text{condition on } x\}$$

and read it out loud as "the set of all x such that ...." For example,

$$\{x \mid x \geq 18\}$$

is read out loud as "the set of all x such that x is greater than or equal to 18." The breakdown is as follows.

$\{x \mid x \geq 18\}$ the set of
$\{x \mid x \geq 18\}$ all x
$\{x \mid x \geq 18\}$ such that
$\{x \mid x \geq 18\}$ x is greater than or equal to 18

◇

Definition 1.3.11 Interval Notation. Interval notation describes a collection of numbers by telling you where the collection "starts" and "stops". For example, in Figure 1.3.9, the interval starts at 18. To the right, the interval extends forever and has no end, so we use the ∞ symbol (meaning "infinity"). This particular interval is denoted:

$$[18, \infty)$$

Why use "[" on one side and ")" on the other? The square bracket tells us that 18 *is* part of the interval and the round parenthesis tells us that ∞ is *not* part of the interval. (And how could it be, since ∞ is not even a number?)

There are four types of infinite intervals. Take note of the different uses of round parentheses and square brackets.

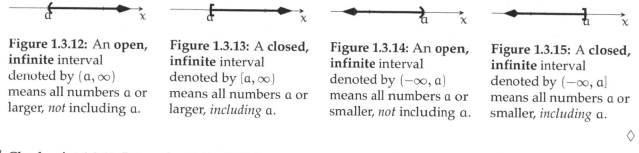

Figure 1.3.12: An **open, infinite** interval denoted by (a, ∞) means all numbers a or larger, *not* including a.

Figure 1.3.13: A **closed, infinite** interval denoted by $[a, \infty)$ means all numbers a or larger, *including* a.

Figure 1.3.14: An **open, infinite** interval denoted by $(-\infty, a)$ means all numbers a or smaller, *not* including a.

Figure 1.3.15: A **closed, infinite** interval denoted by $(-\infty, a]$ means all numbers a or smaller, *including* a.

◇

Checkpoint 1.3.16 Interval and Set-Builder Notation from Number Lines. For each interval expressed in the number lines, give the interval notation and set-builder notation.

a.

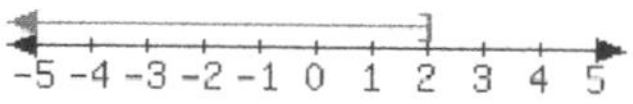

b.

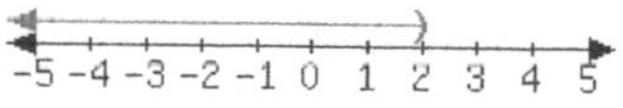

c.

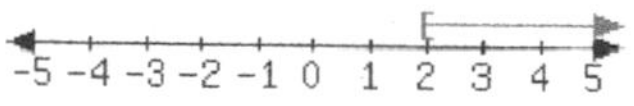

Explanation.

a. Since all numbers less than or equal to 2 are shaded, the set-builder notation is $\{x \mid x \leq 2\}$. The shaded interval "starts" at $-\infty$ and ends at 2 (including 2) so the interval notation is $(-\infty, 2]$.

b. Since all numbers less than to 2 are shaded, the set-builder notation is $\{x \mid x < 2\}$. The shaded interval "starts" at $-\infty$ and ends at 2 (excluding 2) so the interval notation is $(-\infty, 2)$.

c. Since all numbers greater than or equal to 2 are shaded, the set-builder notation is $\{x \mid x \geq 2\}$. The shaded interval starts at 2 (including 2) and "ends" at ∞, so the interval notation is $[2, \infty)$.

Remark 1.3.17 Alternative Convention for Sketching Intervals. When graphing an interval, an alternative convention is to use open circles and filled-in circles. An open circle can be used in place of a round parenthesis, and a filled-in circle can be used in place of a square bracket, as in this example which corresponds to the interval $(a, b]$.

1.3.3 Reading Questions

1.   How many inequality symbols are there?

2.   What is the difference between the interval $[3, \infty)$ and the interval $(3, \infty)$? More generally, what do square brackets and round parentheses mean in the context of interval notation?

3.   The set of numbers $\{x \mid x \leq 10\}$ is being expressed using notation.

1.3.4 Exercises

Review and Warmup

1.   Write the decimal number as a fraction.
      0.65

2.   Write the decimal number as a fraction.
      0.75

3.   Write the decimal number as a fraction.
      8.85

4.   Write the decimal number as a fraction.
      9.45

5.   Write the decimal number as a fraction.
      0.108

6.   Write the decimal number as a fraction.
      0.274

7.   Write the fraction as a decimal number.

      a. $\frac{4}{5}$

      b. $\frac{7}{8}$

8.   Write the fraction as a decimal number.

      a. $\frac{5}{8}$

      b. $\frac{1}{4}$

9.   Write the mixed number as a decimal number.

      a. $3\frac{5}{16} = $ _____

      b. $1\frac{11}{20} = $ _____

10.   Write the mixed number as a decimal number.

      a. $3\frac{1}{16} = $ _____

      b. $1\frac{1}{8} = $ _____

Ordering Numbers Use the $>$ symbol to arrange the following numbers in order from greatest to least. For example, your answer might look like $4 > 3 > 2 > 1 > 0$.

11.
         5   −10   −1   7   −5

12.
            7   3   8   −1   −6

13.
      9.02   −3.9   −4.17   −4.71   −4.81

14.
         −8.8   8.8   3.47   7.64   −8.7

15.
      −7   3 $-\frac{39}{5}$ 5 $-\frac{33}{7}$

16.
         $-\frac{31}{4}$ $\frac{1}{2}$ $\frac{26}{3}$ −9   −7

17.
      $\frac{1}{3}$ 9 π −2 $\frac{2}{3}$ $\frac{\pi}{2}$

18.
         2    $\frac{1}{3}$ $\frac{\pi}{2}$ 0 $\sqrt{2}$ $\frac{1}{2}$

True/False

19. Decide if each comparison is true or false.

   a. $-8 = -9$ ($\square$ True $\square$ False)

   b. $-1 \neq -1$ ($\square$ True $\square$ False)

   c. $-6 > -6$ ($\square$ True $\square$ False)

   d. $-10 \neq 9$ ($\square$ True $\square$ False)

   e. $7 \geq -5$ ($\square$ True $\square$ False)

   f. $2 = 2$ ($\square$ True $\square$ False)

20. Decide if each comparison is true or false.

   a. $-8 \leq -8$ ($\square$ True $\square$ False)

   b. $-7 \geq -7$ ($\square$ True $\square$ False)

   c. $-7 \leq 5$ ($\square$ True $\square$ False)

   d. $0 < -4$ ($\square$ True $\square$ False)

   e. $7 > 7$ ($\square$ True $\square$ False)

   f. $-10 \neq -10$ ($\square$ True $\square$ False)

21. Decide if each comparison is true or false.

   a. $-\frac{1}{9} > -\frac{2}{18}$ ($\square$ True $\square$ False)

   b. $-\frac{20}{6} = \frac{20}{6}$ ($\square$ True $\square$ False)

   c. $\frac{0}{7} \neq \frac{0}{7}$ ($\square$ True $\square$ False)

   d. $\frac{6}{9} = \frac{6}{9}$ ($\square$ True $\square$ False)

   e. $-\frac{10}{5} < -\frac{20}{10}$ ($\square$ True $\square$ False)

   f. $-\frac{5}{2} > \frac{43}{8}$ ($\square$ True $\square$ False)

22. Decide if each comparison is true or false.

   a. $-\frac{10}{3} \geq -\frac{30}{9}$ ($\square$ True $\square$ False)

   b. $\frac{31}{4} = \frac{11}{6}$ ($\square$ True $\square$ False)

   c. $\frac{5}{3} < \frac{19}{8}$ ($\square$ True $\square$ False)

   d. $\frac{8}{4} = \frac{16}{8}$ ($\square$ True $\square$ False),

   e. $-\frac{62}{7} \leq \frac{47}{8}$ ($\square$ True $\square$ False)

   f. $\frac{43}{5} \neq -\frac{3}{2}$ ($\square$ True $\square$ False)

Comparisons Choose $<$, $>$, or $=$ to make a true statement.

23. $-\frac{9}{8}$ ($\square<$ $\square>$ $\square=$) $-\frac{5}{3}$

24. $-\frac{8}{5}$ ($\square<$ $\square>$ $\square=$) $-\frac{2}{3}$

25. $\frac{2}{3} + \frac{5}{2}$ ($\square<$ $\square>$ $\square=$) $\frac{3}{4} \div \frac{3}{5}$

26. $\frac{2}{5} + \frac{4}{3}$ ($\square<$ $\square>$ $\square=$) $\frac{1}{5} \div \frac{4}{5}$

27. $\frac{10}{9} \div \frac{10}{9}$ ($\square<$ $\square>$ $\square=$) $\frac{4}{10} - \frac{2}{5}$

28. $\frac{12}{11} \div \frac{12}{11}$ ($\square<$ $\square>$ $\square=$) $\frac{5}{10} - \frac{1}{2}$

29. $-5\frac{2}{3}$ ($\square<$ $\square>$ $\square=$) -5

30. $-9\frac{1}{2}$ ($\square<$ $\square>$ $\square=$) -9

31. $-9\frac{1}{2}$ ($\square<$ $\square>$ $\square=$) 3

32. $-2\frac{1}{3}$ ($\square<$ $\square>$ $\square=$) 1

33. $\left|-\frac{3}{4}\right|$ ($\square<$ $\square>$ $\square=$) $|0.75|$

34. $\left|-\frac{2}{5}\right|$ ($\square<$ $\square>$ $\square=$) $|0.4|$

Set-builder and Interval Notation For each interval expressed in the number lines, give the interval notation and set-builder notation.

35.

   a.   b.   c.

36.

   a.   b.   c.

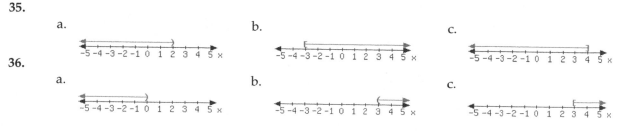

For the interval expressed in the number line, write it using set-builder notation and interval notation.

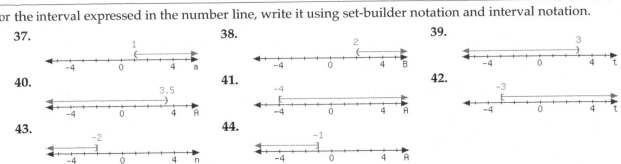

37.

38.

39.

40.

41.

42.

43.

44.

Convert to Interval Notation A set is written using set-builder notation. Write it using interval notation.

45. $\{x \mid x \le -7\}$ **46.** $\{x \mid x \le 2\}$ **47.** $\{x \mid x \ge 5\}$ **48.** $\{x \mid x \ge 7\}$

49. $\{x \mid x < 9\}$ **50.** $\{x \mid x < -9\}$ **51.** $\{x \mid x > -7\}$ **52.** $\{x \mid x > -5\}$

53. $\{x \mid -3 > x\}$ **54.** $\{x \mid -9 > x\}$ **55.** $\{x \mid 2 \ge x\}$ **56.** $\{x \mid 4 \ge x\}$

57. $\{x \mid 7 \le x\}$ **58.** $\{x \mid 9 \le x\}$ **59.** $\{x \mid -10 < x\}$ **60.** $\{x \mid -7 < x\}$

61. $\left\{x \mid \dfrac{3}{7} < x\right\}$ **62.** $\left\{x \mid \dfrac{4}{7} < x\right\}$ **63.** $\left\{x \mid x \le -\dfrac{5}{3}\right\}$ **64.** $\left\{x \mid x \le -\dfrac{6}{7}\right\}$

65. $\{x \mid x \le 0\}$ **66.** $\{x \mid 0 < x\}$

1.4 Equations and Inequalities as True/False Statements

This section introduces the concepts of algebraic *equations* and *inequalities*, and what it means for a number to be a *solution* to an equation or inequality.

1.4.1 Equations, Inequalities, and Solutions

An **equation** is two algebraic expressions with an equals sign between them. The two expressions can be relatively simple or more complicated:

A simple equation:

$$x + 1 = 2$$

A more complicated equation:

$$\left(x^2 + y^2 - 1\right)^3 = x^2 y^3$$

An **inequality** is similar to an equation, but the sign between the expressions is $<$, $\leq$, $>$, $\geq$, or $\neq$.

A simple inequality:

$$x \geq 15$$

A more complicated inequality:

$$x^2 + y^2 < 1$$

The simplest equations and inequalities have numbers and no variables. When this happens, the equation is either *true* or *false*. The following equations and inequalities are *true* statements:

$$2 = 2 \qquad -4 = -4 \qquad 2 > 1 \qquad -2 < -1 \qquad 3 \geq 3$$

The following equations and inequalities are *false* statements:

$$2 = 1 \qquad -4 = 4 \qquad 2 < 1 \qquad -2 \geq -1 \qquad 0 \neq 0$$

There will be times when doing algebra will lead us to an equation like $2 = 1$, which of course we know to be a false equation. To recognize that this is false, we will write $1 \stackrel{no}{=} 2$. This is different from writing $1 \neq 2$, because that is a *true* inequality. And when we want to explicitly recognize that an equation or inequality is true, we will use a checkmark, like with $2 \stackrel{\checkmark}{=} 2$.

A **linear expression** in one variable is an expression in the form $ax + b$, where a and b are numbers, $a \neq 0$, and x is a variable. For example, $2x + 1$ and $3y + \frac{1}{2}$ are linear expressions.

The following examples are a little harder to identify as linear expressions in one variable, but they are.

- $2x$ is linear, with $b = 0$.

- $y + 3$ is linear, with $a = 1$.

- $17 - q$ is linear, with $a = -1$, $b = 17$ and the two terms are written in reverse order.

- $2.1t + 3 + 8t - 1.4$ is linear (because it simplifies to $10.1t + 1.6$).

Definition 1.4.2 Linear Equation and Linear Inequality. A **linear equation** in one variable is any equation where one side is a linear expression in that variable, and the other side is either a constant number, or is another linear expression in that variable. A **linear inequality** in one variable is defined similarly, just with an inequality symbol instead of an equals sign. $\diamond$

The following are some linear equations in one variable:

$$4 - y = 5 \qquad\qquad 4 - z = 5z \qquad\qquad 0 = \frac{1}{2}p$$

$$3 - 2(q + 2) = 10 \qquad\qquad \sqrt{2}r + 3 = 10 \qquad\qquad \frac{s}{2} + 3 = 5$$

(Note that r is outside the square root symbol.)

In a linear equation in one variable, the variable cannot appear with an exponent (other than 1 or 0), and the variable cannot be inside a root symbol (square root, cube root, etc.), absolute value bars, or in a denominator.

The following are not linear equations in one variable:

$$1 + 2 = 3 \qquad\qquad \text{(There is no variable.)}$$
$$4 - 2y^2 = 5 \qquad\qquad \text{(The exponent of } y \text{ is 2.)}$$
$$\sqrt{2r} + 3 = 10 \qquad\qquad \text{(}r \text{ is inside the square root.)}$$
$$\frac{2}{s} + 3 = 5 \qquad\qquad \text{(}s \text{ is in a denominator.)}$$

Equations arise from real-world math problems, sometimes from simple problems, and sometimes from hard ones.

Example 1.4.3 A parking meter requires you pay \$2.50 for one hour. You have been inserting quarters, dimes, and nickels into the meter, and it says that you have inserted \$1.85. How much more do you need to pay?

You might have a simple way to answer that question, using subtraction. But there is an equation hidden in this story. Since we are asked "How much more do you need to pay?", let's use a variable to represent that: x. We've already paid \$1.85, and in total we need to pay \$2.50. So we need

$$1.85 + x = 2.50$$

This is an equation arising from this scenario.

With the equation in Example 1.4.3, if we substitute in 0.65 for x, the resulting equation is true.

$$1.85 + 0.65 \overset{\checkmark}{=} 2.50$$

If we substitute in any other number for x, the resulting equation is false. This motivates what it means to be a *solution* to an equation.

Definition 1.4.4 When an equation (or inequality) has one variable, a **solution** is any number that you could substitute in for the variable that would result in a true equation (or inequality). ◇

Example 1.4.5 A Solution. Consider the equation $y + 2 = 3$, which has only one variable, y. If we substitute in 1 for y and then simplify:

$$y + 2 = 3$$
$$1 + 2 \overset{?}{=} 3$$
$$3 \overset{\checkmark}{=} 3$$

we get a true equation. So we say that 1 is a solution to $y + 2 = 3$. Notice that we used a question mark at first because we are unsure if the equation is true or false until the end.

If replacing a variable with a value makes a false equation or inequality, that number is not a solution.

Example 1.4.6 Not a Solution. Consider the inequality $x + 4 > 5$, which has only one variable, x. If we substitute in 0 for x and then simplify:

$$x + 4 > 5$$
$$0 + 4 \overset{?}{>} 5$$
$$4 \overset{no}{>} 5$$

we get a false inequality. So we say that 0 is *not* a solution to $x + 4 > 5$.

Example 1.4.7 Allowing Variables to Vary. With the help of technology, it is possible to quickly evaluate expressions as variables vary. In the GeoGebra applet in Figure 1.4.8, you may slide the value of q and see how a computer can quickly calculate each side of the equation to determine if that value of q is a solution.

$q = 0$ Can you find a solution to this equation using the slider?

$$10q^2 - 36 = 40 - 18q$$
$$10(0)^2 - 36 \overset{?}{=} 40 - 18(0)$$
$$-36 \overset{no}{=} 40$$

Figure 1.4.8: Allowing Variables to Vary

1.4.2 Checking Possible Solutions

Given an equation or an inequality (with one variable), checking if some particular number is a solution is just a matter of replacing the value of the variable with the specified number and determining if the resulting equation/inequality is true or false. This may involve some arithmetic and simplification.

Example 1.4.9 Is 8 a solution to $x^2 - 5x = \sqrt{2x} + 20$?
   To find out, substitute in 8 for x and see what happens.

$$x^2 - 5x = \sqrt{2x} + 20$$
$$8^2 - 5(8) \overset{?}{=} \sqrt{2(8)} + 20$$
$$64 - 5(8) \overset{?}{=} \sqrt{16} + 20$$
$$64 - 40 \overset{?}{=} 4 + 20$$
$$24 \overset{\checkmark}{=} 24$$

So yes, 8 is a solution to $x^2 - 5x = \sqrt{2x} + 20$.

Example 1.4.10 Is -5 a solution to $\sqrt{169 - y^2} = y^2 - 2y$?
   To find out, substitute in -5 for y and see what happens.

$$\sqrt{169 - y^2} = y^2 - 2y$$

$$\sqrt{169 - (-5)^2} \overset{?}{=} (-5)^2 - 2(-5)$$

$$\sqrt{169 - 25} \overset{?}{=} 25 - 2(-5)$$

$$\sqrt{144} \overset{?}{=} 25 - (-10)$$

$$12 \overset{\text{no}}{=} 35$$

So no, -5 is not a solution to $\sqrt{169 - y^2} = y^2 - 2y$.
   But is -5 a solution to the *inequality* $\sqrt{169 - y^2} \leq y^2 - 2y$? Yes, because substituting -5 in for y would give you

$$12 \leq 35,$$

which is true.

Checkpoint 1.4.11 Is -3 a solution for x in the equation $2x - 3 = 5 - (4 + x)$? Evaluating the left and right sides gives:

$$2x - 3 \quad \underset{\overset{?}{=}}{\underline{}} \quad 5 - (4 + x)$$

So -3 ($\square$ is $\square$ is not)   a solution to $2x - 3 = 5 - (4 + x)$.

Explanation.   We will substitute x with -3 in the equation and simplify each side to determine if the statement is true or false:

$$2x - 3 = 5 - (4 + x)$$

$$2(-3) - 3 \overset{?}{=} 5 - (4 + (-3))$$

$$-6 - 3 \overset{?}{=} 5 - (1)$$

$$-9 \overset{\text{no}}{=} 4$$

Since $-9 = 4$ is not true, -3 is not a solution for x in the equation $2x - 3 = 5 - (4 + x)$.

Checkpoint 1.4.12 Is $\frac{1}{3}$ a solution for t in the equation $2t = 4\left(t - \frac{1}{2}\right)$? Evaluating the left and right sides gives:

$$2t \quad \underset{\overset{?}{=}}{\underline{}} \quad 4\left(t - \frac{1}{2}\right)$$

So $\frac{1}{3}$ ($\square$ is $\square$ is not)   a solution to $2t = 4\left(t - \frac{1}{2}\right)$.

Explanation.   We will substitute t with $\frac{1}{3}$ in the equation and simplify each side to determine if the statement is true or false:

$$2t = 4\left(t - \frac{1}{2}\right)$$

$$2\left(\frac{1}{3}\right) \overset{?}{=} 4\left(\frac{1}{3} - \frac{1}{2}\right)$$

This is not going to be true, since the left side is positive and the right side is negative. So $\frac{1}{3}$ is not a solution for t in the equation $2t = 4\left(t - \frac{1}{2}\right)$.

Checkpoint 1.4.13 Is -2 a solution to $y^2 + y - 5 \leq y - 1$? Evaluating the left and right sides gives:

$$y^2 + y - 5 \quad\underset{\overset{?}{\leq}}{\leq}\quad y - 1$$

$$\underline{\hspace{3em}} \quad \overset{?}{\leq} \quad \underline{\hspace{3em}}$$

So -2 ($\square$ is $\square$ is not)   a solution to $y^2 + y - 5 \leq y - 1$.

Explanation.   We will substitute y with -2 in the inequality and simplify each side to determine if the statement is true or false:

$$y^2 + y - 5 \leq y - 1$$

$$(-2)^2 + (-2) - 5 \overset{?}{\leq} -2 - 1$$

$$4 - 2 - 5 \overset{?}{\leq} -3$$

$$2 - 5 \overset{?}{\leq} -3$$

$$-3 \overset{\checkmark}{\leq} -3$$

This is true. So -2 is a solution for y in the inequality $y^2 + y - 5 \leq y - 1$.

Checkpoint 1.4.14 Is 2 a solution to $\frac{z+3}{z-1} = \sqrt{18z}$? Evaluating the left and right sides gives:

$$\frac{z+3}{z-1} \quad = \quad \sqrt{18z}$$

$$\underline{\hspace{3em}} \quad \overset{?}{=} \quad \underline{\hspace{3em}}$$

So 2 ($\square$ is $\square$ is not)   a solution to $\frac{z+3}{z-1} = \sqrt{18z}$.

Explanation.   We will substitute z with 2 in the equation and simplify each side to determine if the statement is true or false:

$$\frac{z+3}{z-1} = \sqrt{18z}$$

$$\frac{2+3}{2-1} \overset{?}{=} \sqrt{18(2)}$$

$$\frac{5}{1} \overset{?}{=} \sqrt{36}$$

$$5 \overset{no}{=} 6$$

The equation is false. So 2 is not a solution for z in the equation $\frac{z+3}{z-1} = \sqrt{18z}$.

Checkpoint 1.4.15 Is -3 a solution to $x^2 + x + 1 = \frac{3x+2}{x+2}$? Evaluating the left and right sides gives:

$$x^2 + x + 1 \quad = \quad \frac{3x+2}{x+2}$$

$$\underline{\hspace{3em}} \quad \overset{?}{=} \quad \underline{\hspace{3em}}$$

So -3 ($\square$ is $\square$ is not)   a solution to $x^2 + x + 1 = \frac{3x+2}{x+2}$.

. We will substitute x with -3 in the equation and simplify each side to determine if the statement is true or false:

$$x^2 + x + 1 = \frac{3x + 2}{x + 2}$$

$$(-3)^2 + (-3) + 1 \overset{?}{=} \frac{3(-3) + 2}{-3 + 2}$$

$$9 - 3 + 1 \overset{?}{=} \frac{-9 + 2}{-1}$$

$$6 + 1 \overset{?}{=} \frac{-7}{-1}$$

$$7 \overset{\checkmark}{=} 7$$

This is true. So -3 is a solution for x in the inequality $x^2 + x + 1 \leq \frac{3x+2}{x+2}$.

Example 1.4.16 Cylinder Volume.

A cylinder's volume is related to its radius and its height by:

$$V = \pi r^2 h,$$

where V is the volume, r is the base's radius, and h is the height. If we know the volume is $96\pi\,\text{cm}^3$ and the radius is $4\,\text{cm}$, then we have:

$$96\pi = 16\pi h$$

Is $4\,\text{cm}$ the height of the cylinder? In other words, is 4 a solution to $96\pi = 16\pi h$? We will substitute h in the equation with 4 to check:

$$96\pi = 16\pi h$$

$$96\pi \overset{?}{=} 16\pi \cdot 4$$

$$96\pi \overset{no}{=} 64\pi$$

Since $96\pi = 64\pi$ is false, $h = 4$ does *not* satisfy the equation $96\pi = 16\pi h$.
   Next, we will try $h = 6$:

$$96\pi = 16\pi h$$

$$96\pi \overset{?}{=} 16\pi \cdot 6$$

$$96\pi \overset{\checkmark}{=} 96\pi$$

When $h = 6$, the equation $96\pi = 16\pi h$ is true. This tells us that 6 *is* a solution to $96\pi = 16\pi h$.

Remark 1.4.17 Note that we did not approximate π with 3.14 or any other approximation. We often leave π as π throughout our calculations. If we need to round, we do so as a final step.

Example 1.4.18 Jaylen has budgeted a maximum of $300 for an appliance repair. The total cost of the repair can be modeled by $89 + 110(h - 0.25)$, where $89 is the initial cost and $110 is the hourly labor charge after the first quarter hour. Is 2 hours a solution for h in the inequality $89 + 110(h - 0.25) \leq 300$?

To determine if $h = 2$ satisfies the inequality, we will replace h with 2 and check if the statement is true:

$$89 + 110(h - 0.25) \leq 300$$

$$89 + 110(2 - 0.25) \overset{?}{\leq} 300$$

$$89 + 110(1.75) \overset{?}{\leq} 300$$

$$89 + 192.5 \overset{?}{\leq} 300$$

$$281.5 \overset{\checkmark}{\leq} 300$$

So we find that 2 is a solution for h in the inequality $89 + 110(h - 0.25) \leq 300$. In context, this means that Jaylen would stay within their \$300 budget if there is only 2 hours of labor.

1.4.3 Reading Questions

1. Is the equation in Example 1.4.3, $1.85 + x = 2.50$, a linear equation?

2. Give your own example of an equation in one variable that is not a linear equation.

3. Do you believe it is possible for an inequality to have more than one solution? Do you believe it is possible for an equation to have more than one solution?

4. There are two solutions to the equation in Example 1.4.7. What are they?

1.4.4 Exercises

Review and Warmup

1. Evaluate $6 - x$ for $x = 0$.

2. Evaluate $-1 - x$ for $x = 2$.

3. Evaluate $-8x + 5$ for $x = 4$.

4. Evaluate $5x - 8$ for $x = 7$.

5. Evaluate $-5(t + 9)$ for $t = -2$.

6. Evaluate $-(x + 6)$ for $x = -9$.

7. Evaluate the expression $\frac{1}{7}(x + 1)^2 - 7$ when $x = -8$.

8. Evaluate the expression $\frac{1}{3}(x + 2)^2 - 4$ when $x = -5$.

9. Evaluate the expression $-16t^2 + 64t + 128$ when $t = -2$.

10. Evaluate the expression $-16t^2 + 64t + 128$ when $t = -4$.

Identifying Linear Equations and Inequalities

11. Are the equations below linear equations in one variable?

    a. $-4.12z = 1$ ($\square$ is $\square$ is not)   a linear equation in one variable.

    b. $7 + 4y^2 = 24$ ($\square$ is $\square$ is not)   a linear equation in one variable.

    c. $\sqrt{1 - 0.5p} = 9$ ($\square$ is $\square$ is not)   a linear equation in one variable.

    d. $x - 8z^2 = -11$ ($\square$ is $\square$ is not)   a linear equation in one variable.

    e. $4q + 8 = 0$ ($\square$ is $\square$ is not)   a linear equation in one variable.

    f. $2\pi r = 4\pi$ ($\square$ is $\square$ is not)   a linear equation in one variable.

12. Are the equations below linear equations in one variable?

    a. $\sqrt{-3.3z - 8} = 1$ ($\square$ is $\square$ is not)   a linear equation in one variable.

    b. $1.55z = 4$ ($\square$ is $\square$ is not)   a linear equation in one variable.

    c. $9z - 2V^2 = -26$ ($\square$ is $\square$ is not)   a linear equation in one variable.

    d. $7V^2 - 6 = 9$ ($\square$ is $\square$ is not)   a linear equation in one variable.

    e. $6q - 16 = -1$ ($\square$ is $\square$ is not)   a linear equation in one variable.

    f. $2\pi r = 10\pi$ ($\square$ is $\square$ is not)   a linear equation in one variable.

13. Are the equations below linear equations in one variable?

    a. $V\sqrt{30} = 23$ ($\square$ is $\square$ is not)   a linear equation in one variable.

    b. $-0.44r = -7$ ($\square$ is $\square$ is not)   a linear equation in one variable.

    c. $q^2 + z^2 = 34$ ($\square$ is $\square$ is not)   a linear equation in one variable.

    d. $\pi r^2 = 99\pi$ ($\square$ is $\square$ is not)   a linear equation in one variable.

    e. $4prV = -27$ ($\square$ is $\square$ is not)   a linear equation in one variable.

    f. $6 - 3p = -21$ ($\square$ is $\square$ is not)   a linear equation in one variable.

14. Are the equations below linear equations in one variable?

    a. $z^2 + y^2 = -45$ ($\square$ is $\square$ is not)   a linear equation in one variable.

    b. $V\sqrt{30} = -64$ ($\square$ is $\square$ is not)   a linear equation in one variable.

    c. $9Vyz = -18$ ($\square$ is $\square$ is not)   a linear equation in one variable.

    d. $-2.43V = -52$ ($\square$ is $\square$ is not)   a linear equation in one variable.

    e. $15z - 1 = -34$ ($\square$ is $\square$ is not)   a linear equation in one variable.

    f. $\pi r^2 = 33\pi$ ($\square$ is $\square$ is not)   a linear equation in one variable.

15. Are the inequalities below linear inequalities in one variable?

    a. $-4x^2 - 3z^2 > 1$ ($\square$ is $\square$ is not)   a linear inequality in one variable.

    b. $-2 \geq 5 - 10p$ ($\square$ is $\square$ is not)   a linear inequality in one variable.

    c. $6x^2 - 8V > -81$ ($\square$ is $\square$ is not)   a linear inequality in one variable.

16. Are the inequalities below linear inequalities in one variable?

    a. $-3y^2 - 6q \leq 44$ ($\square$ is $\square$ is not)   a linear inequality in one variable.

    b. $2 > 5 - 14x$ ($\square$ is $\square$ is not)   a linear inequality in one variable.

    c. $2p^2 + 6y^2 < 1$ ($\square$ is $\square$ is not)   a linear inequality in one variable.

17. Are the inequalities below linear inequalities in one variable?

    a. $-3.9y < 80$ ($\square$ is $\square$ is not)   a linear inequality in one variable.

    b. $\sqrt{4r} - 14 < 5$ ($\square$ is $\square$ is not)   a linear inequality in one variable.

    c. $129 \le -5144y - 2965q$ ($\square$ is $\square$ is not)   a linear inequality in one variable.

18. Are the inequalities below linear inequalities in one variable?

    a. $-4.2z \ge -58$ ($\square$ is $\square$ is not)   a linear inequality in one variable.

    b. $-73 \le 3916t + 9643p$ ($\square$ is $\square$ is not)   a linear inequality in one variable.

    c. $\sqrt{4y} + 2 \le 4$ ($\square$ is $\square$ is not)   a linear inequality in one variable.

Checking a Solution for an Equation

19. Is -1 a solution for x in the equation $x - 2 = -1$?   ($\square$ Yes $\square$ No)

20. Is 1 a solution for x in the equation $x - 7 = -5$?   ($\square$ Yes $\square$ No)

21. Is 7 a solution for r in the equation $-6 - r = -13$?   ($\square$ Yes $\square$ No)

22. Is 3 a solution for t in the equation $-8 - t = -11$?   ($\square$ Yes $\square$ No)

23. Is -7 a solution for t in the equation $-9t + 7 = 70$?   ($\square$ Yes $\square$ No)

24. Is 6 a solution for x in the equation $x - 6 = 0$?   ($\square$ Yes $\square$ No)

25. Is -2 a solution for x in the equation $8x - 5 = -7x - 20$?   ($\square$ Yes $\square$ No)

26. Is -8 a solution for y in the equation $-4y + 10 = -7y - 14$?   ($\square$ Yes $\square$ No)

27. Is 7 a solution for y in the equation $8(y + 11) = 19y$?   ($\square$ Yes $\square$ No)

28. Is -3 a solution for y in the equation $3(y - 8) = 11y$?   ($\square$ Yes $\square$ No)

29. Is -10 a solution for r in the equation $4(r - 13) = 11(r + 1)$?   ($\square$ Yes $\square$ No)

30. Is -4 a solution for r in the equation $14(r + 1) = 5(r + 10)$?   ($\square$ Yes $\square$ No)

31. Is $\frac{1}{3}$ a solution for x in the equation $6x - 3 = -2$?   ($\square$ Yes $\square$ No)

32. Is $\frac{17}{9}$ a solution for x in the equation $9x - 10 = 7$?   ($\square$ Yes $\square$ No)

33. Is $\frac{5}{2}$ a solution for x in the equation $-\frac{2}{3}x + 1 = 0$?   ($\square$ Yes $\square$ No)

34. Is $-\frac{5}{6}$ a solution for x in the equation $-\frac{4}{3}x - \frac{2}{3} = \frac{4}{9}$?   ($\square$ Yes $\square$ No)

35. Is 3 a solution for x in the equation $-\frac{10}{3}x - 8 = \frac{9}{4}x - \frac{355}{36}$?   ($\square$ Yes $\square$ No)

36. Is $-\frac{2}{9}$ a solution for y in the equation $\frac{10}{3}y + \frac{9}{4} = -\frac{1}{4}y - \frac{111}{8}$?   ($\square$ Yes $\square$ No)

Checking a Solution for an Inequality Decide whether each value is a solution to the given inequality.

37. $-3x + 24 > 9$

    a. $x = 5$ ($\square$ is $\square$ is not)   a solution.

    b. $x = -5$ ($\square$ is $\square$ is not)   a solution.

    c. $x = 0$ ($\square$ is $\square$ is not)   a solution.

    d. $x = 13$ ($\square$ is $\square$ is not)   a solution.

38. $4x - 5 > 3$

    a. $x = 0$ ($\square$ is $\square$ is not)   a solution.

    b. $x = -8$ ($\square$ is $\square$ is not)   a solution.

    c. $x = 5$ ($\square$ is $\square$ is not)   a solution.

    d. $x = 2$ ($\square$ is $\square$ is not)   a solution.

39. $4x - 18 \geq -2$

    a. $x = 3$ ($\square$ is $\square$ is not) a solution.

    b. $x = 0$ ($\square$ is $\square$ is not) a solution.

    c. $x = 4$ ($\square$ is $\square$ is not) a solution.

    d. $x = 12$ ($\square$ is $\square$ is not) a solution.

40. $-5x - 3 \geq -8$

    a. $x = 5$ ($\square$ is $\square$ is not) a solution.

    b. $x = -7$ ($\square$ is $\square$ is not) a solution.

    c. $x = 1$ ($\square$ is $\square$ is not) a solution.

    d. $x = 0$ ($\square$ is $\square$ is not) a solution.

41. $5x - 8 \leq 7$

    a. $x = 2$ ($\square$ is $\square$ is not) a solution.

    b. $x = 11$ ($\square$ is $\square$ is not) a solution.

    c. $x = 0$ ($\square$ is $\square$ is not) a solution.

    d. $x = 3$ ($\square$ is $\square$ is not) a solution.

42. $2x - 9 \leq 1$

    a. $x = 5$ ($\square$ is $\square$ is not) a solution.

    b. $x = 4$ ($\square$ is $\square$ is not) a solution.

    c. $x = 0$ ($\square$ is $\square$ is not) a solution.

    d. $x = 8$ ($\square$ is $\square$ is not) a solution.

Checking Solutions for Application Problems

43. A triangle's area is 66 square meters. Its height is 12 meters. Suppose we wanted to find how long is the triangle's base. A triangle's area formula is

$$A = \frac{1}{2}bh$$

where A stands for area, b for base and h for height. If we let b be the triangle's base, in meters, we can solve this problem using the equation:

$$66 = \frac{1}{2}(b)(12)$$

Check whether 11 is a solution for b of this equation. ($\square$ Yes $\square$ No)

44. A triangle's area is 114 square meters. Its height is 19 meters. Suppose we wanted to find how long is the triangle's base. A triangle's area formula is

$$A = \frac{1}{2}bh$$

where A stands for area, b for base and h for height. If we let b be the triangle's base, in meters, we can solve this problem using the equation:

$$114 = \frac{1}{2}(b)(19)$$

Check whether 24 is a solution for b of this equation. ($\square$ Yes $\square$ No)

45. When a plant was purchased, it was 2 inches tall. It grows 0.5 inches per day. How many days later will the plant be 8 inches tall?

Assume the plant will be 8 inches tall d days later. We can solve this problem using the equation:

$$0.5d + 2 = 8$$

Check whether 15 is a solution for d of this equation. ($\square$ Yes $\square$ No)

46. When a plant was purchased, it was 1.3 inches tall. It grows 0.6 inches per day. How many days later will the plant be 11.5 inches tall?

Assume the plant will be 11.5 inches tall d days later. We can solve this problem using the equation:

$$0.6d + 1.3 = 11.5$$

Check whether 19 is a solution for d of this equation. ($\square$ Yes $\square$ No)

47. A water tank has 283 gallons of water in it, and it is being drained at the rate of 14 gallons per minute. After how many minutes will there be 31 gallons of water left?

Assume the tank will have 31 gallons of water after m minutes. We can solve this problem using the equation:

$$283 - 14m = 31$$

Check whether 19 is a solution for m of this equation.   ($\square$ Yes $\square$ No)

49. A cylinder's volume is 162π cubic centimeters. Its height is 18 centimeters. Suppose we wanted to find how long is the cylinder's radius. A cylinder's volume formula is

$$V = \pi r^2 h$$

where V stands for volume, r for radius and h for height. Let r represent the cylinder's radius, in centimeters. We can solve this problem using the equation:

$$162\pi = \pi r^2(18)$$

Check whether 9 is a solution for r of this equation.   ($\square$ Yes $\square$ No)

51. A country's national debt was 140 million dollars in 2010. The debt increased at 20 million dollars per year. If this trend continues, when will the country's national debt increase to 640 million dollars? Assume the country's national debt will become 640 million dollars y years after 2010. We can solve this problem using the equation:
$$20y + 140 = 640$$

Check whether 26 is a solution for y of this equation.   ($\square$ Yes $\square$ No)

48. A water tank has 264 gallons of water in it, and it is being drained at the rate of 16 gallons per minute. After how many minutes will there be 40 gallons of water left?

Assume the tank will have 40 gallons of water after m minutes. We can solve this problem using the equation:

$$264 - 16m = 40$$

Check whether 17 is a solution for m of this equation.   ($\square$ Yes $\square$ No)

50. A cylinder's volume is 1280π cubic centimeters. Its height is 20 centimeters. Suppose we wanted to find how long is the cylinder's radius. A cylinder's volume formula is

$$V = \pi r^2 h$$

where V stands for volume, r for radius and h for height. Let r represent the cylinder's radius, in centimeters. We can solve this problem using the equation:

$$1280\pi = \pi r^2(20)$$

Check whether 8 is a solution for r of this equation.   ($\square$ Yes $\square$ No)

52. A country's national debt was 100 million dollars in 2010. The debt increased at 20 million dollars per year. If this trend continues, when will the country's national debt increase to 360 million dollars? Assume the country's national debt will become 360 million dollars y years after 2010. We can solve this problem using the equation:
$$20y + 100 = 360$$

Check whether 13 is a solution for y of this equation.   ($\square$ Yes $\square$ No)

53. A school district has a reserve fund worth 32.8 million dollars. It plans to spend 2.2 million dollars per year. After how many years, will there be 13 million dollars left? Assume there will be 13 million dollars left after y years. We can solve this problem using the equation:

$$32.8 - 2.2y = 13$$

Check whether 11 is a solution for y of this equation.   ($\square$ Yes $\square$ No)

54. A school district has a reserve fund worth 31.1 million dollars. It plans to spend 2.3 million dollars per year. After how many years, will there be 15 million dollars left? Assume there will be 15 million dollars left after y years. We can solve this problem using the equation:

$$31.1 - 2.3y = 15$$

Check whether 8 is a solution for y of this equation.   ($\square$ Yes $\square$ No)

55. A rectangular frame's perimeter is 7 feet. If its length is 2.5 feet, suppose we want to find how long is its width. A rectangle's perimeter formula is

$$P = 2(l + w)$$

where P stands for perimeter, l for length and w for width. We can solve this problem using the equation:

$$7 = 2(2.5 + w)$$

Check whether 1 is a solution for w of this equation.   ($\square$ Yes $\square$ No)

56. A rectangular frame's perimeter is 8.8 feet. If its length is 2.6 feet, suppose we want to find how long is its width. A rectangle's perimeter formula is

$$P = 2(l + w)$$

where P stands for perimeter, l for length and w for width. We can solve this problem using the equation:

$$8.8 = 2(2.6 + w)$$

Check whether 6.2 is a solution for w of this equation.   ($\square$ Yes $\square$ No)

1.5 Solving One-Step Equations

We have learned how to check whether a specific number is a solution to an equation or inequality. In this section, we will begin learning how to *find* the solution(s) to basic equations ourselves.

1.5.1 Imagine Filling in the Blanks

Let's start with a very simple situation—so simple, that you might have success entirely in your head without writing much down. It's not exactly the algebra we hope you will learn, but the example may serve as a good warm up.

Example 1.5.2 A number plus 2 is 6. What is that number?

You may be so familiar with basic arithmetic that you know the answer already. The *algebra* approach is to translate "A number plus 2 is 6" into a math statement—in this case, an equation:

$$x + 2 = 6$$

where x is the number we are trying to find. And then ask what should be substituted in for x to make the equation true.

Now, how do you determine what x is? One valid option is to just *imagine* what number you could put in place of x that would result in a true equation.

- Would 0 work? No, that would mean $0 + 2 = 6$, which is false.

- Would 17 work? No, that would mean $17 + 2 = 6$, which is false.

- Would 4 work? Yes, because $4 + 2 = 6$ is a true equation.

So one solution to $x + 2 = 6$ is 4. No other numbers are going to be solutions, because when you add 2 to something smaller than 4, the result is going to be smaller than 6, and when you add 2 to something larger than 4, the result is going to be larger than 6.

This approach might work for you to solve *very basic* equations, but in general equations are going to be too complicated to solve in your head this way. So we move on to more systematic approaches.

1.5.2 The Basic Principle of Algebra

Let's revisit Example 1.5.2, thinking it through differently.

Example 1.5.3 If a number plus 2 is 6, what is the number?

If a number *plus* 2 is 6, the number is a little smaller than 6, and we should be able to *subtract* 2 from 6 and get that unknown number. Doing that: $6 - 2 = 4$. Thinking things through this way, we are using the *opposite* operation from addition: subtraction.

Let's try this strategy with another riddle.

Example 1.5.4 If a number minus 2 is 6, what is the number? Now we have a number a little larger than 6 in mind. This time, if we *add* 2 to 6 we will find the unknown number. So the unknown number is $6 + 2 = 8$.

Does this strategy work with multiplication and division?

Example 1.5.5 If a number times 2 is 6, what is the number? The mystery number is small, since it gets multiplied by 2 to make 6. If we *divide* 6 by 2, we will find the unknown number. So the unknown number is $\frac{6}{2} = 3$.

Example 1.5.6 If a number divided by 2 equals 6, what is the number? Now we must have had a larger number to start with, since cutting it in half made 6. If we *multiply* 6 by 2, we find the unknown number is $6 \cdot 2 = 12$.

Abbreviation for "pound". Why is "lb" the abbreviation for "pound"? It has a connection to a balance scale, which is the symbol for the Zodiac sign *Libra*.

These examples explore an important principle for solving an equation—applying an opposite arithmetic operation. We can revisit Example 1.5.2 and more intentionally apply this strategy. If a number plus 2 is 6, what is the number? As is common in algebra, we use x to represent the unknown number. The question translates into the math equation

$$x + 2 = 6.$$

Try to envision the equals sign as the middle of a balanced scale. The left side has 2 one-pound objects and a block with unknown weight x lb. Together, the weight on the left is $x + 2$. The right side has 6 one-pound objects. Figure 1.5.7 shows the scale.

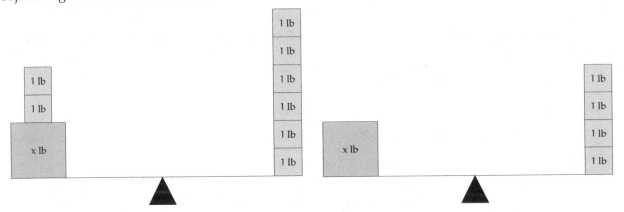

Figure 1.5.7: Balance scale representing $x + 2 = 6$.   **Figure 1.5.8:** Balance scale representing the solution to $x + 2 = 6$, after taking away 2 from each side.

To find the weight of the unknown block, we can take away 2 one-pound blocks from *each* side of the scale (to keep the scale balanced). Figure 1.5.8 shows the solution.

An equation is like a balanced scale, as the two sides of the equation are equal. In the same way that we can take away 2 lb from *each* side of a balanced scale, we can subtract 2 from *each* side of the equation. So instead of two pictures of balance scales, we can use algebra symbols and solve the equation $x + 2 = 6$ in the following manner:

$x + 2 = 6$	a balanced scale
$x + 2 - 2 = 6 - 2$	remove the same quantity from each side
$x = 4$	still balanced; now it tells you the solution

It's important to note that each line shows what is called an **equivalent equation**. In other words, each equation shown is algebraically equivalent to the one above it and will have exactly the same solution(s). The final equivalent equation $x = 4$ tells us that the **solution** to the equation is 4. The **solution set** to this equation is the set that lists every solution to the equation. For this example, the solution set is $\{4\}$.

In Figure 1.5.9, try adding or subtracting something to each side of the equation to find its solution.

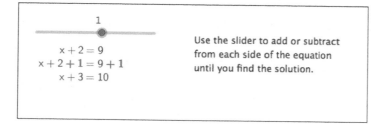

Figure 1.5.9: Allowing Variables to Vary

We have learned we can add or subtract the same number on both sides of the equals sign, just like we can add or remove the same amount of weight on a balanced scale. Can we multiply and divide the same number on both sides of the equals sign? Let's look at Example 1.5.5 again: If a number times 2 is 6, what is the number? Another balance scale can help visualize this.

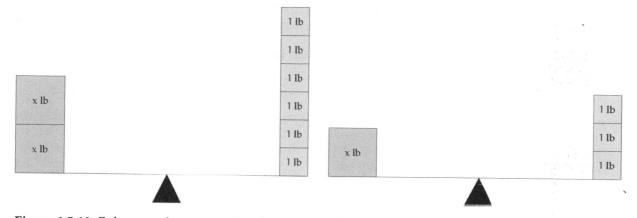

Figure 1.5.10: Balance scale representing the equation $2x = 6$.

Figure 1.5.11: Balance scale representing the solution to $2x = 6$, after cutting each side in half.

Currently, the scale is balanced. If we cut the weight in half on both sides, the scale should still be balanced.

We can see from the scale that $x = 3$ is correct. Removing half of the weight from each side of the scale is like dividing both sides of an equation by 2:

$$2x = 6$$
$$\frac{2x}{2} = \frac{6}{2}$$
$$x = 3$$

The equivalent equation in this example is $x = 3$, which tells us that the solution to the equation is 3 and the solution set is {3}.

Remark 1.5.12 Note that when we divide each side of an equation by a number, we use the fraction line in place of the division symbol. The fact that $\frac{6}{2} = 6 \div 2$ is a reminder that the fraction line and division symbol have the same purpose. The division symbol is rarely used in later math courses.

Similarly, we could multiply each side of an equation by 2, just like we can keep a scale balanced if we double the weight on each side. We will summarize these properties.

Fact 1.5.13 Properties of Equivalent Equations. *If there is an equation Left = Right, we can do the following to obtain an equivalent equation.*

$Left + c = Right + c$ $Left - c = Right - c$ $(Left) \cdot c = (Right) \cdot c$ $\dfrac{Left}{c} = \dfrac{Right}{c}$

(add the same number to each side)   *(subtract the same number from each side)*   *(multiply each side of the equation by the same non-zero number)*   *(divide each side of the equation by the same non-zero number)*

1.5.3 Solving One-Step Equations and Stating Solution Sets

Notice that when we solved equations in Subsection 1.5.2, the final equation looked like x = number, where the variable x is separated from other numbers and stands alone on one side of the equals sign. The goal of solving any equation is to *isolate the variable* in this same manner.

Putting together both strategies (applying the opposite operation and balancing equations like a scale) that we just explored, we summarize how to solve a one-step linear equation.

Process 1.5.14 Steps to Solving Simple (One-Step) Linear Equations.

Apply *Apply the opposite operation to both sides of the equation. If a number was added to the variable, subtract that number, and vice versa. If the variable was multiplied by a number, divide by that number, and vice versa.*

Check *Check the solution. This means, verify that what you think is the solution actually solves the equation. For one reason, it's human to have made a simple arithmetic mistake, and by checking you will protect yourself from this. For another reason, there are situations where solving an equation will tell you that certain numbers are possible solutions, but they do not actually solve the original equation. Checking solutions will catch these situations.*

Summarize *State the solution set, or in the case of application problems, summarize the result using a complete sentence and appropriate units.*

Let's look at a few examples.

Example 1.5.15 Solve for y in the equation $7 + y = 3$.

Explanation.

To isolate y, we need to remove 7 from the left side. Since 7 is being *added* to y, we need to *subtract* 7 from each side of the equation.

$$7 + y = 3$$
$$7 + y - 7 = 3 - 7$$
$$y = -4$$

We should always check the solution when we solve equations. For this problem, we will substitute y in the original equation with -4:

$$7 + y = 3$$
$$7 + (-4) \overset{?}{=} 3$$
$$3 \overset{\checkmark}{=} 3$$

The solution -4 is checked, so the solution set is $\{-4\}$.

Checkpoint 1.5.16 Solve for z in the equation $-7.3 + z = 5.1$.

Explanation. There are two ways to think about this one, but the overall goal is to remove that -7.3 from the left side. Since that negative number is being added to z, we could *subtract* -7.3 from both sides. It is just as effective to *add* positive 7.3.

$$-7.3 + z = 5.1$$
$$-7.3 + z + 7.3 = 5.1 + 7.3$$
$$z = 12.4$$

We will check the solution by substituting z in the original equation with 12.4:

$$-7.3 + z = 5.1$$
$$-7.3 + (12.4) \overset{?}{=} 5.1$$
$$5.1 \overset{\checkmark}{=} 5.1$$

The solution 12.4 is checked and the solution set is $\{12.4\}$.

Checkpoint 1.5.17 Solve for a in the equation $10 = -2a$.

Explanation. To isolate the variable a, we need to divide each side by -2 (because a is being *multiplied* by -2). One common mistake is to add 2 to each side. This would not isolate a, but would instead leave us with the expression $-2a + 2$ on the right-hand side.

$$10 = -2a$$
$$\frac{10}{-2} = \frac{-2a}{-2}$$
$$-5 = a$$

We will check the solution by substituting a in the original equation with -5:

$$10 = -2a$$
$$10 \overset{?}{=} -2(-5)$$
$$10 \overset{\checkmark}{=} 10$$

The solution -5 is checked and the solution set is $\{-5\}$.

Note that in solving the equation in Checkpoint 1.5.17 we found that $-5 = a$, and did not bother to write $a = -5$. All that really matters is that we ended with a clear statement of what a must be equal to.

Example 1.5.18 The formula for a circle's circumference is $c = \pi d$, where c stands for circumference, d stands for diameter, and π is a constant with the value of $3.1415926\ldots$. If a circle's circumference is 12π ft, find this circle's diameter.

Explanation. The circumference is given as 12π feet. Approximating π with 3.14, this means the circumference is approximately 37.68 ft. It is nice to have a rough understanding of how long the circumference is, but if we use 3.14 instead of π, we are using a slightly smaller number than π, and the result of any calculations we do would not be as accurate. This is why we will use the symbol π throughout solving this equation and round only at the end in the conclusion summary (if necessary).

We will substitute c in the formula with 12π and solve for d:

$$c = \pi d$$
$$12\pi = \pi d$$
$$\frac{12\pi}{\pi} = \frac{\pi d}{\pi}$$
$$12 = d$$

So the circle's diameter is 12 ft.

Example 1.5.19 Solve for b in $-b = 2$.

Explanation.   Note that b is not yet isolated as there is a negative sign in front of it. One way to solve for b is to "negate" both sides:

$$-b = 2$$
$$-(-b) = -(2)$$
$$b = -2$$

We removed the negative sign from $-b$ by negating both sides. A second way to remove the negative sign -1 from $-b$ is to divide both sides by -1. If you view the original $-b$ as $-1 \cdot b$, then this approach resembles the solution from Checkpoint 1.5.17.

$$-b = 2$$
$$-1 \cdot b = 2$$
$$\frac{-1 \cdot b}{-1} = \frac{2}{-1}$$
$$b = -2$$

A third way to remove the original negative sign is to use the fact that $-1 \cdot (-b) = b$. So we could multiply on each side by -1.

$$-b = 2$$
$$-1 \cdot (-b) = -1 \cdot (2)$$
$$b = -2$$

We will check the solution by substituting b in the original equation with -2:

$$-b = 2$$
$$-(-2) \overset{\checkmark}{=} 2$$

The solution -2 is checked and the solution set is $\{-2\}$.

1.5.4 Solving One-Step Equations Involving Fractions

When equations have fractions, solving them will make use of the same principles. You may need to use fraction arithmetic, and there may be special considerations that will make the calculations easier. So we have separated the following examples.

Example 1.5.20 Solve for g in $\frac{2}{3} + g = \frac{1}{2}$.

Explanation.

In Section 2.3, we will learn a skill to avoid fraction operations entirely in equations like this one. For now, let's solve the equation by using subtraction to isolate g:

$$\frac{2}{3} + g = \frac{1}{2}$$
$$\frac{2}{3} + g - \frac{2}{3} = \frac{1}{2} - \frac{2}{3}$$
$$g = \frac{3}{6} - \frac{4}{6}$$
$$g = -\frac{1}{6}$$

We will check the solution by substituting g in the original equation with $-\frac{1}{6}$:

$$\frac{2}{3} + g = \frac{1}{2}$$
$$\frac{2}{3} + \left(-\frac{1}{6}\right) \overset{?}{=} \frac{1}{2}$$
$$\frac{4}{6} + \left(-\frac{1}{6}\right) \overset{?}{=} \frac{1}{2}$$
$$\frac{3}{6} \overset{\checkmark}{=} \frac{1}{2}$$

The solution $-\frac{1}{6}$ is checked and the solution set is $\left\{-\frac{1}{6}\right\}$.

Checkpoint 1.5.21 Solve for q in the equation $q - \frac{3}{7} = \frac{3}{2}$.

Explanation. To remove the $\frac{3}{7}$ from the left side, we need to *add* $\frac{3}{7}$ to each side of the equation.

$$q - \frac{3}{7} = \frac{3}{2}$$
$$q - \frac{3}{7} + \frac{3}{7} = \frac{3}{2} + \frac{3}{7}$$
$$q = \frac{21}{14} + \frac{6}{14}$$
$$q = \frac{27}{14}$$

We will check the solution by substituting q in the original equation with $\frac{27}{14}$:

$$q - \frac{3}{7} = \frac{3}{2}$$
$$\frac{27}{14} - \frac{3}{7} \overset{?}{=} \frac{3}{2}$$
$$\frac{27}{14} - \frac{6}{14} \overset{?}{=} \frac{3}{2}$$
$$\frac{21}{14} \overset{?}{=} \frac{3}{2}$$
$$\frac{3}{2} \overset{\checkmark}{=} \frac{3}{2}$$

The solution $\frac{27}{14}$ is checked and the solution set is $\left\{\frac{27}{14}\right\}$.

Example 1.5.22 Solve for c in $\frac{c}{5} = 4$.

Explanation.

Note that the fraction line here implies division, so our variable c is being divided by 5. The opposite operation is to *multiply* by 5:

$$\frac{c}{5} = 4$$

$$5 \cdot \frac{c}{5} = 5 \cdot 4$$

$$c = 20$$

We will check the solution by substituting c in the original equation with 20:

$$\frac{c}{5} = 4$$

$$\frac{20}{5} \overset{\checkmark}{=} 4$$

The solution 20 is checked and the solution set is {20}.

Example 1.5.23 Solve for d in $-\frac{1}{3}d = 6$.

Explanation.   It's true that in this example, the variable d is *multiplied* by $-\frac{1}{3}$. This means that *dividing* each side by $-\frac{1}{3}$ would be a valid strategy for solving this equation. However, dividing by a fraction could lead to human error, so consider this alternative strategy: multiply by -3.

$$-\frac{1}{3}d = 6$$

$$(-3) \cdot \left(-\frac{1}{3}d\right) = (-3) \cdot 6$$

$$d = -18$$

If you choose to divide each side by $-\frac{1}{3}$, that will work out as well:

$$-\frac{1}{3}d = 6$$

$$\frac{-\frac{1}{3}d}{-\frac{1}{3}} = \frac{6}{-\frac{1}{3}}$$

$$d = \frac{6}{1} \cdot \frac{-3}{1} \qquad\qquad \text{Review fraction division in A.2.}$$

$$d = -18$$

This gives the same solution.

We will check the solution by substituting d in the original equation with -18:

$$-\frac{1}{3}d = 6$$

$$-\frac{1}{3} \cdot (-18) \overset{?}{=} 6$$

$$6 \overset{\checkmark}{=} 6$$

The solution -18 is checked and the solution set is {-18}.

Example 1.5.24 Solve for x in $\frac{3x}{4} = 10$.

Explanation. The variable x appears to have *two* operations that apply to it: first multiplication by 3, and then division by 4. But note that

$$\frac{3x}{4} = \frac{3}{4} \cdot \frac{x}{1} = \frac{3}{4}x.$$

If we view the left side this way, we can get away with solving the equation in one step, by multiplying on each side by the reciprocal of $\frac{3}{4}$.

$$\frac{3x}{4} = 10$$
$$\frac{3}{4}x = 10$$
$$\frac{4}{3} \cdot \frac{3}{4}x = \frac{4}{3} \cdot 10$$
$$x = \frac{4}{3} \cdot \frac{10}{1}$$
$$x = \frac{40}{3}$$

We will check the solution by substituting x in the original equation with $\frac{40}{3}$:

$$\frac{3x}{4} = 10$$
$$\frac{3\left(\frac{40}{3}\right)}{4} \stackrel{?}{=} 10$$
$$\frac{40}{4} \stackrel{?}{=} 10$$
$$10 \stackrel{\checkmark}{=} 10$$

The solution $\frac{40}{3}$ is checked and the solution set is $\left\{\frac{40}{3}\right\}$.

Checkpoint 1.5.25 Solve for H in the equation $\frac{-7H}{12} = \frac{2}{3}$.

Explanation. The left side is effectively the same things as $-\frac{7}{12}H$, so multiplying by $-\frac{12}{7}$ will isolate H.

$$\frac{-7H}{12} = \frac{2}{3}$$
$$-\frac{7}{12}H = \frac{2}{3}$$
$$\left(-\frac{12}{7}\right) \cdot \left(-\frac{7}{12}H\right) = \left(-\frac{12}{7}\right) \cdot \frac{2}{3}$$
$$H = -\frac{4}{7} \cdot \frac{2}{1}$$
$$H = -\frac{8}{7}$$

We will check the solution by substituting H in the original equation with $-\frac{8}{7}$:

$$\frac{-7H}{12} = \frac{2}{3}$$
$$\frac{-7\left(-\frac{8}{7}\right)}{12} \stackrel{?}{=} \frac{2}{3}$$
$$\frac{8}{12} \stackrel{?}{=} \frac{2}{3}$$
$$\frac{2}{3} \stackrel{\checkmark}{=} \frac{2}{3}$$

The solution $-\frac{8}{7}$ is checked and the solution set is $\left\{-\frac{8}{7}\right\}$.

1.5.5 Reading Questions

1. If you imagine the equation $2x + 3 = 11$ as a balance scale with boxes on each side, how many boxes do you imagine on the left side? How many *types* of boxes do you imagine on the left side?

2. What is the opposite operation of multiplying by a negative number?

3. Every time you solve an equation, there is something you should do to guarantee success. Describe what that thing is that you should do.

1.5.6 Exercises

Review and Warmup

1. Add the following.

    a. $-10 + (-1)$

    b. $-4 + (-6)$

    c. $-1 + (-8)$

2. Add the following.

    a. $-10 + (-2)$

    b. $-6 + (-7)$

    c. $-1 + (-10)$

3. Add the following.

    a. $2 + (-9)$

    b. $9 + (-2)$

    c. $7 + (-7)$

4. Add the following.

    a. $3 + (-6)$

    b. $5 + (-3)$

    c. $7 + (-7)$

5. Add the following.

    a. $-8 + 3$

    b. $-4 + 8$

    c. $-4 + 4$

6. Add the following.

    a. $-10 + 4$

    b. $-1 + 10$

    c. $-4 + 4$

7. Evaluate the following.

    a. $\frac{-27}{-3}$

    b. $\frac{42}{-6}$

    c. $\frac{-64}{8}$

8. Evaluate the following.

    a. $\frac{-12}{-2}$

    b. $\frac{20}{-4}$

    c. $\frac{-24}{8}$

9. Do the following multiplications.

    a. $9 \cdot \frac{2}{3}$

    b. $12 \cdot \frac{2}{3}$

    c. $15 \cdot \frac{2}{3}$

10. Do the following multiplications.

    a. $28 \cdot \frac{2}{7}$

    b. $35 \cdot \frac{2}{7}$

    c. $42 \cdot \frac{2}{7}$

11. Evaluate the following.

    a. $\frac{-8}{-1}$

    b. $\frac{7}{-1}$

    c. $\frac{100}{-100}$

    d. $\frac{-15}{-15}$

    e. $\frac{12}{0}$

    f. $\frac{0}{-4}$

12. Evaluate the following.

    a. $\frac{-7}{-1}$

    b. $\frac{4}{-1}$

    c. $\frac{150}{-150}$

    d. $\frac{-18}{-18}$

    e. $\frac{12}{0}$

    f. $\frac{0}{-9}$

Solving One-Step Equations with Addition/Subtraction Solve the equation.

13. $y + 7 = 17$

14. $r + 5 = 9$

15. $r + 1 = -3$

16. $t + 8 = -1$

17. $3 = t + 8$

18. $4 = x + 6$

19. $-10 = x - 7$

20. $-10 = x - 9$

21. $y + 79 = 0$

22. $y + 51 = 0$

23. $r - 3 = -1$

24. $r - 10 = -4$

25. $0 = t - 59$

26. $0 = t - 25$

27. $-13 = x - 10$

28. $-15 = x - 6$

29. $x - (-9) = 13$

30. $y - (-5) = 10$

31. $-5 = y - (-3)$

32. $-1 = r - (-5)$

33. $5 + r = -4$

34. $3 + t = -4$

35. $-8 = -9 + t$

36. $2 = -3 + x$

37. $x + \dfrac{7}{6} = \dfrac{5}{6}$ 38. $x + \dfrac{3}{4} = \dfrac{3}{4}$ 39. $\dfrac{10}{9} = y - \dfrac{8}{9}$ 40. $\dfrac{4}{7} = y - \dfrac{2}{7}$

41. $-\dfrac{4}{3} + r = -\dfrac{5}{6}$ 42. $-\dfrac{10}{9} + r = -\dfrac{17}{18}$ 43. $\dfrac{6}{5} + m = -\dfrac{1}{8}$ 44. $\dfrac{10}{9} + p = -\dfrac{1}{4}$

Solving One-Step Equations with Multiplication/Division Solve the equation.

45. $7t = 42$ 46. $4x = 40$ 47. $36 = -3x$ 48. $42 = -6y$

49. $0 = -26c$ 50. $0 = 40A$ 51. $\dfrac{1}{6}C = 8$ 52. $\dfrac{1}{3}m = 3$

53. $-5 = \dfrac{p}{9}$ 54. $-1 = \dfrac{q}{6}$ 55. $\dfrac{3}{8}y = 9$ 56. $\dfrac{7}{13}t = 14$

57. $\dfrac{2}{3}a = 3$ 58. $\dfrac{7}{3}c = 6$ 59. $\dfrac{8}{3} = -\dfrac{A}{10}$ 60. $\dfrac{5}{6} - \dfrac{C}{10}$

61. $2m = -7$ 62. $8p = -5$ 63. $-16 = -10q$ 64. $-15 = -10y$

65. $\dfrac{7}{8} = \dfrac{r}{32}$ 66. $\dfrac{3}{4} = \dfrac{a}{12}$ 67. $-\dfrac{c}{54} = \dfrac{2}{9}$ 68. $-\dfrac{A}{35} = \dfrac{10}{7}$

69. $-\dfrac{C}{16} = -\dfrac{5}{4}$ 70. $-\dfrac{m}{20} = -\dfrac{7}{10}$ 71. $-\dfrac{3}{7} = \dfrac{9p}{10}$ 72. $-\dfrac{7}{4} = \dfrac{8q}{9}$

73. $\dfrac{x}{18} = \dfrac{5}{2}$ 74. $\dfrac{x}{21} = \dfrac{5}{3}$ 75. $\dfrac{9}{4} = \dfrac{x}{20}$ 76. $\dfrac{3}{5} = \dfrac{x}{45}$

Comparisons

77. Solve the equation.

   a. $6r = 36$

   b. $6 + x = 36$

78. Solve the equation.

   a. $2r = 20$

   b. $2 + x = 20$

79. Solve the equation.

   a. $20 = -5t$

   b. $20 = -5 + y$

80. Solve the equation.

   a. $24 = -3t$

   b. $24 = -3 + y$

81. Solve the equation.

   a. $-t = 6$

   b. $-x = -6$

82. Solve the equation.

   a. $-x = 14$

   b. $-t = -14$

83. Solve the equation.

   a. $-\dfrac{1}{2}r = 7$

   b. $-\dfrac{1}{2}b = -7$

84. Solve the equation.

   a. $-\dfrac{1}{6}a = 4$

   b. $-\dfrac{1}{6}y = -4$

85. Solve the equation.

   a. $30 = -\dfrac{10}{7}b$

   b. $-30 = -\dfrac{10}{7}m$

86. Solve the equation.

   a. $20 = -\dfrac{5}{8}A$

   b. $-20 = -\dfrac{5}{8}b$

87. Solve the equation.

   a. $8r = 24$

   b. $45x = 80$

88. Solve the equation.

   a. $3t = 6$

   b. $20r = 64$

89. Solve the equation.

   a. $35 = -7t$

   b. $80 = -35y$

90. Solve the equation.

   a. $28 = -7t$

   b. $60 = -9x$

Challenge

91. Write a linear equation whose solution is $x = 5$. You may not write an equation whose left side is just "x" or whose right side is just "x."

   There are infinitely many correct answers to this problem. *Be creative.* After finding an equation that works, see if you can come up with a different one that also works.

92. Fill in the blanks with the numbers 18 and 67 (using each number only once) to create an equation where x has the greatest possible value.

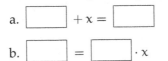

   a. $\boxed{} + x = \boxed{}$

   b. $\boxed{} = \boxed{} \cdot x$

1.6 Solving One-Step Inequalities

In this section, we learn that solving basic inequalities is not that different from solving basic equations.

With one small complication, we can use very similar properties to Fact 1.5.13 when we solve inequalities (as opposed to equations). Here are some numerical examples.

Add to both sides $\qquad$ If $2 < 4$, then $2 + 1 \overset{\checkmark}{<} 4 + 1$.

Subtract from both sides $\qquad$ If $2 < 4$, then $2 - 1 \overset{\checkmark}{<} 4 - 1$.

Multiply on both sides by a *positive* number $\qquad$ If $2 < 4$, then $3 \cdot 2 \overset{\checkmark}{<} 3 \cdot 4$.

Divide on both sides by a *positive* number $\qquad$ If $2 < 4$, then $\frac{2}{2} \overset{\checkmark}{<} \frac{4}{2}$.

However, something interesting happens when we multiply or divide by the same *negative* number on both sides of an inequality: the direction reverses! To understand why, consider Figure 1.6.2, where the numbers 2 and 4 are multiplied by the negative number -1.

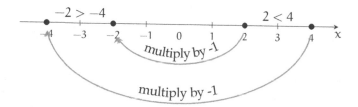

Figure 1.6.2: When two numbers are multiplied by a negative number, their relationship changes.

So even though $2 < 4$, if we multiply both sides by -1, we have the false inequality $-2 \overset{no}{<} -4$. The *true* inequality is $-2 > -4$.

Fact 1.6.3 Changing the Direction of the Inequality Sign. *When we multiply or divide each side of an inequality by the same* negative *number, the inequality sign must change direction. Do* not *change the inequality sign when multiplying/dividing by a positive number, or when adding/subtracting by any number.*

Example 1.6.4 Solve the inequality $-2x \geq 12$. State the solution set graphically, using interval notation, and using set-builder notation. (Interval notation and set-builder notation are discussed in Section 1.3.)

Explanation. To solve this inequality, we will divide each side by -2:

$$-2x \geq 12$$
$$\frac{-2x}{-2} \leq \frac{12}{-2} \qquad \text{Note the change in direction.}$$
$$x \leq -6$$

Note that the inequality sign changed direction at the step where we divided each side of the inequality by a *negative* number.

When we solve a linear *inequality*, there are usually infinitely many solutions. (Unlike when we solve a linear equation and only have one solution.) For this example, any number less than or equal to -6 is a solution.

There are at least three ways to represent the solution set for the solution to an inequality: graphically, with set-builder notation, and with interval notation. Graphically, we represent the solution set as:

Using interval notation, we write the solution set as $(-\infty, -6]$. Using set-builder notation, we write the solution set as $\{x \mid x \leq -6\}$.

As with equations, we should check solutions to catch both human mistakes as well as for possible extraneous solutions (numbers which were *possible* solutions according to algebra, but which actually do not solve the inequality).

Since there are infinitely many solutions, it's impossible to literally check them all. We found that all values of x for which $x \leq -6$ are solutions. One approach is to check that one number less than -6 (any number, your choice) satisfies the inequality. *And* that -6 satisfies the inequality. *And* that one number greater than -6 (any number, your choice) does *not* satsify the inequality.

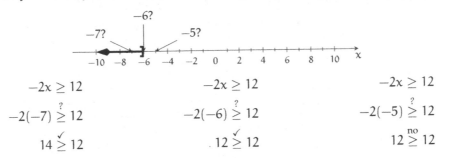

$$-2x \geq 12 \qquad\qquad -2x \geq 12 \qquad\qquad -2x \geq 12$$
$$-2(-7) \overset{?}{\geq} 12 \qquad -2(-6) \overset{?}{\geq} 12 \qquad -2(-5) \overset{?}{\geq} 12$$
$$14 \overset{\checkmark}{\geq} 12 \qquad\qquad 12 \overset{\checkmark}{\geq} 12 \qquad\qquad 12 \overset{no}{\geq} 12$$

Thus both -7 and -6 are solutions, while -5 is not. This is evidence that our solution set is correct, and it's valuable in that making these checks would likely help us catch an error if we had made one. While it certainly does take time and space to make three checks like this, it has its value.

Example 1.6.5 Solve the inequality $t + 7 < 5$. State the solution set graphically, using interval notation, and using set-builder notation.

Explanation. To solve this inequality, we will subtract 7 from each side. There is not much difference between this process and solving the *equation* $t + 7 = 5$, because we are not going to multiply or divide by negative numbers.

$$t + 7 < 5$$
$$t + 7 - 7 < 5 - 7$$
$$t < -2$$

Note again that the direction of the inequality did not change, since we did not multiply or divide each side of the inequality by a negative number at any point.

Graphically, we represent this solution set as:

Using interval notation, we write the solution set as $(-\infty, -2)$. Using set-builder notation, we write the solution set as $\{t \mid t < -2\}$.

We should check that some number less than -2 *is* a solution, but that -2 and some number greater than -2 are *not* solutions.

$$t + 7 < 5 \qquad\qquad t + 7 < 5 \qquad\qquad t + 7 < 5$$
$$-10 + 7 \overset{?}{<} 5 \qquad\qquad -2 + 7 \overset{?}{<} 5 \qquad\qquad 0 + 7 \overset{?}{<} 5$$

$$-3 \overset{\checkmark}{<} 5 \qquad\qquad 5 \overset{no}{<} 5 \qquad\qquad 7 \overset{no}{<} 5$$

So our solution is reasonably checked.

Checkpoint 1.6.6 Solve the inequality $x - 5 > -4$. State the solution set using interval notation and using set-builder notation.

Explanation. To solve this inequality, we will add 5 to each side.

$$x - 5 > -4$$
$$x - 5 + 5 > -4 + 5$$
$$x > 1$$

Note again that the direction of the inequality did not change, since we did not multiply or divide each side of the inequality by a negative number at any point.

Graphically, we represent this solution set as:

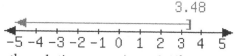

Using interval notation, we write the solution set as $(1, \infty)$. Using set-builder notation, we write the solution set as $\{x \mid x > 1\}$.

We should check that some number less than 1 is *not* a solution, that 1 itself is *not* a solution, and that some number greater than 1 *is* a solution.

$$x - 5 > -4 \qquad x - 5 > -4 \qquad x - 5 > -4$$
$$0 - 5 \overset{?}{>} -4 \qquad 1 - 5 \overset{?}{>} -4 \qquad 10 - 5 \overset{?}{>} -4$$
$$-5 \overset{no}{>} -4 \qquad\quad -4 \overset{no}{>} -4 \qquad\quad 5 \overset{\checkmark}{>} -4$$

So our solution is reasonably checked

Checkpoint 1.6.7 Solve the inequality $-\frac{1}{2}z \geq -1.74$. State the solution set using interval notation and using set-builder notation.

Explanation. To solve this inequality, we will multiply by -2 to each side.

$$-\frac{1}{2}z \geq -1.74$$
$$(-2)\left(-\frac{1}{2}z\right) \leq (-2)(-1.74)$$
$$z \leq 3.48$$

In this exercise, we *did* multiply by a negative number and so the direction of the inequality sign changed. Graphically, we represent this solution set as:

3.48

Using interval notation, we write the solution set as $(-\infty, 3.48]$. Using set-builder notation, we write the solution set as $\{z \mid z \leq 3.48\}$.

We should check that some number less than 3.48 *is* a solution, that 3.48 itself *is* a solution, and also that some number greater than 3.48 is *not* a solution.

$$-\frac{1}{2}z \geq -1.74 \qquad -\frac{1}{2}z \geq -1.74 \qquad -\frac{1}{2}z \geq -1.74$$

$$-\frac{1}{2}(0) \overset{?}{\geq} -1.74 \qquad -\frac{1}{2}(3.48) \overset{?}{\geq} -1.74 \qquad -\frac{1}{2}(10) \overset{?}{\geq} -1.74$$

$$0 \overset{\checkmark}{\geq} -1.74 \qquad -1.74 \overset{\checkmark}{\geq} -1.74 \qquad -5 \overset{no}{\geq} -1.74$$

So our solution is reasonably checked.

Reading Questions

1. What are three ways to express the solution set to a linear inequality?

2. When you go through the motions of solving a simple linear inequality, what step(s) might you need to take where something special happens that you don't have to worry about when solving a simple linear equation?

3. Why does checking the solution set to an inequality take more effort than checking the solution set to an equation?

Exercises

Review and Warmup

1. Add the following.
    a. $-9 + (-3)$
    b. $-7 + (-6)$
    c. $-2 + (-9)$

2. Add the following.
    a. $-9 + (-1)$
    b. $-5 + (-3)$
    c. $-2 + (-7)$

3. Add the following.
    a. $4 + (-8)$
    b. $10 + (-2)$
    c. $5 + (-5)$

4. Add the following.
    a. $5 + (-9)$
    b. $7 + (-3)$
    c. $5 + (-5)$

5. Add the following.
    a. $-6 + 5$
    b. $-4 + 9$
    c. $-6 + 6$

6. Add the following.
    a. $-8 + 1$
    b. $-1 + 6$
    c. $-6 + 6$

7. Evaluate the following.
    a. $\frac{-27}{-9}$
    b. $\frac{35}{-5}$
    c. $\frac{-35}{7}$

8. Evaluate the following.
    a. $\frac{-72}{-8}$
    b. $\frac{28}{-7}$
    c. $\frac{-60}{6}$

9. Do the following multiplications.
    a. $12 \cdot \frac{3}{4}$
    b. $16 \cdot \frac{3}{4}$
    c. $20 \cdot \frac{3}{4}$

10. Do the following multiplications.

  a. $20 \cdot \frac{4}{5}$

  b. $25 \cdot \frac{4}{5}$

  c. $30 \cdot \frac{4}{5}$

11. Evaluate the following.

  a. $\frac{-5}{-1}$

  b. $\frac{9}{-1}$

  c. $\frac{120}{-120}$

  d. $\frac{-15}{-15}$

  e. $\frac{8}{0}$

  f. $\frac{0}{-7}$

12. Evaluate the following.

  a. $\frac{-4}{-1}$

  b. $\frac{7}{-1}$

  c. $\frac{170}{-170}$

  d. $\frac{-18}{-18}$

  e. $\frac{8}{0}$

  f. $\frac{0}{-2}$

Solving One-Step Inequalities using Addition/Subtraction Solve this inequality.

13. $x + 5 > 6$

14. $x + 5 > 9$

15. $x - 1 \le 7$

16. $x - 1 \le 6$

17. $2 \le x + 9$

18. $3 \le x + 7$

19. $3 > x - 10$

20. $4 > x - 9$

Solving One-Step Inequalities using Multiplication/Division Solve this inequality.

21. $5x \le 10$

22. $5x \le 20$

23. $7x > 10$

24. $4x > 1$

25. $-2x \ge 8$

26. $-3x \ge 9$

27. $6 \ge -3x$

28. $16 \ge -4x$

29. $7 < -x$

30. $8 < -x$

31. $-x \le 9$

32. $-x \le 10$

33. $\frac{1}{3}x > 2$

34. $\frac{2}{9}x > 8$

35. $-\frac{4}{5}x \le 8$

36. $-\frac{5}{2}x \le 15$

37. $-12 < \frac{6}{7}x$

38. $-21 < \frac{7}{5}x$

39. $-16 < -\frac{8}{7}x$

40. $-18 < -\frac{9}{8}x$

41. $5x > -15$

42. $2x > -8$

43. $-6 < -2x$

44. $-6 < -3x$

45. $\frac{5}{6} \ge \frac{x}{12}$

46. $\frac{7}{6} \ge \frac{x}{36}$

47. $-\frac{z}{24} < -\frac{5}{8}$

48. $-\frac{z}{40} < -\frac{9}{8}$

Challenge

49. Choose the correct inequality or equal sign to make the relation true.

  a. Let x and y be integers, such that $x < y$.

  Then $x - y$ ($\Box <$ $\Box >$ $\Box =$) $y - x$.

  b. Let x and y be integers, such that $1 < x < y$.

  Then xy ($\Box <$ $\Box >$ $\Box =$) $x + y$.

  c. Let x and y be rational numbers, such that $0 < x < y < 1$.

  Then xy ($\Box <$ $\Box >$ $\Box =$) $x + y$.

  d. Let x and y be integers, such that $x < y$.

  Then $x + 2y$ ($\Box <$ $\Box >$ $\Box =$) $2x + y$.

1.7 Algebraic Properties and Simplifying Expressions

We know that if we have two apples and add three more, then our result is the same as if we'd had three apples and added two more. In this section, we'll examine this and other basic properties we know about numbers, and extend them to variable expressions.

1.7.1 Identities and Inverses

We start with some definitions. The number 0 is called the **additive identity**. It gets this name because adding 0 to a number does not change the "identity" of that number. If the sum of two numbers is the additive identity, 0, these two numbers are called **additive inverses**. For example, 2 is the additive inverse of -2, and the additive inverse of -2 is 2.

Similarly, the number 1 is called the **multiplicative identity**. It gets this name because multiplying a number by 1 does not change the "identity" of that number. If the product of two numbers is the multiplicative identity, 1, these two numbers are called **multiplicative inverses**. For example, 2 is the multiplicative inverse of $\frac{1}{2}$, and the multiplicative inverse of $-\frac{2}{3}$ is $-\frac{3}{2}$. The multiplicative inverse of a number is also called the **reciprocal** of that number.

1.7.2 Introduction to Algebraic Properties

Commutative Property. When we compute the area of a rectangle, we generally multiply the length by the width. Does the result change if we multiply the width by the length?

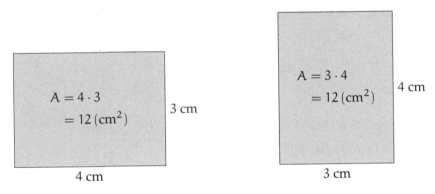

Figure 1.7.2: Horizontal and Vertical Rectangles

We can see $3 \cdot 2 = 2 \cdot 3$. If we denote the length of a rectangle with ℓ and the width with w, this implies $\ell w = w \ell$. The fact that we can reverse the order is known as the **commutative property of multiplication**. There is a similar property for addition, as with $1 + 2 = 2 + 1$, called the **commutative property of addition**. However, there is no commutative property of subtraction or division, because for example $2 - 1 \neq 1 - 2$ and $\frac{4}{2} \neq \frac{2}{4}$.

Associative Property. Let's extend the rectangle to a rectangular prism with width $w = 4$ cm, depth $d = 3$ cm, and height $h = 2$ cm. To compute the volume of this solid, we multiply the width, depth and height, which we write as wdh.

In the following figure, on the left side, we multiply the width and depth first, and then multiply the height. On the right side, we multiply the width and height first, and then multiply the depth. Let's compare the products.

Figure 1.7.3: $(4 \cdot 3) \cdot 2 = 24$ **Figure 1.7.4:** $4 \cdot (3 \cdot 2) = 24$

We can see $(wd)h = w(dh)$. We haven't changed the order that the three variables are written left to right, but we have moved parentheses to change what operation is highest priority in the order of operations. This is known as the **associative property of multiplication**. Theres is a similar property for addition, as with $(1+2)+3 = 1+(2+3)$, called the **associative property of addition**. However, there is no associative property of subtraction or division, because for example $(3-2)-1 \neq 3-(2-1)$ and $(2 \div 2) \div 2 \neq 2 \div (2 \div 2)$.

Distributive Property.   The final property we'll explore is called the **distributive property**, which involves both multiplication and addition. To conceptualize this property, let's consider what happens if we buy 3 boxes that each contain one apple and one pear. This will have the same total cost as if we'd bought 3 apples and 3 pears. We write this algebraically:

$$3(a+p) = 3a + 3p.$$

Visually, we can see that it's just a means of re-grouping: $(🍎 + 🍐) + (🍎 + 🍐) + (🍎 + 🍐) = (🍎 + 🍎 + 🍎) + (🍐 + 🍐 + 🍐)$.

1.7.3 Summary of Algebraic Properties

List 1.7.5: Algebraic Properties

Let a, b, and c represent real numbers, variables, or algebraic expressions. Then the following properties hold:

Commutative Property of Multiplication $a \cdot b = b \cdot a$

Associative Property of Multiplication $a \cdot (b \cdot c) = (a \cdot b) \cdot c$

Commutative Property of Addition $a + b = b + a$

Associative Property of Addition $a + (b + c) = (a + b) + c$

Distributive Property $a(b + c) = ab + ac$

Let's practice these properties in the following exercises.

Checkpoint 1.7.6

    a. Use the commutative property of multiplication to write an equivalent expression to $53m$.

    b. Use the associative property of multiplication to write an equivalent expression to $3(5n)$.

    c. Use the commutative property of addition to write an equivalent expression to $q + 84$.

    d. Use the associative property of addition to write an equivalent expression to $x + (20 + c)$.

    e. Use the distributive property to write an equivalent expression to $3(r + 7)$ that has no grouping symbols.

Explanation.

    a. To use the commutative property of multiplication, we change the order in which two factors are multiplied:

$$53m$$
$$= m \cdot 53.$$

    b. To use the associative property of multiplication, we leave factors written in their original order, but change the grouping symbols so that a different multiplication has higher priority:

$$3(5n)$$
$$= (3 \cdot 5)n.$$

    You may further simplify by carrying out the multiplication between the two numbers:

$$3(5n)$$
$$= (3 \cdot 5)n$$
$$= 15n.$$

    c. To use the commutative property of addition, we change the order in which two terms are added:

$$q + 84$$
$$= 84 + q.$$

    d. To use the associative property of addition, we leave terms written in their original order, but change the grouping symbols so that a different addition has higher priority:

$$x + (20 + c)$$
$$= (x + 20) + c.$$

    e. To use the distributive property, we multiply the number outside the parentheses, 3, with each term inside the parentheses:

$$3(r + 7)$$
$$= 3 \cdot r + 3 \cdot 7$$
$$= 3r + 21.$$

1.7.4 Applying the Commutative, Associative, and Distributive Properties

Like Terms.   One of the main ways that we will use the commutative, associative, and distributive properties is to simplify expressions. In order to do this, we need to recognize **like terms**, as discussed in Section 1.2. We combine like terms when we take an expression like $2a + 3a$ and write the result as $5a$. The formal process actually involves using the distributive property:

$$2a + 3a = (2 + 3)a$$
$$= 5a$$

In practice, however, it's more helpful to think of this as having 2 of an object and then an additional 3 of that same object. In total, we then have 5 of that object.

Example 1.7.7 Where possible, simplify the following expressions by combining like terms.

   a. $6c + 12c - 5c$ b. $-5q^2 - 3q^2$ c. $x - 5y + 4x$ d. $2x - 3y + 4z$

Explanation.

   a. All three terms are like terms, so they may combined. We combine them two at a time:

$$6c + 12c - 5c = 18c - 5c$$
$$= 13c$$

   b. The two terms $-5q^2$ and $-3q^2$ are like terms, so we may combine them:

$$-5q^2 - 3q^2 = -8q^2$$

   c. The two terms x and $4x$ are like terms, while the other term is different. Using the associative and commutative properties of addition in the first step allows us to place the two like terms next to each other, and then combine them:

$$x - 5y + 4x = x + 4x + (-5y)$$
$$= 1x + 4x + (-5y)$$
$$= 5x - 5y$$

Note the expression x is the same as $1x$. Usually we don't write the "1" as it is implied. However, it's helpful when combining like terms to remember that $x = 1x$. (Similarly, $-x$ is equal to $-1x$, which can be helpful when combining $-x$ with like terms.)

   d. The expression $2x - 3y + 4z$ cannot be simplified as there are no like terms.

Adding Expressions.   When we add an expression like $4x - 5$ to an expression like $3x - 7$, we write them as follows:

$$(4x - 5) + (3x - 7)$$

In order to remove the given sets of parentheses and apply the commutative property of addition, we will rewrite the subtraction operation as "adding the opposite":

$$4x + (-5) + 3x + (-7)$$

At this point we can apply the commutative property of addition and then combine like terms. Here's how the entire problem will look:

$$\begin{aligned}(4x - 5) + (3x - 7) &= 4x + (-5) + 3x + (-7) \\ &= 4x + 3x + (-5) + (-7) \\ &= 7x + (-12) \\ &= 7x - 12\end{aligned}$$

Remark 1.7.8 Once we become more comfortable simplifying such expressions, we will simply write this kind of simplification in one step:

$$(4x - 5) + (3x - 7) = 7x - 12$$

Example 1.7.9 Use the associative, commutative, and distributive properties to simplify the following expressions as much as possible.

a. $(2x + 3) + (4x + 5)$

b. $(-5x + 3) + (4x - 7)$

Explanation.

a. We will remove parentheses, and then combine like terms:

$$\begin{aligned}(2x + 3) + (4x + 5) &= 2x + 3 + 4x + 5 \\ &= 2x + 4x + 3 + 5 \\ &= 6x + 8\end{aligned}$$

b. We will remove parentheses, and then combine like terms:

$$\begin{aligned}(-5x + 3) + (4x - 7) &= -5x + 3 + 4x + (-7) \\ &= -x + (-4) \\ &= -x - 4\end{aligned}$$

Applying the Distributive Property with Negative Coefficients.   Applying the distributive property in an expression such as $2(3x + 4)$ is fairly straightforward, in that this becomes $2(3x) + 2(4)$ which we then simplify to $6x + 8$. Applying the distributive property is a little trickier when subtraction or a negative constant is involved, for example, with the expression $2(3x - 4)$. Recalling that subtraction is defined as "adding the opposite," we can change the subtraction of positive 4 to the addition of negative 4:

$$2\big(3x + (-4)\big)$$

Now when we distribute, we obtain:

$$2(3x) + 2(-4)$$

As a final step, we see that this simplifies to:

$$6x - 8$$

Remark 1.7.10 We can also extend the distributive property to use subtraction, and state that $a(b - c) = ab - ac$. With this property, we would simplify $2(3x - 4)$ more efficiently:

$$\begin{aligned}2(3x - 4) &= 2(3x) - 2(4) \\ &= 6x - 8\end{aligned}$$

Example 1.7.11 Apply the distributive property to each expression and simplify it as much as possible.

a. $-3(5x + 7)$ b. $2(-4x - 1)$

Explanation.

a. We will distribute -3 to the $5x$ and 7:

$$-3(5x + 7) = -3(5x) + (-3)(7)$$
$$= -15x - 21$$

b. We will distribute 2 to the $-4x$ and -1:

$$2(-4x - 1) = 2(-4x) - 2(1)$$
$$= -8x - 2$$

Checkpoint 1.7.12 Use the distributive property to write an equivalent expression to $-4(y - 7)$ that has no grouping symbols.

Explanation. To use the distributive property, we multiply the number outside the parentheses, -4, with each term inside the parentheses:

$$-4(y - 7) = -4 \cdot y - 4(-7)$$
$$= -4y + 28$$

Subtracting Expressions. To subtract one expression from another expression, such as $(5x + 9) - (3x + 2)$, we will again rely on the fact that subtraction is defined as "adding the opposite." To add the *opposite* of an expression, we will technically distribute a constant factor of -1 and simplify from there:

$$(5x + 9) - (3x + 2) = (5x + 9) + (-1)(3x + 2)$$
$$= 5x + 9 + (-1)(3x) + (-1)(2)$$
$$= 5x + 9 + (-3x) + (-2)$$
$$= 2x + 7$$

Remark 1.7.13 The above example demonstrates *how* we apply the distributive property in order to subtract two expressions. But in practice, it can be pretty cumbersome. A shorter (and often clearer) approach is to instead subtract every term in the expression we are subtracting, which is shown like this:

$$(5x + 9) - (3x + 2) = 5x + 9 - 3x - 2$$
$$= 2x + 7$$

Example 1.7.14 Use the associative, commutative, and distributive properties to simplify the following expressions as much as possible.

a. $(-6x + 4) - (3x - 7)$ b. $(-2x - 5) - (-4x - 6)$

Explanation.

a. We will remove parentheses using the distributive property, and then combine like terms:

$$(-6x + 4) - (3x - 7) = -6x + 4 - 3x - (-7)$$
$$= -6x + 4 - 3x + 7$$
$$= -9x + 11$$

b. We will remove parentheses using the distributive property, and then combine like terms:

$$(-2x - 5) - (-4x - 6) = -2x - 5 - (-4x) - (-6)$$

$$= -2x - 5 + 4x + 6$$
$$= 2x + 1$$

1.7.5 The Role of the Order of Operations in Applying the Commutative, Associative, and Distributive Properties

When simplifying an expression such as $3 + 4(5x + 7)$, we need to respect the order of operations. Since the terms inside the parentheses are not like terms, there is nothing to simplify there. The next highest priority operation is multiplying the 4 by $(5x + 7)$. This must be done *before* anything happens with the adding of that 3. We cannot say $3 + 4(5x + 7) = 7(5x + 7)$, because that would mean we treated the addition as having higher priority than the multiplication.

So to simplify $3 + 4(5x + 7)$, we will first examine the multiplication of 4 with $(5x + 7)$, and here we may apply the distributive property. After that, we will use the commutative and associative properties:

$$3 + 4(5x + 7) = 3 + 4(5x) + 4(7)$$
$$= 3 + 20x + 28$$
$$= 20x + 3 + 28$$
$$= 20x + 31$$

Example 1.7.15 Simplify the following expressions using the commutative, associative, and distributive properties.

    a. $4 - (3x - 9)$ b. $5x + 9(-2x + 3)$ c. $5(x - 9) + 4(x + 4)$

Explanation.

    a. We will remove parentheses using the distributive property, and then combine like terms:

$$4 - (3x - 9) = 4 - 3x - (-9)$$
$$= 4 - 3x + 9$$
$$= -3x + 13$$

    b. We will remove parentheses using the distributive property, and then combine like terms:

$$5x + 9(-2x + 3) = 5x + 9(-2x) + 9(3)$$
$$= 5x - 18x + 27$$
$$= -13x + 27$$

    c. We will remove parentheses using the distributive property, and then combine like terms:

$$5(x - 9) + 4(x + 4) = 5x - 45 + 4x + 16$$
$$= 9x - 29$$

Checkpoint 1.7.16 Use the distributive property to simplify $6 - 7(-8 + 7r)$ completely.

Explanation. We first use distributive property to get rid of parentheses, and then combine like terms:

$$
\begin{aligned}
6 - 7(-8 + 7r) &= 6 + (-7)(-8 + 7r) \\
&= 6 + (-7)(-8) + (-7)(7r) \\
&= 6 + 56 - 49r \\
&= 62 - 49r \\
&= -49r + 62
\end{aligned}
$$

Note that either of the last two expressions are acceptable final answers.

1.7.6 Reading Questions

1. Why is the number 1 known as the "multiplicative identity"?

2. Consider the expression $138 + 25 + 5$. By the order of operations, you would add this as $(138 + 25) + 5$. (Meaning you would start by adding $138 + 25$.)
   Which property of algebra allows you to view that as $138 + (25 + 5)$? (Meaning you could start with an easy $25 + 5$, and follow with an easy $138 + 30$.)

3. Describe a certin thing that you should watch out for when it comes to using the distributive law. (It is something that has to do with negative numbers and/or subtraction.)

1.7.7 Exercises

Review and Warmup

1. Count the number of terms in each expression.
   a. $-6s - 3y$
   b. $-9x - 6z$
   c. $9s^2 + y - 9y^2 + 7t$
   d. $4z + 6x^2 - 3t + 7y$

2. Count the number of terms in each expression.
   a. $-5t^2 + 5t^2$
   b. $8t - 7z^2 + 5 - 5s^2$
   c. $7y$
   d. $2y + 6z + x$

3. List the terms in each expression.
   a. $-2.9t - 5x + 5.7y$
   b. $-7.7z + 0.6s$
   c. $6.9y + 4.5z - 8.5 + 1.6t$
   d. $5.1z - 6y$

4. List the terms in each expression.
   a. $-1.3t^2 + 3.2z + 3.7x$
   b. $3.7z$
   c. $8.4y^2 - 3z$
   d. $8.2t + 3.6t^2$

5. List the terms in each expression.
   a. $0.3t - 6.7s^2 + 1.7t + 7.9t^2$
   b. $-0.9x - 5.7x^2 + 6.5$
   c. $5.5y^2 + 6.7z^2$
   d. $0.6t^2 - 7.2s - 5s^2$

6. List the terms in each expression.
   a. $1.9t^2 + 1.5 - 0.3y + 6.7t$
   b. $6.6t + 6.2x^2$
   c. $2.1t - 8.8t^2 - 2s + 3.6x$
   d. $-1.9z + 4.4y^2$

7. Simplify each expression, if possible, by combining like terms.

   a. $4t - 9 + 4s - 6s$

   b. $t + 7x$

   c. $-6s - 7$

   d. $-9x + 3x$

8. Simplify each expression, if possible, by combining like terms.

   a. $5t^2 + t$

   b. $5y + 5y - 7y + 9t$

   c. $2t^2 - 7s^2 + 4s$

   d. $4x + 2 + 9s^2 + s$

These exercises involve the concepts of like terms and the commutative, associative, and distributive properties.

9. What is the additive inverse of -7?

10. What is the additive inverse of -4?

11. What is the multiplicative inverse of -2?

12. What is the multiplicative inverse of -3?

13. Use the associative property of addition to write an equivalent expression to $x + (51 + m)$.

14. Use the associative property of addition to write an equivalent expression to $m + (24 + r)$.

15. Use the associative property of addition to write an equivalent expression to $7 + (13 + n)$.

16. Use the associative property of addition to write an equivalent expression to $20 + (1 + q)$.

17. Use the associative property of multiplication to write an equivalent expression to $7(5x)$.

18. Use the associative property of multiplication to write an equivalent expression to $4(9r)$.

19. Use the commutative property of addition to write an equivalent expression to $a + 92$.

20. Use the commutative property of addition to write an equivalent expression to $b + 57$.

21. Use the commutative property of addition to write an equivalent expression to $4t + 11$.

22. Use the commutative property of addition to write an equivalent expression to $2p + 53$.

23. Use the commutative property of addition to write an equivalent expression to $10(m + 53)$.

24. Use the commutative property of addition to write an equivalent expression to $5(n + 18)$.

25. Use the commutative property of multiplication to write an equivalent expression to $84q$.

26. Use the commutative property of multiplication to write an equivalent expression to $49x$.

27. Use the commutative property of multiplication to write an equivalent expression to $14 + 7r$.

28. Use the commutative property of multiplication to write an equivalent expression to $79 + 2t$.

29. Use the commutative property of multiplication to write an equivalent expression to $5(b + 45)$.

30. Use the commutative property of multiplication to write an equivalent expression to $9(y + 87)$.

31. Use the distributive property to write an equivalent expression to $4(m + 6)$ that has no grouping symbols.

32. Use the distributive property to write an equivalent expression to $5(m + 8)$ that has no grouping symbols.

33. Use the distributive property to write an equivalent expression to $-10(n-8)$ that has no grouping symbols.

34. Use the distributive property to write an equivalent expression to $-4(q+1)$ that has no grouping symbols.

35. Use the distributive property to write an equivalent expression to $-(x-3)$ that has no grouping symbols.

36. Use the distributive property to write an equivalent expression to $-(r-10)$ that has no grouping symbols.

37. Use the distributive property to simplify $7+9(9+5t)$ completely.

38. Use the distributive property to simplify $4+3(7+4b)$ completely.

39. Use the distributive property to simplify $7-8(-4-7q)$ completely.

40. Use the distributive property to simplify $2-8(4+3x)$ completely.

41. Use the distributive property to simplify $4-(-1+5m)$ completely.

42. Use the distributive property to simplify $10-(8-n)$ completely.

43. Use the distributive property to simplify $7-(-6q-5)$ completely.

44. Use the distributive property to simplify $4-(9x+4)$ completely.

45. Use the distributive property to simplify $\frac{9}{7}(-6-7r)$ completely.

46. Use the distributive property to simplify $\frac{6}{5}(-6+3t)$ completely.

47. Use the distributive property to simplify $\frac{3}{10}(-9+\frac{3}{4}b)$ completely.

48. Use the distributive property to simplify $\frac{9}{5}(7+\frac{3}{7}c)$ completely.

49. The expression $c+m+r$ would be ambiguous if we did not have a left-to-right reading convention. Use grouping symbols to emphasize the order that these additions should be carried out.
Use the associative property of addition to write an equivalent (but different) algebraic expression.

50. The expression $m+y+r$ would be ambiguous if we did not have a left-to-right reading convention. Use grouping symbols to emphasize the order that these additions should be carried out.
Use the associative property of addition to write an equivalent (but different) algebraic expression.

51. A student has (correctly) simplified an algebraic expression in the following steps. Between each pair of steps, identify the algebraic property that justifies moving from one step to the next.

$$8(n+6)+9n$$

($\square$ commutative property of addition $\quad\square$ commutative property of multiplication $\quad\square$ associative property of addition $\quad\square$ associative property of multiplication $\quad\square$ distributive property)

$$=(8n+48)+9n$$

($\square$ commutative property of addition $\quad\square$ commutative property of multiplication $\quad\square$ associative property of addition $\quad\square$ associative property of multiplication $\quad\square$ distributive property)

$$=(48+8n)+9n$$

(□ commutative property of addition □ commutative property of multiplication □ associative property of addition □ associative property of multiplication □ distributive property)

$$= 48 + (8n + 9n)$$

(□ commutative property of addition □ commutative property of multiplication □ associative property of addition □ associative property of multiplication □ distributive property)

$$= 48 + (8 + 9)\, n$$

$$= 48 + 17n$$

(□ commutative property of addition □ commutative property of multiplication □ associative property of addition □ associative property of multiplication □ distributive property)

$$= 17n + 48$$

52. A student has (correctly) simplified an algebraic expression in the following steps. Between each pair of steps, identify the algebraic property that justifies moving from one step to the next.

$$5(q + 2) + 7q$$

(□ commutative property of addition □ commutative property of multiplication □ associative property of addition □ associative property of multiplication □ distributive property)

$$= (5q + 10) + 7q$$

(□ commutative property of addition □ commutative property of multiplication □ associative property of addition □ associative property of multiplication □ distributive property)

$$= (10 + 5q) + 7q$$

(□ commutative property of addition □ commutative property of multiplication □ associative property of addition □ associative property of multiplication □ distributive property)

$$= 10 + (5q + 7q)$$

(□ commutative property of addition □ commutative property of multiplication □ associative property of addition □ associative property of multiplication □ distributive property)

$$= 10 + (5 + 7)\, q$$

$$= 10 + 12q$$

(□ commutative property of addition □ commutative property of multiplication □ associative property of addition □ associative property of multiplication □ distributive property)

$$= 12q + 10$$

53. The number of students enrolled in math courses at Portland Community College has grown over the years. The formulas

$$M = 0.31x + 3.3 \quad W = 0.43x + 4.3 \quad N = 0.01x + 0.1$$

describe the numbers (of thousands) of men, women, and gender-non-binary students enrolled in math courses at PCC x years after 2005. (Note this is an exercise using randomized numbers, not actual data.) Give a simplified formula for the total number T of thousands of students at PCC taking math classes x years after 2005. Be sure to give the entire formula, starting with T=.

54. The number of students enrolled in math courses at Portland Community College has grown over the years. The formulas

$$M = 0.35x + 5.3 \quad W = 0.56x + 3.4 \quad N = 0.01x + 0.2$$

describe the numbers (of thousands) of men, women, and gender-non-binary students enrolled in math courses at PCC x years after 2005. (Note this is an exercise using randomized numbers, not actual data.) Give a simplified formula for the total number T of thousands of students at PCC taking math classes x years after 2005. Be sure to give the entire formula, starting with T=.

55. Fully simplify $(-3x + 5) + (x - 3)$.

56. Fully simplify $(4x + 1) + (-x + 7)$.

57. Fully simplify $(-5x - 7) + (-x - 3)$.

58. Fully simplify $(6x - 3) + (-x - 6)$.

59. Fully simplify $(7x + 1) + (-x + 2)$.

60. Fully simplify $(-8x - 6) + (-x - 6)$.

61. Fully simplify $-9(-3x - 7) - 5(7x - 8)$.

62. Fully simplify $-9x + 3 + 6(x - 2)$.

63. Fully simplify $2(6x - 7) - 7(-5x - 3)$.

64. Fully simplify $-3(4x + 1) + 7(9x - 5)$.

65. Fully simplify $-4(9x - 5) - 8(-3x - 1)$.

66. Fully simplify $5(6x + 9) + 9(-6x + 3)$.

67. Fully simplify $6(2x - 3) - (3x + 7)$.

68. Fully simplify $-7(9x + 5) + 2(-6x + 9)$.

1.8 Modeling with Equations and Inequalities

One purpose of learning math is to be able to model real-life situations and then use the model to ask and answer questions about the situation. In this lesson, we will examine the basics of modeling to set up an equation (or inequality).

1.8.1 Setting Up Equations for Rate Models

To set up an equation modeling a real world scenario, the first thing we need to do is identify what variable we will use. The variable we use will be determined by whatever is unknown in our problem statement. Once we've identified and defined our variable, we'll use the numerical information provided to set up our equation.

Example 1.8.2 A savings account starts with \$500. Each month, an automatic deposit of \$150 is made. Write an equation that represents the number of months it will take for the balance to reach \$1,700.

Explanation.

To set up an equation, we might start by making a table in order to identify a general pattern for the total amount in the account after m months. In Figure 1.8.3, we find the pattern is that after m months, the total amount saved is $500 + 150m$.

Using this pattern, we determine that an equation representing when the total savings equals \$1700 is:

$$500 + 150m = 1700$$

Months Since Saving Started	Total Amount Saved (in Dollars)
0	500
1	$500 + 150 = 650$
2	$500 + 150(2) = 800$
3	$500 + 150(3) = 950$
4	$500 + 150(4) = 1100$
$\vdots$	$\vdots$
m	$500 + 150m$

Figure 1.8.3: Amount in Savings Account

Right now we are not interested in actually solving this equation and finding the number of months m until the savings has reached \$1700. The skill of *setting up* that equation is challenging enough, and this section only focuses on that setup.

Example 1.8.4 A bathtub contains $2.5\,\text{ft}^3$ of water. More water is being poured in at a rate of $1.75\,\text{ft}^3$ per minute. Write an equation representing when the amount of water in the bathtub will reach $6.25\,\text{ft}^3$.

Explanation.

Since this problem refers to *when* the amount of water will reach a certain amount, we immediately know that the unknown quantity is time. As the volume of water in the tub is measured in ft^3 per minute, we know that time needs to be measured in minutes. We'll define t to be the number of minutes that water is poured into the tub. To determine this equation, we'll start by making a table of values:

Minutes Water Has Been Poured	Total Amount of Water (in ft^3)
0	2.5
1	$2.5 + 1.75 = 4.25$
2	$2.5 + 1.75(2) = 6$
3	$2.5 + 1.75(3) = 7.75$
$\vdots$	$\vdots$
t	$2.5 + 1.75t$

Figure 1.8.5: Amount of Water in the Bathtub

Using this pattern, we determine that the equation representing when the amount will be 6.25 ft³ is:

$$2.5 + 1.75t = 6.25$$

1.8.2 Setting Up Equations for Percent Problems

Section A.4 reviews some basics of working with percentages, and even solves some one-step equations that are set up using percentages. Here we look at some scenarios where there is an equation to set up based on percentages, but it things are a little more complicated than with a one-step equation. One important fact is that when doing math with percentages, we always start by rewriting the percentage as a decimal. For example, 18% should be written as 0.18 if you are going to us it to do algebra or arithmetic.

Example 1.8.6 Jakobi's annual salary as a nurse in Portland, Oregon, is $73,290. His salary increased by 4% from last year. Write a linear equation modeling this scenario, where the unknown value is Jakobi's salary last year.

Explanation. We want to work with Jakobi's salary last year. So we'll introduce s, defined to be Jakobi's salary last year (in dollars). To set up the equation, we need to think about how he arrived at this year's salary. To get to this year's salary, his employer took last year's salary and added 4% to it. Conceptually, this means we have:

$$(\text{last year's salary}) + (4\% \text{ of last year's salary}) = (\text{this year's salary})$$

We'll represent 4% of last year's salary with $0.04s$ since 0.04 is the decimal representation of 4%. This means that the equation we set up is:

$$s + 0.04s = 73290$$

Checkpoint 1.8.7 Kirima offered to pay the bill and tip at a restaurant where she and her friends had dinner. In total she paid $150, which made the tip come out to a little more than 19%. We'd like to know what was the bill before tip. Set up an equation for this situation.

Explanation. A common mistake is to translate a question like this into "what is 19% of $150?" as a way to calculate the tip amount, and then subtract that from $150. But that is not how tipping works. The 19% is applied to the *original bill*, not the *final total*. If we let x represent the original bill, then:

$$\underset{x}{\text{bill}} \underset{+}{\text{plus}} \underset{0.19}{\text{19\%}} \underset{\cdot}{\text{of}} \underset{x}{\text{bill}} \underset{=}{\text{is}} \underset{150}{\$150}$$

Example 1.8.8 The price of a refrigerator after a 15% discount is $612. Write a linear equation modeling this scenario, where the original price of the refrigerator (before the discount was applied) is the unknown quantity.

Explanation. We'll let c be the original price of the refrigerator. To obtain the discounted price, we take the original price and subtract 15% of that amount. Conceptually, this looks like:

$$(\text{original price}) - (15\% \text{ of the original price}) = (\text{discounted price})$$

Since the amount of the discount is 15% of the original price, we'll represent this with $0.15c$. The equation we set up is then:

$$c - 0.15c = 612$$

Checkpoint 1.8.9 A shirt is on sale at 20% off. The current price is $51.00. Write an equation based on this scenario where the variable represents the shirt's original price.

Explanation.   Let x represent the original price of the shirt. Since 20% is removed to bring the cost to $51, we can set up the equation:

$$\underset{\substack{| \\ x}}{\text{original}} \quad \underset{\substack{| \\ -}}{\text{minus}} \quad \underset{\substack{| \\ 0.20 \cdot}}{\text{20\%}} \quad \underset{\substack{\\ }}{\text{of}} \quad \underset{\substack{| \\ x}}{\text{original}} \quad \underset{\substack{| \\ =}}{\text{is}} \quad \underset{\substack{| \\ 51}}{\text{\$51}}$$

1.8.3 Setting Up Inequalities for Models

In general, we'll model using inequalities when we want to determine a maximum or minimum value. To identify that an inequality is needed instead of an equality, we'll look for phrases like *at least, at most, at a minimum* or *at a maximum*.

Example 1.8.10 The car share company car2go has a one-time registration fee of $5 and charges $14.99 per hour for use of their vehicles. Hana wants to use car2go and has a maximum budget of $300. Write a linear inequality representing this scenario, where the unknown quantity is the number of hours she uses their vehicles.

Explanation.   We'll let h be the number of hours that Hana uses car2go. We need the initial cost and the cost from the hourly charge to be less than or equal to $300, which we set up as:

$$5 + 14.99h \leq 300$$

Example 1.8.11 When an oil tank is decommissioned, it is drained of its remaining oil and then re-filled with an inert material, such as sand. A cylindrical oil tank has a volume of 275 gal and is being filled with sand at a rate of 700 gal per hour. Write a linear inequality representing this scenario, where the time it takes for the tank to overflow with sand is the unknown quantity.

Explanation.   The unknown in this scenario is time, so we'll define t to be the number of hours that sand is poured into the tank. (Note that we chose hours based on the rate at which the sand is being poured.) We'll represent the amount of sand poured in as 700t as each hour an additional 700 gal are added. Given that we want to know when this amount exceeds 275 gal, we set this equation up as:

$$700t > 275$$

1.8.4 Translating Phrases into Algebraic Expressions and Equations/Inequalities

Void of context, there are certain short phrases and expressions in English that have mathematical meaning, and might show up in a modeling scenario. The following table shows how to translate some of these common phrases into algebraic expressions.

English Phrases	Math Expressions
the sum of 2 and a number	$x + 2$ or $2 + x$
2 more than a number	$x + 2$ or $2 + x$
a number increased by 2	$x + 2$ or $2 + x$
a number and 2 together	$x + 2$ or $2 + x$
the difference between a number and 2	$x - 2$
the difference of 2 and a number	$2 - x$
2 less than a number	$x - 2$ (*not* $2 - x$)
a number decreased by 2	$x - 2$
2 decreased by a number	$2 - x$
2 subtracted from a number	$x - 2$
a number subtracted from 2	$2 - x$
the product of 2 and a number	$2x$
twice a number	$2x$
a number times 2	$x \cdot 2$ or $2x$
two thirds of a number	$\frac{2}{3}x$
25% of a number	$0.25x$
the quotient of a number and 2	$x/2$
the quotient of 2 and a number	$2/x$
the ratio of a number and 2	$x/2$
the ratio of 2 and a number	$2/x$

Table 1.8.12: Translating English Phrases into Math Expressions

We can extend this to setting up equations and inequalities. Let's look at some examples. The key is to break a complicated phrase or sentence into smaller parts, identifying key vocabulary such as "is," "of," "greater than," "at most," etc.

English Sentences	Math Equations and Inequalities
The sum of 2 and a number is 6.	$x + 2 = 6$
2 less than a number is at least 6.	$x - 2 \geq 6$
Twice a number is at most 6.	$2x \leq 6$
6 is the quotient of a number and 2.	$6 = \frac{x}{2}$
4 less than twice a number is greater than 10.	$2x - 4 > 10$
Twice the difference between 4 and a number is 10.	$2(4 - x) = 10$
The product of 2 and the sum of 3 and a number is less than 10.	$2(x + 3) < 10$
The product of 2 and a number, subtracted from 5, yields 8.	$5 - 2x = 8$
Two thirds of a number subtracted from 10 is 2.	$10 - \frac{2}{3}x = 2$
25% of the sum of 7 and a number is 2.	$0.25(x + 7) = 2$

Table 1.8.13: Translating English Sentences into Math Equations

A certain amount of practice with translating these English phrases and sentences into math expressions, equations, and inequalities can be helpful for word problems that do have context. In the exercises for this section, you will find such practice exercises.

1.8.5 Reading Questions

1. It is common to come across a word problem where there is some kind of rate. In a problem like that, it can help you to understand the pattern if you make a [　　　　].

2. It is common to come across a word problem where some percent is either added or subtracted from an unknown original value. With the approach described in theis section for setting up an equation, how many times will you use the variable in such an equation?

3. Is there any difference between these three phrases, or do they all mean the same thing?

   - ten subtracted from a number

   - ten less than a number

   - ten minus a number

1.8.6 Exercises

Review and Warmup

1. Identify a variable you might use to represent each quantity. And identify what units would be most appropriate.

   a. Let [　] be the area of a house, measured in [　　　　　　].

   b. Let [　] be the age of a dog, measured in [　　　　　　].

   c. Let [　] be the amount of time passed since a driver left Seattle, Washington, bound for Portland, Oregon, measured in [　　　　　].

2. Identify a variable you might use to represent each quantity. And identify what units would be most appropriate.

   a. Let [　] be the age of a person, measured in [　　　　　].

   b. Let [　] be the distance traveled by a driver that left Portland, Oregon, bound for Boise, Idaho, measured in [　　　　].

   c. Let [　] be the surface area of the walls of a room, measured in [　　　　　　].

Modeling with Linear Equations

3. Sherial's annual salary as a radiography technician is $38,494.00. Her salary increased by 1.3% from last year. What was her salary last year?
   Assume her salary last year was s dollars. Write an equation to model this scenario. There is no need to solve it.

4. Ken's annual salary as a radiography technician is $42,066.00. His salary increased by 2.6% from last year. What was his salary last year?
   Assume his salary last year was s dollars. Write an equation to model this scenario. There is no need to solve it.

5. A bicycle for sale costs $180.71, which includes 6.3% sales tax. What was the cost before sales tax?

   Assume the bicycle's price before sales tax is p dollars. Write an equation to model this scenario. There is no need to solve it.

6. A bicycle for sale costs $210.60, which includes 5.3% sales tax. What was the cost before sales tax?

   Assume the bicycle's price before sales tax is p dollars. Write an equation to model this scenario. There is no need to solve it.

7. The price of a washing machine after 25% discount is $172.50. What was the original price of the washing machine (before the discount was applied)?

   Assume the washing machine's price before the discount is p dollars. Write an equation to model this scenario. There is no need to solve it.

8. The price of a washing machine after 15% discount is $221.00. What was the original price of the washing machine (before the discount was applied)?

   Assume the washing machine's price before the discount is p dollars. Write an equation to model this scenario. There is no need to solve it.

9. The price of a restaurant bill, including an 10% gratuity charge, was $110.00. What was the price of the bill before gratuity was added?

   Assume the bill without gratuity is b dollars. Write an equation to model this scenario. There is no need to solve it.

10. The price of a restaurant bill, including an 17% gratuity charge, was $11.70. What was the price of the bill before gratuity was added?

    Assume the bill without gratuity is b dollars. Write an equation to model this scenario. There is no need to solve it.

11. In May 2016, the median rent price for a one-bedroom apartment in a city was reported to be $904.50 per month. This was reported to be an increase of 0.5% over the previous month. Based on this reporting, what was the median price of a one-bedroom apartment in April 2016?

    Assume the median price of a one-bedroom apartment in April 2016 was p dollars. Write an equation to model this scenario. There is no need to solve it.

12. In May 2016, the median rent price for a one-bedroom apartment in a city was reported to be $1,002.00 per month. This was reported to be an increase of 0.2% over the previous month. Based on this reporting, what was the median price of a one-bedroom apartment in April 2016?

    Assume the median price of a one-bedroom apartment in April 2016 was p dollars. Write an equation to model this scenario. There is no need to solve it.

13. Briana is driving an average of 41 miles per hour, and she is 123 miles away from home. After how many hours will she reach his home?

    Assume Briana will reach home after h hours. Write an equation to model this scenario. There is no need to solve it.

14. Ryan is driving an average of 44 miles per hour, and he is 83.6 miles away from home. After how many hours will he reach his home?

    Assume Ryan will reach home after h hours. Write an equation to model this scenario. There is no need to solve it.

15. Uhaul charges an initial fee of $31.90 and then $0.89 per mile to rent a 15-foot truck for a day. If the total bill is $182.31, how many miles were driven?

    Assume m miles were driven. Write an equation to model this scenario. There is no need to solve it.

16. Uhaul charges an initial fee of $34.10 and then $0.75 per mile to rent a 15-foot truck for a day. If the total bill is $94.85, how many miles were driven?

    Assume m miles were driven. Write an equation to model this scenario. There is no need to solve it.

17. A cat litter box has a rectangular base that is 24 inches by 12 inches. What will the height of the cat litter be if 3 cubic feet of cat litter is poured? (Hint: $1 \text{ ft}^3 = 1728 \text{ in}^3$) Assume h inches will be the height of the cat litter if 3 cubic feet of cat litter is poured. Write an equation to model this scenario. There is no need to solve it.

18. A cat litter box has a rectangular base that is 24 inches by 24 inches. What will the height of the cat litter be if 4 cubic feet of cat litter is poured? (Hint: $1 \text{ ft}^3 = 1728 \text{ in}^3$) Assume h inches will be the height of the cat litter if 4 cubic feet of cat litter is poured. Write an equation to model this scenario. There is no need to solve it.

19. Ibuprofen for infants comes in a liquid form and contains 30 milligrams of ibuprofen for each 0.75 milliliters of liquid. If a child is to receive a dose of 50 milligrams of ibuprofen, how many milliliters of liquid should they be given? Assume l milliliters of liquid should be given. Write an equation to model this scenario. There is no need to solve it.

20. Ibuprofen for infants comes in a liquid form and contains 35 milligrams of ibuprofen for each 0.875 milliliters of liquid. If a child is to receive a dose of 60 milligrams of ibuprofen, how many milliliters of liquid should they be given? Assume l milliliters of liquid should be given. Write an equation to model this scenario. There is no need to solve it.

21. The property taxes on a 2400-square-foot house are $2,832.00 per year. Assuming these taxes are proportional, what are the property taxes on a 1600-square-foot house? Assume property taxes on a 1600-square-foot house is t dollars. Write an equation to model this scenario. There is no need to solve it.

22. The property taxes on a 1900-square-foot house are $2,489.00 per year. Assuming these taxes are proportional, what are the property taxes on a 1500-square-foot house? Assume property taxes on a 1500-square-foot house is t dollars. Write an equation to model this scenario. There is no need to solve it.

Modeling with Linear Inequalities

23. A truck that hauls water is capable of carrying a maximum of 1800 lb. Water weighs $8.3454 \frac{\text{lb}}{\text{gal}}$, and the plastic tank on the truck that holds water weighs 74 lb. Assume the truck can carry a maximum of g gallons of water. Write an *inequality* to model this scenario. There is no need to solve it.

24. A truck that hauls water is capable of carrying a maximum of 2800 lb. Water weighs $8.3454 \frac{\text{lb}}{\text{gal}}$, and the plastic tank on the truck that holds water weighs 80 lb. Assume the truck can carry a maximum of g gallons of water. Write an *inequality* to model this scenario. There is no need to solve it.

25. Lindsay's maximum lung capacity is 6.8 liters. If her lungs are full and she exhales at a rate of 0.8 liters per second, write an *inequality* that models when she will still have at least 0.56 liters of air left in his lungs. There is no need to solve it.

26. Lily's maximum lung capacity is 7.3 liters. If her lungs are full and she exhales at a rate of 0.8 liters per second, write an *inequality* that models when she will still have at least 3.94 liters of air left in his lungs. There is no need to solve it.

27. A swimming pool is being filled with water from a garden hose at a rate of 9 gallons per minute. If the pool already contains 100 gallons of water and can hold up to 334 gallons, set up an *inequality* modeling how much time can pass without the pool overflowing. There is no need to solve it.

28. A swimming pool is being filled with water from a garden hose at a rate of 7 gallons per minute. If the pool already contains 10 gallons of water and can hold up to 108 gallons, set up an *inequality* modeling how much time can pass without the pool overflowing. There is no need to solve it.

29. An engineer is designing a cylindrical springform pan (the kind of pan a cheesecake is baked in). The pan needs to be able to hold a volume at least 33 cubic inches and have a diameter of 6 inches. Write an *inequality* modeling possible height of the pan. There is no need to solve it.

30. An engineer is designing a cylindrical springform pan (the kind of pan a cheesecake is baked in). The pan needs to be able to hold a volume at least 96 cubic inches and have a diameter of 7 inches. Write an *inequality* modeling possible height of the pan. There is no need to solve it.

Translating English Phrases into Math Expressions and Equations Translate the following phrase or sentence into a math expression or equation (whichever is appropriate).

31. five more than a number

32. one less than a number

33. the sum of a number and eight

34. the difference between a number and four

35. the difference between one and a number

36. the difference between seven and a number

37. four subtracted from a number

38. ten added to a number

39. seven decreased by a number

40. three increased by a number

41. a number decreased by ten

42. a number increased by six

43. four times a number, decreased by five

44. ten times a number, decreased by nine

45. six less than four times a number

46. two less than eight times a number

47. nine less than the quotient of three and a number

48. five more than the quotient of six and a number

49. Three times a number is twenty-four.

50. Nine times a number is thirty-six.

51. The sum of forty and a number is fifty-six.

52. The sum of eighteen and a number is twenty-three.

53. The quotient of a number and three is thirteen thirds.

54. The quotient of a number and thirty-one is one thirty-first.

55. The quotient of three and a number is one eighth.

56. The quotient of twenty and a number is five thirds.

57. The sum of four times a number and ten is 194.

58. The sum of twice a number and twenty-two is eighty-eight.

59. Two less than six times a number is sixty-four.

60. Two less than four times a number is 118.

61. The product of eight and a number, added to eight, is 344.

62. The product of six and a number, increased by four, is 178.

63. The product of three and a number added to seven, is sixty-nine.

64. The product of eight and a number increased by three, is 424.

65. one seventh of a number

66. one fourth of a number

67. twenty-seven forty-seconds of a number

68. seventeen forty-fourths of a number

69. a number decreased by two twelfths of itself

70. a number increased by eight thirtieths of itself

71. A number decreased by two thirds is three elevenths of that number.

72. A number increased by one sixth is three elevenths of that number.

73. One less than the product of three elevenths and a number gives two ninths of that number.

74. Three more than the product of two thirds and a number gives one third of that number.

Challenge

75. Last year, Joan received a 1% raise. This year, she received a 2% raise. Her current wage is $11.07 an hour. What was her wage before the two raises?

1.9 Variables, Expressions, and Equations Chapter Review

1.9.1 Variables and Evaluating Expressions

In Section 1.1 we covered the definitions of variables and expressions, and how to evaluate an expression with a particular number.

Evaluating Expressions. When we evaluate an expression's value, we substitute each variable with its given value.

Example 1.9.1 Evaluate the value of $\frac{5}{9}(F - 32)$ if $F = 212$.

$$\frac{5}{9}(F - 32) = \frac{5}{9}(212 - 32)$$
$$= \frac{5}{9}(180)$$
$$= 100$$

Substituting a Negative Number. When we substitute a variable with a negative number, it's important to use parentheses around the number.

Example 1.9.2 Evaluate the following expressions if $x = -3$.

a. $x^2 = (-3)^2$
   $= 9$

b. $x^3 = (-3)^3$
   $= (-3)(-3)(-3)$
   $= -27$

c. $-x^2 = -(-3)^2$
   $= -9$

d. $-x^3 = -(-3)^3$
   $= -(-27)$
   $= 27$

1.9.2 Combining Like Terms

In Section 1.2 we covered the definitions of a term and how to combine like terms.

Example 1.9.3 List the terms in the expression $5x - 3y + \frac{2w}{3}$.

Explanation. The expression has three terms that are being added, $5x$, $-3y$ and $\frac{2w}{3}$.

Example 1.9.4 Simplify the expression $5x - 3x^2 + 2x + 5x^2$, if possible, by combining like terms.

Explanation. This expression has four terms: $5x$, $-3x^2$, $2x$, and $5x^2$. Both $5x$ and $2x$ are like terms; also $-3x^2$ and $5x^2$ are like terms. When we combine like terms, we get:

$$5x - 3x^2 + 2x + 5x^2 = 7x + 2x^2$$

Note that we cannot combine $7x$ and $2x^2$ because x and x^2 represent different quantities.

1.9.3 Comparison Symbols and Notation for Intervals

The following are symbols used to compare numbers.

Symbol	Means	True	True	False
$=$	equals	$13 = 13$	$\frac{5}{4} = 1.25$	$5 \overset{no}{=} 6$
$>$	is greater than	$13 > 11$	$\pi > 3$	$9 \overset{no}{>} 9$
$\geq$	is greater than or equal to	$13 \geq 11$	$3 \geq 3$	$11.2 \overset{no}{\geq} 10.2$
$<$	is less than	$-3 < 8$	$\frac{1}{2} < \frac{2}{3}$	$2 \overset{no}{<} -2$
$\leq$	is less than or equal to	$-3 \leq 8$	$3 \leq 3$	$\frac{4}{5} \overset{no}{\leq} \frac{3}{5}$
$\neq$	is not equal to	$10 \neq 20$	$\frac{1}{2} \neq 1.2$	$\frac{3}{8} \overset{no}{\neq} 0.375$

Table 1.9.5: Comparison Symbols

The following are some examples of set-builder notation and interval notation.

Graph	Set-builder Notation	Interval Notation
number line, closed at 1, arrow right	$\{x \mid x \geq 1\}$	$[1, \infty)$
number line, open at 1, arrow right	$\{x \mid x > 1\}$	$(1, \infty)$
number line, closed at 1, arrow left	$\{x \mid x \leq 1\}$	$(-\infty, 1]$
number line, open at 1, arrow left	$\{x \mid x < 1\}$	$(-\infty, 1)$

1.9.4 Equations and Inequalities as True/False Statements

In Section 1.4 we covered the definitions of an equation and an inequality, as well as how to verify if a particular number is a solution to them.

Checking Possible Solutions. Given an equation or an inequality (with one variable), checking if some particular number is a solution is just a matter of replacing the value of the variable with the specified number and determining if the resulting equation/inequality is true or false. This may involve some amount of arithmetic simplification.

Example 1.9.6 Is -5 a solution to $2(x + 3) - 2 = 4 - x$?

Explanation. To find out, substitute in -5 for x and see what happens.

$$2(x + 3) - 2 = 4 - x$$
$$2((-5) + 3) - 2 \overset{?}{=} 4 - (-5)$$
$$2(-2) - 2 \overset{?}{=} 9$$
$$-4 - 2 \overset{?}{=} 9$$
$$-6 \overset{no}{=} 9$$

So no, -5 is not a solution to $2(x + 3) - 2 = 4 - x$.

1.9.5 Solving One-Step Equations

In Section 1.5 we covered to to add, subtract, multiply, or divide on both sides of an equation to isolate the variable, summarized in Fact 1.5.13. We also learned how to state our answer, either as a solution or a solution set. Last, we discussed how to solve equations with fractions.

Solving One-Step Equations. When we solve linear equations, we use Properties of Equivalent Equations and follow an algorithm to solve a linear equation.

Example 1.9.7 Solve for g in $\frac{1}{2} = \frac{2}{3} + g$.

Explanation.

We will subtract $\frac{2}{3}$ on both sides of the equation:

$$\frac{1}{2} = \frac{2}{3} + g$$
$$\frac{1}{2} - \frac{2}{3} = \frac{2}{3} + g - \frac{2}{3}$$
$$\frac{3}{6} - \frac{4}{6} = g$$
$$-\frac{1}{6} = g$$

We will check the solution by substituting g in the original equation with $-\frac{1}{6}$:

$$\frac{1}{2} = \frac{2}{3} + g$$
$$\frac{1}{2} \overset{?}{=} \frac{2}{3} + \left(-\frac{1}{6}\right)$$
$$\frac{1}{2} \overset{?}{=} \frac{4}{6} + \left(-\frac{1}{6}\right)$$
$$\frac{1}{2} \overset{\checkmark}{=} \frac{3}{6}$$

The solution $-\frac{1}{6}$ is checked and the solution set is $\left\{-\frac{1}{6}\right\}$.

1.9.6 Solving One-Step Inequalities

In Section 1.6 we covered how solving inequalities is very much like how we solve equations, except that if we multiply or divide by a negative we switch the inequality sign.

Solving One-Step Inequalities. When we solve linear inequalities, we also use Properties of Equivalent Equations with one small complication: When we multiply or divide by the same *negative* number on both sides of an inequality, the direction reverses!

Example 1.9.8 Solve the inequality $-2x \geq 12$. State the solution set with both interval notation and set-builder notation.

Explanation. To solve this inequality, we will divide each side by -2:

$$-2x \geq 12$$
$$\frac{-2x}{-2} \leq \frac{12}{-2} \qquad \text{Note the change in direction.}$$
$$x \leq -6$$

- The inequality's solution set in interval notation is $(-\infty, -6]$.

- The inequality's solution set in set-builder notation is $\{x \mid x \leq -6\}$.

1.9.7 Algebraic Properties and Simplifying Expressions

In Section 1.7 we covered the definitions of the identities and inverses, and the various algebraic properties. We then learned about the order of operations.

Example 1.9.9 Use the associative, commutative, and distributive properties to simplify the expression $5x + 9(-2x + 3)$ as much as possible.

Explanation.   We will remove parentheses by the distributive property, and then combine like terms:

$$\begin{aligned}
5x + 9(-2x + 3) &= 5x + 9(-2x + 3) \\
&= 5x + 9(-2x) + 9(3) \\
&= 5x - 18x + 27 \\
&= -13x + 27
\end{aligned}$$

1.9.8 Modeling with Equations and Inequalities

In Section 1.8 we covered how to translate phrases into mathematics, and how to set up equations and inequalities for application models.

Modeling with Equations and Inequalities.   To set up an equation modeling a real world scenario, the first thing we need to do is to identify what variable we will use. The variable we use will be determined by whatever is unknown in our problem statement. Once we've identified and defined our variable, we'll use the numerical information provided in the equation to set up our equation.

Example 1.9.10 A bathtub contains $2.5\,\text{ft}^3$ of water. More water is being poured in at a rate of $1.75\,\text{ft}^3$ per minute. When will the amount of water in the bathtub reach $6.25\,\text{ft}^3$?

Explanation.   Since the question being asked in this problem starts with "when," we immediately know that the unknown is time. As the volume of water in the tub is measured in ft^3 per minute, we know that time needs to be measured in minutes. We'll defined t to be the number of minutes that water is poured into the tub. Since each minute there are $1.75\,\text{ft}^3$ of water added, we will add the expression $1.75t$ to 2.5 to obtain the total amount of water. Thus the equation we set up is:

$$2.5 + 1.75t = 6.25$$

1.9.9 Exercises

Variables and Evaluating Expressions

1. Evaluate the expression y^2:

  a. For $y = 8$.

  b. For $y = -3$.

2. Evaluate the expression y^2:

  a. For $y = 5$.

  b. For $y = -7$.

3. Evaluate $\dfrac{2r - 9}{9r}$ for $r = -9$.

4. Evaluate $\dfrac{6r - 2}{9r}$ for $r = 5$.

5. Evaluate the expression $\dfrac{1}{3}(x + 4)^2 - 4$ when $x = -7$.

6. Evaluate the expression $\dfrac{1}{4}(x + 4)^2 - 2$ when $x = -8$.

To convert a temperature measured in degrees Fahrenheit to degrees Celsius, there is a formula:

$$C = \frac{5}{9}(F - 32)$$

where C represents the temperature in degrees Celsius and F represents the temperature in degrees Fahrenheit.

7. If a temperature is 5°F, what is that temperature measured in Celsius?

8. If a temperature is 14°F, what is that temperature measured in Celsius?

The percentage of births in the U.S. delivered via C-section can be given by the following formula for the years since 1996:

$$p = 0.8(y - 1996) + 21$$

In this formula y is a year after 1996 and p is the percentage of births delivered via C-section for that year.

9. What percentage of births in the U.S. were delivered via C-section in the year 2001?

of births in the U.S. were delivered via C-section in the year 2001.

10. What percentage of births in the U.S. were delivered via C-section in the year 2003?

of births in the U.S. were delivered via C-section in the year 2003.

Combining Like Terms

11. Count the number of terms in each expression.

a. $8t + y + 8s^2$

b. $3t - 5x$

c. $-5z^2 + 7z$

d. $-3y^2 - 3x - 5x + 2z^2$

12. Count the number of terms in each expression.

a. $-9t^2 + 9t^2 + 6z^2$

b. $2t - 9t + 5s - 1$

c. $6x^2 - 7s + x + 9y$

d. $9t^2 + 8z^2$

13. List the terms in each expression.

a. $-6.9t - 1.1x + 3.4x^2$

b. $0.7s^2 + 5.3y^2 - 1.5$

c. $-3.4x^2 - 2.1t$

d. $-7.9s - 8.6t^2$

14. List the terms in each expression.

a. $-5.2t^2 + 7.1z + 1.4t^2 - 0.5s$

b. $1.3t - 7.7x$

c. $-5.6x^2 + 8.5y - 8.9x^2$

d. $-0.1y$

Simplify each expression, if possible, by combining like terms.

15. a. $-\frac{1}{2}t - \frac{3}{7} - \frac{9}{2}t^2 - t^2$

b. $-\frac{5}{3}s^2 - \frac{1}{6}s^2 + 9z^2 + \frac{1}{6}s$

c. $-2t + \frac{5}{8}z$

d. $-\frac{3}{7}y^2 - 2y^2 + \frac{6}{7}$

16. a. $\frac{2}{3}t^2 + \frac{9}{7}t^2$

b. $-\frac{2}{3}y^2 + \frac{7}{6}s^2 - \frac{3}{8}s^2$

c. $\frac{7}{4}z + s^2 + \frac{1}{3}z^2$

d. $-9z^2 + 2y^2 + \frac{3}{4}z$

Comparison Symbols and Notation for Intervals

17. Decide if each comparison is true or false.

a. $-\frac{3}{3} \neq -\frac{6}{6}$ ($\square$ True $\square$ False)

b. $\frac{29}{4} < \frac{7}{4}$ ($\square$ True $\square$ False)

c. $-\frac{5}{9} < -\frac{5}{9}$ ($\square$ True $\square$ False)

d. $\frac{7}{4} \geq -\frac{58}{7}$ ($\square$ True $\square$ False)

e. $\frac{19}{4} > -\frac{15}{8}$ ($\square$ True $\square$ False)

f. $\frac{82}{9} = -\frac{41}{5}$ ($\square$ True $\square$ False)

18. Decide if each comparison is true or false.

a. $-\frac{6}{3} = -\frac{12}{6}$ ($\square$ True $\square$ False)

b. $\frac{9}{2} < \frac{9}{2}$ ($\square$ True $\square$ False)

c. $-\frac{16}{3} > \frac{27}{8}$ ($\square$ True $\square$ False)

d. $\frac{11}{6} \leq -\frac{6}{4}$ ($\square$ True $\square$ False)

e. $\frac{9}{2} \geq -\frac{76}{8}$ ($\square$ True $\square$ False)

f. $\frac{77}{9} \neq \frac{5}{2}$ ($\square$ True $\square$ False)

19. Choose $<$, $>$, or $=$ to make a true statement.
$\frac{2}{3} + \frac{4}{5}$ ($\square <$ $\square >$ $\square =$) $\frac{4}{3} \div \frac{1}{4}$

20. Choose $<$, $>$, or $=$ to make a true statement.
$\frac{3}{2} + \frac{1}{3}$ ($\square <$ $\square >$ $\square =$) $\frac{4}{5} \div \frac{4}{5}$

21. For each interval expressed in the number lines, give the interval notation and set-builder notation.

a.   b.   c.

22. For each interval expressed in the number lines, give the interval notation and set-builder notation.

a.   b.   c.

23. A set is written using set-builder notation. Write it using interval notation.
$\{x \mid x \leq 6\}$

24. A set is written using set-builder notation. Write it using interval notation.
$\{x \mid x \leq 8\}$

Equations and Inequalities as True/False Statements

25. Is -2 a solution for x in the equation $-6x - 10 = 2x + 6$?   ($\square$ Yes $\square$ No)

26. Is -10 a solution for x in the equation $3x + 5 = 2x - 4$?   ($\square$ Yes $\square$ No)

27. Is $\frac{3}{4}$ a solution for x in the equation $-\frac{5}{9}x - \frac{1}{2} = -\frac{67}{54}$?   ($\square$ Yes $\square$ No)

28. Is 6 a solution for y in the equation $\frac{3}{7}y + \frac{1}{6} = \frac{5}{21}$?   ($\square$ Yes $\square$ No)

29. When a plant was purchased, it was 1 inches tall. It grows 0.6 inches per day. How many days later will the plant be 12.4 inches tall?

Assume the plant will be 12.4 inches tall d days later. We can solve this problem using the equation:

$$0.6d + 1 = 12.4$$

Check whether 22 is a solution for d of this equation.   ($\square$ Yes $\square$ No)

30. When a plant was purchased, it was 2.4 inches tall. It grows 0.7 inches per day. How many days later will the plant be 11.5 inches tall?

Assume the plant will be 11.5 inches tall d days later. We can solve this problem using the equation:

$$0.7d + 2.4 = 11.5$$

Check whether 15 is a solution for d of this equation.   ($\square$ Yes $\square$ No)

Solving One-Step Equations

31. Solve the equation.
$r - 4 = 4$

32. Solve the equation.
$t - 10 = -7$

33. Solve the equation.
$\frac{6}{7} + p = -\frac{5}{8}$

34. Solve the equation.
$\frac{6}{5} + x = -\frac{7}{6}$

35. Solve the equation.
$\frac{5}{3} = \frac{x}{27}$

36. Solve the equation.
$\frac{9}{4} = \frac{x}{28}$

37. Solve the equation.
a. $2y = 16$
b. $2 + x = 16$

38. Solve the equation.
a. $6y = 36$
b. $6 + t = 36$

39. Solve the equation.
a. $54 = -9r$
b. $54 = -9 + x$

40. Solve the equation.
a. $14 = -7r$
b. $14 = -7 + x$

41. Solve the equation.
a. $30 = -\frac{10}{7}m$
b. $-30 = -\frac{10}{7}p$

42. Solve the equation.
a. $20 = -\frac{4}{5}p$
b. $-20 = -\frac{4}{5}A$

Solving One-Step Inequalities Solve this inequality.

43. $5 > x - 6$

44. $1 > x - 10$

45. $2x \leq 6$

46. $3x \leq 6$

47. $-3x \geq 12$

48. $-4x \geq 12$

49. $\frac{7}{2}x > 7$

50. $\frac{8}{7}x > 8$

51. $-\frac{9}{5}x \leq 9$

52. $-\frac{10}{7}x \leq 40$

Algebraic Properties and Simplifying Expressions

53. What is the additive inverse of -8?

54. What is the additive inverse of -6?

55. What is the multiplicative inverse of -4?

56. What is the multiplicative inverse of -1?

57. Use the associative property of addition to write an equivalent expression to $a + (19 + y)$.

58. Use the associative property of addition to write an equivalent expression to $q + (18 + p)$.

59. Use the associative property of multiplication to write an equivalent expression to $7(5m)$.

60. Use the associative property of multiplication to write an equivalent expression to $4(9p)$.

61. Use the commutative property of addition to write an equivalent expression to $4q + 91$.

62. Use the commutative property of addition to write an equivalent expression to $7y + 56$.

63. Use the commutative property of multiplication to write an equivalent expression to $21r$.

64. Use the commutative property of multiplication to write an equivalent expression to $87a$.

65. Use the distributive property to write an equivalent expression to $6(c + 10)$ that has no grouping symbols.

66. Use the distributive property to write an equivalent expression to $4(r + 7)$ that has no grouping symbols.

67. Use the distributive property to simplify $8 - 7(-9 - 7n)$ completely.

68. Use the distributive property to simplify $6 - 9(-9 - 10m)$ completely.

69. Use the distributive property to simplify $3p - 5p(7 - 10p^2)$ completely.

70. Use the distributive property to simplify $8q - 2q(1 - 10q^4)$ completely.

71. Fully simplify $-(-5x - 4) + 3(7x + 8)$.

72. Fully simplify $2(x + 8) - 4(-x + 3)$.

Modeling with Equations and Inequalities

73. A bicycle for sale costs \$139.36, which includes 7.2% sales tax. What was the cost before sales tax?
    Assume the bicycle's price before sales tax is p dollars. Write an equation to model this scenario. There is no need to solve it.

74. A bicycle for sale costs \$169.76, which includes 6.1% sales tax. What was the cost before sales tax?
    Assume the bicycle's price before sales tax is p dollars. Write an equation to model this scenario. There is no need to solve it.

75. The price of a washing machine after 5% discount is \$180.50. What was the original price of the washing machine (before the discount was applied)?
    Assume the washing machine's price before the discount is p dollars. Write an equation to model this scenario. There is no need to solve it.

76. The price of a washing machine after 25% discount is \$157.50. What was the original price of the washing machine (before the discount was applied)?
    Assume the washing machine's price before the discount is p dollars. Write an equation to model this scenario. There is no need to solve it.

77. Lisa is driving an average of 53 miles per hour, and she is 106 miles away from home. After how many hours will she reach his home?
    Assume Lisa will reach home after h hours. Write an equation to model this scenario. There is no need to solve it.

78. Emiliano is driving an average of 57 miles per hour, and he is 228 miles away from home. After how many hours will he reach his home?
    Assume Emiliano will reach home after h hours. Write an equation to model this scenario. There is no need to solve it.

Translate the following phrase or sentence into a math expression or equation (whichever is appropriate).

79. seven less than eight times a number

80. three less than three times a number

81. ten more than the quotient of seven and a number

82. seven more than the quotient of ten and a number

83. One less than three times a number yields sixty-eight.

84. One less than eight times a number yields 335.

85. The product of five and a number increased by three, yields 125.

86. The product of three and a number added to six, yields forty-five.

87. A number increased by three fourths is three tenths of that number.

88. A number decreased by two sevenths is three tenths of that number.

Chapter 2

Linear Equations and Inequalities

2.1 Solving Multistep Linear Equations

We learned how to solve one-step equations in Section 1.5. In this section, we will solve equations that need more than one step.

2.1.1 Solving Two-Step Equations

Example 2.1.2 A water tank can hold up to 140 gallons of water, but it starts with only 5 gallons. A tap is turned on, pouring 15 gallons of water into the tank every minute. After how many minutes will the tank be full? Let's find a pattern first.

Minutes Since Tap Was Turned on	Amount of Water in the Tank (in Gallons)
0	5
1	$15 \cdot 1 + 5 = 20$
2	$15 \cdot 2 + 5 = 35$
3	$15 \cdot 3 + 5 = 50$
4	$15 \cdot 4 + 5 = 65$
$\vdots$	$\vdots$
m	$15m + 5$

We can see that after m minutes, the tank has $15m + 5$ gallons of water. This makes sense since the tap pours 15 gallons into the tank for each of m minutes, and it has 5 gallons to start with. To find when the tank will be full with 140 gallons, we can write the equation

$$15m + 5 = 140$$

Figure 2.1.3: Amount of Water in the Tank

First, we need to isolate the variable term, $15m$. In other words, we need to "remove" the 5 from the left side of the equals sign. We can do this by subtracting 5 from both sides of the equation. Once the variable term is isolated, we can eliminate its coefficient and solve for m.

87

The full process is:

$$15m + 5 = 140$$
$$15m + 5 - 5 = 140 - 5$$
$$15m = 135$$
$$\frac{15m}{15} = \frac{135}{15}$$
$$m = 9$$

We should check the solution by substituting m with 9 in the original equation:

$$15m + 5 = 140$$
$$15(9) + 5 \stackrel{?}{=} 140$$
$$135 + 5 \stackrel{\checkmark}{=} 140$$

The solution 9 is checked.

This problem had *context*. It was not simply solving an equation, rather it comes with the story of the tank filling with water. So we report a conclusion that uses that context: In summary, the tank will be full after 9 minutes.

In solving the two-step equation in Example 2.1.2, we first isolated the variable expression $15m$ and then eliminated the coefficient of 15 by dividing each side of the equation by 15. These two steps are at the heart of our approach to solving linear equations. For more complicated equations, we may need to simplify one or both sides first. Below is a general approach that summarizes all of this.

Process 2.1.4 Steps to Solve Linear Equations.

Simplify *Simplify the expressions on each side of the equation by distributing and combining like terms.*

Separate *Use addition or subtraction to separate the variable terms and constant terms so that they are on different sides of the equation.*

Clear Coefficient *Use multiplication or division to eliminate the variable term's coefficient.*

Check *Check the solution in the original equation. Substitute values into the original equation and use the order of operations to simplify both sides. It's important to use the order of operations alone rather than properties like the distributive law. Otherwise you might repeat the same arithmetic errors made while solving and fail to catch an incorrect solution.*

Summarize *State the solution set. Or in the case of an application problem, summarize the result in a complete sentence using appropriate units.*

Example 2.1.5 Solve for y in the equation $7 - 3y = -8$.

Explanation.   To solve, we first separate the variable terms and constant terms to different sides of the equation. Then we eliminate the variable term's coefficient.

$$7 - 3y = -8$$
$$7 - 3y - 7 = -8 - 7$$
$$-3y = -15$$
$$\frac{-3y}{-3} = \frac{-15}{-3}$$
$$y = 5$$

Checking the solution $y = 5$:

$$7 - 3y = -8$$
$$7 - 3(5) \stackrel{?}{=} -8$$
$$7 - 15 \stackrel{\checkmark}{=} -8$$

So the solution to the equation $7 - 3y = -8$ is 5 and the solution set is $\{5\}$.

2.1.2 Solving Multistep Linear Equations

Example 2.1.6 Ahmed has saved $2,500.00 in his savings account and is going to start saving $550.00 per month. Julia has saved $4,600.00 in her savings account and is going to start saving $250.00 per month. If this situation continues, how many months will it take Ahmed catch up with Julia in savings?

Ahmed saves $550.00 per month, so he can save 550m dollars in m months. With the $2,500.00 he started with, after m months he has $550m + 2500$ dollars. Similarly, after m months, Julia has $250m + 4600$ dollars. To find when those two accounts will have the same amount of money, we can write the equation

$$550m + 2500 = 250m + 4600.$$

$$550m + 2500 = 250m + 4600$$
$$550m + 2500 - 2500 = 250m + 4600 - 2500$$
$$550m = 250m + 2100$$
$$550m - 250m = 250m + 2100 - 250m$$
$$300m = 2100$$
$$\frac{300m}{300} = \frac{2100}{300}$$
$$m = 7$$

Checking the solution 7:

$$550m + 2500 = 250m + 4600$$
$$550(7) + 2500 \stackrel{?}{=} 250(7) + 4600$$
$$3850 + 2500 \stackrel{?}{=} 1750 + 4600$$
$$6350 \stackrel{\checkmark}{=} 6350$$

Ahmed will catch up with Julia's savings after 7 months.

Example 2.1.7 Solve for x in $5 - 2x = 5x - 9$.

Explanation.

$$5 - 2x = 5x - 9$$
$$5 - 2x - 5 = 5m - 9 - 5$$
$$-2x = 5x - 14$$
$$-2x - 5x = 5x - 14 - 5x$$
$$-7x = -14$$
$$\frac{-7x}{-7} = \frac{-14}{-7}$$
$$x = 2$$

Checking the solution 2:

$$5 - 2x = 5x - 9$$
$$5 - 2(2) \stackrel{?}{=} 5(2) - 9$$
$$5 - 4 \stackrel{?}{=} 10 - 9$$
$$1 \stackrel{\checkmark}{=} 1$$

Therefore the solution is 2 and the solution set is $\{2\}$.

Example 2.1.8 In Example 2.1.7, we could have moved variable terms to the right side of the equals sign, and number terms to the left side. We chose not to. There's no reason we *couldn't* have moved variable terms to the right side though. Let's compare:

$$5 - 2x = 5x - 9$$
$$5 - 2x + 9 = 5x - 9 + 9$$
$$14 - 2x = 5x$$
$$14 - 2x + 2x = 5x + 2x$$
$$14 = 7x$$
$$\frac{14}{7} = \frac{7x}{7}$$

$$2 = x$$

Lastly, we could save a step by moving variable terms and number terms in one step:

$$5 - 2x = 5x - 9$$
$$5 - 2x + 2x + 9 = 5x - 9 + 2x + 9$$
$$14 = 7x$$
$$\frac{14}{7} = \frac{7x}{7}$$
$$2 = x$$

For the sake of a slow and careful explanation, the examples in this chapter will move variable terms and number terms separately.

Checkpoint 2.1.9 Solve the equation.

$$9y + 3 = y + 83$$

Explanation.   The first step is to subtract terms in order to separate the variable and non-variable terms.

$$9y + 3 = y + 83$$
$$9y + 3 - \mathbf{y} - \mathbf{3} = y + 83 - \mathbf{y} - \mathbf{3}$$
$$8y = 80$$
$$\frac{8y}{8} = \frac{80}{8}$$
$$y = 10$$

The solution to this equation is 10. To stress that this is a value assigned to y, some report $y = 10$. We can also say that the solution set is $\{10\}$, or that $y \in \{10\}$. If we substitute 10 in for y in the original equation $9y + 3 = y + 83$, the equation will be true. Please check this on your own; it is an important habit.

The next example requires combining like terms.

Example 2.1.10 Solve for n in $n - 9 + 3n = n - 3n$.

Explanation.   To start solving this equation, we'll need to combine like terms. After this, we can put all terms containing n on one side of the equation and finish solving for n.

$$n - 9 + 3n = n - 3n$$
$$4n - 9 = -2n$$
$$4n - 9 - 4n = -2n - 4n$$
$$-9 = -6n$$
$$\frac{-9}{-6} = \frac{-6n}{-6}$$
$$\frac{3}{2} = n$$

Checking the solution $\frac{3}{2}$:

$$n - 9 + 3n = n - 3n$$
$$\frac{3}{2} - 9 + 3\left(\frac{3}{2}\right) \stackrel{?}{=} \frac{3}{2} - 3\left(\frac{3}{2}\right)$$
$$\frac{3}{2} - 9 + \frac{9}{2} \stackrel{?}{=} \frac{3}{2} - \frac{9}{2}$$
$$\frac{12}{2} - 9 \stackrel{?}{=} -\frac{6}{2}$$
$$6 - 9 \stackrel{\checkmark}{=} -3$$

The solution to the equation $n - 9 + 3n = n - 3n$ is $\frac{3}{2}$ and the solution set is $\left\{\frac{3}{2}\right\}$.

Checkpoint 2.1.11 Solve the equation.

$$-6 + 7 = -5t - t - 11$$

Explanation. The first step is simply to combine like terms.

$$-6 + 7 = -5t - t - 11$$
$$1 = -6t - 11$$
$$1 + \mathbf{11} = -6t - 11 + \mathbf{11}$$
$$12 = -6t$$
$$\frac{12}{-6} = \frac{-6t}{-6}$$
$$-2 = t$$
$$t = -2$$

The solution to this equation is -2. To stress that this is a value assigned to t, some report $t = -2$. We can also say that the solution set is $\{-2\}$, or that $t \in \{-2\}$. If we substitute -2 in for t in the original equation $-6 + 7 = -5t - t - 11$, the equation will be true. Please check this on your own; it is an important habit.

We should be careful when we distribute a negative sign into the parentheses, like in the next example.

Example 2.1.12 Solve for a in $4 - (3 - a) = -2 - 2(2a + 1)$.

Explanation. To solve this equation, we will simplify each side of the equation, manipulate it so that all variable terms are on one side and all constant terms are on the other, and then solve for a:

$$4 - (3 - a) = -2 - 2(2a + 1)$$
$$4 - 3 + a = -2 - 4a - 2$$
$$1 + a = -4 - 4a$$
$$1 + a + 4a = -4 - 4a + 4a$$
$$1 + 5a = -4$$
$$1 + 5a - 1 = -4 - 1$$
$$5a = -5$$
$$\frac{5a}{5} = \frac{-5}{5}$$
$$a = -1$$

Checking the solution -1:

$$4 - (3 - a) = -2 - 2(2a + 1)$$
$$4 - (3 - (-1)) \stackrel{?}{=} -2 - 2(2(-1) + 1)$$
$$4 - (4) \stackrel{?}{=} -2 - 2(-1)$$
$$0 \stackrel{?}{=} -2 + 2$$
$$0 \stackrel{\checkmark}{=} 0$$

Therefore the solution to the equation is -1 and the solution set is $\{-1\}$.

2.1.3 Revisiting Applications from Section 1.8

In Section 1.8, we set up equations given some background information, but we didn't try to solve the equations yet. Now we can do that.

Example 2.1.13 Here we revisit Example 1.8.2.

A savings account starts with $500. Each month, an automatic deposit of $150 is made. Find the number of months it will take for the balance to reach $1,700.

Explanation.

To set up an equation, we might start by making a table in order to identify a general pattern for the total amount in the account after m months. In Figure 2.1.14, we find the pattern is that after m months, the total amount saved is $500 + 150m$. Using this pattern, we determine that an equation representing when the total savings equals \$1700 is:

$$500 + 150m = 1700$$

Months Since Saving Started	Total Amount Saved (in Dollars)
0	500
1	$500 + 150 = 650$
2	$500 + 150(2) = 800$
3	$500 + 150(3) = 950$
4	$500 + 150(4) = 1100$
$\vdots$	$\vdots$
m	$500 + 150m$

Figure 2.1.14: Amount in Savings Account

To solve this equation, we can start by subtracting 500 from each side. Then we cna divide each side by 150.

$$500 + 150m = 1700$$
$$500 + 150m - 500 = 1700 - 500$$
$$150m = 1200$$
$$\frac{150m}{150} = \frac{1200}{150}$$
$$m = 8$$

Checking the solution 8:

$$500 + 150m = 1700$$
$$500 + 150(8) \stackrel{?}{=} 1700$$
$$500 + 1200 \stackrel{\checkmark}{=} 1700$$

So 8 is the solution, and it checks out. This means it will take 8 months for the account balance to reach \$1700.

Example 2.1.15 Here we revisit Example 1.8.4.

A bathtub contains 2.5 ft^3 of water. More water is being poured in at a rate of 1.75 ft^3 per minute. How long will it be until the amount of water in the bathtub reaches 6.25 ft^3?

Explanation.

Since this problem refers to *when* the amount of water will reach a certain amount, we immediately know that the unknown quantity is time. As the volume of water in the tub is measured in ft^3 per minute, we know that time needs to be measured in minutes. We'll define t to be the number of minutes that water is poured into the tub. To determine this equation, we'll start by making a table of values:

Minutes Water Has Been Poured	Total Amount of Water (in ft^3)
0	2.5
1	$2.5 + 1.75 = 4.25$
2	$2.5 + 1.75(2) = 6$
3	$2.5 + 1.75(3) = 7.75$
$\vdots$	$\vdots$
t	$2.5 + 1.75t$

Figure 2.1.16: Amount of Water in the Bathtub

Using this pattern, we determine that the equation representing when the amount will be 6.25 ft^3 is:

$$2.5 + 1.75t = 6.25$$

To solve this equation, we can start by subtracting 2.5 from each side. Then we cna divide each side by 1.75.

$$2.5 + 1.75t = 6.25$$
$$2.5 + 1.75t - 2.5 = 6.25 - 2.5$$
$$1.75t = 3.75$$
$$\frac{1.75t}{1.75} = \frac{3.75}{1.75}$$
$$t = \frac{375}{175} = \frac{15}{7} \approx 2.143$$

Checking the solution $\frac{15}{7}$:

$$2.5 + 1.75t = 6.25$$
$$2.5 + 1.75\left(\frac{15}{7}\right) \overset{?}{=} 6.25$$
$$2.5 + \frac{7}{4} \cdot \frac{15}{7} \overset{?}{=} 6.25$$
$$2.5 + \frac{15}{4} \overset{?}{=} 6.25$$
$$2.5 + 3.75 \overset{\checkmark}{=} 6.25$$

So $\frac{15}{7}$ (about 2.143) is the solution, and it checks out. This means it will take about 2.143 minutes for the tub to fill to 6.25 ft^3.

Example 2.1.17 Here we revisit Example 1.8.6.

Jakobi's annual salary as a nurse in Portland, Oregon, is \$73,290. His salary increased by 4% from last year. What was Jakobi's salary last year?

Explanation. We need to find Jakobi's salary last year. So we'll introduce s, defined to be Jakobi's salary last year (in dollars). To set up the equation, we need to think about how he arrived at this year's salary. To get to this year's salary, his employer took last year's salary and added 4% to it. Conceptually, this means we have:

$$\text{(last year's salary)} + \text{(4\% of last year's salary)} = \text{(this year's salary)}$$

We'll represent 4% of last year's salary with $0.04s$ since 0.04 is the decimal representation of 4%. This means that the equation we set up is:

$$s + 0.04s = 73290$$

To solve this equation, we can start by simplifing the left side, and proceed from there.

$$s + 0.04s = 73290$$
$$1s + 0.04s = 73290$$
$$1.04s = 73290$$
$$\frac{1.04s}{1.04} = \frac{73290}{1.04}$$
$$s \approx 70471.15$$

Checking the solution 70471.15:

$$s + 0.04s = 73290$$
$$70471.15 + 0.04(70471.15) \overset{?}{=} 73290$$
$$70471.15 + 2818.846 \overset{?}{=} 73290$$
$$73289.996 \overset{?}{=} 73290$$

In the check, those values are not equal, but they are very close. And it is reasonable to believe the only reason they are at all different comes from when we rounded the real solution to 70471.15. So Jakobi's salary was \$70471.15 last year.

Checkpoint 2.1.18 Here we revisit Exercise 1.8.7.

Kirima offered to pay the bill and tip at a restaurant where she and her friends had dinner. In total she paid \$150, which made the tip come out to a little more than 19%. What was the bill before tip?

Explanation. A common mistake is to translate a question like this into "what is 19% of \$150?" as a way to calculate the tip amount, and then subtract that from \$150. But that is not how tipping works. If we let x represent the original bill, then:

$$\underset{\text{bill}}{x} \underset{\text{plus}}{+} \underset{19\%}{0.19} \underset{\text{of}}{\cdot} \underset{\text{bill}}{x} \underset{\text{is}}{=} \underset{\$150}{150}$$

$$1.00x + 0.19x = 150$$
$$1.19x = 150$$
$$\frac{1.19x}{1.19} = \frac{150}{1.19}$$
$$x \approx 126.05$$

So the original bill was about $126.05.

Example 2.1.19 Here we revisit Example 1.8.8.
The price of a refrigerator after a 15% discount is $612. What was the price before the discount?

Explanation.   We'll let c be the original price of the refrigerator. To obtain the discounted price, we take the original price and subtract 15% of that amount. Conceptually, this looks like:

$$(\text{original price}) - (15\% \text{ of the original price}) = (\text{discounted price})$$

Since the amount of the discount is 15% of the original price, we'll represent this with $0.15c$. The equation we set up is then:
$$c - 0.15c = 612$$

To solve this equation, we can start by simplifing the left side, and proceed from there.

$$c - 0.15c = 612$$
$$1.00c - 0.15c = 612$$
$$0.85c = 612$$
$$\frac{0.85c}{0.85} = \frac{612}{0.85}$$
$$c = 720$$

Checking the solution 720:

$$c - 0.15c = 612$$
$$720 - 0.15(720) \stackrel{?}{=} 612$$
$$720 - 108 \stackrel{\checkmark}{=} 612$$

The solution 720 checks out. So the refrigerator cost $720 before the discount was applied.

Checkpoint 2.1.20 Here we revisit Exercise 1.8.9.

A shirt is on sale at 20% off. The current price is $51.00. What was the shirt's original price?

Explanation.   Let x represent the original price of the shirt. Since 20% is removed to bring the cost to $51, we can set up and solve the equation:

$$\underset{\text{original}}{x} \underset{\text{minus}}{-} \underset{20\%}{0.20} \underset{\text{of}}{\cdot} \underset{\text{original}}{x} \underset{\text{is}}{=} \underset{\$51}{51}$$

$$1.00x - 0.20x = 51$$
$$0.8x = 51$$
$$\frac{0.8x}{0.8} = \frac{51}{0.8}$$
$$x = 63.75$$

The shirt's original price was $63.75.

2.1.4 Differentiating between Simplifying Expressions, Evaluating Expressions and Solving Equations

Let's look at the following similar, yet different examples.

Example 2.1.21 Simplify the expression $10 - 3(x + 2)$.
Explanation.

$$10 - 3(x + 2) = 10 - 3x - 6$$
$$= -3x + 4$$

An equivalent result is $4 - 3x$. Note that our final result is an *expression*.

Example 2.1.22 Evaluate the expression $10 - 3(x + 2)$ when $x = 2$.
Explanation.   We will substitute $x = 2$ into the expression:

$$10 - 3(x + 2) = 10 - 3(2 + 2)$$
$$= 10 - 3(4)$$
$$= 10 - 12$$
$$= -2$$

So when $x = 2$, $10 - 3(x + 2) = -2$.
   Note that our final result here is a *numerical value*.

Example 2.1.23 Solve the equation $10 - 3(x + 2) = x - 16$.
Explanation.

$$10 - 3(x + 2) = x - 16$$
$$10 - 3x - 6 = x - 16$$
$$-3x + 4 = x - 16$$
$$-3x + 4 - 4 = x - 16 - 4$$
$$-3x = x - 20$$
$$-3x - x = x - 20 - x$$
$$-4x = -20$$
$$\frac{-4x}{-4} = \frac{-20}{-4}$$
$$x = 5$$

So the solution set is $\{5\}$. (We should probably check that.)
   Note that our final result here is a *solution set*.

Here is a summary collection of the distinctions that you should understand between simplifying expressions, evaluating expressions and solving equations.

List 2.1.24: A summary the differences among simplifying expressions, evaluating expressions and solving equations.

> - An expression like $10 - 3(x + 2)$ can be simplified to $-3x + 4$ (as in Example 2.1.21). However we cannot "solve" an expression like this.
>
> - As variables take different values, an expression can be evaluated to different values. In Example 2.1.22, when $x = 2$, $10 - 3(x + 2) = -2$; but when $x = 3$, $10 - 3(x + 2) = -5$.
>
> - An equation connects two expressions with an equals sign. In Example 2.1.23, $10 - 3(x + 2) = x - 16$ has the expression $10 - 3(x + 2)$ on the left side of equals sign, and the expression $x - 16$ on the right side.
>
> - When we solve the equation $10 - 3(x + 2) = x - 16$, we are looking for a number which makes those two expressions have the same value. In Example 2.1.23, we found the solution to be 5. It makes both $10 - 3(x + 2)$ and $x - 16 =$ equal to -11.

2.1.5 Reading Questions

1. Describe the five steps that you might need to go through when solving a general linear equation in one variable.

2. In percent questions like tipping at a restaurant when you know the total bill, or purchasing something where sales tax is applied and you know the total charge, describe a common misunderstanding of what number to apply the percentage to.

3. Explain what is wrong with saying "I need to solve $3x + x - 8$."

2.1.6 Exercises

Warmup and Review Solve the equation.

1.	$r + 4 = 1$	**2.**	$r + 1 = -7$	**3.**	$t - 7 = 1$	**4.**	$t - 4 = -2$
5.	$21 = -3t$	**6.**	$10 = -5x$	**7.**	$\frac{5}{4}t = 3$	**8.**	$\frac{4}{5}a = 9$

Solving Two-Step Equations Solve the equation.

9.	$7c + 4 = 25$	**10.**	$4A + 2 = 30$	**11.**	$10C - 1 = -101$	**12.**	$6m - 5 = -11$
13.	$-6 = 3p + 3$	**14.**	$-70 = 9q + 2$	**15.**	$18 = 6y - 6$	**16.**	$-28 = 3t - 4$
17.	$-3a + 4 = 22$	**18.**	$-6c + 1 = 13$	**19.**	$-9A - 9 = 18$	**20.**	$-4C - 6 = -30$
21.	$9 = -m + 2$	**22.**	$17 = -p + 7$	**23.**	$8q + 80 = 0$	**24.**	$5y + 35 = 0$

Application Problems for Solving Two-Step Equations

25. A gym charges members $25 for a registration fee, and then $20 per month. You became a member some time ago, and now you have paid a total of $405 to the gym. How many months have passed since you joined the gym?

⬜ months have passed since you joined the gym.

26. Your cell phone company charges a $16 monthly fee, plus $0.17 per minute of talk time. One month your cell phone bill was $75.50. How many minutes did you spend talking on the phone that month?

   You spent ⬜ talking on the phone that month.

27. A school purchased a batch of T-shirts from a company. The company charged $6 per T-shirt, and gave the school a $65 rebate. If the school had a net expense of $2,575 from the purchase, how many T-shirts did the school buy?

   The school purchased ⬜ T-shirts.

28. James hired a face-painter for a birthday party. The painter charged a flat fee of $75, and then charged $5.50 per person. In the end, James paid a total of $141. How many people used the face painter's service?

   ⬜ people used the face-painter's service.

29. A certain country has 465.5 million acres of forest. Every year, the country loses 6.65 million acres of forest mainly due to deforestation for farming purposes. If this situation continues at this pace, how many years later will the country have only 206.15 million acres of forest left? (Use an equation to solve this problem.)

   After ⬜ years, this country would have 206.15 million acres of forest left.

30. Randi has $86 in his piggy bank. He plans to purchase some Pokemon cards, which costs $1.95 each. He plans to save $52.85 to purchase another toy. At most how many Pokemon cards can he purchase?

   Write an equation to solve this problem.

   Randi can purchase at most ⬜ Pokemon cards.

Solving Equations with Variable Terms on Both Sides Solve the equation.

31. $10p + 5 = p + 59$

32. $8q + 8 = q + 29$

33. $-4y + 3 = -y - 27$

34. $-10r + 7 = -r - 56$

35. $6 - 2a = 5a + 55$

36. $3 - 5c = 5c + 103$

37. $8A + 6 = 5A + 8$

38. $2C + 6 = 10C + 5$

39. a. $9m + 4 = 2m + 32$

   b. $2r + 4 = 9r - 17$

40. a. $6p + 10 = 2p + 42$

   b. $2n + 10 = 6n - 6$

Application Problems for Solving Equations with Variable Terms on Both Sides Use a linear equation to solve the word problem.

41. Two trees are 8 feet and 13.5 feet tall. The shorter tree grows 3 feet per year; the taller tree grows 2.5 feet per year. How many years later would the shorter tree catch up with the taller tree?

   It would take the shorter tree ⬜ years to catch up with the taller tree.

42. Massage Heaven and Massage You are competitors. Massage Heaven has 2700 registered customers, and it gets approximately 550 newly registered customers every month. Massage You has 6700 registered customers, and it gets approximately 350 newly registered customers every month.

How many months would it take Massage Heaven to catch up with Massage You in the number of registered customers?

These two companies would have approximately the same number of registered customers $\boxed{}$ months later.

43. Two truck rental companies have different rates. V-Haul has a base charge of $55.00, plus $0.65 per mile. W-Haul has a base charge of $50.40, plus $0.70 per mile. For how many miles would these two companies charge the same amount?

If a driver drives $\boxed{}$ miles, those two companies would charge the same amount of money.

44. Massage Heaven and Massage You are competitors. Massage Heaven has 9800 registered customers, but it is losing approximately 300 registered customers every month. Massage You has 2650 registered customers, and it gets approximately 350 newly registered customers every month. How many months would it take Massage Heaven to catch up with Massage You in the number of registered customers?

These two companies would have approximately the same number of registered customers $\boxed{}$ months later.

45. Anthony has $75.00 in his piggy bank, and he spends $2.00 every day. Ken has $10.00 in his piggy bank, and he saves $4.50 every day.

If they continue to spend and save money this way, how many days later would they have the same amount of money in their piggy banks?

$\boxed{}$ days later, Anthony and Ken will have the same amount of money in their piggy banks.

46. Penelope has $100.00 in her piggy bank, and she spends $1.50 every day. Haley has $8.00 in her piggy bank, and she saves $2.50 every day.

If they continue to spend and save money this way, how many days later would they have the same amount of money in their piggy banks?

$\boxed{}$ days later, Penelope and Haley will have the same amount of money in their piggy banks.

Solving Linear Equations with Like Terms Solve the equation.

47. $5C + 2C + 2 = 16$

48. $2m + 5m + 2 = 58$

49. $8p + 9 + 3 = 60$

50. $5q + 4 + 2 = 21$

51. $-1 + 8 = -2y - y - 20$

52. $-4 + 2 = -5r - r - 56$

53. $3y + 6 - 6y = 27$

54. $5y + 10 - 6y = 19$

55. $-7r + 5 + r = -37$

56. $-5r + 8 + r = 4$

57. $52 = -10m - 3 - m$

58. $-87 = -7p - 7 - p$

59. $3 - q - q = -2 + (-5)$

60. $9 - y - y = -6 + 17$

61. $4 - 3r - 10 = -6$

62. $2 - 10a - 7 = -5$

63. $b - 9 - 8b = -7 - 2b + 28$

64. $A - 6 - 3A = -5 - 8A + 5$

65. $-6B + 4B = 2 - 3B - 3$

66. $-9m + 5m = 9 - 10m - 57$

67. $5p + 5 = -6p + 5 - 10p$

68. $2q + 9 = -4q + 9 - 10q$

69. $-9 + 11 = 8y - 10 - 3y + 5 - 6y$

70. $-6 + (-10) = 5r - 10 - 8r + 4 + 2r$

Application Problems for Solving Linear Equations with Like Terms

71. A 130-meter rope is cut into two segments. The longer segment is 10 meters longer than the shorter segment. Write and solve a linear equation to find the length of each segment. Include units.

The segments are ☐ and ☐ long.

72. In a doctor's office, the receptionist's annual salary is $135,000 less than that of the doctor. Together, the doctor and the receptionist make $207,000 per year. Find each person's annual income.

The receptionist's annual income is ☐. The doctor's annual income is ☐.

73. Selena and Charity went picking strawberries. Selena picked 100 fewer strawberries than Charity did. Together, they picked 214 strawberries. How many strawberries did Charity pick?

Charity picked ☐ strawberries.

74. Stephanie and Haley collect stamps. Haley collected 30 fewer than three times the number of Stephanie's stamps. Altogether, they collected 626 stamps. How many stamps did Stephanie and Haley collect?

Stephanie collected ☐ stamps. Haley collected ☐ stamps.

75. Emily and Sherial sold girl scout cookies. Emily's sales were $35 more than five times of Sherial's. Altogether, their sales were $725. How much did each girl sell?

Emily's sales were ☐. Sherial's sales were ☐.

76. A hockey team played a total of 129 games last season. The number of games they won was 13 more than three times of the number of games they lost.

Write and solve an equation to answer the following questions.

The team lost ☐ games. The team won ☐ games.

77. After a 55% increase, a town has 1395 people. What was the population before the increase?

Before the increase, the town's population was ☐.

78. After a 45% increase, a town has 145 people. What was the population before the increase?

Before the increase, the town's population was ☐.

Solving Linear Equations Involving Distribution Solve the equation.

79. $4(r + 2) = 28$

80. $10(a + 10) = 190$

81. $7(b - 7) = -91$

82. $3(A - 4) = -6$

83. $72 = -9(B + 1)$

84. $-66 = -6(m + 5)$

85. $12 = -3(n - 9)$

86. $72 = -9(q - 3)$

87. $-(y - 8) = 9$

88. $-(r - 2) = 10$

89. $-7 = -(8 - a)$

90. $4 = -(5 - b)$

91. $2(5A - 7) = 56$

92. $8(9B - 7) = 88$

93. $18 = -3(3 - 3m)$

94. $-2 = -2(7 - 2n)$

95. $4 + 6(q + 7) = 76$

96. $2 + 8(y + 6) = 42$

97. $5 - 10(r + 6) = 5$

98. $4 - 7(a + 6) = -101$

99. $28 = 4 - 8(b - 6)$

100. $37 = 10 - 3(A - 6)$

101. $4 - 8(B - 6) = 124$

102. $2 - 10(m - 6) = 2$

103. $9 = 10 - (2 - n)$

104. $-1 = 8 - (4 - q)$

105. $2 - (x + 7) = -15$

106. $5 - (r + 9) = -8$

107. a. $6 + (a + 5) = 1$

b. $6 - (a + 5) = 1$

108. a. $3 + (b + 2) = 4$

b. $3 - (b + 2) = 4$

Solve the equation.

109. $5(A + 9) - 10(A - 1) = 60$

110. $3(B + 3) - 8(B - 6) = 67$

111. $1 + 9(m - 5) = -53 - (1 - 4m)$

112. $4 + 7(n - 3) = -17 - (6 - 4n)$

113. $8(q - 6) - q = 68 - 3(2 + 5q)$

114. $6(x - 10) - x = -39 - 3(7 + 5x)$

115. $7(-8r + 4) = 14(-3 - 5r)$

116. $5(-8a + 8) = 10(-10 - 5a)$

117. $5 + 2(3 - 5b) = -3(b - 3) + 2$

118. $14 + 5(5 - 3A) = -3(A - 12) + 3$

Application Problems for Solving Linear Equations Involving Distribution

119. A rectangle's perimeter is 78 cm. Its base is 26 cm.

Its height is [　　　　　　].

120. A rectangle's perimeter is 50 m. Its width is 8 m. Use an equation to solve for the rectangle's length.

Its length is [　　　　　　].

121. A rectangle's perimeter is 112 in. Its length is 8 in longer than its width. Use an equation to find the rectangle's length and width.

Its width is [　　　　　　].

Its length is [　　　　　　].

122. A rectangle's perimeter is 180 cm. Its length is 2 times as long as its width. Use an equation to find the rectangle's length and width.

It's width is [　　　　　　].

Its length is [　　　　　　].

123. A rectangle's perimeter is 92 ft. Its length is 4 ft shorter than four times its width. Use an equation to find the rectangle's length and width.

Its width is [　　　　　　].

Its length is [　　　　　　].

124. A rectangle's perimeter is 170 ft. Its length is 1 ft longer than three times its width. Use an equation to find the rectangle's length and width.

Its width is [　　　　　　].

Its length is [　　　　　　].

Comparisons

125. Solve the equation.

    a. $-t + 9 = 9$

    b. $-A + 9 = -9$

    c. $-c - 9 = 9$

    d. $-x - 9 = -9$

126. Solve the equation.

    a. $-b + 3 = 3$

    b. $-p + 3 = -3$

    c. $-q - 3 = 3$

    d. $-r - 3 = -3$

127. a. Solve $r + 1 = 6$.

    b. Evaluate $r + 1$ when $r = 5$.

128. a. Solve $r - 5 = 4$.

    b. Evaluate $r - 5$ when $r = 9$.

129. a. Solve $5(r - 6) - 3 = -18$.

    b. Evaluate $5(r - 6) - 3$ when $r = 3$.

    c. Simplify $5(r - 6) - 3$.

130. a. Solve $4(t + 2) - 9 = 11$.

    b. Evaluate $4(t + 2) - 9$ when $t = 3$.

    c. Simplify $4(t + 2) - 9$.

131. Choose True or False for the following questions about the difference between expressions and equations.

   a. $9x - 7$ is an expression.   ($\square$ True $\square$ False)

   b. We can check whether $x = 1$ is a solution of $9x - 7 = -7x + 9$.   ($\square$ True $\square$ False)

   c. $9x - 7 = -7x + 9$ is an equation.   ($\square$ True $\square$ False)

   d. $-7x + 9$ is an equation.   ($\square$ True $\square$ False)

   e. $9x - 7 = -7x + 9$ is an expression.   ($\square$ True $\square$ False)

   f. We can evaluate $9x - 7$ when $x = 1$ ($\square$ True $\square$ False)

   g. We can evaluate $9x - 7 = -7x + 9$ when $x = 1$ ($\square$ True $\square$ False)

   h. We can check whether $x = 1$ is a solution of $9x - 7$.   ($\square$ True $\square$ False)

132. Choose True or False for the following questions about the difference between expressions and equations.

   a. $7x - 9$ is an equation.   ($\square$ True $\square$ False)

   b. $-9x + 7 = 7x - 9$ is an equation.   ($\square$ True $\square$ False)

   c. We can evaluate $-9x + 7 = 7x - 9$ when $x = 1$ ($\square$ True $\square$ False)

   d. We can evaluate $-9x + 7$ when $x = 1$ ($\square$ True $\square$ False)

   e. We can check whether $x = 1$ is a solution of $-9x + 7 = 7x - 9$.   ($\square$ True $\square$ False)

   f. $-9x + 7 = 7x - 9$ is an expression.   ($\square$ True $\square$ False)

   g. We can check whether $x = 1$ is a solution of $-9x + 7$.   ($\square$ True $\square$ False)

   h. $-9x + 7$ is an expression.   ($\square$ True $\square$ False)

Challenge

133. Think of a number. Add four to your number. Now double that. Then add six. Then halve it. Finally, subtract 7. What is the result? Do you always get the same result, regardless of what number you start with? How does this work? Explain using algebra.

134. Write a linear equation whose solution is $x = -9$. You may not write an equation whose left side is just "x" or whose right side is just "x."

There are infinitely many correct answers to this problem. Be creative. After finding an equation that works, see if you can come up with a different one that also works.

2.2 Solving Multistep Linear Inequalities

We learned how to solve one-step inequalities in Section 1.6. In this section, we will solve linear inequalities that need more than one step.

2.2.1 Solving Multistep Inequalities

When solving a linear inequality, we follow the same steps in Process 2.1.4. The only difference is that when we multiply or divide by a negative number on both sides of an inequality, the direction of the inequality symbol must switch.

Process 2.2.2 Steps to Solve Linear Inequalities.

Simplify *Simplify the expressions on each side of the inequality by distributing and combining like terms.*

Separate *Use addition or subtraction to isolate the variable terms and constant terms (numbers) so that they are on different sides of the inequality symbol.*

Clear Coefficient *Use multiplication or division to eliminate the variable term's coefficient. If you multiply or divide each side by a negative number, switch the direction of the inequality symbol.*

Check *A solution to a linear inequality has a "boundary number". In the original inequality, check a number less than the boundary number, the boundary number itself, and a number greater than the boundary number to confirm what should be a solution is indeed a solution, and what should not is not. (This can be time-consuming, so use your judgment about when you might get away with skipping this.)*

Summarize *State the solution set or (in the case of an application problem) summarize the result in a complete sentence using appropriate units.*

Example 2.2.3 Solve for t in the inequality $-3t + 5 \geq 11$. Write the solution set in both set-builder notation and interval notation.

Explanation.

$$-3t + 5 \geq 11$$
$$-3t + 5 - 5 \geq 11 - 5$$
$$-3t \geq 6$$
$$\frac{-3t}{-3} \leq \frac{6}{-3}$$
$$t \leq -2$$

Note that when we divided both sides of the inequality by -3, we had to switch the direction of the inequality symbol. At this point we think that the solution set in set-builder notation is $\{t \mid t \leq -2\}$, and the solution set in interval notation is $(-\infty, -2]$.

Since there are infinitely many solutions, it's impossible to literally check them all. We believe that all values of t for which $t \leq -2$ are solutions. We check that one number less than -2 (any number, your choice) satisfies the inequality. *And* that -2 satisfies the inequality. *And* that one number greater than -2 (any number, your choice) does *not* satisfy the inequality. We choose to check the values -10, -2, and 0.

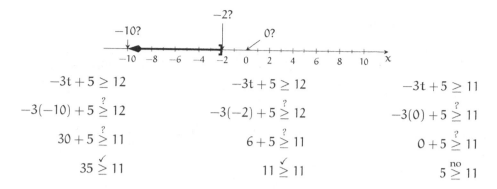

$-3t + 5 \geq 12$	$-3t + 5 \geq 12$	$-3t + 5 \geq 11$
$-3(-10) + 5 \stackrel{?}{\geq} 12$	$-3(-2) + 5 \stackrel{?}{\geq} 12$	$-3(0) + 5 \stackrel{?}{\geq} 11$
$30 + 5 \stackrel{?}{\geq} 11$	$6 + 5 \stackrel{?}{\geq} 11$	$0 + 5 \stackrel{?}{\geq} 11$
$35 \stackrel{\checkmark}{\geq} 11$	$11 \stackrel{\checkmark}{\geq} 11$	$5 \stackrel{\text{no}}{\geq} 11$

So both -10 and -2 are solutions as expected, while 0 is not. This is evidence that our solution set is correct, and it's valuable in that making these checks would likely help us catch an error if we had made one. While it certainly does take time and space to make three checks like this, it has its value.

Example 2.2.4 Solve for z in the inequality $(6z+5)-(2z-3) > -12$. Write the solution set in both set-builder notation and interval notation.

Explanation.

$$(6z + 5) - (2z - 3) > -12$$
$$6z + 5 - 2z + 3 > -12$$
$$4z + 8 > -12$$
$$4z + 8 - 8 > -12 - 8$$
$$4z > -20$$
$$\frac{4z}{4} > \frac{-20}{4}$$
$$z > -5$$

Note that we divided both sides of the inequality by 4 and since this is a positive number we *did not* need to switch the direction of the inequality symbol. At this point we think that the solution set in set-builder notation is $\{z \mid z > -5\}$, and the solution set in interval notation is $(-5, \infty)$.

Since there are infinitely many solutions, it's impossible to literally check them all. We believe that all values of z for which $z > -5$ are solutions. We check that one number less than -5 (any number, your choice) does *not* satisfy the inequality. *And* that -5 does *not* satisfy the inequality. *And* that one number greater than -5 (any number, your choice) *does* satisfy the inequality. We choose to check the values -10, -5, and 0.

$(6z + 5) - (2z - 3) > -12$	$(6z + 5) - (2z - 3) > -12$	$(6z + 5) - (2z - 3) > -12$
$(6(-10) + 5) - (2(-10) - 3) \stackrel{?}{>} -12$	$(6(-5) + 5) - (2(-5) - 3) \stackrel{?}{>} -12$	$(6(0) + 5) - (2(0) - 3) \stackrel{?}{>} -12$
$(-60 + 5) - (-20 - 3) \stackrel{?}{>} -12$	$(-30 + 5) - (-10 - 3) \stackrel{?}{>} -12$	$(0 + 5) - (0 - 3) \stackrel{?}{>} -12$
$-55 - (-23) \stackrel{?}{>} -12$	$-25 - (-13) \stackrel{?}{>} -12$	$5 - (-3) \stackrel{?}{>} -12$

$$-32 \overset{\text{no}}{>} -12 \qquad\qquad -12 \overset{\text{no}}{>} -12 \qquad\qquad 8 \overset{\checkmark}{>} -12$$

So both -10 and -5 are not solutions as expected, while 0 is a solution. This is evidence that our solution set is correct. The solution set in set-builder notation is $\{z \mid z > -5\}$. The solution set in interval notation is $(-5, \infty)$.

Checkpoint 2.2.5 Solve for x in $-2 - 2(2x + 1) > 4 - (3 - x)$. Write the solution set in both set-builder notation and interval notation.

Explanation.

$$-2 - 2(2x + 1) > 4 - (3 - x)$$
$$-2 - 4x - 2 > 4 - 3 + x$$
$$-4x - 4 > x + 1$$
$$-4x - 4 - x > x + 1 - x$$
$$-5x - 4 > 1$$
$$-5x - 4 + 4 > 1 + 4$$
$$-5x > 5$$
$$\frac{-5x}{-5} < \frac{5}{-5}$$
$$x < -1$$

Note that when we divided both sides of the inequality by -5, we had to switch the direction of the inequality symbol. We should check the solution set, but we omit that here. The solution set in set-builder notation is $\{x \mid x < -1\}$. The solution set in interval notation is $(-\infty, -1)$.

Example 2.2.6 When a stopwatch started, the pressure inside a gas container was 4.2 atm (one atm is standard atmospheric pressure). As the container was heated, the pressure increased by 0.7 atm per minute. The maximum pressure the container can handle was 21.7 atm. Heating must be stopped once the pressure reaches 21.7 atm. Over what time interval was the container in a safe state?

Explanation. The pressure increases by 0.7 atm per minute, so it increases by $0.7m$ after m minutes. Counting in the original pressure of 4.2 atm, pressure in the container can be modeled by $0.7m + 4.2$, where m is the number of minutes since the stop watch started.

The container is safe when the pressure is 21.7 atm or lower. We can write and solve this inequality:

$$0.7m + 4.2 \le 21.7$$
$$0.7m + 4.2 - 4.2 \le 21.7 - 4.2$$
$$0.7m \le 17.5$$
$$\frac{0.7m}{0.7} \le \frac{17.5}{0.7}$$
$$m \le 25$$

In summary, the container was safe as long as $m \le 25$. Assuming that m also must be greater than or equal to zero, this means $0 \le m \le 25$. We can write this as the time interval as $[0, 25]$. Thus the container was safe between 0 minutes and 25 minutes.

2.2.2 Reading Questions

1.   When solving an inequality, what are the conditions when you have to reverse the direction of the inequality symbol?

2.   How is the solution set to a linear inequality different from the solution set to a linear equation?

2.2.3 Exercises

Review and Warmup Solve this inequality.

1. $x + 3 > 8$ 2. $x + 4 > 6$ 3. $4 > x - 9$ 4. $5 > x - 7$ 5. $5x \le 10$

6. $2x \le 8$ 7. $6 \ge -2x$ 8. $6 \ge -3x$

9. $\dfrac{4}{7}x > 8$ 10. $\dfrac{5}{4}x > 20$

11.   A swimming pool is being filled with water from a garden hose at a rate of 10 gallons per minute. If the pool already contains 70 gallons of water and can hold 230 gallons, after how long will the pool overflow?

   Assume m minutes later, the pool would overflow. Write an equation to model this scenario. There is no need to solve it.

12.   An engineer is designing a cylindrical springform pan. The pan needs to be able to hold a volume of 248 cubic inches and have a diameter of 12 inches. What's the minimum height it can have? (Hint: The formula for the volume of a cylinder is $V = \pi r^2 h$).

   Assume the pan's minimum height is h inches. Write an equation to model this scenario. There is no need to solve it.

Solving Multistep Linear Inequalities Solve this inequality.

13. $9x + 4 > 31$ 14. $10x + 10 > 70$ 15. $26 \ge 3x - 4$

16. $18 \ge 4x - 2$ 17. $45 \le 9 - 4x$ 18. $21 \le 6 \quad 5x$

19. $-6x - 2 < -44$ 20. $-7x - 9 < -23$ 21. $3 \ge -8x + 3$

22. $2 \ge -9x + 2$ 23. $-4 > 5 - x$ 24. $-7 > 1 - x$

25. $3(x + 2) \ge 12$ 26. $4(x + 6) \ge 56$ 27. $7t + 5 < 5t + 11$

28. $8t + 2 < 2t + 62$ 29. $-7z + 8 < -z - 46$ 30. $-8z + 5 \le -z - 16$

Solve this inequality.

31. $a - 8 - 5a > -6 - 6a + 10$ 32. $a - 10 - 7a > -2 - 9a + 4$

33. $-6p + 4 - 6p \ge 2p + 4$ 34. $-9p + 10 - 4p \ge 3p + 10$

35. $44 < -4(p - 7)$ 36. $-10 < -5(p - 3)$

37. $-(x - 10) \ge 16$ 38. $-(x - 6) \ge 11$

39. $4 \le 8 - 4(z - 9)$ 40. $81 \le 9 - 9(z - 6)$

41. $5 - (y + 8) < -9$ 42. $1 - (y + 6) < 1$

43. $1 + 10(x - 8) < -38 - (6 - 3x)$ 44. $2 + 8(x - 3) < -19 - (6 - 5x)$

Applications

45. You are riding in a taxi and can only pay with cash. You have to pay a flat fee of $25, and then pay $2.60 per mile. You have a total of $155 in your pocket. Let x be the number of miles the taxi will drive you. You want to know how many miles you can afford.

   a. Write an inequality to represent this situation in terms of how many miles you can afford.

   b. Solve this inequality. At most how many miles can you afford?

   c. Use interval notation to express the number of miles you can afford.

46. You are riding in a taxi and can only pay with cash. You have to pay a flat fee of $30, and then pay $3.30 per mile. You have a total of $261 in your pocket. Let x be the number of miles the taxi will drive you. You want to know how many miles you can afford.

   a. Write an inequality to represent this situation in terms of how many miles you can afford.

   b. Solve this inequality. At most how many miles can you afford?

   c. Use interval notation to express the number of miles you can afford.

47. A car rental company offers the following two plans for renting a car.
   Plan A: $30 per day and 16 cents per mile
   Plan B: $47 per day with free unlimited mileage
   How many miles must one drive in order to justify choosing Plan B?

   One must drive more than [   ] miles to justify choosing Plan B. In other words, it's more economical to use plan B if your number of miles driven will be in the interval [   ].

48. A car rental company offers the following two plans for renting a car.
   Plan A: $27 per day and 18 cents per mile
   Plan B: $50 per day with free unlimited mileage
   How many miles must one drive in order to justify choosing Plan B?

   One must drive more than [   ] miles to justify choosing Plan B. In other words, it's more economical to use plan B if your number of miles driven will be in the interval [   ].

49. You are offered two different sales jobs. The first company offers a straight commission of 8% of the sales. The second company offers a salary of $240 per week *plus* 4% of the sales. How much would you have to sell in a week in order for the straight commission offer to be at least as good?

   You'd have to sell more than [   ] worth of goods for the straight commission to be better for you. In other words, the dollar amount of goods sold would have to be in the interval [   ].

50. You are offered two different sales jobs. The first company offers a straight commission of 7% of the sales. The second company offers a salary of $370 per week *plus* 4% of the sales. How much would you have to sell in a week in order for the straight commission offer to be at least as good?

   You'd have to sell more than [   ] worth of goods for the straight commission to be better for you. In other words, the dollar amount of goods sold would have to be in the interval [   ].

2.3 Linear Equations and Inequalities with Fractions

This section discusses a technique that might make it easier for you to solve linear equations and inequalities when there are fractions present.

2.3.1 Introduction

So far, in our last step of solving for a variable we have divided each side of the equation by a constant, as in:

$$2x = 10$$
$$\frac{2x}{2} = \frac{10}{2}$$
$$x = 5$$

If we have a coefficient that is a fraction, we *could* proceed in exactly the same manner:

$$\frac{1}{2}x = 10$$
$$\frac{\frac{1}{2}x}{\frac{1}{2}} = \frac{10}{\frac{1}{2}}$$
$$x = 10 \cdot \frac{2}{1} = 20$$

What if our equation or inequality was more complicated though, for example $\frac{1}{4}x + \frac{2}{3} = \frac{1}{6}$? We would have to first do a lot of fraction arithmetic in order to then divide each side by the coefficient of x. An alternate approach is to instead *multiply* each side of the equation by just the right number that eliminates the denominator(s). In the equation $\frac{1}{2}x = 10$, we could simply multiply each side of the equation by 2, which would eliminate the denominator of 2:

$$\frac{1}{2}x = 10$$
$$2 \cdot \left(\frac{1}{2}x\right) = 2 \cdot 10$$
$$x = 20$$

For more complicated equations, multiply each side of the equation by the least common denominator (LCD) of all fractions appearing in the equation. In this way we can take one step to turn an equation full of fractions into an equation with no fractions.

2.3.2 Eliminating Denominators

Example 2.3.2
Deshawn planted a sapling in his yard that was 4 ft tall. The tree will grow $\frac{2}{3}$ of a foot every year. How many years will it take for his tree to be 10 ft tall? Since the tree grows $\frac{2}{3}$ of a foot every year, we can use a table to help write a formula modeling the tree's growth:

Years Passed	Tree's Height (ft)
0	4
1	$4 + \frac{2}{3}$
2	$4 + \frac{2}{3} \cdot 2$
$\vdots$	$\vdots$
y	$4 + \frac{2}{3}y$

From this, we've determined that y years since the tree was planted, the tree's height will be $4 + \frac{2}{3}y$ feet. To find when Deshawn's tree will be 10 feet tall, we set up the equation

$$4 + \frac{2}{3}y = 10$$

To solve the equation, we take note of the fraction and its denominator 3. As the very first step, multiplying by 3 on each side will leave us with no fractions.

$$4 + \frac{2}{3}y = 10$$

$$3 \cdot \left(4 + \frac{2}{3}y\right) = 3 \cdot 10$$

$$3 \cdot 4 + 3 \cdot \frac{2}{3}y = 30$$

$$12 + 2y = 30$$

$$2y = 18$$

$$y = 9$$

Now we will check the solution 9 in the equation $4 + \frac{2}{3}y = 10$:

$$4 + \frac{2}{3}y = 10$$

$$4 + \frac{2}{3}(9) \stackrel{?}{=} 10$$

$$4 + 6 \stackrel{\checkmark}{=} 10$$

In summary, it will take 9 years for Deshawn's tree to reach 10 feet tall. The point of this example was to demonstrate that clearing denominators can make an equation fairly easy to solve.

Example 2.3.3 Solve for x in $\frac{1}{4}x + \frac{2}{3} = \frac{1}{6}$.

Explanation.   To solve this equation, we first need to identify the LCD of all fractions in the equation. On the left side we have $\frac{1}{4}$ and $\frac{2}{3}$. On the right side we have $\frac{1}{6}$. The LCD of $3, 4$, and 6 is 12, so we will multiply each side of the equation by 12 in order to eliminate *all* of the denominators:

$$\frac{1}{4}x + \frac{2}{3} = \frac{1}{6}$$

$$12 \cdot \left(\frac{1}{4}x + \frac{2}{3}\right) = 12 \cdot \frac{1}{6}$$

$$12 \cdot \left(\frac{1}{4}x\right) + 12 \cdot \left(\frac{2}{3}\right) = 12 \cdot \frac{1}{6}$$

$$3x + 8 = 2$$

$$3x = -6$$

$$\frac{3x}{3} = \frac{-6}{3}$$

$$x = -2$$

Checking the solution -2:

$$\frac{1}{4}x + \frac{2}{3} = \frac{1}{6}$$

$$\frac{1}{4}(-2) + \frac{2}{3} \stackrel{?}{=} \frac{1}{6}$$

$$-\frac{2}{4} + \frac{2}{3} \stackrel{?}{=} \frac{1}{6}$$

$$-\frac{6}{12} + \frac{8}{12} \stackrel{?}{=} \frac{1}{6}$$

$$\frac{2}{12} \stackrel{\checkmark}{=} \frac{1}{6}$$

The solution is therefore -2 and the solution set is $\{-2\}$.

Checkpoint 2.3.4 Solve for z in $-\frac{2}{5}z - \frac{3}{2} = -\frac{1}{2}z + \frac{4}{5}$.

Explanation.   The first thing we need to do is identify the LCD of all denominators in this equation. Since the denominators are 2 and 5, the LCD is 10. So as our first step, we will multiply each side of the equation by 10 in order to eliminate all denominators:

$$-\frac{2}{5}z - \frac{3}{2} = -\frac{1}{2}z + \frac{4}{5}$$

$$10 \cdot \left(-\frac{2}{5}z - \frac{3}{2}\right) = 10 \cdot \left(-\frac{1}{2}z + \frac{4}{5}\right)$$

$$10\left(-\frac{2}{5}z\right) - 10\left(\frac{3}{2}\right) = 10\left(-\frac{1}{2}z\right) + 10\left(\frac{4}{5}\right)$$

$$-4z - 15 = -5z + 8$$

$$z - 15 = 8$$

$$z = 23$$

Checking the solution 23:

$$-\frac{2}{5}z - \frac{3}{2} = -\frac{1}{2}z + \frac{4}{5}$$

$$-\frac{2}{5}(23) - \frac{3}{2} \overset{?}{=} -\frac{1}{2}(23) + \frac{4}{5}$$

$$-\frac{46}{5} - \frac{3}{2} \overset{?}{=} -\frac{23}{2} + \frac{4}{5}$$

$$-\frac{46}{5} \cdot \frac{2}{2} - \frac{3}{2} \cdot \frac{5}{5} \overset{?}{=} -\frac{23}{2} \cdot \frac{5}{5} + \frac{4}{5} \cdot \frac{2}{2}$$

$$-\frac{92}{10} - \frac{15}{10} \overset{?}{=} -\frac{115}{10} + \frac{8}{10}$$

$$-\frac{107}{10} \overset{\checkmark}{=} -\frac{107}{10}$$

Thus the solution is 23 and so the solution set is $\{23\}$.

Example 2.3.5 Solve for a in the equation $\frac{2}{3}(a+1) + 5 = \frac{1}{3}$.

Explanation.

There are two fractions appearing here, but both have the same denominator 3. So we can multiply by 3 on each side to clear denominators.

$$\frac{2}{3}(a+1) + 5 = \frac{1}{3}$$

$$3 \cdot \left(\frac{2}{3}(a+1) + 5\right) = 3 \cdot \frac{1}{3}$$

$$3 \cdot \frac{2}{3}(a+1) + 3 \cdot 5 = 1$$

$$2(a+1) + 15 = 1$$

$$2a + 2 + 15 = 1$$

$$2a + 17 = 1$$

$$2a = -16$$

$$a = -8$$

Check the solution -8 in the equation $\frac{2}{3}(a+1) + 5 = \frac{1}{3}$, we find that:

$$\frac{2}{3}(a+1) + 5 = \frac{1}{3}$$

$$\frac{2}{3}(-8+1) + 5 \overset{?}{=} \frac{1}{3}$$

$$\frac{2}{3}(-7) + 5 \overset{?}{=} \frac{1}{3}$$

$$-\frac{14}{3} + \frac{15}{3} \overset{\checkmark}{=} \frac{1}{3}$$

The solution is therefore -8 and the solution set is $\{-8\}$.

Example 2.3.6 Solve for b in the equation $\frac{2b+1}{3} = \frac{2}{5}$.

Explanation.

The structure of the equation is a little different from previous examples, but we can still see two denominators 3 and 5, and find their LCM is 15.

$$\frac{2b+1}{3} = \frac{2}{5}$$

$$15 \cdot \frac{2b+1}{3} = 15 \cdot \frac{2}{5}$$

$$5(2b+1) = 6$$

$$10b+5 = 6$$

$$10b = 1$$

$$b = \frac{1}{10}$$

Checking the solution $\frac{1}{10}$:

$$\frac{2b+1}{3} = \frac{2}{5}$$

$$\frac{2\left(\frac{1}{10}\right)+1}{3} \stackrel{?}{=} \frac{2}{5}$$

$$\frac{\frac{1}{5}+1}{3} \stackrel{?}{=} \frac{2}{5}$$

$$\frac{\frac{1}{5}+\frac{5}{5}}{3} \stackrel{?}{=} \frac{2}{5}$$

$$\frac{\frac{6}{5}}{3} \stackrel{?}{=} \frac{2}{5}$$

$$\frac{6}{5} \cdot \frac{1}{3} \stackrel{\checkmark}{=} \frac{2}{5}$$

The solution is $\frac{1}{10}$ and the solution set is $\left\{\frac{1}{10}\right\}$.

Example 2.3.7 Suppose we want to know the total cost for a box of cereal that weighs 18 ounces, assuming it costs the same per ounce as the 21-ounce box. Letting C be this unknown cost (in dollars), we could set up the following proportion:

$$\frac{\text{cost in dollars}}{\text{weight in oz}} = \frac{\text{cost in dollars}}{\text{weight in oz}}$$

$$\frac{\$3.99}{21\,\text{oz}} = \frac{\$C}{18\,\text{oz}}$$

We take a moment to rewrite the equation without units:

$$\frac{3.99}{21} = \frac{C}{18}$$

Next we want to recognize that each side contains a fraction. Our usual approach for solving this type of equation is to multiply each side by the least common denominator (LCD). In this case, the LCD of 21 and 18 is 126. As with many other proportions we solve, it is often easier to just multiply each side by the common denominator of $18 \cdot 21$, which we know will make each denominator cancel:

$$\frac{3.99}{21} = \frac{C}{18}$$

$$18 \cdot 21 \cdot \frac{3.99}{21} = \frac{C}{18} \cdot 18 \cdot 21$$

$$18 \cdot \cancel{21} \frac{3.99}{\cancel{21}} = \frac{C}{\cancel{18}} \cdot \cancel{18} \cdot 21$$

$$71.82 = 21C$$

$$\frac{71.82}{21} = \frac{21C}{21}$$

$$C = 3.42$$

So assuming the cost is proportional to the cost of the 21-ounce box, the cost for an 18-ounce box of cereal would be $3.42.

Example 2.3.8 In a science lab, a container had 21 ounces of water at 9:00 AM. Water has been evaporating at the rate of 3 ounces every 5 minutes. When will there be 8 ounces of water left?

Explanation. Since the container has been losing 3 oz of water every 5 minutes, it loses $\frac{3}{5}$ oz every minute. In m minutes since 9:00 AM, the container would lose $\frac{3}{5}m$ oz of water. Since the container had 21 oz of water at the beginning, the amount of water in the container can be modeled by $21 - \frac{3}{5}m$ (in oz).

To find when there would be 8 oz of water left, we write and solve this equation:

Checking the solution $\frac{65}{3}$:

$$21 - \frac{3}{5}m = 8$$

$$5 \cdot \left(21 - \frac{3}{5}x\right) = 5 \cdot 8$$

$$5 \cdot 21 - 5 \cdot \frac{3}{5}x = 40$$

$$105 - 3m = 40$$

$$105 - 3m - 105 = 40 - 105$$

$$-3m = -65$$

$$\frac{-3m}{-3} = \frac{-65}{-3}$$

$$m = \frac{65}{3}$$

$$21 - \frac{3}{5}m = 8$$

$$21 - \frac{3}{5}\left(\frac{65}{3}\right) \overset{?}{=} 8$$

$$21 - 13 \overset{\checkmark}{=} 8$$

Therefore the solution is $\frac{65}{3}$. As a mixed number, this is $21\frac{2}{3}$. In context, this means that 21 minutes and 40 seconds after 9:00 AM, at 9:21:40 AM, the container will have 8 ounces of water left.

2.3.3 Creating and Solving Proportions

Proportions can be used to solve many real-life applications where two quantities vary together. For example, if your home is worth more, your property tax will be more. If you have a larger amount of liquid Tylenol, you have more milligrams of the drug dissolved in that liquid. The key to using proportions is to first set up a ratio where all values are known. We then set up a second ratio that will be proportional to the first, but has an unknown value.

Example 2.3.9 Property taxes for a residential property are proportional to the assessed value of the property. A certain home is assessed at $234,100 and its annual property taxes are $2,518.92. What are the annual property taxes for the house next door that is assessed at $287,500?

Explanation. Let T be the annual property taxes (in dollars) for a property assessed at $287,500. We can write and solve this proportion:

$$\frac{\text{tax}}{\text{property value}} = \frac{\text{tax}}{\text{property value}}$$

$$\frac{2518.92}{234100} = \frac{T}{287500}$$

The least common denominator of this proportion is rather large, so we will instead multiply each side by 234100 and 287500 and simplify from there:

$$\frac{2518.92}{234100} = \frac{T}{287500}$$

$$234100 \cdot 287500 \cdot \frac{2518.92}{234100} = \frac{T}{287500} \cdot 234100 \cdot 287500$$

$$287500 \cdot 2518.92 = T \cdot 234100$$

$$\frac{287500 \cdot 2518.92}{234100} = \frac{234100T}{234100}$$

$$T \approx 3093.50$$

The property taxes for a property assessed at \$287,500 are \$3,093.50.

Example 2.3.10 Tagging fish is a means of estimating the size of the population of fish in a lake. A sample of fish is taken, tagged, and then redistributed into the lake. Later when another sample is taken, some of those fish will have tags. The number of tagged fish are assumed to be proportional to the total number of fish. We can look at that relationship from the perspective of the entire lake, or just the second sample, and we get two ratios that should be proportional.

$$\frac{\text{number of tagged fish in sample}}{\text{number of fish in sample}} = \frac{\text{number of tagged fish total}}{\text{number of fish total}}$$

Assume that 90 fish are caught and tagged. Once they are redistributed, a sample of 200 fish is taken. Of these, 7 are tagged. Estimate how many fish total are in the lake.

Explanation.   Let n be the number of fish in the lake. We can set up a proportion for this scenario:

$$\frac{7}{200} = \frac{90}{n}$$

To solve for n, which is in a denominator, we'll need to multiply each side by both 200 and n:

$$\frac{7}{200} = \frac{90}{n}$$

$$200 \cdot n \cdot \frac{7}{200} = \frac{90}{n} \cdot 200 \cdot n$$

$$200 \cdot n \cdot \frac{7}{200} = \frac{90}{n} \cdot 200 \cdot n$$

$$7n = 1800$$

$$\frac{7n}{7} = \frac{1800}{7}$$

$$n \approx 2471.4286$$

According to this sample, we can estimate that there are about 2471 fish in the lake.

Checkpoint 2.3.11 Infant Tylenol contains 160 mg of acetaminophen in each 5 mL of liquid. If Bao's baby is prescribed 60 mg of acetaminophen, how many milliliters of liquid should he give the baby?

Explanation. Assume Bao should give q milliliters of liquid medicine, so we can set up the following proportion:

$$\frac{\text{amount of liquid medicine in mL}}{\text{amount of acetaminophen in mg}} = \frac{\text{amount of liquid medicine in mL}}{\text{amount of acetaminophen in mg}}$$

$$\frac{5\,\text{mL}}{160\,\text{mg}} = \frac{q\,\text{mL}}{60\,\text{mg}}$$

$$\frac{5}{160} = \frac{q}{60}$$

$$160 \cdot 60 \cdot \frac{5}{160} = \frac{q}{60} \cdot 160 \cdot 60$$

$$60 \cdot 5 = q \cdot 160$$

$$300 = 160q$$

$$\frac{300}{160} = \frac{160q}{160}$$

$$q = 1.875$$

So to give 60 mg of acetaminophen to his baby, Bao should give 1.875 mL of liquid medication.

Example 2.3.12 Sarah is an architect and she's making a scale model of a building. The actual building will be 30 ft tall. In the model, the height of the building will be 2 in. How tall should she make the model of a person who is 5 ft 6 in tall so that the model is to scale?

Explanation. Let h be the height of the person in Sarah's model, which we'll measure in inches. We'll create a proportion that compares the building and person's heights in the model to their heights in real life:

$$\frac{\text{height of model building in inches}}{\text{height of actual building in feet}} = \frac{\text{height of model person in inches}}{\text{height of actual person in feet}}$$

$$\frac{2\,\text{in}}{30\,\text{ft}} = \frac{h\,\text{in}}{5\,\text{ft}\,6\text{in}}$$

Before we can just eliminate the units, we'll need to convert 5 ft 6 in to feet:

$$\frac{2\,\text{in}}{30\,\text{ft}} = \frac{h\,\text{in}}{5.5\,\text{ft}}$$

Now we can remove the units and continue solving:

$$\frac{2}{30} = \frac{h}{5.5}$$

$$30 \cdot 5.5 \cdot \frac{2}{30} = \frac{h}{5.5} \cdot 30 \cdot 5.5$$

$$5.5 \cdot 2 = h \cdot 30$$

$$11 = 30h$$

$$\frac{11}{30} = \frac{30h}{30}$$

$$\frac{11}{30} = h$$

$$h \approx 0.3667$$

Sarah should make the model of a person who is 5 ft 6 in tall be $\frac{11}{30}$ inches (about 0.3667 inches) tall.

2.3.4 Solving Inequalities with Fractions

The notion of clearing denominators can also apply when solving a linear inequality. Remember that with inequalities, the only difference in the process is that the inequality sign reverses direction whenever we multiply or divide each side by a negative number.

Example 2.3.13 Solve for x in the inequality $\frac{3}{4}x - 2 > \frac{4}{5}x$. Write the solution set in both set-builder notation and interval notation.

Explanation. The LCM of the denominators is 20, so we start out multiplying each side of the inequality by 20.

$$\frac{3}{4}x - 2 > \frac{4}{5}x$$

$$20 \cdot \left(\frac{3}{4}x - 2\right) > 20 \cdot \frac{4}{5}x$$

$$20 \cdot \frac{3}{4}x - 20 \cdot 2 > 16x$$

$$15x - 40 > 16x$$

$$15x - 40 - 15x > 16x - 15x$$

$$-40 > x$$

$$x < -40$$

The solution set in set-builder notation is $\{x \mid x < -40\}$. Note that it's equivalent to write $\{x \mid -40 > x\}$, but it's easier to understand if we write x first in an inequality. The solution set in interval notation is $(-\infty, -40)$.

Checkpoint 2.3.14 Solve for y in the inequality $\frac{4}{7} - \frac{4}{3}y \le \frac{2}{3}$. Write the solution set in both set-builder notation and interval notation.

Explanation. The LCM of the denominators is 21, so we start out multiplying each side of the inequality by 21.

$$\frac{4}{7} - \frac{4}{3}y \le \frac{2}{3}$$

$$21 \cdot \left(\frac{4}{7} - \frac{4}{3}y\right) \le 21 \cdot \left(\frac{2}{3}\right)$$

$$21\left(\frac{4}{7}\right) - 21\left(\frac{4}{3}y\right) \le 21\left(\frac{2}{3}\right)$$

$$12 - 28y \le 14$$

$$-28y \le 2$$

$$\frac{-28y}{-28} \ge \frac{2}{-28}$$

$$y \ge -\frac{1}{14}$$

Note that when we divided each side of the inequality by -28, the inequality symbol reversed direction. The solution set in set-builder notation is $\left\{y \mid y \ge -\frac{1}{14}\right\}$. The solution set in interval notation is $\left[-\frac{1}{14}, \infty\right)$.

Example 2.3.15 In a certain class, a student's grade is calculated by the average of their scores on three tests. Aidan scored 78% and 54% on the first two tests. If he wants to earn at least a grade of C (70%), what's the lowest score he needs to earn on the third exam?

Explanation. Assume Aidan will score x% on the third test. To make his average test score greater than or equal to 70%, we write and solve this inequality:

$$\frac{78 + 54 + x}{3} \geq 70$$
$$\frac{132 + x}{3} \geq 70$$
$$3 \cdot \frac{132 + x}{3} \geq 3 \cdot 70$$
$$132 + x \geq 210$$
$$x \geq 78$$

To earn at least a C grade, Aidan needs to score at least 78% on the third test.

2.3.5 Reading Questions

1. What does LCD stand for? And what does it really *mean*?

2. When you clear denominators from an equation like $\frac{2}{3}x + 5 = \frac{2}{7}$, you will multiply by 21. At first, what are the *two* things that you multiply by 21, possibly requiring you to use some parentheses?

3. What is a proportional equation?

2.3.6 Exercises

Review and Warmup

1. Multiply: $4 \cdot \frac{2}{3}$

2. Multiply: $7 \cdot \frac{3}{8}$

3. Multiply: $25 \cdot \left(-\frac{6}{5}\right)$

4. Multiply: $30 \cdot \left(-\frac{7}{10}\right)$

5. Do the following multiplications.
   a. $32 \cdot \frac{5}{8}$
   b. $40 \cdot \frac{5}{8}$
   c. $48 \cdot \frac{5}{8}$

6. Do the following multiplications.
   a. $14 \cdot \frac{5}{7}$
   b. $21 \cdot \frac{5}{7}$
   c. $28 \cdot \frac{5}{7}$

Solving Linear Equations with Fractions Solve the equation.

7. $\frac{x}{10} + 95 = 2x$

8. $\frac{r}{7} + 68 = 5r$

9. $\frac{t}{4} + 5 = 9$

10. $\frac{b}{9} + 3 = 9$

11. $6 - \frac{c}{5} = 0$

12. $2 - \frac{B}{9} = -3$

13. $-3 = 9 - \frac{4C}{3}$

14. $-1 = 5 - \frac{2n}{7}$

15. $2p = \frac{3p}{2} + 6$

16. $2x = \dfrac{5x}{8} + 44$

17. $80 = \dfrac{4}{9}y + 4y$

18. $36 = \dfrac{2}{5}t + 2t$

19. $78 - \dfrac{7}{8}b = 4b$

20. $51 - \dfrac{5}{6}c = 2c$

21. $3B = \dfrac{2}{7}B + 1$

22. $3C = \dfrac{10}{9}C + 8$

23. $\dfrac{5}{4} - 7n = 2$

24. $\dfrac{9}{2} - 4p = 2$

25. $\dfrac{3}{8} - \dfrac{1}{8}x = 1$

26. $\dfrac{7}{4} - \dfrac{1}{4}y = 8$

27. $\dfrac{2t}{9} - 6 = -\dfrac{74}{9}$

28. $\dfrac{4b}{7} - 4 = -\dfrac{68}{7}$

29. $\dfrac{2}{5} + \dfrac{8}{5}c = 3c$

30. $\dfrac{4}{9} + \dfrac{8}{9}B = 3B$

31. $\dfrac{4C}{7} - \dfrac{30}{7} = -\dfrac{2}{7}C$

32. $\dfrac{2n}{5} - \dfrac{6}{5} = -\dfrac{1}{5}n$

33. $\dfrac{10p}{9} + \dfrac{7}{10} = p$

34. $\dfrac{6x}{7} + \dfrac{5}{6} = x$

35. $\dfrac{4y}{3} - 69 = -\dfrac{5}{2}y$

36. $\dfrac{6t}{7} - 47 = -\dfrac{5}{2}t$

37. $-\dfrac{9}{10}a + 42 = \dfrac{3a}{20}$

38. $-\dfrac{5}{2}c + 19 = \dfrac{9c}{4}$

39. $\dfrac{3B}{10} - 10B = \dfrac{3}{20}$

40. $\dfrac{5C}{6} - 6C = \dfrac{7}{12}$

41. $\dfrac{9n}{2} + \dfrac{8}{7} = \dfrac{1}{8}n$

42. $\dfrac{7p}{6} + \dfrac{8}{5} = \dfrac{1}{4}p$

43. $\dfrac{5}{4}x = \dfrac{2}{7} + \dfrac{4x}{3}$

44. $\dfrac{1}{2}y = \dfrac{5}{3} + \dfrac{2y}{5}$

45. $\dfrac{7}{8} = \dfrac{t}{32}$

46. $\dfrac{9}{4} = \dfrac{a}{12}$

47. $-\dfrac{c}{15} = \dfrac{10}{3}$

48. $-\dfrac{B}{35} = \dfrac{10}{7}$

49. $-\dfrac{C}{12} = -\dfrac{3}{4}$

50. $-\dfrac{n}{20} = -\dfrac{7}{10}$

51. $-\dfrac{3}{7} = \dfrac{8p}{9}$

52. $-\dfrac{3}{4} = \dfrac{9x}{7}$

53. $\dfrac{9}{10} = \dfrac{y+3}{50}$

54. $\dfrac{5}{6} = \dfrac{t+1}{30}$

55. $\dfrac{7}{4} = \dfrac{a-7}{7}$

56. $\dfrac{3}{10} = \dfrac{c-7}{5}$

57. $\dfrac{A-6}{4} = \dfrac{A+2}{6}$

58. $\dfrac{C-10}{2} = \dfrac{C+10}{4}$

59. $\dfrac{n+5}{6} - \dfrac{n-7}{12} = \dfrac{5}{3}$

60. $\dfrac{p+9}{4} - \dfrac{p-4}{8} = \dfrac{15}{8}$

61. $\dfrac{x}{3} - 1 = \dfrac{x}{6}$

62. $\dfrac{y}{7} - 9 = \dfrac{y}{10}$

63. $\dfrac{t}{4} - 1 = \dfrac{t}{5} + 2$

64. $\dfrac{a}{2} - 1 = \dfrac{a}{6} + 1$

65. $\dfrac{4}{9}c + \dfrac{2}{9} = \dfrac{7}{9}c + \dfrac{1}{3}$

66. $\dfrac{5}{3}A + \dfrac{4}{3} = \dfrac{8}{3}A + 2$

Solve the equation.

67. $\dfrac{5C+8}{2} - \dfrac{4-C}{4} = \dfrac{3}{7}$

68. $\dfrac{3n+8}{4} - \dfrac{1-n}{8} = \dfrac{2}{3}$

69. $33 = \dfrac{p}{5} + \dfrac{p}{6}$

70. $26 = \dfrac{x}{3} + \dfrac{x}{10}$

71. $-2y - \dfrac{4}{5} = \dfrac{7}{5}y + \dfrac{4}{3}$

72. $\dfrac{4}{9}t - 1 = \dfrac{3}{4}t - 4$

Solve the equation.

73. $-\dfrac{5}{2}a - 1 = \dfrac{7}{4}a - \dfrac{3}{10}$

74. $\dfrac{7}{8}c - \dfrac{3}{2} = -\dfrac{3}{4}c + \dfrac{2}{3}$

75. a. $-\dfrac{A}{5} + 2 = -3$

   b. $\dfrac{-t}{5} + 2 = -3$

   c. $\dfrac{y}{-5} + 2 = -3$

   d. $\dfrac{-r}{-5} + 2 = -3$

76. a. $-\dfrac{C}{5} + 3 = 1$

   b. $\dfrac{-q}{5} + 3 = 1$

   c. $\dfrac{c}{-5} + 3 = 1$

   d. $\dfrac{-p}{-5} + 3 = 1$

Applications

77. Kimball is jogging in a straight line. He got a head start of 10 meters from the starting line, and he ran 5 meters every 8 seconds. After how many seconds will Kimball be 30 meters away from the starting line?

   Kimball will be 30 meters away from the starting line ☐ seconds since he started running.

78. Brent is jogging in a straight line. He started at a place 36 meters from the starting line, and ran toward the starting line at the speed of 5 meters every 7 seconds. After how many seconds will Brent be 21 meters away from the starting line?

   Brent will be 21 meters away from the starting line ☐ seconds since he started running.

79. Joseph had only $7.00 in his piggy bank, and he decided to start saving more. He saves $4.00 every 5 days. After how many days will he have $23.00 in the piggy bank?

   Joseph will save $23.00 in his piggy bank after ☐ days.

80. Brandon has saved $41.00 in his piggy bank, and he decided to start spending them. He spends $2.00 every 7 days. After how many days will he have $31.00 left in the piggy bank?

   Brandon will have $31.00 left in his piggy bank after ☐ days.

81. According to a salad recipe, each serving requires 2 teaspoons of vegetable oil and 8 teaspoons of vinegar. If 17 teaspoons of vegetable oil were used, how many teaspoons of vinegar should be used?

   If 17 teaspoons of vegetable oil were used, ☐ teaspoons of vinegar should be used.

82. According to a salad recipe, each serving requires 5 teaspoons of vegetable oil and 20 teaspoons of vinegar. If 84 teaspoons of vinegar were used, how many teaspoons of vegetable oil should be used?

   If 84 teaspoons of vinegar were used, ☐ teaspoons of vegetable oil should be used.

83. Jay makes $108 every eight hours he works. How much will he make if he works twenty-four hours this week?

   If Jay works twenty-four hours this week, he will make ☐.

84. Casandra makes $198 every twelve hours she works. How much will she make if she works thirty hours this week?

   If Casandra works thirty hours this week, she will make ☐.

85. A mutual fund consists of 63% stock and 37% bond. In other words, for each 63 dollars of stock, there are 37 dollars of bond. For a mutual fund with $2,810.00 of stock, how many dollars of bond are there?

     For a mutual fund with $2,810.00 of stock, there are approximately [   ] of bond.

86. A mutual fund consists of 72% stock and 28% bond. In other words, for each 72 dollars of stock, there are 28 dollars of bond. For a mutual fund with $2,460.00 of bond, how many dollars of stock are there?

     For a mutual fund with $2,460.00 of bond, there are approximately [   ] of stock.

87. Eileen jogs every day. Last month, she jogged 6.5 hours for a total of 37.05 miles. At this speed, if Eileen runs 31.5 hours, how far can she run?

     At this speed, Eileen can run [   ] in 31.5 hours.

88. Donna jogs every day. Last month, she jogged 16.5 hours for a total of 57.75 miles. At this speed, how long would it take Donna to run 140 miles?

     At this speed, Donna can run 140 mi in [   ].

89. Kimball purchased 5.3 pounds of apples at the total cost of $7.42. If he purchases 6.6 pounds of apples at this store, how much would it cost?

     It would cost [   ] to purchase 6.6 pounds of apples.

90. Alejandro purchased 3.1 pounds of apples at the total cost of $6.20. If the price doesn't change, how many pounds of apples can Alejandro purchase with $12.20?

     With $12.20, Alejandro can purchase [   ] of apples.

91. Dawn collected a total of 1411 stamps over the past 17 years. At this rate, how many stamps would she collect in 27 years?

     At this rate, Dawn would collect [   ] stamps in 27 years.

92. Corey collected a total of 1330 stamps over the past 14 years. At this rate, how many years would it take he to collect 2090 stamps?

     At this rate, Corey can collect 2090 stamps in [   ] years.

93. In a city, the owner of a house valued at 260 thousand dollars needs to pay $821.60 in property tax. At this tax rate, how much property tax should the owner pay if a house is valued at 650 thousand dollars?

     The owner of a 650-thousand-dollar house should pay [   ] in property tax.

94. In a city, the owner of a house valued at 480 thousand dollars needs to pay $2,299.20 in property tax. At this tax rate, if the owner of a house paid $3,113.50 of property tax, how much is the house worth?

     If the owner of a house paid $3,113.50 of property tax, the house is worth [   ] thousand dollars.

95. To try to determine the health of the Rocky Mountain elk population in the Wenaha Wildlife Area, the Oregon Department of Fish and Wildlife caught, tagged, and released 39 Rocky Mountain elk. A week later, they returned and observed 42 Rocky Mountain elk, 9 of which had tags. Approximately how many Rocky Mountain elk are in the Wenaha Wildlife Area?

     There are approximately [   ] elk in the wildlife area.

96. To try to determine the health of the black-tailed deer population in the Jewell Meadow Wildlife Area, the Oregon Department of Fish and Wildlife caught, tagged, and released 28 black-tailed deer. A week later, they returned and observed 63 black-tailed deer, 18 of which had tags. Approximately how many black-tailed deer are in the Jewell Meadow Wildlife Area?

There are approximately [   ] deer in the wildlife area.

97. A restaurant used 1015 lb of vegetable oil in 25 days. At this rate, how many pounds of vegetable oil will be used in 42 days?

The restaurant will use [   ] of vegetable oil in 42 days.

98. A restaurant used 735.9 lb of vegetable oil in 33 days. At this rate, 1271.1 lb of oil will last how many days?

The restaurant will use 1271.1 lb of vegetable oil in [   ] days.

Solving Inequalities with Fractions Solve this inequality.

99. $\frac{x}{3} + 30 \geq 2x$

100. $\frac{x}{4} + 44 \geq 3x$

101. $\frac{3}{4} - 6y < 6$

102. $\frac{5}{4} - 3y < 5$

103. $-\frac{1}{6}t > \frac{4}{5}t - 58$

104. $-\frac{1}{2}t > \frac{2}{7}t - 11$

105. $\frac{9}{10} \geq \frac{x}{40}$

106. $\frac{7}{10} \geq \frac{x}{60}$

107. $-\frac{z}{8} < -\frac{3}{2}$

108. $-\frac{z}{24} < -\frac{9}{4}$

109. $\frac{x}{7} - 4 \leq \frac{x}{3}$

110. $\frac{x}{7} - 4 \leq \frac{x}{5}$

111. $\frac{y-8}{6} \geq \frac{y+1}{4}$

112. $\frac{y-5}{6} \geq \frac{y+6}{4}$

Solve this inequality.

113. $\frac{5}{4} < \frac{x+1}{6} - \frac{x-10}{12}$

114. $\frac{3}{2} < \frac{x+8}{6} - \frac{x-4}{12}$

Applications

115. Your grade in a class is determined by the average of three test scores. You scored 75 and 87 on the first two tests. To earn at least 82 for this course, how much do you have to score on the third test? Let x be the score you will earn on the third test.

    a. Write an inequality to represent this situation.

    b. Solve this inequality. What is the minimum that you have to earn on the third test in order to earn a 82 for the course?

    c. You cannot score over 100 on the third test. Use interval notation to represent the range of scores you can earn on the third test in order to earn at least 82 for this course.

116. Your grade in a class is determined by the average of three test scores. You scored 70 and 85 on the first two tests. To earn at least 77 for this course, how much do you have to score on the third test? Let x be the score you will earn on the third test.

    a. Write an inequality to represent this situation.

    b. Solve this inequality. What is the minimum that you have to earn on the third test in order to earn a 77 for the course?

c. You cannot score over 100 on the third test. Use interval notation to represent the range of scores you can earn on the third test in order to earn at least 77 for this course.

Challenge

117. The ratio of girls to boys in a preschool is 2 to 7. If there are 63 kids in the school, how many girls are there in the preschool?

2.4 Special Solution Sets

Most of the time after solving a linear equation in one variable, you have an equivalent equation similar to, say $x = 3$, that explicitly tells you what value the variable needs to be. And there is only one solution, 3 in this case. Similarly, after solving a linear inequality, you typically have a statement like $x < 5$, and the solution set is represented with either $(-\infty, 5)$ in interval notation or $\{x \mid x < 5\}$ in set-builder notation.

Occasionally you run into a linear equation or inequality that doesn't work this way. A linear equation might have may more solutions than just one. Or it might have none at all. An inequality might have no solutions, or maybe every real number is a solution. In this section we explore these equations and inequalities.

2.4.1 Special Solution Sets

Recall that for the equation $x + 2 = 5$, there is only one number which will make the equation true: 3. This means that the solution is 3, and we write the **solution set** as $\{3\}$. We say the equation's solution set has one **element**, 3.

We'll now explore equations that have *all* real numbers as solutions or *no* real numbers at all as solutions.

Example 2.4.2 Solve for x in $3x = 3x + 4$.

To solve this equation, we need to move all terms containing x to one side of the equals sign:

$$3x = 3x + 4$$
$$3x - 3x = 3x + 4 - 3x$$
$$0 = 4$$

Notice that x is no longer present in the equation. What value can we substitute into x everywhere that you see x in the equation to make $0 = 4$ true? Nothing! There is no x to substitute a value into and change the equation from being $0 = 4$. We say this equation has no solution. Or, the equation has an empty solution set. We can write this as $\emptyset$, or $\{\ \}$, which are the symbols for the **empty set** (not to be confused with the number 0.)

The equation $0 = 4$ is known a **false statement**. It is false no matter what x is. It indicates there is no solution to the original equation.

Example 2.4.3 Solve for x in $2x + 1 = 2x + 1$.

We will move all terms containing x to one side of the equals sign:

$$2x + 1 = 2x + 1$$
$$2x + 1 - 2x = 2x + 1 - 2x$$
$$1 = 1$$

At this point, x is no longer present in the equation. What value can we substitute into x to make $1 = 1$ true? Any number! This means that all real numbers are solutions to the equation $2x + 1 = 2x + 1$. We say this equation's solution set contains *all real numbers*. We can write this set using set-builder notation as $\{x \mid x \text{ is a real number}\}$ or using interval notation as $(-\infty, \infty)$.

The equation $1 = 1$ is unambiguously true, since it is true no matter what x is. It indicates that all real numbers are solutions to the original linear equation.

Remark 2.4.4 What would have happened if we had continued solving after we obtained $1 = 1$ in Example 2.4.3?

$$1 = 1$$
$$1 - 1 = 1 - 1$$
$$0 = 0$$

As we can see, all we found was another unambiguously true equation.

Warning 2.4.5 Note that there is a very important difference between when our solving process ends with $0 = 0$ and when it ends with $x = 0$. The first equation is true for all real numbers, and the solution set is $(-\infty, \infty)$. The second has only one solution, 0, and the solution set can be written as $\{0\}$.

Example 2.4.6 Solve for t in the inequality $4t + 5 > 4t + 2$.

To solve for t, we will first subtract $4t$ from each side to get all terms containing t on one side:

$$4t + 5 > 4t + 2$$
$$4t + 5 - 4t > 4t + 2 - 4t$$
$$5 > 2$$

Notice that again, the variable t is no longer contained in the inequality. We then need to consider which values of t make the inequality true. The answer is that *all values* of t make $5 > 2$, which we know is a very strange sentence. So our solution set is all real numbers, which we can write as $\{t \mid t \text{ is a real number}\}$, or as $(-\infty, \infty)$.

Example 2.4.7 Solve for x in the inequality $-5x + 1 \leq -5x$.

To solve for x, we will first add $5x$ to each side to get all terms containing x on one side:

$$-5x + 1 \leq -5x$$
$$-5x + 1 + 5x \leq -5x + 5x$$
$$1 \leq 0$$

Once more, the variable x is absent. So we can ask ourselves, "For which values of x is $1 \leq 0$ true?" The answer is *none*, and so there is no solution to this inequality. We can write the solution set using $\emptyset$.

Remark 2.4.8 Again consider what would have happened if we had continued solving after we obtained $1 \leq 0$ in Example 2.4.7.

$$1 \leq 0$$
$$1 - 1 \leq 0 - 1$$
$$0 \leq -1$$

As we can see, all we found was another false statement—a different inequality that is not true for any real number.

Let's summarize the two special cases when solving linear equations and inequalities.

List 2.4.9: Special Solution Sets for Equations and Inequalities

---

All Real Numbers When solving an equation or inequality boils down to an unambiguously true equation or inequality such as $2 = 2$ or $0 < 2$, all real numbers are solutions. We write this solution set as either $(-\infty, \infty)$ or $\{x \mid x \text{ is a real number}\}$.

No Solution When solving an equation or inequality boils down to a *false statement* such as $0 = 2$ or $0 > 2$, no real number is a solution. We write this solution set as either $\{\,\}$ or $\emptyset$ or write the words "no solution exists."

2.4.2 Further Examples

Example 2.4.10 Solve for a in $\frac{2}{3}(a + 1) - \frac{5}{6} = \frac{2}{3}a$.

To solve this equation for a, we recall the technique of multiplying each side of the equation by the LCD of all fractions. Here, this means that we will multiply each side by 6 as our first step. After that, we'll be able to simplify each side of the equation and continue solving for a:

$$\frac{2}{3}(a + 1) - \frac{5}{6} = \frac{2}{3}a$$
$$6 \cdot \left(\frac{2}{3}(a + 1) - \frac{5}{6}\right) = 6 \cdot \frac{2}{3}a$$
$$6 \cdot \frac{2}{3}(a + 1) - 6 \cdot \frac{5}{6} = 6 \cdot \frac{2}{3}a$$
$$4(a + 1) - 5 = 4a$$
$$4a + 4 - 5 = 4a$$
$$4a - 1 = 4a$$
$$4a - 1 - 4a = 4a - 4a$$
$$-1 = 0$$

The statement $-1 = 0$ is false, so the equation has no solution. We can write the solution set as the empty set, $\emptyset$.

Example 2.4.11 Solve for x in the equation $3(x + 2) - 8 = (5x + 4) - 2(x + 1)$.

To solve for x, we will first need to simplify the left side and right side of the equation as much as possible by distributing and combining like terms:

$$3(x + 2) - 8 = (5x + 4) - 2(x + 1)$$
$$3x + 6 - 8 = 5x + 4 - 2x - 2$$
$$3x - 2 = 3x + 2$$

From here, we'll want to subtract $3x$ from each side:

$$3x - 2 - 3x = 3x + 2 - 3x$$
$$-2 = 2$$

As the equation $-2 = 2$ is not true for any value of x, there is no solution to this equation. We can write the solution set as the empty set, $\emptyset$.

Example 2.4.12 Solve for z in the inequality $\frac{3z}{5} + \frac{1}{2} \le \left(\frac{z}{10} + \frac{3}{4}\right) + \left(\frac{z}{2} - \frac{1}{4}\right)$.

To solve for z, we will first need to multiply each side of the inequality by the LCD, which is 20. After that, we'll finish solving by putting all terms containing a variable on one side of the inequality:

$$\frac{3z}{5} + \frac{1}{2} \le \left(\frac{z}{10} + \frac{3}{4}\right) + \left(\frac{z}{2} - \frac{1}{4}\right)$$

$$20 \cdot \left(\frac{3z}{5} + \frac{1}{2}\right) \le 20 \cdot \left(\left(\frac{z}{10} + \frac{3}{4}\right) + \left(\frac{z}{2} - \frac{1}{4}\right)\right)$$

$$20 \cdot \left(\frac{3z}{5}\right) + 20 \cdot \left(\frac{1}{2}\right) \le 20 \cdot \left(\frac{z}{10} + \frac{3}{4}\right) + 20 \cdot \left(\frac{z}{2} - \frac{1}{4}\right)$$

$$20 \cdot \left(\frac{3z}{5}\right) + 20 \cdot \left(\frac{1}{2}\right) \le 20 \cdot \left(\frac{z}{10}\right) + 20 \cdot \left(\frac{3}{4}\right) + 20 \cdot \left(\frac{z}{2}\right) - 20 \cdot \left(\frac{1}{4}\right)$$

$$12z + 10 \le 2z + 15 + 10z - 5$$

$$12z + 10 \le 12z + 10$$

$$12z + 10 - 12z \le 12z + 10 - 12z$$

$$10 \le 10$$

As the equation $10 \le 10$ is true for all values of z, all real numbers are solutions to this inequality. Thus the solution set is $\{z \mid z \text{ is a real number}\}$, or $(-\infty, \infty)$ in interval notation.

2.4.3 Reading Questions

1. Given a linear equation in one variable, what are the possibilities for how many solutions it could have? One solution? Two solutions? Other possibilities?

2. How will you know when a linear equation or inequality has no solutions?

3. How will you know when all numbers are solutions to a linear equation or inequality?

2.4.4 Exercises

Review and Warmup Solve the equation.

1.	$5a + 2 = 12$	**2.**	$10c + 1 = 51$	**3.**	$-5A - 8 = -43$
4.	$-8C - 5 = 35$	**5.**	$-10m + 8 = -m - 10$	**6.**	$-7p + 2 = -p - 52$
7.	$16 = -4(q - 6)$	**8.**	$130 = -10(y - 10)$		

Solving Equations with Special Solution Sets Solve the equation.

9.	$6r = 6r + 4$	**10.**	$4a = 4a + 7$
11.	$10c + 2 = 10c + 2$	**12.**	$6A + 6 = 6A + 6$
13.	$3C - 2 - 4C = -7 - C + 5$	**14.**	$9m - 5 - 10m = -9 - m + 4$
15.	$-7 - 10p + 3 = -p + 13 - 9p$	**16.**	$-5 - 6q + 1 = -q + 12 - 5q$
17.	$8(y - 9) = 8(y - 4)$	**18.**	$6(r - 5) = 6(r - 3)$

19. $2(5 - 4a) - (8a - 10) = 22 - 2(6 + 8a)$

20. $4(9 - 2b) - (8b - 5) = 16 - 2(7 + 8b)$

21. $15 - 4(5 + 5A) = -21A - (5 - A)$

22. $19 - 3(8 + 4C) = -13C - (5 - C)$

23. Solve the equation.

    a. $9m + 3 = 3m + 3$

    b. $9m + 3 = 9m + 3$

    c. $9m + 3 = 9m + 6$

24. Solve the equation.

    a. $7p + 7 = 5p + 7$

    b. $7p + 7 = 7p + 7$

    c. $7p + 7 = 7p + 10$

Solving Inequalities with Special Solution Sets Solve this inequality.

25. $10x > 10x + 9$

26. $2x > 2x + 6$

27. $-4x \leq -4x - 8$

28. $-4x \leq -4x - 1$

29. $-7 + 6x + 14 \geq 6x + 7$

30. $-1 + 6x + 4 \geq 6x + 3$

31. $-6 + 8x + 16 < 8x + 10$

32. $-10 + 8x + 16 < 8x + 6$

33. $-10 - 6z + 4 > -z + 5 - 5z$

34. $-10 - 10z + 8 > -z + 1 - 9z$

35. $2(k - 8) \leq 2(k - 1)$

36. $4(k - 6) \leq 4(k - 3)$

37. $4x \leq 4x + 8$

38. $6x \leq 6x + 5$

39. $4(2 - 10m) - (8m - 4) > 7 - 2(10 + 24m)$

40. $4(7 - 4m) - (6m - 4) > 9 - 2(5 + 11m)$

Challenge

41. Fill in the right side of the equation to create a linear equation that meets the description.

    a. Create a linear equation with solution set {2}.

        $16(x + 4)$

    b. Create a linear equation with *infinitely many solutions*.

        $16(x + 4)$

2.5 Isolating a Linear Variable

In this section, we solve for a variable in a linear equation, even when there is more than one variable.

2.5.1 Solving for a Variable

The formula of calculating a rectangle's area is $A = \ell w$, where ℓ stands for the rectangle's length, and w stands for width. So when a rectangle's length and width are given, we can easily calculate its area.

But what if we know a rectangle's *area* and *length*, and we need to calculate its width?

If a rectangle's area is $12\,\mathrm{m}^2$, and its length is $4\,\mathrm{m}$, we could find its width this way:

$$A = \ell w$$
$$12 = 4w$$
$$\frac{12}{4} = \frac{4w}{4}$$
$$3 = w$$
$$w = 3$$

We can go through the same motions without using the specific numbers for A and ℓ:

$$A = \ell w$$
$$\frac{A}{\ell} = \frac{\ell w}{\ell}$$
$$\frac{A}{\ell} = w$$
$$w = \frac{A}{\ell}$$

Now if we want to find the width when $A = 12$ and $\ell = 4$, we have a formula: $w = \frac{A}{\ell}$. But the formula could also quickly tell us the width when $A = 100$ and $\ell = 20$, or when when $A = 23.47$ and $\ell = 2.71$, or any other variation. This formula, $w = \frac{A}{\ell}$, is a handy version of the original equation in situations where w is the unknown.

Remark 2.5.2 Note that in solving for A, we divided each side of the equation by ℓ. The operations that we apply, and the order in which we do them, are determined by the operations in the original equation. In the original equation $A = \ell w$, we saw that w was *multiplied* by ℓ, and so we knew that in order to undo that operation, we would need to *divide* each side by ℓ. We continue to use this process of "un-doing" operations throughout this section.

Example 2.5.3 Solve for R in $P = R - C$. (This is the relationship between profit, revenue, and cost.)

Explanation.   To solve for R, we first want to note that C is *subtracted* from R. To undo this, we *add* C to each side of the equation:

$$P = \overset{\downarrow}{R} - C$$
$$P + C = \overset{\downarrow}{R} - C + C$$
$$P + C = \overset{\downarrow}{R}$$
$$R = P + C$$

Example 2.5.4 Solve for x in $y = mx + b$. (This is a line's equation in slope-intercept form, studied more in Section 3.5.)

Explanation. In the equation $y = mx + b$, we see that x is multiplied by m and then b is added to that. Our first step will be to isolate mx, which we'll do by subtracting b from each side of the equation:

$$y = m\overset{\downarrow}{x} + b$$

$$y - b = m\overset{\downarrow}{x} + b - b$$

$$y - b = m\overset{\downarrow}{x}$$

Now that we have mx by itself, we note that x is multiplied by m. To undo this, we divide each side of the equation by m:

$$\frac{y - b}{m} = \frac{m\overset{\downarrow}{x}}{m}$$

$$\frac{y - b}{m} = \overset{\downarrow}{x}$$

$$x = \frac{y - b}{m}$$

Warning 2.5.5 It's important to note in Example 2.5.4 that each *side* was divided by m. We can't simply divide y by m, as the equation would no longer be equivalent.

Example 2.5.6 Solve for b in $A = \frac{1}{2}bh$. (This is the area formula for a triangle.)

Explanation. To solve for b, we need to determine what operations need to be undone. The expression $\frac{1}{2}bh$ has multiplication between $\frac{1}{2}$ and b and h. As a first step, we will multiply each side of the equation by 2 in order to eliminate the $\frac{1}{2}$:

$$A = \frac{1}{2}\overset{\downarrow}{b}h$$

$$2 \cdot A = 2 \cdot \frac{1}{2}\overset{\downarrow}{b}h$$

$$2A = \overset{\downarrow}{b}h$$

Next we undo the multiplication between b and h by dividing each side by h:

$$\frac{2A}{h} = \frac{\overset{\downarrow}{b}h}{h}$$

$$\frac{2A}{h} = \overset{\downarrow}{b}$$

$$b = \frac{2A}{h}$$

Checkpoint 2.5.7 Solve for y in $2x + 5y = 10$. (This is a linear equation in standard form, studied more in Section 3.7.)

Explanation.   To solve for y, we first isolate $5y$ by subtracting $2x$ from each side of the equation. After that, we can divide each side by 5 to finish solving for y:

$$2x + 5\overset{\downarrow}{y} = 10$$

$$2x + 5\overset{\downarrow}{y} - 2x = 10 - 2x$$

$$5\overset{\downarrow}{y} = 10 - 2x$$

$$\frac{5\overset{\downarrow}{y}}{5} = \frac{10 - 2x}{5}$$

$$y = \frac{10 - 2x}{5}$$

Example 2.5.8 Solve for F in $C = \frac{5}{9}(F - 32)$. (This represents the relationship between temperature in degrees Celsius and degrees Fahrenheit.)

Explanation.   To solve for F, note that it is contained inside parentheses. To isolate the expression $F - 32$, we want to eliminate the $\frac{5}{9}$ outside those parentheses. One way we can undo this multiplication is to divide each side by $\frac{5}{9}$. A better technique is to multiply each side by the reciprocal of $\frac{5}{9}$, which is $\frac{9}{5}$:

$$C = \frac{5}{9}(\overset{\downarrow}{F} - 32)$$

$$\frac{9}{5} \cdot C = \frac{9}{5} \cdot \frac{5}{9}(\overset{\downarrow}{F} - 32)$$

$$\frac{9}{5}C = \overset{\downarrow}{F} - 32$$

Now that we have $F - 32$, we simply need to add 32 to each side to finish solving for F:

$$\frac{9}{5}C + 32 = \overset{\downarrow}{F} - 32 + 32$$

$$\frac{9}{5}C + 32 = \overset{\downarrow}{F}$$

$$F = \frac{9}{5}C + 32$$

2.5.2 Reading Questions

1.   Suppose you want to solve the equation $mq + b = T$ for q. What would be wrong with dividing on each side by m to get $\frac{mq}{m} + b = \frac{T}{m}$?

2.   How do you undo dividing by R?

2.5.3 Exercises

Review and Warmup Solve the equation.

1. $8q + 4 = 52$

2. $5y + 3 = 53$

3. $-10r - 1 = 29$

4. $-4a - 9 = -29$

5. $-5b + 3 = -b - 21$

6. $-10A + 7 = -A - 20$

7. $-63 = -7(B - 1)$

8. $4 = -4(m - 5)$

Solving for a Variable

9. a. Solve $t + 5 = 13$ for t.

b. Solve $y + r = p$ for y.

10. a. Solve $t + 1 = 7$ for t.

b. Solve $r + b = c$ for r.

11. a. Solve $x - 9 = -7$ for x.

b. Solve $y - C = -7$ for y.

12. a. Solve $x - 5 = -3$ for x.

b. Solve $t - y = -3$ for t.

13. a. Solve $-y + 1 = -9$ for y.

b. Solve $-r + A = a$ for r.

14. a. Solve $-y + 3 = -7$ for y.

b. Solve $-x + q = r$ for x.

15. a. Solve $3r = 30$ for r.

b. Solve $at = m$ for t.

16. a. Solve $5r = 10$ for r.

b. Solve $ct = y$ for t.

17. a. Solve $\frac{r}{3} = 10$ for r.

b. Solve $\frac{x}{y} = n$ for x.

18. a. Solve $\frac{t}{5} = 4$ for t.

b. Solve $\frac{r}{q} = y$ for r.

19. a. Solve $4t + 3 = 35$ for t.

b. Solve $xy + C = n$ for y.

20. a. Solve $6x + 6 = 24$ for x.

b. Solve $by + a = r$ for y.

21. a. Solve $xt = n$ for x.

b. Solve $xt = n$ for t.

22. a. Solve $yt = x$ for y.

b. Solve $yt = x$ for t.

23. a. Solve $y + x = C$ for y.

b. Solve $y + x = C$ for x.

24. a. Solve $r + x = t$ for r.

b. Solve $r + x = t$ for x.

25. a. Solve $br + B = q$ for B.

b. Solve $br + B = q$ for b.

26. a. Solve $xt + m = C$ for m.

b. Solve $xt + m = C$ for x.

27. a. Solve $y = Cn + c$ for n.

b. Solve $y = Cn + c$ for C.

28. a. Solve $t = aq + r$ for q.

b. Solve $t = aq + r$ for a.

29. a. Solve $10 = \frac{1}{2}b \cdot 2$ for b.

b. Solve $A = \frac{1}{2}b \cdot h$ for b.

30. a. Solve $8 = \frac{1}{2}b \cdot 2$ for b.

b. Solve $A = \frac{1}{2}b \cdot h$ for b.

31. Solve these linear equations for y.

a. $\frac{y}{5} + 10 = 12$

b. $\frac{y}{x} + 10 = a$

32. Solve these linear equations for y.

a. $\frac{y}{5} + 1 = 3$

b. $\frac{y}{t} + 1 = c$

33. Solve this linear equation for x.

$$y = mx - b$$

34. Solve this linear equation for x.

$$y = -mx + b$$

35. Solve this linear equation for r.

$$C = 2\pi r$$

36. Solve this linear equation for h.

$$V = \pi r^2 h$$

37. Solve this linear equation for t.

$$\frac{t}{x} + A = C$$

38. Solve this linear equation for x.

$$\frac{x}{t} + q = b$$

39. Solve this linear equation for x.

$$\frac{x}{2} + r = a$$

40. Solve this linear equation for y.

$$\frac{y}{9} + x = m$$

41. Solve this linear equation for b.

$$A = r - \frac{9b}{n}$$

42. Solve this linear equation for A.

$$t = B - \frac{9A}{c}$$

43. Solve this linear equation for x.

$$Ax + By = C$$

44. Solve this linear equation for y.

$$Ax + By = C$$

Solve the linear equation for y.

45. $-35x - 5y = 10$

46. $20x - 5y = 65$

47. $8x + 2y = 30$

48. $14x - 2y = -10$

49. $4x - y = 18$

50. $2x - y = -8$

51. $4x - 6y = -36$

52. $8x - 6y = -36$

53. $7y - 3x = 5$

54. $6x - 8y = 5$

55. $21x + 87y = 110$

56. $24y - 51x = 97$

2.6 Linear Equations and Inequalities Chapter Review

2.6.1 Solving Multistep Linear Equations

In Section 2.1 we covered the steps to solve a linear equation and the differences between simplifying expressions, evaluating expressions and solving equations.

Example 2.6.1 Solve for a in $4 - (3 - a) = -2 - 2(2a + 1)$.

Explanation. To solve this equation, we will simplify each side of the equation, manipulate it so that all variable terms are on one side and all constant terms are on the other, and then solve for a:

$$4 - (3 - a) = -2 - 2(2a + 1)$$
$$4 - 3 + a = -2 - 4a - 2$$
$$1 + a - -4 - 4a$$
$$1 + a + 4a = -4 - 4a + 4a$$
$$1 + 5a = -4$$
$$1 + 5a - 1 = -4 - 1$$
$$5a = -5$$
$$\frac{5a}{5} = \frac{-5}{5}$$
$$a = -1$$

Checking the solution -1 in the original equation, we get:

$$4 - (3 - a) = -2 - 2(2a + 1)$$
$$4 - (3 - (-1)) \stackrel{?}{=} -2 - 2(2(-1) + 1)$$
$$4 - (4) \stackrel{?}{=} -2 - 2(-1)$$
$$0 \stackrel{\checkmark}{=} 0$$

Therefore the solution to the equation is -1 and the solution set is $\{-1\}$.

2.6.2 Solving Multistep Linear Inequalities

In Section 2.2 we covered how solving inequalities is very much like how we solve equations, except that if we multiply or divide by a negative we switch the inequality sign.

Example 2.6.2 Solve for x in $-2 - 2(2x + 1) > 4 - (3 - x)$. Write the solution set in both set-builder notation and interval notation.

Explanation.

$$-2 - 2(2x + 1) > 4 - (3 - x)$$
$$-2 - 4x - 2 > 4 - 3 + x$$
$$-4x - 4 > x + 1$$
$$-4x - 4 - x > x + 1 - x$$

$$-5x - 4 > 1$$
$$-5x - 4 + 4 > 1 + 4$$
$$-5x > 5$$
$$\frac{-5x}{-5} < \frac{5}{-5}$$
$$x < -1$$

Note that when we divided both sides of the inequality by -5, we had to switch the direction of the inequality symbol.

The solution set in set-builder notation is $\{x \mid x < -1\}$. The solution set in interval notation is $(-\infty, -1)$.

2.6.3 Linear Equations and Inequalities with Fractions

In Section 2.3 we covered how to eliminate denominators in an equation with the LCD to help solve the equation.

Example 2.6.3 Solve for x in $\frac{1}{4}x + \frac{2}{3} = \frac{1}{6}$.

Explanation.

We'll solve by multiplying each side of the equation by 12:

$$\frac{1}{4}x + \frac{2}{3} = \frac{1}{6}$$
$$12 \cdot \left(\frac{1}{4}x + \frac{2}{3}\right) = 12 \cdot \frac{1}{6}$$
$$12 \cdot \left(\frac{1}{4}x\right) + 12 \cdot \left(\frac{2}{3}\right) = 12 \cdot \frac{1}{6}$$
$$3x + 8 = 2$$
$$3x = -6$$
$$\frac{3x}{3} = \frac{-6}{3}$$
$$x = -2$$

Checking the solution:

$$\frac{1}{4}x + \frac{2}{3} = \frac{1}{6}$$
$$\frac{1}{4}(-2) + \frac{2}{3} \overset{?}{=} \frac{1}{6}$$
$$-\frac{2}{4} + \frac{2}{3} \overset{?}{=} \frac{1}{6}$$
$$-\frac{6}{12} + \frac{8}{12} \overset{?}{=} \frac{1}{6}$$
$$\frac{2}{12} \overset{?}{=} \frac{1}{6}$$
$$\frac{1}{6} \overset{\checkmark}{=} \frac{1}{6}$$

The solution is therefore -2. We write the solution set s $\{-2\}$.

2.6.4 Special Solution Sets

In Section 2.4 we covered linear equations that have no solutions and also linear equations that have infinitely many solutions. When solving linear inequalities, it's also possible that no solution exists or that all real numbers are solutions.

Example 2.6.4

a. Solve for x in the equation $3x = 3x + 4$.

b. Solve for t in the inequality $4t + 5 > 4t + 2$.

Explanation.

a. To solve this equation, we need to move all terms containing x to one side of the equals sign:

$$3x = 3x + 4$$
$$3x - 3x = 3x + 4 - 3x$$
$$0 = 4$$

This equation has no solution. We write the solution set as ∅, which is the symbol for the empty set.

b. To solve for t, we will first subtract 4t from each side to get all terms containing t on one side:

$$4t + 5 > 4t + 2$$
$$4t + 5 - 4t > 4t + 2 - 4t$$
$$5 > 2$$

All values of the variable t make the inequality true. The solution set is all real numbers, which we can write as {t | t is a real number} in set notation, or $(-\infty, \infty)$ in interval notation.

2.6.5 Isolating a Linear Variable

In Section 2.5 we covered how to solve an equation when there are multiple variables in the equation.

Example 2.6.5 Solve for x in $y = mx + b$.

Explanation.

$$y = mx + b$$
$$y - b = mx + b - b$$
$$y - b = mx$$
$$\frac{y - b}{m} = \frac{mx}{m}$$
$$\frac{y - b}{m} = x$$

2.6.6 Exercises

1. a. Solve $3(x + 7) - 7 = 35$.

    b. Evaluate $3(x + 7) - 7$ when $x = 7$.

    c. Simplify $3(x + 7) - 7$.

2. a. Solve $5(y - 4) + 7 = 22$.

    b. Evaluate $5(y - 4) + 7$ when $y = 7$.

    c. Simplify $5(y - 4) + 7$.

3. Solve the equation.
$-16 = -7b - 8 - b$

4. Solve the equation.
$14 = -3A - 2 - A$

5. Solve the equation.
$5 + 9(B - 3) = -7 - (8 - 2B)$

6. Solve the equation.
$3 + 10(m - 8) = -74 - (3 - 2m)$

7. Solve the equation.
$-6 - 7n + 3 = -n + 9 - 6n$

8. Solve the equation.
$-9 - 9q + 2 = -q + 7 - 8q$

9. Solve the equation.
$$21 = \frac{x}{5} + \frac{x}{2}$$

10. Solve the equation.
$$22 = \frac{r}{3} + \frac{r}{8}$$

11. Solve the equation.
$$\frac{t-1}{6} = \frac{t+4}{8}$$

12. Solve the equation.
$$\frac{b-5}{4} = \frac{b+1}{6}$$

13. Solve this inequality.
$$3 - (y+6) < -11$$

14. Solve this inequality.
$$4 - (y+9) < 0$$

15. Solve this inequality.
$$8(k-7) \leq 8(k-3)$$

16. Solve this inequality.
$$10(k-5) \leq 10(k-1)$$

17. Solve this inequality.
$$5 + 9(x-7) < -34 - (4-4x)$$

18. Solve this inequality.
$$1 + 8(x-10) < -87 - (4-2x)$$

19. Solve this inequality.
$$-\frac{1}{4}t > \frac{2}{3}t - 22$$

20. Solve this inequality.
$$-\frac{5}{6}t > \frac{4}{3}t - 26$$

21. Solve this linear equation for x.
$$Ax + By = C$$

22. Solve this linear equation for y.
$$Ax + By = C$$

23. Solve this linear equation for B.
$$C = a - \frac{7B}{x}$$

24. Solve this linear equation for m.
$$r = c - \frac{8m}{t}$$

25. Matthew has $87 in his piggy bank. He plans to purchase some Pokemon cards, which costs $2.85 each. He plans to save $52.80 to purchase another toy. At most how many Pokemon cards can he purchase? Write an equation to solve this problem.

   Matthew can purchase at most [   ] Pokemon cards.

26. Chris has $89 in his piggy bank. He plans to purchase some Pokemon cards, which costs $2.25 each. He plans to save $71 to purchase another toy. At most how many Pokemon cards can he purchase? Write an equation to solve this problem.

   Chris can purchase at most [   ] Pokemon cards.

27. Use a linear equation to solve the word problem.

   Daniel has $95.00 in his piggy bank, and he spends $3.50 every day. Sydney has $40.00 in her piggy bank, and she saves $1.50 every day.

   If they continue to spend and save money this way, how many days later would they have the same amount of money in their piggy banks?

   [   ] days later, Daniel and Sydney will have the same amount of money in their piggy banks.

28. Use a linear equation to solve the word problem.

   Sean has $100.00 in his piggy bank, and he spends $2.50 every day. Kurt has $8.00 in his piggy bank, and he saves $1.50 every day.

   If they continue to spend and save money this way, how many days later would they have the same amount of money in their piggy banks?

   [   ] days later, Sean and Kurt will have the same amount of money in their piggy banks.

29. Use a linear equation to solve the word problem.

   Massage Heaven and Massage You are competitors. Massage Heaven has 4200 registered customers, and it gets approximately 700 newly registered customers every month. Massage You has 9450 registered customers, and it gets approximately 350 newly registered customers every month. How many months would it take Massage Heaven to catch up with Massage You in the number of registered customers?

These two companies would have approximately the same number of registered customers ☐ months later.

30. Use a linear equation to solve the word problem.

Two truck rental companies have different rates. V-Haul has a base charge of $60.00, plus $0.35 per mile. W-Haul has a base charge of $45.40, plus $0.45 per mile. For how many miles would these two companies charge the same amount?

If a driver drives ☐ miles, those two companies would charge the same amount of money.

31. A rectangle's perimeter is 146 ft. Its length is 2 ft shorter than four times its width. Use an equation to find the rectangle's length and width.

Its width is ☐.

Its length is ☐.

32. A rectangle's perimeter is 216 ft. Its length is 4 ft longer than three times its width. Use an equation to find the rectangle's length and width.

Its width is ☐.

Its length is ☐.

Chapter 3

Graphing Lines

3.1 Cartesian Coordinates

When we model a relationship between two variables visually, we use the *Cartesian coordinate system*. This section covers the basic vocabulary and ideas that come with the Cartesian coordinate system.

The Cartesian coordinate system identifies the location of every point in a plane. Basically, the system gives every point in a plane its own "address" in relation to a starting point. We'll use a street grid as an analogy. Here is a map with Carl's home at the center. The map also shows some nearby businesses. Assume each unit in the grid represents one city block.

René Descartes. Several ideas and conventions used in mathematics are attributed to (or at least named after) René Descartes[1]. The Cartesian coordinate system is one of these.

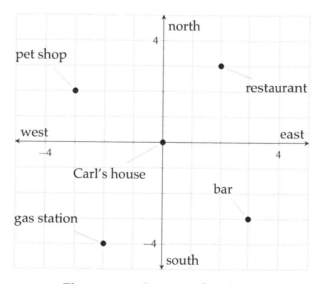

Figure 3.1.2: Carl's neighborhood

---

[1]en.wikipedia.org/wiki/René_Descartes

If Carl has an out-of-town guest who asks him how to get to the restaurant, Carl could say:

"First go 2 blocks east (to the right on the map), then go 3 blocks north (up on the map)."

Two numbers are used to locate the restaurant. In the Cartesian coordinate system, these numbers are called **coordinates** and they are written as the **ordered pair** $(2, 3)$. The first coordinate, 2, represents distance traveled from Carl's house to the east (or to the right horizontally on the graph). The second coordinate, 3, represents distance to the north (up vertically on the graph).

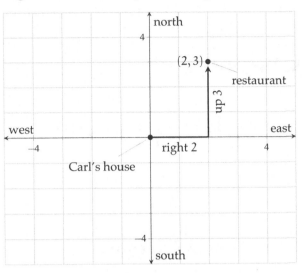

Figure 3.1.3: Carl's path to the restaurant

To travel from Carl's home to the pet shop, he would go 3 blocks west, and then 2 blocks north. In the Cartesian coordinate system, the *positive* directions are to the *right* horizontally and *up* vertically. The *negative* directions are to the *left* horizontally and *down* vertically. So the pet shop's Cartesian coordinates are $(-3, 2)$.

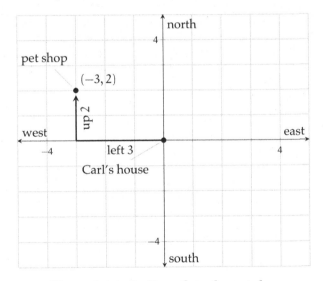

Figure 3.1.4: Carl's path to the pet shop

Remark 3.1.5 It's important to know that the order of Cartesian coordinates is (horizontal, vertical). This idea of communicating horizontal information *before* vertical information is consistent throughout most of mathematics.

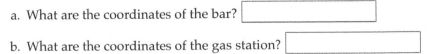 **Checkpoint 3.1.6** Use Figure 3.1.2 to answer the following questions.

a. What are the coordinates of the bar? [   ]

b. What are the coordinates of the gas station? [   ]

c. What are the coordinates of Carl's house? [   ]

Warning 3.1.7 Notation Issue: Coordinates or Interval? Unfortunately, the notation for an ordered pair looks exactly like interval notation for an open interval. *Context* will help you understand if $(1, 3)$ indicates the point 1 unit right of the origin and 3 units up, or if $(1, 3)$ indicates the interval of all real numbers between 1 and 3.

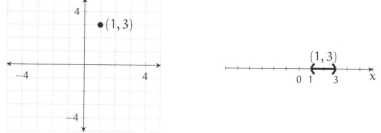

Traditionally, the variable x represents numbers on the horizontal axis, so it is called the x-**axis**. The variable y represents numbers on the vertical axis, so it is called the y-**axis**. The axes meet at the point $(0, 0)$, which is called the **origin**. Every point in the plane is represented by an **ordered pair**, (x, y).

In a Cartesian coordinate system, the map of Carl's neighborhood would look like this:

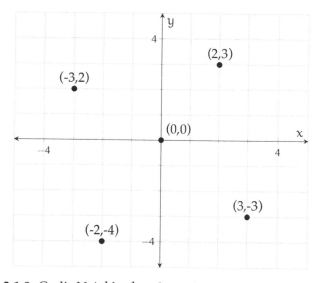

Figure 3.1.8: Carl's Neighborhood in a Cartesian Coordinate System

Definition 3.1.9 Cartesian Coordinate System. The Cartesian coordinate system[2] is a coordinate system that specifies each point uniquely in a plane by a pair of numerical coordinates, which are the signed (positive/negative) distances to the point from two fixed perpendicular directed lines, measured in the same unit of length. Those two reference lines are called the **horizontal axis** and **vertical axis**, and the point where they meet is the **origin**. The horizontal and vertical axes are often called the x-**axis** and y-**axis**.

The plane based on the x-axis and y-axis is called a **coordinate plane**. The ordered pair used to locate a point is called the point's **coordinates**, which consists of an x-**coordinate** and a y-**coordinate**. For example, the point $(1, 2)$, has x-coordinate 1, and y-coordinate 2. The origin has coordinates $(0, 0)$.

A Cartesian coordinate system is divided into four **quadrants**, as shown in Figure 3.1.10. The quadrants are traditionally labeled with Roman numerals.

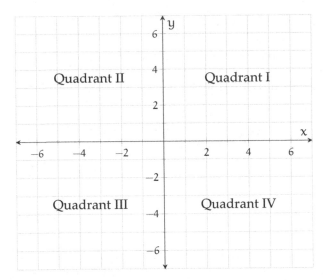

Figure 3.1.10: A Cartesian grid with four quadrants marked

◊

Example 3.1.11 On paper, sketch a Cartesian coordinate system with units, and then plot the following points: $(3,2), (-5,-1), (0,-3), (4,0)$.

Explanation.

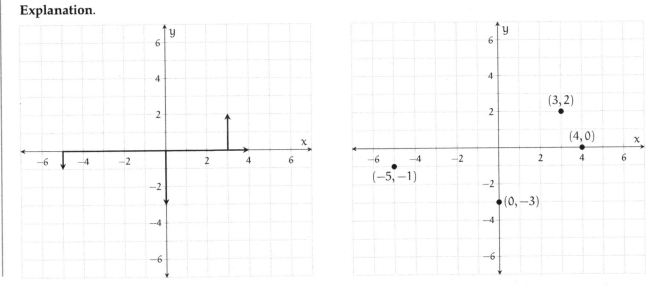

[2]en.wikipedia.org/wiki/Cartesian_coordinate_system

Reading Questions

1.   What are the coordinates of the gas station in the map of Carl's neighborhood?

2.   A Cartesian coordinate system has seven "places" within that are worth noting. What are they? (For example, one of them is Quadrant I.)

Exercises

Identifying Coordinates Locate each point in the graph:

1.

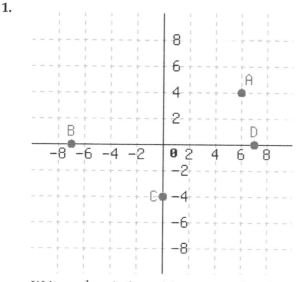

2.

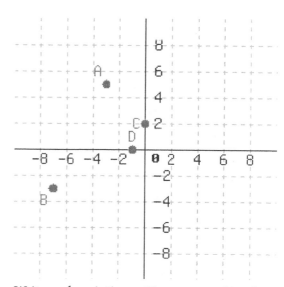

Write each point's position as an ordered pair, like $(1, 2)$.

$A = \underline{\hspace{1cm}}$ $B = \underline{\hspace{1cm}}$
$C = \underline{\hspace{1cm}}$ $D = \underline{\hspace{1cm}}$

Write each point's position as an ordered pair, like $(1, 2)$.

$A = \underline{\hspace{1cm}}$ $B = \underline{\hspace{1cm}}$
$C = \underline{\hspace{1cm}}$ $D = \underline{\hspace{1cm}}$

Creating Sketches of Graphs

3.   Sketch the points $(8, 2)$, $(5, 5)$, $(-3, 0)$, and $(2, -6)$ on a Cartesian plane.

4.   Sketch the points $(1, -4)$, $(-3, 5)$, $(0, 4)$, and $(-2, -6)$ on a Cartesian plane.

5.   Sketch the points $(208, -50)$, $(97, 112)$, $(-29, 103)$, and $(-80, -172)$ on a Cartesian plane.

6.   Sketch the points $(110, 38)$, $(-205, 52)$, $(-52, 125)$, and $(-172, -80)$ on a Cartesian plane.

7.   Sketch the points $(5.5, 2.7)$, $(-7.3, 2.75)$, $\left(-\frac{10}{3}, \frac{1}{2}\right)$, and $\left(-\frac{28}{5}, -\frac{29}{4}\right)$ on a Cartesian plane.

8.   Sketch the points $(1.9, -3.3)$, $(-5.2, -8.11)$, $\left(\frac{7}{11}, \frac{15}{2}\right)$, and $\left(-\frac{16}{3}, \frac{19}{5}\right)$ on a Cartesian plane.

9.   Sketch a Cartesian plane and shade the quadrants where the x-coordinate is negative.

10. Sketch a Cartesian plane and shade the quadrants where the y-coordinate is positive.

11. Sketch a Cartesian plane and shade the quadrants where the x-coordinate has the same sign as the y-coordinate.

12. Sketch a Cartesian plane and shade the quadrants where the x-coordinate and the y-coordinate have opposite signs.

Cartesian Plots in Context

13. This graph gives the minimum estimates of the wolf population in Washington from 2008 through 2015.

14. Here is a graph of the foreign-born US population (in millions) during Census years 1960 to 2010.

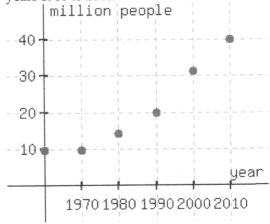

What are the Cartesian coordinates for the point representing the year 2011?

[   ]

Between 2011 and 2012, the wolf population

grew by [   ] wolves.

List at least three ordered pairs in the graph.

What are the Cartesian coordinates for the point representing the year 1980?

[   ]

Between 1980 and 2000, the US population

that is foreign-born increased by [   ]

million people.

List at least three ordered pairs in the graph.

Regions in the Cartesian Plane

15. The point $(3, -10)$ is in Quadrant (☐ I ☐ II ☐ III ☐ IV) .
The point $(-5, 7)$ is in Quadrant (☐ I ☐ II ☐ III ☐ IV) .
The point $(8, 9)$ is in Quadrant (☐ I ☐ II ☐ III ☐ IV) .
The point $(-3, -9)$ is in Quadrant (☐ I ☐ II ☐ III ☐ IV) .

16. The point $(6, 4)$ is in Quadrant (☐ I ☐ II ☐ III ☐ IV) .
The point $(4, -5)$ is in Quadrant (☐ I ☐ II ☐ III ☐ IV) .
The point $(-10, -4)$ is in Quadrant (☐ I ☐ II ☐ III ☐ IV) .
The point $(-10, 4)$ is in Quadrant (☐ I ☐ II ☐ III ☐ IV) .

17. Assume the point (x, y) is in Quadrant II, locate the following points:
The point $(-x, y)$ is in Quadrant (☐ I ☐ II ☐ III ☐ IV) .
The point $(x, -y)$ is in Quadrant (☐ I ☐ II ☐ III ☐ IV) .
The point $(-x, -y)$ is in Quadrant (☐ I ☐ II ☐ III ☐ IV) .

18. Assume the point (x, y) is in Quadrant IV, locate the following points:
The point $(-x, y)$ is in Quadrant (☐ I ☐ II ☐ III ☐ IV) .
The point $(x, -y)$ is in Quadrant (☐ I ☐ II ☐ III ☐ IV) .

The point $(-x, -y)$ is in Quadrant   ($\square$ I $\square$ II $\square$ III $\square$ IV) .

19. Answer the following questions on the coordinate system:

For the point (x, y), if $x > 0$ and $y > 0$, then the point is in/on   ($\square$ Quadrant I $\square$ Quadrant II $\square$ Quadrant III $\square$ Quadrant IV $\square$ the x-axis $\square$ the y-axis) .

For the point (x, y), if $x > 0$ and $y < 0$, then the point is in/on   ($\square$ Quadrant I $\square$ Quadrant II $\square$ Quadrant III $\square$ Quadrant IV $\square$ the x-axis $\square$ the y-axis) .

For the point (x, y), if $y = 0$, then the point is in/on   ($\square$ Quadrant I $\square$ Quadrant II $\square$ Quadrant III $\square$ Quadrant IV $\square$ the x-axis $\square$ the y-axis) .

For the point (x, y), if $x < 0$ and $y < 0$, then the point is in/on   ($\square$ Quadrant I $\square$ Quadrant II $\square$ Quadrant III $\square$ Quadrant IV $\square$ the x-axis $\square$ the y-axis) .

For the point (x, y), if $x = 0$, then the point is in/on   ($\square$ Quadrant I $\square$ Quadrant II $\square$ Quadrant III $\square$ Quadrant IV $\square$ the x-axis $\square$ the y-axis) .

For the point (x, y), if $x < 0$ and $y > 0$, then the point is in/on   ($\square$ Quadrant I $\square$ Quadrant II $\square$ Quadrant III $\square$ Quadrant IV $\square$ the x-axis $\square$ the y-axis) .

Plotting Points and Choosing a Scale

20. What would be the difficulty with trying to plot $(12, 4)$, $(13, 5)$, and $(310, 208)$ all on the same graph?

21. The points $(3, 5)$, $(5, 6)$, $(7, 7)$, and $(9, 8)$ all lie on a straight line. What can go wrong if you make a plot of a Cartesian plane with these points marked, and you don't have tick marks that are evenly spaced apart?

3.2 Graphing Equations

We have graphed *points* in a coordinate system, and now we will graph *lines* and *curves*.

A **graph** of an equation is a picture of that equation's solution set. For example, the graph of $y = -2x + 3$ is shown in Figure 3.2.3(c). The graph plots the ordered pairs whose coordinates make $y = -2x + 3$ true. Figure 3.2.2 shows a few points that make the equation true.

$y = -2x + 3$	(x, y)
$5 \overset{\checkmark}{=} -2(-1) + 3$	$(-1, 5)$
$3 \overset{\checkmark}{=} -2(0) + 3$	$(0, 3)$
$1 \overset{\checkmark}{=} -2(1) + 3$	$(1, 1)$
$-1 \overset{\checkmark}{=} -2(2) + 3$	$(2, -1)$
$-3 \overset{\checkmark}{=} -2(3) + 3$	$(3, -3)$
$-5 \overset{\checkmark}{=} -2(4) + 3$	$(4, -5)$

Figure 3.2.2

Figure 3.2.2 tells us that the points $(-1, 5)$, $(0, 3)$, $(1, 1)$, $(2, -1)$, $(3, -3)$, and $(4, -5)$ are all solutions to the equation $y = -2x + 3$, and so they should all be shaded as part of that equation's graph. You can see them in Figure 3.2.3(a). But there are many more points that make the equation true. More points are plotted in Figure 3.2.3(b). Even more points are plotted in Figure 3.2.3(c)—so many, that together the points look like a straight line.

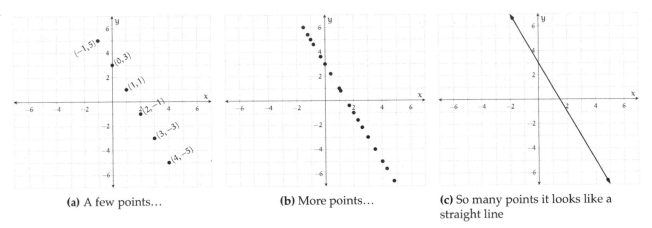

(a) A few points…   (b) More points…   (c) So many points it looks like a straight line

Figure 3.2.3: Graphs of the Equation $y = -2x + 3$

The graph of an equation shades all the points (x, y) that make the equation true once the x- and y-values are substituted in. Typically, there are *so many* points shaded, that the final graph appears to be a continuous line or curve that you could draw with one stroke of a pen.

Checkpoint 3.2.4 The point $(4, -5)$ is on the graph in Figure 3.2.3.(c). What happens when you substitute these values into the equation $y = -2x + 3$?

$$y \quad = \quad -2x + 3$$
$$\underline{} \overset{?}{=} \underline{}$$

This equation is   ($\square$ true $\square$ false)   .

Checkpoint 3.2.5 Decide whether $(5, -2)$ and $(-10, -7)$ are on the graph of the equation $y = -\frac{3}{5}x + 1$.
At $(5, -2)$:

$$y \;=\; -\tfrac{3}{5}x + 1$$
$$\underline{\qquad \overset{?}{=} \qquad\qquad\qquad\qquad}$$

This equation is   ($\square$ true $\square$ false) and $(5, -2)$ is ($\square$ part of $\square$ not part of) the graph of $y = -\frac{3}{5}x + 1$.
At $(-10, -7)$:

$$y \;=\; -\tfrac{3}{5}x + 1$$
$$\underline{\qquad \overset{?}{=} \qquad\qquad\qquad\qquad}$$

This equation is   ($\square$ true $\square$ false) and $(-10, -7)$ is ($\square$ part of $\square$ not part of) the graph of $y = -\frac{3}{5}x + 1$.

Explanation.   If the point $(5, -2)$ is on $y = -\frac{3}{5}x + 1$, once we substitute $x = 5$ and $y = 2$ into the line's equation, the equation should be true. Let's try:

$$y = -\frac{3}{5}x + 1$$
$$-2 \overset{?}{=} -\frac{3}{5}(5) + 1$$
$$-2 \overset{\checkmark}{=} -3 + 1$$

Because this last equation is true, we can say that $(5, -2)$ is on the graph of $y = -\frac{3}{5}x + 1$.
However if we substitute $x = -10$ and $y = -7$ into the equation, it leads to $-7 = 7$, which is false. This tells us that $(-10, -7)$ is *not* on the graph.

To make our own graph of an equation with two variables x and y, we can choose some reasonable x-values, then calculate the corresponding y-values, and then plot the (x, y)-pairs as points. For many algebraic equations, connecting those points with a smooth curve will produce an excellent graph.

Example 3.2.6 Let's plot a graph for the equation $y = -2x + 5$. We use a table to organize our work:

x	$y = -2x + 5$	Point
-2		
-1		
0		
1		
2		

x	$y = -2x + 5$	Point
-2	$-2(-2) + 5 = 9$	$(-2, 9)$
-1	$-2(-1) + 5 = 7$	$(-1, 7)$
0	$-2(0) + 5 = 5$	$(0, 5)$
1	$-2(1) + 5 = 3$	$(1, 3)$
2	$-2(2) + 5 = 1$	$(2, 1)$

(a) Set up the table   (b) Complete the table

Figure 3.2.7: Making a table for $y = -2x + 5$

We use points from the table to graph the equation in Figure 3.2.8. First, we need a coordinate system to draw on. We will eventually need to see the x-values -2, -1, 0, 1, and 2. So drawing an x-axis that runs from -5 to 5 will be good enough. We will eventually need to see the y-values 9, 7, 5, 3, and 1. So drawing a y-axis that runs from -1 to 10 will be good enough.

Axes should always be labeled using the variable names they represent. In this case, with "x" and "y". The axes should have tick marks that are spaced evenly. In this case it is fine to place the tick marks one unit apart (on both axes). Labeling at least some of the tick marks is necessary for a reader to understand the scale. Here we label the even-numbered ticks.

Then, connect the points with a smooth curve. Here, the curve is a straight line. Lastly, we can communicate that the graph extends further by sketching arrows on both ends of the line.

All that we have decided so far is drawn in Figure 3.2.8(a).	Next we carefully plot each point from the table in Figure 3.2.8(b). It's not necessary to label each point's coordinates, but we do so here.	Last we connect the points with a smooth curve. Here, the "curve" is a straight line. We communicate that the line extends further by putting arrowheads on both ends.

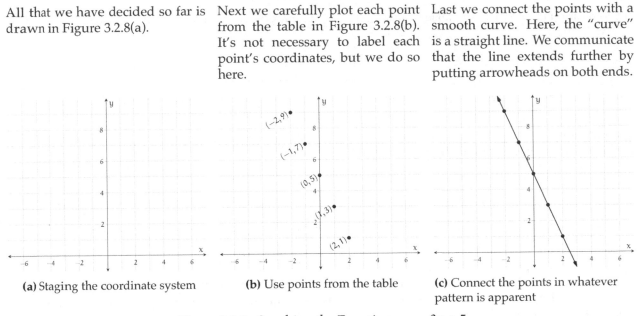

(a) Staging the coordinate system   (b) Use points from the table   (c) Connect the points in whatever pattern is apparent

Figure 3.2.8: Graphing the Equation $y = -2x + 5$

Remark 3.2.9 Note that our choice of x-values in the table was arbitrary. As long as we determine the coordinates of enough points to indicate the behavior of the graph, we may choose whichever x-values we like. Having a few negative x-values will be good. For simpler calculations, it's fine to choose -2, -1, 0, 1, and 2. However sometimes the equation has context that suggests using other x-values, as in the next examples.

Example 3.2.10 The gas tank in Sofia's car holds 14 gal of fuel. Over the course of a long road trip, her car uses fuel at an average rate of $0.032 \frac{\text{gal}}{\text{mi}}$. If Sofia fills the tank at the beginning of a long trip, then the amount of fuel remaining in the tank, y, after driving x miles is given by the equation $y = 14 - 0.032x$. Make a suitable table of values and graph this equation.

Explanation.   Choosing x-values from -2 to 2, as in our previous example, wouldn't make sense here. Sofia cannot drive a negative number of miles, and any long road trip is longer than 2 miles. So in this context, choose x-values that reflect the number of miles Sofia might drive in a day.

x	$y = 14 - 0.032x$	Point
20	13.36	$(20, 13.36)$
50	12.4	$(50, 12.4)$
80	11.44	$(80, 11.44)$
100	10.8	$(100, 10.8)$
200	7.6	$(200, 7.6)$

Figure 3.2.11: Make the table

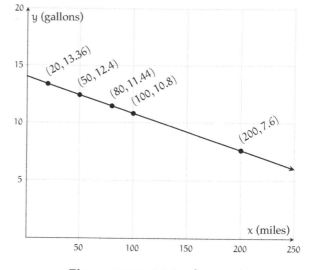

Figure 3.2.12: Make the graph

In Figure 3.2.12, notice how both axes are also labeled with *units* ("gallons" and "miles"). When the equation you plot has context like this example, including the units in the axes labels is very important to help anyone who reads your graph to understand it better.

In the table, x-values ran from 20 to 200, while y-values ran from 13.36 down to 7.6. So it was appropriate to make the x-axis cover something like from 0 to 250, and make the y-axis cover something like from 0 to 20. The scales on the two axes ended up being different.

Example 3.2.13 Plot a graph for the equation $y = \frac{4}{3}x - 4$.

Explanation. This equation doesn't have any context to help us choose x-values for a table. We could use x-values like -2, -1, and so on. But note the fraction in the equation. If we use an x-value like -2, we will have to multiply by the fraction $\frac{4}{3}$ which will leave us still holding a fraction. And then we will have to subtract 4 from that fraction. Since we know that everyone can make mistakes with that kind of arithmetic, maybe we can avoid it with a more wise selection of x-values.

If we use only multiples of 3 for the x-values, then multiplying by $\frac{4}{3}$ will leave us with an integer, which will be easy to subtract 4 from. So we decide to use -6, -3, 0, 3, and 6 for x.

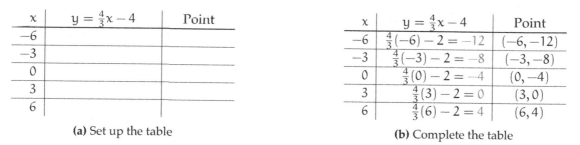

x	$y = \frac{4}{3}x - 4$	Point
-6		
-3		
0		
3		
6		

(a) Set up the table

x	$y = \frac{4}{3}x - 4$	Point
-6	$\frac{4}{3}(-6) - 2 = -12$	$(-6, -12)$
-3	$\frac{4}{3}(-3) - 2 = -8$	$(-3, -8)$
0	$\frac{4}{3}(0) - 2 = -4$	$(0, -4)$
3	$\frac{4}{3}(3) - 2 = 0$	$(3, 0)$
6	$\frac{4}{3}(6) - 2 = 4$	$(6, 4)$

(b) Complete the table

Figure 3.2.14: Making a table for $y = \frac{4}{3}x - 4$

We use points from the table to graph the equation. First, plot each point carefully. Then, connect the points with a smooth curve. Here, the curve is a straight line. Lastly, we can communicate that the graph extends further by sketching arrows on both ends of the line.

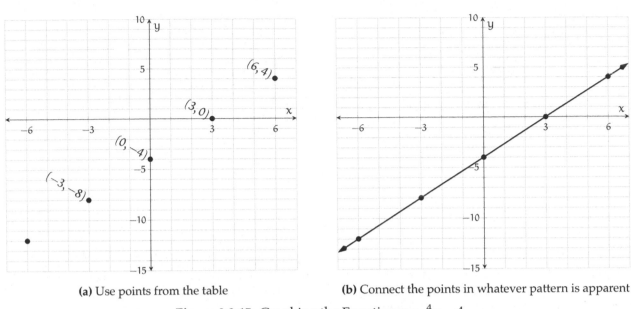

(a) Use points from the table   (b) Connect the points in whatever pattern is apparent

Figure 3.2.15: Graphing the Equation $y = \frac{4}{3}x - 4$

Not all equations make a straight line once they are plotted.

Example 3.2.16 Build a table and graph the equation $y = x^2$. Use x-values from -3 to 3.

Explanation.

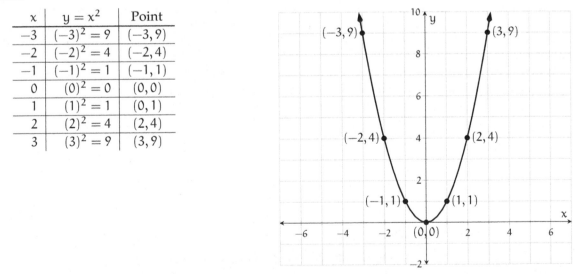

x	$y = x^2$	Point
-3	$(-3)^2 = 9$	$(-3, 9)$
-2	$(-2)^2 = 4$	$(-2, 4)$
-1	$(-1)^2 = 1$	$(-1, 1)$
0	$(0)^2 = 0$	$(0, 0)$
1	$(1)^2 = 1$	$(0, 1)$
2	$(2)^2 = 4$	$(2, 4)$
3	$(3)^2 = 9$	$(3, 9)$

In this example, the points do not fall on a straight line. Many algebraic equations have graphs that are non-linear, where the points do not fall on a straight line. We connected the points with a smooth curve, sketching from left to right.

Reading Questions

1. When a point like $(5, 8)$ is on the graph of an equation, where the equation has variables x and y, what happens when you substitute in 5 for x and 8 for y?

2. What are all the things to label when you set up a Cartesian coordinate system?

3. When you start making a table for some equation, you have to choose some x-values. Explain three different ways to choose those x-values that were demonstrated in this section.

4. What is an example of an equation that does not make a straight line once you make a graph of it?

Exercises

Testing Points as Solutions Consider the equation

1. $y = 7x + 10$
   Which of the following ordered pairs are solutions to the given equation? There may be more than one correct answer.
   □ $(-5, -25)$ □ $(-4, -18)$
   □ $(2, 25)$ □ $(0, 12)$

2. $y = 8x + 6$
   Which of the following ordered pairs are solutions to the given equation? There may be more than one correct answer.
   □ $(-4, -26)$ □ $(0, 11)$
   □ $(5, 50)$ □ $(-3, -18)$

3. $y = -3x - 8$
   Which of the following ordered pairs are solutions to the given equation? There may be more than one correct answer.
   □ $(9, -35)$ □ $(0, -8)$ □ $(-4, 6)$
   □ $(-6, 10)$

4. $y = -2x - 2$
   Which of the following ordered pairs are solutions to the given equation? There may be more than one correct answer.
   □ $(4, -10)$ □ $(-9, 16)$
   □ $(0, -2)$ □ $(-4, 11)$

5. $y = \frac{2}{3}x - 4$
   Which of the following ordered pairs are solutions to the given equation? There may be more than one correct answer.
   □ $(0, 0)$ □ $(-6, -6)$
   □ $(-15, -14)$ □ $(15, 6)$

6. $y = \frac{2}{3}x - 1$
   Which of the following ordered pairs are solutions to the given equation? There may be more than one correct answer.
   □ $(12, 7)$ □ $(0, 0)$ □ $(-6, 0)$
   □ $(-15, -11)$

7. $y = -\frac{3}{4}x - 3$
   Which of the following ordered pairs are solutions to the given equation? There may be more than one correct answer.
   □ $(0, -3)$ □ $(8, -5)$
   □ $(-20, 14)$ □ $(-16, 9)$

8. $y = -\frac{3}{4}x - 5$
   Which of the following ordered pairs are solutions to the given equation? There may be more than one correct answer.
   □ $(-16, 10)$ □ $(-4, -2)$
   □ $(4, -4)$ □ $(0, -5)$

Tables for Equations Make a table for the equation.

9.   The first row is an example.

x	$y = -x + 6$	Points
−3	9	(−3, 9)
−2	_____	_____
−1	_____	_____
0	_____	_____
1	_____	_____
2	_____	_____

10.   The first row is an example.

x	$y = -x + 7$	Points
−3	10	(−3, 10)
−2	_____	_____
−1	_____	_____
0	_____	_____
1	_____	_____
2	_____	_____

11.   The first row is an example.

x	$y = 5x + 5$	Points
−3	−10	(−3, −10)
−2	_____	_____
−1	_____	_____
0	_____	_____
1	_____	_____
2	_____	_____

12.   The first row is an example.

x	$y = 6x + 1$	Points
−3	−17	(−3, −17)
−2	_____	_____
−1	_____	_____
0	_____	_____
1	_____	_____
2	_____	_____

13.   The first row is an example.

x	$y = -2x + 8$	Points
−3	14	(−3, 14)
−2	_____	_____
−1	_____	_____
0	_____	_____
1	_____	_____
2	_____	_____

14.   The first row is an example.

x	$y = -5x + 4$	Points
−3	19	(−3, 19)
−2	_____	_____
−1	_____	_____
0	_____	_____
1	_____	_____
2	_____	_____

15.   The first row is an example.

x	$y = \frac{3}{2}x + 7$	Points
−6	−2	(−6, −2)
−4	_____	_____
−2	_____	_____
0	_____	_____
2	_____	_____
4	_____	_____

16.   The first row is an example.

x	$y = \frac{3}{8}x - 5$	Points
−24	−14	(−24, −14)
−16	_____	_____
−8	_____	_____
0	_____	_____
8	_____	_____
16	_____	_____

17.   The first row is an example.

x	$y = -\frac{5}{4}x + 4$	Points
−12	19	(−12, 19)
−8	_____	_____
−4	_____	_____
0	_____	_____
4	_____	_____
8	_____	_____

18.   The first row is an example.

x	$y = -\frac{5}{6}x - 4$	Points
−18	11	(−18, 11)
−12	_____	_____
−6	_____	_____
0	_____	_____
6	_____	_____
12	_____	_____

19.

x	$y = 7x$

20.

x	$y = 12x$

21.

x	$y = 8x + 8$

22.

x	$y = 10x + 2$

23.

x	$y = \frac{5}{3}x - 8$

24.

x	$y = \frac{18}{7}x - 6$

25.

x	$y = -\frac{5}{9}x - 4$

26.

x	$y = -\frac{6}{5}x - 1$

Cartesian Plots in Context

27. A certain water heater will cost you $900 to buy and have installed. This water heater claims that its operating expense (money spent on electricity or gas) will be about $31 per month. According to this information, the equation $y = 900 + 31x$ models the total cost of the water heater after x months, where y is in dollars. Make a table of at least five values and plot a graph of this equation.

28. You bought a new Toyota Corolla for $18,600 with a zero interest loan over a five-year period. That means you'll have to pay $310 each month for the next five years (sixty months) to pay it off. According to this information, the equation $y = 18600 - 310x$ models the loan balance after x months, where y is in dollars. Make a table of at least five values and plot a graph of this equation. Make sure to include a data point representing when you will have paid off the loan.

29. The pressure inside a full propane tank will rise and fall if the ambient temperature rises and falls. The equation $P = 0.1963(T + 459.67)$ models this relationship, where the temperature T is measured in °F and the pressure and the pressure P is measured in $\frac{lb}{in^2}$. Make a table of at least five values and plot a graph of this equation. Make sure to use T-values that make sense in context.

30. A beloved coworker is retiring and you want to give her a gift of week-long vacation rental at the coast that costs $1400 for the week. You might end up paying for it yourself, but you ask around to

see if the other 29 office coworkers want to split the cost evenly. The equation $y = \frac{1400}{x}$ models this situation, where x people contribute to the gift, and y is the dollar amount everyone contributes. Make a table of at least five values and plot a graph of this equation. Make sure to use x-values that make sense in context.

Graphs of Equations

31. Create a table of ordered pairs and then make a plot of the equation $y = 2x + 3$.

32. Create a table of ordered pairs and then make a plot of the equation $y = 3x + 5$.

33. Create a table of ordered pairs and then make a plot of the equation $y = -4x + 1$.

34. Create a table of ordered pairs and then make a plot of the equation $y = -x - 4$.

35. Create a table of ordered pairs and then make a plot of the equation $y = \frac{5}{2}x$.

36. Create a table of ordered pairs and then make a plot of the equation $y = \frac{4}{3}x$.

37. Create a table of ordered pairs and then make a plot of the equation $y = -\frac{2}{5}x - 3$.

38. Create a table of ordered pairs and then make a plot of the equation $y = -\frac{3}{4}x + 2$.

39. Create a table of ordered pairs and then make a plot of the equation $y = x^2 + 1$.

40. Create a table of ordered pairs and then make a plot of the equation $y = (x - 2)^2$. Use x-values from 0 to 4.

41. Create a table of ordered pairs and then make a plot of the equation $y = -3x^2$.

42. Create a table of ordered pairs and then make a plot of the equation $y = -x^2 - 2x - 3$.

3.3 Exploring Two-Variable Data and Rate of Change

This section is about examining data that has been plotted on a Cartesian coordinate system, and then making observations. In some cases, we'll be able to turn those observations into useful mathematical calculations.

3.3.1 Modeling data with two variables

Using mathematics, we can analyze data from the world around us. We can use what we discover to understand the world better and make predictions. Here's an example with economic data from the US, plotted in a Cartesian plane.

For the years from 1990 to 2013, consider what percent of all income was held by the top 1% of wage earners. The table in Figure 3.3.2 gives the numbers, but any pattern there might not be apparent when looking at the data organized this way. Plotting the data in a Cartesian coordinates sytem can make an overall pattern or trend become visible.

year	%	year	%
1990	14	2002	17
1991	13	2003	18
1992	15	2004	20
1993	14	2005	22
1994	14	2006	23
1995	15	2007	24
1996	17	2008	21
1997	18	2009	18
1998	19	2010	20
1999	20	2011	20
2000	22	2012	22
2001	18	2013	20

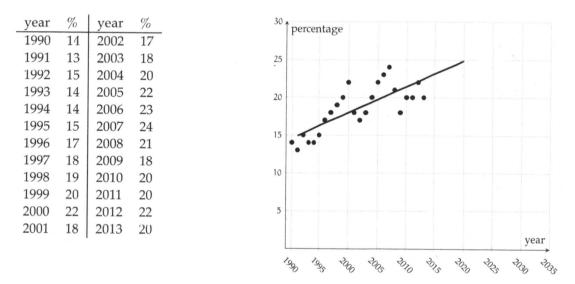

Figure 3.3.2: Share of all income held by the top 1% of wage earners

If this trend continues, what percentage of all income will the top 1% have in the year 2030? If we model data in the chart with the trend line, we can estimate the value to be 28.6 %. This is one way math is used in real life.

Does that trend line have an equation like those we looked at in Section 3.2? Is it even correct to look at this data set and decide that a straight line is a good model?

3.3.2 Patterns in Tables

Example 3.3.3 Find a pattern in each table. What is the missing entry in each table? Can you describe each pattern in words and/or mathematics?

black	white
big	small
short	tall
few	

USA	Washington
UK	London
France	Paris
Mexico	

1	2
2	4
3	6
5	

Figure 3.3.4: Patterns in 3 tables

Explanation.

black	white
big	small
short	tall
few	*many*

USA	Washington
UK	London
France	Paris
Mexico	*Mexico City*

1	2
2	4
3	6
5	10

Figure 3.3.5: Patterns in 3 tables

First table Each word on the right has the opposite meaning of the word to its left.

Second table Each city on the right is the capital of the country to its left.

Third table Each number on the right is double the number to its left.

We can view each table as assigning each input in the left column a corresponding output in the right column. In the first table, for example, when the input "big" is on the left, the output "small" is on the right. The first table's function is to output a word with the opposite meaning of each input word. (This is not a numerical example.)

The third table *is* numerical. And its function is to take a number as input, and give twice that number as its output. Mathematically, we can describe the pattern as "$y = 2x$," where x represents the input, and y represents the output. Labeling the table mathematically, we have Figure 3.3.6.

x (input)	y (output)
1	2
2	4
3	6
5	10
10	20

Pattern: $y = 2x$

Figure 3.3.6: Table with a mathematical pattern

The equation $y = 2x$ summarizes the pattern in the table. For each of the following tables, find an equation that describes the pattern you see. Numerical pattern recognition may or may not come naturally for you. Either way, pattern recognition is an important mathematical skill that anyone can develop. Solutions for these exercises provide some ideas for recognizing patterns.

Checkpoint 3.3.7 Write an equation in the form $y = \ldots$ suggested by the pattern in the table.

x	y
0	10
1	11
2	12
3	13

Explanation. One approach to pattern recognition is to look for a relationship in each row. Here, the y-value in each row is always 10 more than the x-value. So the pattern is described by the equation $y = x + 10$.

Checkpoint 3.3.8 Write an equation in the form $y = \ldots$ suggested by the pattern in the table.

x	y
0	−1
1	2
2	5
3	8

Explanation. The relationship between x and y in each row is not as clear here. Another popular approach for finding patterns: in each column, consider how the values change from one row to the next. From row to row, the x-value increases by 1. Also, the y-value increases by 3 from row to row.

	x	y	
	0	−1	
+1 →	1	2	← +3
+1 →	2	5	← +3
+1 →	3	8	← +3

Since row-to-row change is always 1 for x and is always 3 for y, the *rate of change* from one row to another row is always the same: 3 units of y for every 1 unit of x. This suggests that $y = 3x$ *might* be a good equation for the table pattern. But if we try to make a table with that pattern:

x	y using $y = 3x$	Actual y
0	0	−1
1	3	2
2	6	5
3	9	8

We find that the values from $y = 3x$ are 1 too large. So now we make an adjustment. The equation $y = 3x - 1$ describes the pattern in the table.

Checkpoint 3.3.9 Write an equation in the form $y = \ldots$ suggested by the pattern in the table.

x	y
0	0
1	1
2	4
3	9

Explanation. Looking for a relationship in each row here, we see that each y-value is the square of the corresponding x-value. That may not be obvious to you. It comes down to recognizing what square numbers are. So the equation is $y = x^2$.

What if we had tried the approach we used in the previous exercise, comparing change from row to row in each column?

$$
\begin{array}{cc}
x & y \\
0 & 0 \\
+1 \rightarrow \quad 1 & 1 \quad \leftarrow +1 \\
+1 \rightarrow \quad 2 & 4 \quad \leftarrow +3 \\
+1 \rightarrow \quad 3 & 9 \quad \leftarrow +5 \\
\end{array}
$$

Here, the rate of change is *not* constant from one row to the next. While the x-values are increasing by 1 from row to row, the y-values increase more and more from row to row. Do you notice that there is a pattern there as well? Mathematicians are interested in relationships with patterns.

3.3.3 Rate of Change

For an hourly wage-earner, the amount of money they earn depends on how many hours they work. If a worker earns $15 per hour, then 10 hours of work corresponds to $150 of pay. Working *one* additional hour will change 10 hours to 11 hours; and this will cause the $150 in pay to rise by *fifteen* dollars to $165 in pay. Any time we compare how one amount changes (dollars earned) as a consequence of another amount changing (hours worked), we are talking about a **rate of change**.

Given a table of two-variable data, between any two rows we can compute a **rate of change**.

Example 3.3.10 The following data, given in both table and graphed form, gives the counts of invasive cancer diagnoses in Oregon over a period of time. (wonder.cdc.gov)

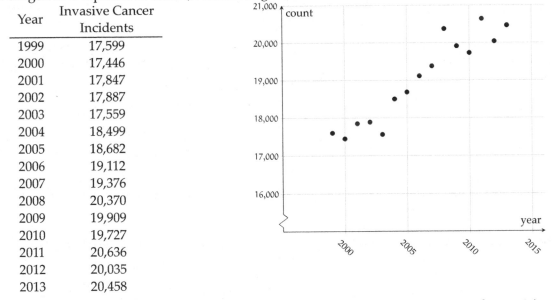

Year	Invasive Cancer Incidents
1999	17,599
2000	17,446
2001	17,847
2002	17,887
2003	17,559
2004	18,499
2005	18,682
2006	19,112
2007	19,376
2008	20,370
2009	19,909
2010	19,727
2011	20,636
2012	20,035
2013	20,458

What is the **rate of change** in Oregon invasive cancer diagnoses between 2000 and 2010? The total (net) change in diagnoses over that timespan is

$$19727 - 17446 = 2281$$

meaning that there were 2281 more invasive cancer incidents in 2010 than in 2000. Since 10 years passed (which you can calculate as $2010 - 2000$), the rate of change is 2281 diagnoses per 10 years, or

$$\frac{2281 \text{ diagnoses}}{10 \text{ year}} = 228.1 \frac{\text{diagnoses}}{\text{year}}.$$

We read that last quantity as "228.1 diagnoses per year." This rate of change means that between the years 2000 and 2010, there were 228.1 more diagnoses *each* year, on average. This is just an average over those ten years—it does not mean that the diagnoses grew by exactly this much each year. % We dare not interpret *why* that increase existed, % just that it did. % If you are interested in examining causal relationships that exist in real life, % we strongly recommend a statistics course or two in your future!

Checkpoint 3.3.11 Use the data in Example 3.3.10 to find the rate of change in Oregon invasive cancer diagnoses between 1999 and 2002.

And what was the rate of change between 2003 and 2011?

Explanation. To find the rate of change between 1999 and 2002, calculate

$$\frac{17887 - 17599}{2002 - 1999} = 96.$$

So the rate of change was 96.
To find the rate of change between 2003 and 2011, calculate

$$\frac{20636 - 17559}{2011 - 2003} = 384.625.$$

So the rate of change was 384.625.

We are ready to give a formal definition for "rate of change". Considering our work from Example 3.3.10 and Checkpoint 3.3.11, we settle on:

Definition 3.3.12 Rate of Change. If (x_1, y_1) and (x_2, y_2) are two data points from a set of two-variable data, then the **rate of change** between them is

$$\frac{\text{change in } y}{\text{change in } x} = \frac{\Delta y}{\Delta x} = \frac{y_2 - y_1}{x_2 - x_1}.$$

(The Greek letter delta, Δ, is used to represent "change in" since it is the first letter of the Greek word for "difference.") ◊

In Example 3.3.10 and Checkpoint 3.3.11 we found three rates of change. Figure 3.3.13 highlights the three pairs of points that were used to make these calculations.

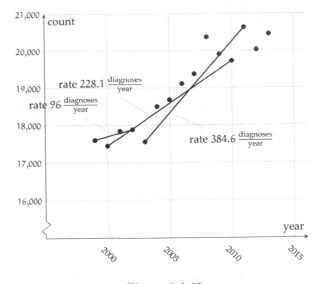

Figure 3.3.13

Note how the larger the numerical rate of change between two points, the steeper the line is that connects them. This is such an important observation, we'll put it in an official remark.

Remark 3.3.14 The rate of change between two data points is intimately related to the steepness of the line segment that connects those points.

1. The steeper the line, the larger the rate of change, and vice versa.

2. If one rate of change between two data points equals another rate of change between two different data points, then the corresponding line segments will have the same steepness.

3. We always measure rate of change from left to right. When a line segment between two data points slants up from left to right, the rate of change between those points will be positive. When a line segment between two data points slants down from left to right, the rate of change between those points will be negative.

In the solution to Checkpoint 3.3.8, the key observation was that the rate of change from one row to the next was constant: 3 units of increase in y for every 1 unit of increase in x. Graphing this pattern in Figure 3.3.15, we see that every line segment here has the same steepness, so the whole picture is a straight line.

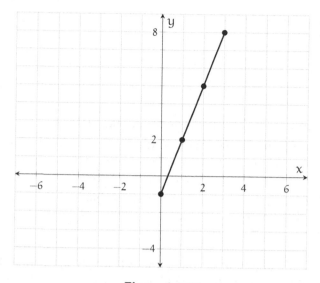

Figure 3.3.15

Whenever the rate of change is constant no matter which two (x, y)-pairs (or data pairs) are chosen from a data set, then you can conclude the graph will be a straight line *even without making the graph*. We call this kind of relationship a **linear** relationship. We'll study linear relationships in more detail throughout this chapter. Right now in this section, we feel it is important to simply identify if data has a linear relationship or not.

Checkpoint 3.3.16 Is there a linear relationship in the table?

x	y
-8	3.1
-5	2.1
-2	1.1
1	0.1

($\square$ The relationship is linear $\square$ The relationship is not linear)

Explanation. From one x-value to the next, the change is always 3. From one y-value to the next, the change is always -1. So the rate of change is always $\frac{-1}{3} = -\frac{1}{3}$. Since the rate of change is constant, the data have a linear relationship.

Checkpoint 3.3.17 Is there a linear relationship in the table?

x	y
11	208
13	210
15	214
17	220

($\square$ The relationship is linear $\square$ The relationship is not linear)

Explanation. The rate of change between the first two points is $\frac{210-208}{13-11} = 1$. The rate of change between the last two points is $\frac{220-214}{17-15} = 3$. This is one way to demonstrate that the rate of change differs for different pairs of points, so this pattern is not linear.

Checkpoint 3.3.18 Is there a linear relationship in the table?

x	y
3	−2
6	−8
8	−12
12	−20

(☐ The relationship is linear   ☐ The relationship is not linear)

Explanation.   The changes in x from one row to the next are $+3, +2$, and $+8$. That's not a consistent pattern, but we need to consider rates of change between points. The rate of change between the first two points is $\frac{-8-(-2)}{6-3} = -2$. The rate of change between the next two points is $\frac{-12-(-8)}{8-6} = -2$. And the rate of change between the last two points is $\frac{-20-(-12)}{12-8} = -2$. So the rate of change, -2, is constant regardless of which pairs we choose. That means these pairs describe a linear relationship.

Let's return to the data that we opened the section with, in Figure 3.3.2. Is that data linear? Well, yes and no. To be completely honest, it's not linear. It's easy to pick out pairs of points where the steepness changes from one pair to the next. In other words, the points do not all fall into a single line.

However if we step back, there does seem to be an overall upward trend that is captured by the line someone has drawn over the data. Points *on this line* do have a linear pattern. Let's estimate the rate of change between some points on this line. We are free to use any points to do this, so let's make this calculation easier by choosing points we can clearly identify on the graph: $(1991, 15)$ and $(2020, 25)$.

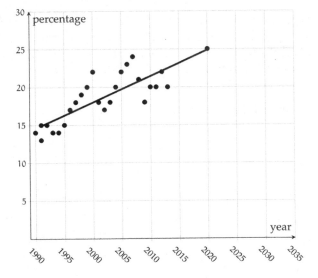

Figure 3.3.19: Share of all income held by the top 1%, United States, 1990–2013 (www.epi.org)

The rate of change between those two points is

$$\frac{(25-15)\text{ percentage points}}{(2020-1991)\text{years}} = \frac{10\text{ percentage points}}{29\text{years}} \approx 0.3448 \frac{\text{percentage points}}{\text{year}}.$$

So we might say that *on average* the rate of change expressed by this data is 0.3448 percentage points per year.

3.3.4 Reading Questions

1. Given a table of data with x- and y-values, explain how to calculate the rate of change from one row to the next.

2. If there is a table of data with x- and y-values, and the plot of all that data makes a straight line, what is true about the rates of change as you move from row to row in the table?

3. What does it mean for a rate of change to be positive (or negative) with regard to a graph with two points plotted?

3.3.5 Exercises

Finding Patterns Write an equation in the form $y = \ldots$ suggested by the pattern in the table.

1.

x	y
-2	-6
-1	-3
0	0
1	3
2	6

2.

x	y
3	12
4	16
5	20
6	24
7	28

3.

x	y
5	13
6	14
7	15
8	16
9	17

4.

x	y
6	12
7	13
8	14
9	15
10	16

5.

x	y
15	20
0	5
8	13
16	21
4	9

6.

x	y
17	12
13	8
16	11
8	3
3	-2

7.

x	y
25	5
4	2
1	1
9	3
16	4

8.

x	y
-5	5
-1	1
-2	2
5	5
1	1

9.

x	y
5	25
6	36
7	49
8	64
9	81

10.

x	y
2	4
4	16
6	36
8	64
10	100

11.

x	y
42	$\frac{1}{42}$
94	$\frac{1}{94}$
93	$\frac{1}{93}$
11	$\frac{1}{11}$
15	$\frac{1}{15}$

12.

x	y
53	$\frac{1}{53}$
60	$\frac{1}{60}$
35	$\frac{1}{35}$
83	$\frac{1}{83}$
13	$\frac{1}{13}$

Linear Relationships Does the following table show that x and y have a linear relationship? (□ yes □ no)

13.

x	y
0	32
1	39
2	46
3	53
4	60
5	67

14.

x	y
0	92
1	100
2	108
3	116
4	124
5	132

15.

x	y
6	60
7	57
8	54
9	51
10	48
11	45

16.

x	y
0	60
1	58
2	56
3	54
4	52
5	50

17.

x	y
4	34
5	50
6	82
7	146
8	274
9	530

18.

x	y
9	523
10	1035
11	2059
12	4107
13	8203
14	16395

19.

x	y
0	4
1	5
2	12
3	31
4	68
5	129

20.

x	y
2	25
3	44
4	81
5	142
6	233
7	360

21.

x	y
-8	60.57
-7	60.86
-6	61.15
-5	61.44
-4	61.73
-3	62.02

22.

x	y
1	39.95
2	41.35
3	42.75
4	44.15
5	45.55
6	46.95

23.

x	y
9	150
11	166
14	190
16	206
18	222
19	230

24.

x	y
3	67
5	83
7	99
10	123
14	155
19	195

Calculating Rate of Change

25. This table gives population estimates for Portland, Oregon from 1990 through 2014.

Year	Population	Year	Population
1990	487849	2003	539546
1991	491064	2004	533120
1992	493754	2005	534112
1993	497432	2006	538091
1994	497659	2007	546747
1995	498396	2008	556442
1996	501646	2009	566143
1997	503205	2010	585261
1998	502945	2011	593859
1999	503637	2012	602954
2000	529922	2013	609520
2001	535185	2014	619360
2002	538803		

Find the rate of change in Portland population between 1991 and 1996.
And what was the rate of change between 2008 and 2014?
List all the years where there is a negative rate of change between that year and the next year.

26. This table and graph gives population estimates for Portland, Oregon from 1990 through 2014.

Year	Population	Year	Population
1990	487849	2003	539546
1991	491064	2004	533120
1992	493754	2005	534112
1993	497432	2006	538091
1994	497659	2007	546747
1995	498396	2008	556442
1996	501646	2009	566143
1997	503205	2010	585261
1998	502945	2011	593859
1999	503637	2012	602954
2000	529922	2013	609520
2001	535185	2014	619360
2002	538803		

Between what two years that are two years apart was the rate of change highest?
What was that rate of change?

3.4 Slope

In Section 3.3, we observed that a constant rate of change between points produces a linear relationship, whose graph is a straight line. Such a constant rate of change has a special name, *slope*, and we'll explore slope in more depth here.

3.4.1 What is slope?

Given a graph with points, when the rate of change from one point to the next never changes, those points must fall on a straight line, as in Figure 3.4.2. Rather than say "constant rate of change" in every such situation, there is a specific word for this.

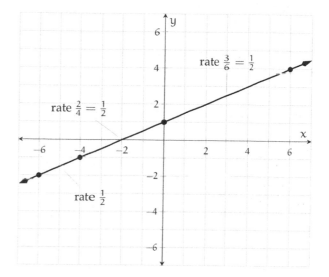

Figure 3.4.2: Between successive points, the rate of change is always 1/2.

Definition 3.4.3 Slope. When x and y are two variables where the rate of change between any two points is always the same, we call this common rate of change the **slope**. Since having a constant rate of change means the graph will be a straight line, its also called the **slope of the line**.   ◊

Considering the definition for rate of change, this means that when x and y are two variables where the rate of change between any two points is always the same, then you can calculate slope, m, by finding two distinct data points (x_1, y_1) and (x_2, y_2), and calculating

$$m = \frac{\text{change in } y}{\text{change in } x} = \frac{\Delta y}{\Delta x} = \frac{y_2 - y_1}{x_2 - x_1}.$$ (3.4.1)

A slope is a rate of change. So if there are units for the horizontal and vertical variables, then there will be units for the slope. The slope will be measured in $\frac{\text{vertical units}}{\text{horizontal units}}$. If the slope is nonzero, we say that there is a **linear relationship** between x and y. When the slope is 0, we say that y is **constant** with respect to x.

Slope m. Why is the letter m commonly used as the symbol for "slope?" Some believe that it comes from the French word "monter" which means "to climb."

Here are some scenarios with different slopes. As you read each scenario, note how a slope is more meaningful with units.

- If a tree grows 2.5 feet every year, its rate of change in height is the same from year to year. So the height and time have a linear relationship where the slope is 2.5 $\frac{\text{ft}}{\text{yr}}$.

- If a company loses 2 million dollars every year, its rate of change in reserve funds is the same from year to year. So the company's reserve funds and time have a linear relationship where the slope is -2 million dollars per year.

- If Sakura is an adult who has stopped growing, her rate of change in height is the same from year to year—it's zero. So the slope is $0 \frac{\text{in}}{\text{yr}}$. Sakura's height is constant with respect to time.

Remark 3.4.4 A useful phrase for remembering the definition of slope is "rise over run." Here, "rise" refers to "change in y," Δy, and "run" refers to "change in x," Δx. Be careful though. As we have learned, the horizontal direction comes *first* in mathematics, followed by the vertical direction. The phrase "rise over run" reverses this. (It's a bit awkward to say, but the phrase "run under rise" puts the horizontal change first.)

Example 3.4.5 Yara's Savings. On Dec. 31, Yara had only \$50 in her savings account. For the the new year, she resolved to deposit \$20 into her savings account each week, without withdrawing any money from the account.

Yara keeps her resolution, and her account balance increases steadily by \$20 each week. That's a constant rate of change, so her account balance and time have a linear relationship with slope $20 \frac{\text{dollars}}{\text{wk}}$.

We can model the balance, y, in dollars, in Yara's savings account x weeks after she started making deposits with an equation. Since Yara started with \$50 and adds \$20 each week, then x weeks after she started making deposits,

$$y = 50 + 20x \tag{3.4.2}$$

where y is a dollar amount. Notice that the slope, $20 \frac{\text{dollars}}{\text{wk}}$, serves as the multiplier for x weeks.

We can also consider Yara's savings using a table as in Figure 3.4.6.

	x, weeks since DEC. 31	y, savings account balance (dollars)	
	0	50	
x increases by 1 ⟶	1	70	⟵ y increases by 20
x increases by 1 ⟶	2	90	⟵ y increases by 20
x increases by 2 ⟶	4	130	⟵ y increases by 40
x increases by 3 ⟶	7	190	⟵ y increases by 60
x increases by 5 ⟶	12	290	⟵ y increases by 100

Figure 3.4.6: Yara's savings

In first few rows of the table, we see that when the number of weeks x increases by 1, the balance y increases by 20. The row-to-row rate of change is $\frac{20\,\text{dollars}}{1\,\text{wk}} = 20 \frac{\text{dollars}}{\text{wk}}$, the slope. In any table for a linear relationship, whenever x increases by 1 unit, y will increase by the slope.

In further rows, notice that as row-to-row change in x increases, row-to-row change in y increases proportionally to preserve the constant rate of change. Looking at the change in the last two rows of the table, we see x increases by 5 and y increases by 100, which gives a rate of change of $\frac{100\,\text{dollars}}{5\,\text{wk}} = 20 \frac{\text{dollars}}{\text{wk}}$, the value of the slope again.

On a graph of Yara's savings, we can "see" the rates of change between consecutive rows of the table by including **slope triangles**.

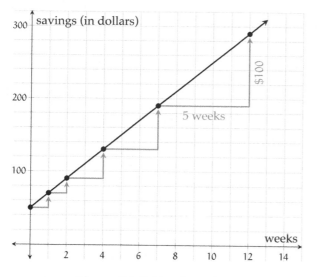

Figure 3.4.7: Yara's savings

The large slope triangle indicates that when 5 weeks pass, Yara saves $100. This is the rate of change between the last two rows of the table, $\frac{100}{5} = 20 \frac{\text{dollars}}{\text{wk}}$. The smaller slope triangles indicate, from left to right, the rates of change $\frac{20\,\text{dollars}}{1\,\text{wk}}$, $\frac{20\,\text{dollars}}{1\,\text{wk}}$, $\frac{40\,\text{dollars}}{2\,\text{wk}}$, and $\frac{60\,\text{dollars}}{3\,\text{wk}}$ respectively. All of these rates simplify to the slope, $20 \frac{\text{dollars}}{\text{wk}}$.

Every slope triangle on the graph of Yara's savings has the same shape (geometrically, they are called similar triangles) since the ratio of vertical change to horizontal change is always $20 \frac{\text{dollars}}{\text{wk}}$. On any graph of any line, we can draw a slope triangle and compute slope as "rise over run."

Of course, we could draw a slope triangle on the other side of the line:

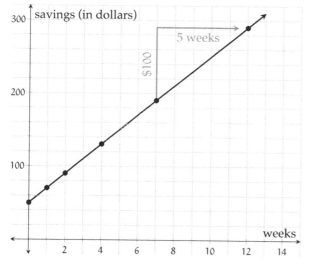

Figure 3.4.8: Yara's savings

This slope triangle works just as well for identifying "rise" and "run," but it focuses on vertical change before horizontal change. For consistency with mathematical conventions, we will generally draw slope triangles showing horizontal change followed by vertical change, as in Figure 3.4.7.

Example 3.4.9 The following graph of a line models the amount of gas, in gallons, in Kiran's gas tank as they drive their car. Find the line's slope, and interpret its meaning in this context.

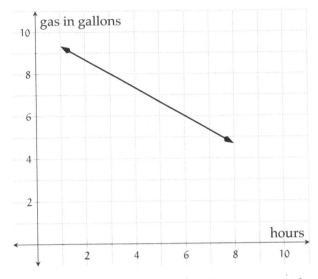

Figure 3.4.10: Amount of gas in Kiran's gas tank

Explanation.   To find a line's slope using its graph, we first identify two points on it, and then draw a slope triangle. Naturally, we would want to choose two points whose x- and y-coordinates are easy to identify exactly based on the graph. We will pick the two points where $x = 3$ and $x = 6$, because they are right on grid line crossings:

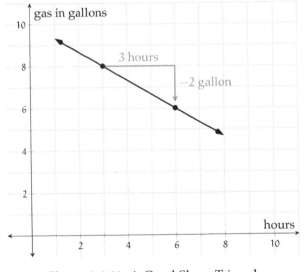

Figure 3.4.11: A Good Slope Triangle

Notice that the *change* in y is negative, because the amount of gas is decreasing. Since we chose points with integer coordinates, we can easily calculate the slope:

$$\text{slope} = \frac{-2\,\text{gallons}}{3\,\text{miles}} = -\frac{2}{3}\,\frac{\text{gal}}{\text{mi}}.$$

In the given context, this slope implies gas in the tank is *decreasing* at the rate of $\frac{2}{3}\frac{\text{gal}}{\text{h}}$. Since this slope is written as a fraction, another way to understand it is that Kiran is using up 2 gallons of gas every 3 hours.

Checkpoint 3.4.12 Below is a line's graph.

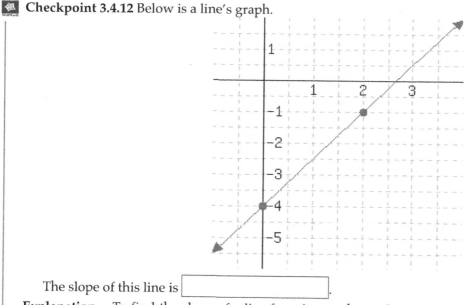

The slope of this line is [   ].

Explanation. To find the slope of a line from its graph, we first need to identify two points that the line passes through. It is wise to choose points with integer coordinates. For this problem, we choose $(0, -4)$ and $(2, -1)$.

Next, we sketch a slope triangle and find the *rise* and *run*. In the sketch below, the rise is 3 and the run is 2.

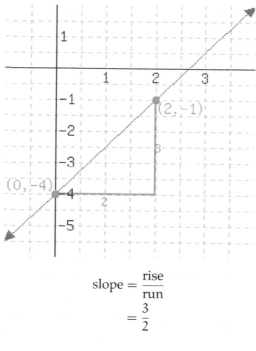

$$\text{slope} = \frac{\text{rise}}{\text{run}}$$
$$= \frac{3}{2}$$

This line's slope is $\frac{3}{2}$.

Checkpoint 3.4.13 Make a table and plot the equation $y = \frac{3}{4}x + 2$, which makes a straight line. Use the plot to determine the slope of this line.

Explanation.   First, we choose some x-values to make a table, and compute the corresponding y-values.

x	$y = \frac{3}{4}x + 2$	Point
-2	$\frac{3}{4}(-2) + 2 = 0.5$	$(-2, 0.5)$
-1	$\frac{3}{4}(-1) + 2 = 1.25$	$(-1, 1.25)$
0	$\frac{3}{4}(0) + 2 = 2$	$(0, 2)$
1	$\frac{3}{4}(1) + 2 = 2.75$	$(1, 2.75)$
2	$\frac{3}{4}(2) + 2 = 3.5$	$(2, 3.5)$
3	$\frac{3}{4}(3) + 2 = 4.25$	$(3, 4.25)$
4	$\frac{3}{4}(4) + 2 = 5$	$(4, 5)$
5	$\frac{3}{4}(5) + 2 = 5.75$	$(5, 5.75)$

This table lets us plot the graph and identify a slope triangle that is easy to work with.

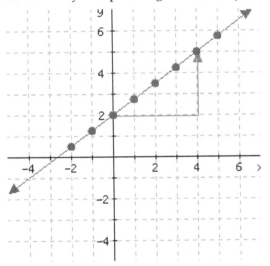

Since the slope triangle runs 4 units and then rises 3 units, the slope is $\frac{3}{4}$.

3.4.2 Comparing Slopes

It's useful to understand what it means for different slopes to appear on the same coordinate system.

Example 3.4.14 Effie, Ivan and Cleo are in a foot race. Figure 3.4.15 models the distance each has traveled in the first few seconds. Each runner takes a second to accelerate up to their running speed, but then runs at a constant speed. So they are then traveling with a constant rate of change, and the straight line portions of their graphs have a slope. Find each line's slope, and interpret its meaning in this context. What comparisons can you make with these runners?

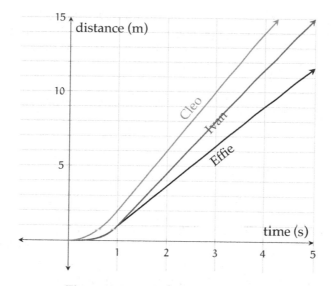

Figure 3.4.15: A three-way foot race

We will draw slope triangles to find each line's slope.

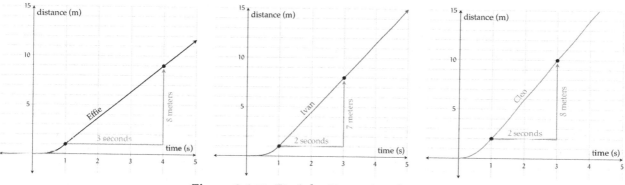

Figure 3.4.16: Find the Slope of Each Line

Using the slope equation (3.4.1), we have:

- Effie's slope is $\frac{8\,\text{m}}{3\,\text{s}} \approx 2.666\,\frac{\text{m}}{\text{s}}$.

- Ivan's slope is $\frac{7\,\text{m}}{2\,\text{s}} = 3.5\,\frac{\text{m}}{\text{s}}$.

- Cleo's slope is $\frac{8\,\text{m}}{2\,\text{s}} = 4\,\frac{\text{m}}{\text{s}}$.

In a time-distance graph, the slope of a line represents speed. The slopes in these examples and the running speeds of these runners are measured in $\frac{\text{m}}{\text{s}}$. A relationship we can see is that the more sharply a line is slanted, the bigger the slope is. This should make sense because for each passing second, the faster person travels longer, making a slope triangle's height taller. This means that, numerically, we can tell that Cleo is the fastest runner (and Effie is the slowest) just by comparing the slopes $4 > 3.5 > 2.666$.

Checkpoint 3.4.17 Jogging on Mt. Hood. Kato is training for a race up the slope of Mt. Hood, from Sandy to Government Camp, and then back. The graph below models his elevation from his starting point as time passes. Find the slopes of the three line segments, and interpret their meanings in this context.

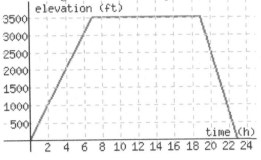

a. What is the slope of the first segment?

b. What is the slope of the second segment?

c. What is the slope of the third segment?

Explanation. The first segment started at $(0, 0)$ and stopped at $(7, 3500)$. This implies, Kato started at the starting point, traveled 7 hours and reached a point 3500 feet higher in elevation from the starting point. The slope of the line is

$$\frac{\Delta y}{\Delta x} = \frac{3500\,\text{ft}}{7\,\text{h}} = 500\,\frac{\text{ft}}{\text{h}}.$$

In context, Kato was running, gaining 500 feet in elevation per hour.

What happened in the second segment, which started at $(7, 3500)$ and ended at $(19, 3500)$? This implies he started this portion 3500 feet higher in elevation from the starting point, and didn't change elevation for 19 hours. The slope of the line is

$$\frac{\Delta y}{\Delta x} = \frac{0\,\text{ft}}{12\,\text{h}} = 0\,\frac{\text{ft}}{\text{h}}$$

In context, Kato was running but neither gaining nor losing elevation.

The third segment started from $(19, 3500)$ and stopped at $(23, 0)$. This implies, Kato started this part of his trip from a spot 3500 feet higher in elevation from the starting point, traveled for 4 hours and returned to the starting elevation. The slope of the line is

$$\frac{\Delta y}{\Delta x} = \frac{-3500\,\text{ft}}{4\,\text{h}} = -875\,\frac{\text{ft}}{\text{h}}$$

In context, Kato was running, dropping in elevation by 875 feet per hour.

Some important properties are demonstrated in Exercise 3.4.17.

Fact 3.4.18 The Relationship Between Slope and Increase/Decrease. *In a linear relationship, as the x-value increases (in other words as you read its graph from left to right):*

- *if the y-values increase (in other words, the line goes upward), its slope is positive.*

- *if the y-values decrease (in other words, the line goes downward), its slope is negative.*

- *if the y-values don't change (in other words, the line is flat, or horizontal), its slope is 0.*

These properties are summarized graphically in Figure 3.4.19.

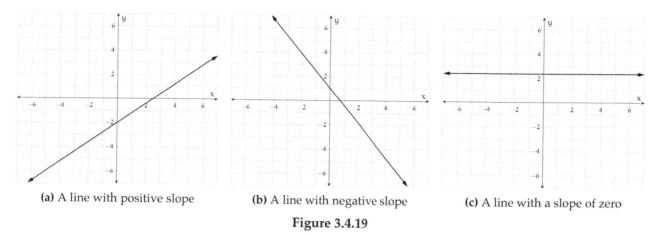

(a) A line with positive slope   **(b)** A line with negative slope   **(c)** A line with a slope of zero

Figure 3.4.19

3.4.3 Finding Slope by Two Given Points

Several times in this section we computed a slope by drawing a slope triangle. That's not really necessary if you have coordinates for two points that a line passes through. In fact, sometimes it's impractical to draw a slope triangle.[1] Here we will stress how to find a line's slope without drawing a slope triangle.

Example 3.4.20 Your neighbor planted a sapling from Portland Nursery in his front yard. Ever since, for several years now, it has been growing at a constant rate. By the end of the third year, the tree was 15 ft tall; by the end of the sixth year, the tree was 27 ft tall. What's the tree's rate of growth (i.e. the slope)?

We *could* sketch a graph for this scenario, and include a slope triangle. If we did that, it would look like:

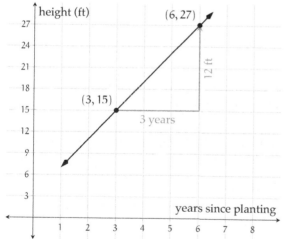

By the slope triangle and Equation (3.4.1) we have:

$$\text{slope} = m = \frac{\Delta y}{\Delta x}$$
$$= \frac{12\,\text{ft}}{3\,\text{yr}}$$
$$= 4\,\frac{\text{ft}}{\text{yr}}$$

So the tree is growing at a rate of $4\,\frac{\text{ft}}{\text{yr}}$.

Figure 3.4.21: Height of a Tree

But hold on. Did we really *need* this picture? The "rise" of 12 came from a subtraction of two y-values: $27 - 15$. And the "run" of 3 came from a subtraction of two x-values: $6 - 3$.

Here is a picture-free approach. We know that after 3 yr, the height is 15 ft. As an ordered pair, that

---

[1]For instance if you only have specific information about two points that are too close together to draw a triangle, or if you cannot clearly see precise coordinates where you might start and stop your slope triangle.

information gives us the point $(3, 15)$ which we can label as $(\overset{x_1}{3}, \overset{y_1}{15})$. Similarly, the background information tells us to consider $(6, 27)$, which we label as $(\overset{x_2}{6}, \overset{y_2}{27})$. Here, x_1 and y_1 represent the first point's x-value and y-value, and x_2 and y_2 represent the second point's x-value and y-value.

Now we can write an alternative to Equation (3.4.1):

$$\text{slope} = m = \frac{\Delta y}{\Delta x} = \frac{y_2 - y_1}{x_2 - x_1} \tag{3.4.3}$$

This is known as the **slope formula**. The following graphs help to understand why this formula works. Basically, we are still using a slope triangle to calculate the slope.

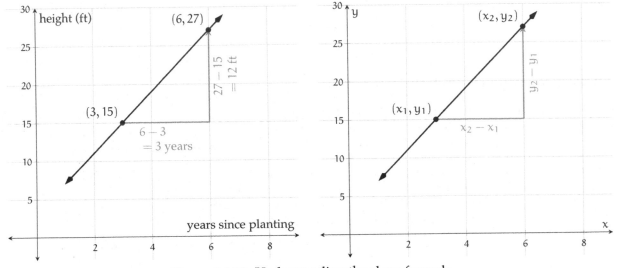

Figure 3.4.22: Understanding the slope formula

Remark 3.4.23 It's important to use subscript instead of superscript in the slope equation, because y^2 means to take the number y and square it. Whereas y_2 tells you that there are at least two y-values in the conversation, and y_2 is the second of them.

The beauty of the slope formula (3.4.3) is that to find a line's slope, we don't need to draw a slope triangle any more. Let's look at an example.

Example 3.4.24 A line passes the points $(-5, 25)$ and $(4, -2)$. Find this line's slope.

Explanation. If you are new to this formula, it may help to label each number before using the formula. The two given points are:

$$(\overset{x_1}{-5}, \overset{y_1}{25}) \text{ and } (\overset{x_2}{4}, \overset{y_2}{-2})$$

Now apply the slope formula (3.4.3):

$$\text{slope} = \frac{y_2 - y_1}{x_2 - x_1}$$
$$= \frac{-2 - 25}{4 - (-5)}$$

$$= \frac{-27}{9}$$
$$= -3$$

Note that we used parentheses when substituting negative numbers in x_1 and y_1. This is a good habit to protect yourself from making errors with subtraction and double negatives.

 Checkpoint 3.4.25 A line passes through the points $(-4, 15)$ and $(12, -13)$. Find this line's slope.

Explanation. To find a line's slope, we can use the slope formula:

$$\text{slope} = \frac{y_2 - y_1}{x_2 - x_1}$$

First, we mark which number corresponds to which variable in the formula:

$$(-4, 15) \longrightarrow (x_1, y_1)$$

$$(12, -13) \longrightarrow (x_2, y_2)$$

Now we substitute these numbers into the corresponding variables in the slope formula:

$$\text{slope} = \frac{y_2 - y_1}{x_2 - x_1}$$
$$= \frac{-13 - 15}{12 - (-4)}$$
$$= \frac{-28}{16}$$
$$= -\frac{7}{4}$$

So the line's slope is $-\frac{7}{4}$.

3.4.4 Reading Questions

1. Have you memorized a formula for finding the slope between two points using their coordinates?

2. What is an important thing to do with slope to make it more meaningful in an application problem?

3. Drawing a slope triangle can be helpful to think about slope. But what might happen that could make it impractical to draw a slope triangle?

3.4.5 Exercises

Review and Warmup

1. Reduce the fraction $\frac{7}{56}$.

2. Reduce the fraction $\frac{5}{45}$.

3. Reduce the fraction $\frac{10}{14}$.

4. Reduce the fraction $\frac{25}{40}$.

5. Reduce the fraction $\frac{21}{168}$.

6. Reduce the fraction $\frac{6}{36}$.

7. Reduce the fraction $\dfrac{315}{245}$.   **8.** Reduce the fraction $\dfrac{350}{105}$.   **9.** Reduce the fraction $\dfrac{70}{10}$.

10. Reduce the fraction $\dfrac{112}{14}$.

Slope and Points

11. A line passes through the points $(3, 12)$ and $(9, 36)$. Find this line's slope.

12. A line passes through the points $(5, 18)$ and $(8, 33)$. Find this line's slope.

13. A line passes through the points $(2, 5)$ and $(7, 0)$. Find this line's slope.

14. A line passes through the points $(4, -21)$ and $(10, -51)$. Find this line's slope.

15. A line passes through the points $(-4, -12)$ and $(-6, -14)$. Find this line's slope.

16. A line passes through the points $(-2, 2)$ and $(-7, -8)$. Find this line's slope.

17. A line passes through the points $(-1, 0)$ and $(1, -2)$. Find this line's slope.

18. A line passes through the points $(-1, 2)$ and $(3, -18)$. Find this line's slope.

19. A line passes through the points $(-1, 7)$ and $(-6, 17)$. Find this line's slope.

20. A line passes through the points $(-4, 6)$ and $(-7, 12)$. Find this line's slope.

21. A line passes through the points $(3, 11)$ and $(-6, -13)$. Find this line's slope.

22. A line passes through the points $(21, 14)$ and $(-14, -26)$. Find this line's slope.

23. A line passes through the points $(-8, 5)$ and $(8, -7)$. Find this line's slope.

24. A line passes through the points $(-24, 17)$ and $(16, 2)$. Find this line's slope.

25. A line passes through the points $(4, -4)$ and $(-4, -4)$. Find this line's slope.

26. A line passes through the points $(2, -2)$ and $(-2, -2)$. Find this line's slope.

27. A line passes through the points $(0, -1)$ and $(0, 1)$. Find this line's slope.

28. A line passes through the points $(3, -2)$ and $(3, 3)$. Find this line's slope.

Slope and Graphs

29. Below is a line's graph.

30. Below is a line's graph.

31. Below is a line's graph.

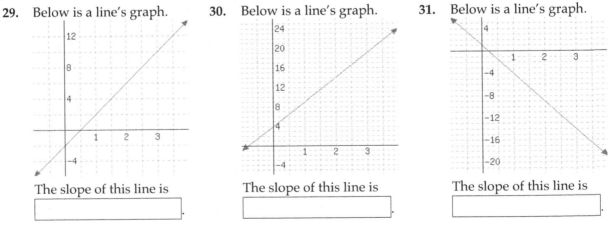

The slope of this line is

⬚ .

The slope of this line is

⬚ .

The slope of this line is

⬚ .

32. Below is a line's graph.

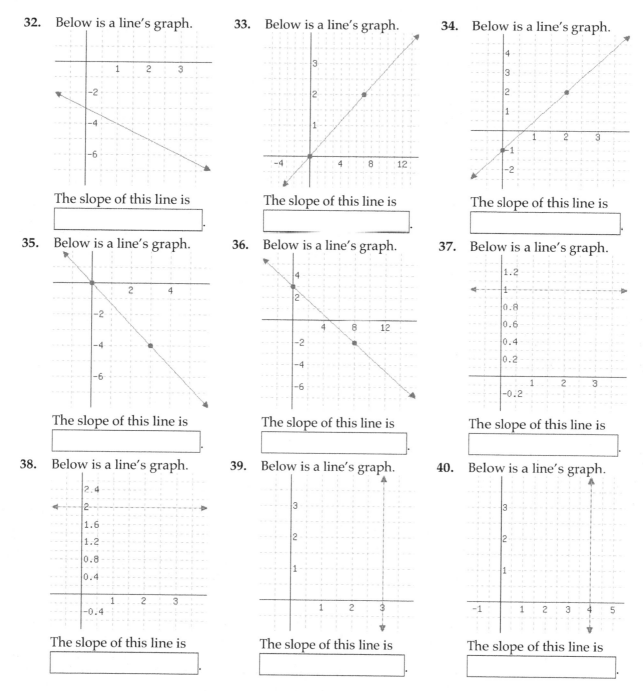

The slope of this line is

33. Below is a line's graph.

The slope of this line is

34. Below is a line's graph.

The slope of this line is

35. Below is a line's graph.

The slope of this line is

36. Below is a line's graph.

The slope of this line is

37. Below is a line's graph.

The slope of this line is

38. Below is a line's graph.

The slope of this line is

39. Below is a line's graph.

The slope of this line is

40. Below is a line's graph.

The slope of this line is

41. Below is a line's graph.

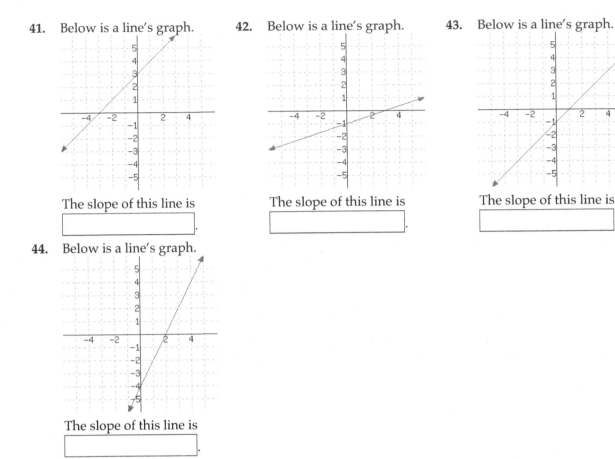

The slope of this line is

.

42. Below is a line's graph.

The slope of this line is

.

43. Below is a line's graph.

The slope of this line is

.

44. Below is a line's graph.

The slope of this line is

.

Slope in Context

45. By your cell phone contract, you pay a monthly fee plus some money for each minute you use the phone during the month. In one month, you spent 270 minutes on the phone, and paid $29.15. In another month, you spent 340 minutes on the phone, and paid $32.30. What is the rate (in dollars per minute) that the phone company is charging you? That is, what is the slope of the line if you plotted the bill versus the number of minutes spent on the phone?

The rate is [   ] per minute.

46. By your cell phone contract, you pay a monthly fee plus some money for each minute you use the phone during the month. In one month, you spent 210 minutes on the phone, and paid $23.45. In another month, you spent 310 minutes on the phone, and paid $27.95. What is the rate (in dollars per minute) that the phone company is charging you? That is, what is the slope of the line if you plotted the bill versus the number of minutes spent on the phone?

The rate is [   ] per minute.

47. A company set aside a certain amount of money in the year 2000. The company spent exactly the same amount from that fund each year on perks for its employees. In 2003, there was still $474,000 left in the fund. In 2007, there was $306,000 left. What is the rate (in dollars per year) at which this company is spending from this fund?

The company is spending [   ] per year on perks for its employees.

48. A company set aside a certain amount of money in the year 2000. The company spent exactly the same amount from that fund each year on perks for its employees. In 2004, there was still $677,000 left in the fund. In 2006, there was $585,000 left. What is the rate (in dollars per year) at which this company is spending from this fund?

The company is spending [   ] per year on perks for its employees.

49. A biologist has been observing a tree's height. Eleven months into the observation, the tree was 16.59 feet tall. Seventeen months into the observation, the tree was 18.33 feet tall. What is the rate at which the tree is growing? In other words, what is the slope if you plotted height versus time?

50. A biologist has been observing a tree's height. Fourteen months into the observation, the tree was 20.24 feet tall. Twenty months into the observation, the tree was 20.9 feet tall. What is the rate at which the tree is growing? In other words, what is the slope if you plotted height versus time?

51. Scientists are conducting an experiment with a gas in a sealed container. The mass of the gas is measured, and the scientists realize that the gas is leaking over time in a linear way. Five minutes since the experiment started, the gas had a mass of 234 grams. Seventeen minutes since the experiment started, the gas had a mass of 156 grams. At what rate is the gas leaking?

52. Scientists are conducting an experiment with a gas in a sealed container. The mass of the gas is measured, and the scientists realize that the gas is leaking over time in a linear way. Eight minutes since the experiment started, the gas had a mass of 119 grams. Fourteen minutes since the experiment started, the gas had a mass of 98.6 grams. At what rate is the gas leaking?

53. The graph plots the number of invasive cancer diagnoses in Oregon over time, and a trend-line has been drawn.

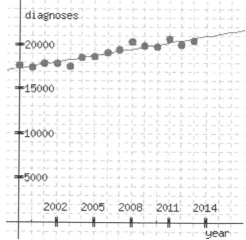

Estimate the slope of the trend-line.

Challenge

54. True or False: A slope of $\frac{1}{7}$ is steeper than a slope of 0.1.   (□ true   □ false)

55. True or False: A slope of $\frac{5}{7}$ is steeper than a slope of 0.7.   (□ true   □ false)

3.5 Slope-Intercept Form

In this section, we will explore what is perhaps the most common way to write the equation of a line. It's known as slope-intercept form.

3.5.1 Slope-Intercept Definition

Recall Example 3.4.5, where Yara had $50 in her savings account when the year began, and decided to deposit $20 each week without withdrawing any money. In that example, we model using x to represent how many weeks have passed. After x weeks, Yara has added 20x dollars. And since she started with $50, she has

$$y = 20x + 50$$

in her account after x weeks. In this example, there is a constant rate of change of 20 dollars per week, so we call that the slope as discussed in Section 3.4. We also saw in Figure 3.4.7 that plotting Yara's balance over time gives us a straight-line graph.

The graph of Yara's savings has some things in common with almost every straight-line graph. There is a slope, and there is a place where the line crosses the y-axis. Figure 3.5.3 illustrates this in the abstract.

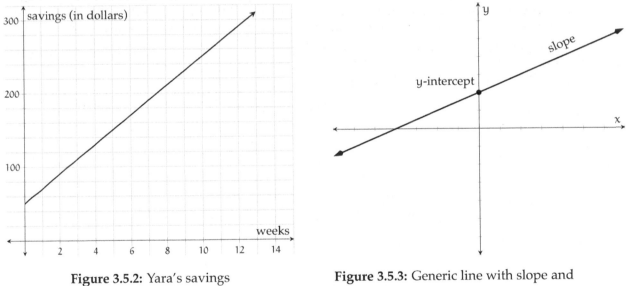

Figure 3.5.2: Yara's savings   **Figure 3.5.3:** Generic line with slope and
                                       y-intercept

We already have an accepted symbol, m, for the slope of a line. The y-**intercept** is a *point* on the y-axis where the line crosses. Since it's on the y-axis, the x-coordinate of this point is 0. It is standard to call the point $(0, b)$ the y-intercept, and call the number b the y-coordinate of the y-intercept.

Checkpoint 3.5.4 Use Figure 3.4.7 to answer this question.

   What was the value of b in the plot of Yara's savings?
   What is the y-intercept?

Explanation.   The line crosses the y-axis at $(0, 50)$, so the value of b is 50. And the y-intercept is $(0, 50)$.

One way to write the equation for Yara's savings was

$$y = 20x + 50$$

where both $m = 20$ and $b = 50$ are immediately visible in the equation. Now we are ready to generalize this.

Definition 3.5.5 Slope-Intercept Form. When x and y have a linear relationship where m is the slope and $(0, b)$ is the y-intercept, one equation for this relationship is

$$y = mx + b \tag{3.5.1}$$

and this equation is called the **slope-intercept form** of the line. It is called this because the slope and y-intercept are immediately discernible from the numbers in the equation. ◊

Checkpoint 3.5.6 What are the slope and y-intercept for each of the following line equations?

Equation	Slope	y-intercept
$y = 3.1x + 1.78$	_____	_____
$y = -17x + 112$	_____	_____
$y = \frac{3}{7}x - \frac{2}{3}$	_____	_____
$y = 13 - 8x$	_____	_____
$y = 1 - \frac{2x}{3}$	_____	_____
$y = 2x$	_____	_____
$y = 3$	_____	_____

Explanation. In the first three equations, simply read the slope m according to slope-intercept form. The slopes are 3.1, -17, and $\frac{3}{7}$.

The fourth equation was written with the terms not in the slope-intercept form order. It could be written $y = -8x + 13$, and then it is clear that its slope is -8. In any case, the slope is the coefficient of x.

The fifth equation is also written with the terms not in the slope-intercept form order. Changing the order of the terms, it could be written $y = -\frac{2x}{3} + 1$, but this still does not match the pattern of slope-intercept form. Considering how fraction multiplication works, $\frac{2x}{3} = \frac{2}{3} \cdot \frac{x}{1} = \frac{2}{3}x$. So we can write this equation as $y = -\frac{2}{3}x + 1$, and we see the slope is $-\frac{2}{3}$.

The last two equations could be written $y = 2x + 0$ and $y = 0x + 3$, allowing us to read their slopes as 2 and 0.

For the y-intercepts, remember that we are expected to answer using an ordered pair $(0, b)$, not just a single number b. We can simply read that the first two y-intercepts are $(0, 1.78)$ and $(0, 112)$.

The third equation does not exactly match the slope-intercept form, until you view it as $y = \frac{3}{7}x + \left(-\frac{2}{3}\right)$, and then you can see that its y-intercept is $\left(0, -\frac{2}{3}\right)$.

With the fourth equation, after rewriting it as $y = -8x + 13$, we can see that its y-intercept is $(0, 13)$.

We already explored rewriting the fifth equation as $y = -\frac{2}{3}x + 1$, where we can see that its y-intercept is $(0, 1)$.

The last two equations could be written $y = 2x + 0$ and $y = 0x + 3$, allowing us to read their y-intercepts as $(0, 0)$ and $(0, 3)$.

Alternatively, we know that y-intercepts happen where $x = 0$, and substituting $x = 0$ into each equation gives you the y-value of the y-intercept.

Remark 3.5.7 The number b is the y-value when $x = 0$. Therefore it is common to refer to b as the **initial value** or **starting value** of a linear relationship.

Example 3.5.8 With a simple equation like $y = 2x + 3$, we can see that this is a line whose slope is 2 and which has initial value 3. So starting at $y = 3$ on the y-axis, each time we increase the x-value by 1, the y-value increases by 2. With these basic observations, we can quickly produce a table and/or a graph.

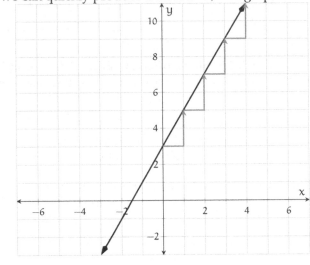

start on	x	y		initial
y-axis ⟶	0	3	⟵	value
increase by 1 ⟶	1	5	⟵	increase by 2
increase by 1 ⟶	2	7	⟵	increase by 2
increase by 1 ⟶	3	9	⟵	increase by 2
increase by 1 ⟶	4	11	⟵	increase by 2

Example 3.5.9 Decide whether data in the table has a linear relationship. If so, write the linear equation in slope-intercept form (3.5.1).

x-values	y-values
0	−4
2	2
5	11
9	23

Explanation.   To assess whether the relationship is linear, we have to recall from Section 3.3 that we should examine rates of change between data points. Note that the changes in y-values are not consistent. However, the rates of change are calculated as follows:

- When x increases by 2, y increases by 6. The first rate of change is $\frac{6}{2} = 3$.

- When x increases by 3, y increases by 9. The second rate of change is $\frac{9}{3} = 3$.

- When x increases by 4, y increases by 12. The third rate of change is $\frac{12}{4} = 3$.

Since the rates of change are all the same, 3, the relationship is linear and the slope m is 3. According to the table, when $x = 0$, $y = -4$. So the starting value, b, is -4. So in slope-intercept form, the line's equation is $y = 3x - 4$.

Checkpoint 3.5.10 Decide whether data in the table has a linear relationship. If so, write the linear equation in slope-intercept form. This may not be as easy as the previous example. Read the solution for a full explanation.

x-values	y-values
3	−2
6	−8
8	−12
11	−18

The data   (□ does   □ does not)   have a linear relationship, because: (□ changes in x are not constant   □ rates of change between data points are constant   □ rates of change between data points are not constant)

The slope-intercept form of the equation for this line is [   ].

Explanation.   To assess whether the relationship is linear, we examine rates of change between data points.

- The first rate of change is $\frac{-6}{3} = -2$.

- The second rate of change is $\frac{-4}{2} = 2$.

- The third rate of change is $\frac{-6}{3} = -2$.

Since the rates of change are all the same, −2, the relationship is linear and the slope m is −2.

So we know that the slope-intercept equation is $y = -2x + b$, but what number is b? The table does not directly tell us what the initial y-value is. One approach is to use any point that we know the line passes through, and use algebra to solve for b. We know the line passes through $(3, -2)$, so

$$y = -2x + b$$
$$-2 = -2(3) + b$$
$$-2 = -6 + b$$
$$4 = b$$

So the equation is $y = -2x + 4$.

3.5.2 Graphing Slope-Intercept Equations

Example 3.5.11 The conversion formula for a Celsius temperature into Fahrenheit is $F = \frac{9}{5}C + 32$. This appears to be in slope-intercept form, except that x and y are replaced with C and F. Suppose you are asked to graph this equation. How will you proceed? You *could* make a table of values as we do in Section 3.2 but that takes time and effort. Since the equation here is in slope-intercept form, there is a nicer way.

Since this equation is for starting with a Celsius temperature and obtaining a Fahrenheit temperature, it makes sense to let C be the horizontal axis variable and F be the vertical axis variable. Note the slope is $\frac{9}{5}$ and the vertical intercept (here, the F-intercept) is $(0, 32)$.

1. Set up the axes using an appropriate window and labels. Considering the freezing temperature of water ($0°$ Celsius or $32°$ Fahrenheit), and the boiling temperature of water ($100°$ Celsius or $212°$ Fahrenheit), it's reasonable to let C run through at least 0 to 100 and F run through at least 32 to 212.

2. Plot the F-intercept, which is at $(0, 32)$.

3. Starting at the F-intercept, use slope triangles to reach the next point. Since our slope is $\frac{9}{5}$, that suggests a "run" of 5 and a "rise" of 9 might work. But as Figure 3.5.12 indicates, such slope triangles are too tiny. You can actually use any fraction equivalent to $\frac{9}{5}$ to plot using the slope, as in $\frac{18}{10}$, $\frac{90}{50}$, $\frac{900}{50}$, or $\frac{45}{25}$

which all reduce to $\frac{9}{5}$. Given the size of our graph, we will use $\frac{90}{50}$ to plot points, where we will try a "run" of 50 and a "rise" of 90.

4. Connect your points with a straight line, use arrowheads, and label the equation.

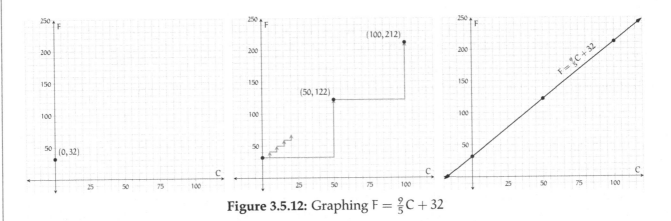

Figure 3.5.12: Graphing $F = \frac{9}{5}C + 32$

Example 3.5.13 Graph $y = -\frac{2}{3}x + 10$.

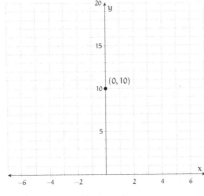 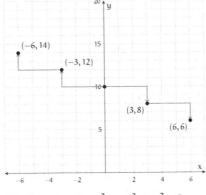 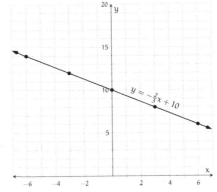

(a) Setting up the axes in an appropriate window and making sure that the y-intercept will be visible, and that any "run" and "rise" amounts we wish to use will not make triangles that are too big or too small.

(b) The slope is $-\frac{2}{3} = \frac{-2}{3} = \frac{2}{-3}$. So we can try using a "run" of 3 and a "rise" of -2 or a "run" of -3 and a "rise" of 2.

(c) Connecting the points with a straight line and adding labels.

Figure 3.5.14: Graphing $y = -\frac{2}{3}x + 10$

Example 3.5.15 Graph $y = 3x + 5$.

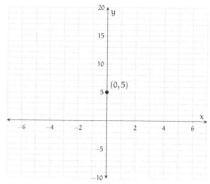

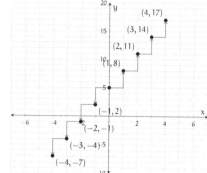

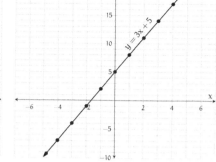

(a) Setting up the axes to make sure that the y-intercept will be visible, and that any "run" and "rise" amounts we wish to use will not make triangles that are too big or too small.

(b) The slope is a whole number 3. Every 1 unit forward causes a change of positive 3 in the y-values.

(c) Connecting the points with a straight line and adding labels.

Figure 3.5.16: Graphing $y = 3x + 5$

3.5.3 Writing a Slope-Intercept Equation Given a Graph

We can write a linear equation in slope-intercept form based on its graph. We need to be able to calculate the line's slope and see its y-intercept.

Checkpoint 3.5.17 Use the graph to write an equation of the line in slope-intercept form.

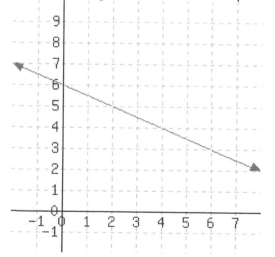

Explanation. On the line, pick two points with easy-to-read integer coordinates so that we can calculate slope. It doesn't matter which two points we use; the slope will be the same.

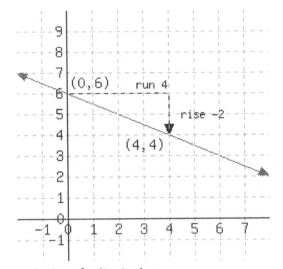

Using the slope triangle, we can calculate the line's slope:

$$\text{slope} = \frac{\Delta y}{\Delta x} = \frac{-2}{4} = -\frac{1}{2}.$$

From the graph, we can see the y-intercept is $(0, 6)$.
With the slope and y-intercept found, we can write the line's equation:

$$y = -\frac{1}{2}x + 6.$$

Checkpoint 3.5.18 There are seven public four-year colleges in Oregon. The graph plots the annual in-state tuition for each school on the x-axis, and the median income of former students ten years after first enrolling on the y-axis.

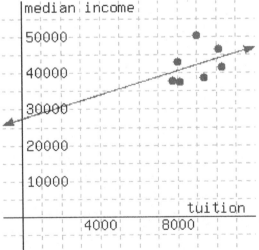

Write an equation for this line in slope-intercept form.

Explanation.   Do your best to identify two points on the line. We go with $(0, 27500)$ and $(11000, 45000)$.

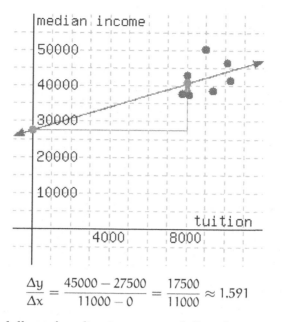

$$\frac{\Delta y}{\Delta x} = \frac{45000 - 27500}{11000 - 0} = \frac{17500}{11000} \approx 1.591$$

So the slope is about 1.591 dollars of median income per dollar of tuition. This is only an estimate since we are not certain the two points we chose are actually on the line.

Estimating the y-intercept to be at $(0, 27500)$, we have $y = 1.591x + 27500$.

3.5.4 Writing a Slope-Intercept Equation Given Two Points

The idea that any two points uniquely determine a line has been understood for thousands of years in many cultures around the world. Once you have two specific points, there is a straightforward process to find the slope-intercept form of the equation of the line that connects them.

Example 3.5.19 Find the slope-intercept form of the equation of the line that passes through the points $(0, 5)$ and $(8, -5)$.

Explanation. We are trying to write down $y = mx + b$, but with specific numbers for m and b. So the first step is to find the slope, m. To do this, recall the slope formula (3.4.3) from Section 3.4. It says that if a line passes through the points (x_1, y_1) and (x_2, y_2), then the slope is found by the formula $m = \frac{y_2 - y_1}{x_2 - x_1}$.

Applying this to our two points $(\overset{x_1 \ y_1}{0, \ 5})$ and $(\overset{x_2 \ y_2}{8, \ -5})$, we see that the slope is:

$$
\begin{aligned}
m &= \frac{y_2 - y_1}{x_2 - x_1} \\
&= \frac{-5 - 5}{8 - 0} \\
&= \frac{-10}{8} = -\frac{5}{4}
\end{aligned}
$$

We are trying to write $y = mx + b$. Since we already found the slope, we know that we want to write $y = -\frac{5}{4}x + b$ but we need a specific number for b. We *happen* to know that one point on this line is $(0, 5)$, which is on the y-axis because its x-value is 0. So $(0, 5)$ is this line's y-intercept, and therefore $b = 5$. So, our equation is

$$y = -\frac{5}{4}x + 5.$$

Example 3.5.20 Find the slope-intercept form of the equation of the line that passes through the points $(3, -8)$ and $(-6, 1)$.

Explanation.   The first step is always to find the slope between our two points: $(\overset{x_1}{3},\overset{y_1}{-8})$ and $(\overset{x_2}{-6},\overset{y_2}{1})$. Using the slope formula (3.4.3) again, we have:

$$\begin{aligned}
m &= \frac{y_2 - y_1}{x_2 - x_1} \\
&= \frac{1 - (-8)}{-6 - 3} \\
&= \frac{9}{-9} \\
&= -1
\end{aligned}$$

Now that we have the slope, we can write $y = -1x + b$, which simplifies to $y = -x + b$. Unlike in Example 3.5.19, we are not given the value of b because neither of our two given points have an x-value of 0. The trick to finding b is to remember that we have two points that we know make the equation true! This means all we have to do is substitute *either* point into the equation for x and y and solve for b. Let's arbitrarily choose $(3, -8)$ to plug in.

$$\begin{aligned}
y &= -x + b \\
-8 &= -(3) + b \qquad\qquad\qquad\text{(Now solve for b.)} \\
-8 &= -3 + b \\
-8 + 3 &= -3 + b + 3 \\
-5 &= b
\end{aligned}$$

In conclusion, the equation for which we were searching is $y = -x - 5$.

Don't be tempted to plug in values for x and y at this point. The general equation of a line in any form should have (at least one, and in this case two) variables in the final answer.

Checkpoint 3.5.21 Find the slope-intercept form of the equation of the line that passes through the points $(-3, 150)$ and $(0, 30)$.

Explanation.   The first step is always to find the slope between our points: $(\overset{x_1}{-3},\overset{y_1}{150})$ and $(\overset{x_2}{0},\overset{y_2}{30})$. Using the slope formula, we have:

$$\begin{aligned}
m &= \frac{y_2 - y_1}{x_2 - x_1} \\
&= \frac{30 - 150}{0 - (-3)} \\
&= \frac{-120}{3} \\
&= -40
\end{aligned}$$

Now we can write $y = -40x + b$ and to find b we need look no further than one of the given points: $(0, 30)$. Since the x-value is 0, the value of b must be 30. So, the slope-intercept form of the line is

$$y = -40x + 30$$

Checkpoint 3.5.22 Find the slope-intercept form of the equation of the line that passes through the points $\left(-3, \frac{3}{4}\right)$ and $\left(-6, -\frac{17}{4}\right)$.

Explanation. First find the slope through our points: $\left(-3, \frac{3}{4}\right)$ and $\left(-6, -\frac{17}{4}\right)$.

$$
\begin{aligned}
m &= \frac{y_2 - y_1}{x_2 - x_1} \\
&= \frac{-\frac{17}{4} - \frac{3}{4}}{-6 - (-3)} \\
&= \frac{\frac{-20}{4}}{-3} \\
&= \frac{-5}{-3} \\
&= \frac{5}{3}
\end{aligned}
$$

So far we have $y = \frac{5}{3}x + b$. Now we need to solve for b since neither of the points given were the vertical intercept. Recall that to do this, we will choose one of the two points and plug it into our equation. We choose $\left(-3, \frac{3}{4}\right)$.

$$
\begin{aligned}
y &= \frac{5}{3}x + b \\
\frac{3}{4} &= \frac{5}{3}(-3) + b \\
\frac{3}{4} &= -5 + b \\
\frac{3}{4} + 5 &= -5 + b + 5 \\
\frac{3}{4} + \frac{20}{4} &= b \\
\frac{23}{4} &= b
\end{aligned}
$$

Lastly, we write our equation.

$$
y = \frac{5}{3}x + \frac{23}{4}
$$

3.5.5 Modeling with Slope-Intercept Form

We can model many relatively simple relationships using slope-intercept form, and then solve related questions using algebra. Here are a few examples.

Example 3.5.23 Uber is a ride-sharing company. Its pricing in Portland factors in how much time and how many miles a trip takes. But if you assume that rides average out at a speed of 30 mph, then their pricing scheme boils down to a base of $7.35 for the trip, plus $3.85 per mile. Use a slope-intercept equation and algebra to answer these questions.

   a. How much is the fare if a trip is 5.3 miles long?

   b. With $100 available to you, how long of a trip can you afford?

Explanation. The rate of change (slope) is $3.85 per mile, and the starting value is $7.35. So the slope-intercept equation is

$$
y = 3.85x + 7.35.
$$

In this equation, x stands for the number of miles in a trip, and y stands for the amount of money to be charged.

If a trip is 5.3 miles long, we substitute $x = 5.3$ into the equation and we have:

$$
\begin{aligned}
y &= 3.85x + 7.35 \\
&= 3.85(5.3) + 7.35 \\
&= 20.405 + 7.35 \\
&= 27.755
\end{aligned}
$$

And the 5.3-mile ride will cost you about \$27.76. (We say "about," because this was all assuming you average 30 mph.)

Next, to find how long of a trip would cost \$100, we substitute $y = 100$ into the equation and solve for x:

$$
\begin{aligned}
y &= 3.85x + 7.35 \\
100 &= 3.85x + 7.35 \\
100 - 7.35 &= 3.85x \\
92.65 &= 3.85x \\
\frac{92.65}{3.85} &= x \\
24.06 &\approx x
\end{aligned}
$$

So with \$100 you could afford a little more than a 24-mile trip.

Checkpoint 3.5.24 In a certain wildlife reservation in Africa, there are approximately 2400 elephants. Sadly, the population has been decreasing by 30 elephants per year. Use a slope-intercept equation and algebra to answer these questions.

   a. If the trend continues, what would the elephant population be 15 years from now?

   b. If the trend continues, how many years will it be until the elephant population dwindles to 1200?

Explanation.   The rate of change (slope) is -30 elephants per year. Notice that since we are losing elephants, the slope is a negative number. The starting value is 2400 elephants. So the slope-intercept equation is

$$y = -30x + 2400.$$

In this equation, x stands for a number of years into the future, and y stands for the elephant population. To estimate the elephant population 15 years later, we substitute x in the equation with 15, and we have:

$$
\begin{aligned}
y &= -30x + 2400 \\
&= -30(15) + 2400 \\
&= -450 + 2400 \\
&= 1950
\end{aligned}
$$

So if the trend continues, there would be 1950 elephants on this reservation 15 years later.

Next, to find when the elephant population would decrease to 1200, we substitute y in the equation with

1200, and solve for x:

$$y = -30x + 2400$$
$$1200 = -30x + 2400$$
$$1200 - 2400 = -30x$$
$$-1200 = -30x$$
$$\frac{-1200}{-30} = x$$
$$40 = x$$

So if the trend continues, 40 years later, the elephant population would dwindle to 1200.

3.5.6 Reading Questions

1. How does "slope-intercept form" get its name?

2. What are two phrases you can use for "b" in a slope-intercept form line equation?

3. Explain the two basic steps to graphing a line when you have the equation in slope-intercept form. (Not counting the step where you draw and label the axes and ticks.)

3.5.7 Exercises

Review and Warmup

1. Evaluate $2A + 10a$ for $A = 1$ and $a = -8$.

2. Evaluate $-5B + 3C$ for $B = 7$ and $C = -9$.

3. Evaluate
$$\frac{y_2 - y_1}{x_2 - x_1}$$
for $x_1 = 14$, $x_2 = -4$, $y_1 = -5$, and $y_2 = 2$:

4. Evaluate
$$\frac{y_2 - y_1}{x_2 - x_1}$$
for $x_1 = 18$, $x_2 = -19$, $y_1 = 12$, and $y_2 = -9$:

Identifying Slope and y-Intercept Find the line's slope and y-intercept.

5. A line has equation $y = 2x + 7$.

This line's slope is ☐.

This line's y-intercept is ☐.

6. A line has equation $y = 3x + 4$.

This line's slope is ☐.

This line's y-intercept is ☐.

7. A line has equation $y = -8x - 10$.

This line's slope is ☐.

This line's y-intercept is ☐.

8. A line has equation $y = -7x - 4$.

This line's slope is ☐.

This line's y-intercept is ☐.

9. A line has equation $y = x - 4$.

This line's slope is ☐.

This line's y-intercept is ☐.

10. A line has equation $y = x + 2$.

This line's slope is ☐.

This line's y-intercept is ☐.

11. A line has equation $y = -x + 5$.

This line's slope is ☐.

This line's y-intercept is ☐.

12. A line has equation $y = -x + 7$.

This line's slope is ☐.

This line's y-intercept is ☐.

13. A line has equation $y = -\dfrac{8}{9}x + 1$.

This line's slope is [   ].

This line's y-intercept is [   ].

14. A line has equation $y = -\dfrac{2}{7}x + 10$.

This line's slope is [   ].

This line's y-intercept is [   ].

15. A line has equation $y = \dfrac{1}{2}x + 8$.

This line's slope is [   ].

This line's y-intercept is [   ].

16. A line has equation $y = \dfrac{1}{4}x - 7$.

This line's slope is [   ].

This line's y-intercept is [   ].

17. A line has equation $y = 1 + 5x$.

This line's slope is [   ].

This line's y-intercept is [   ].

18. A line has equation $y = -7 + 6x$.

This line's slope is [   ].

This line's y-intercept is [   ].

19. A line has equation $y = 7 - x$.

This line's slope is [   ].

This line's y-intercept is [   ].

20. A line has equation $y = 8 - x$.

This line's slope is [   ].

This line's y-intercept is [   ].

Graphs and Slope-Intercept Form   A line's graph is given. What is this line's slope-intercept equation?

21.   **22.**   **23.**

24.   **25.**   **26.**

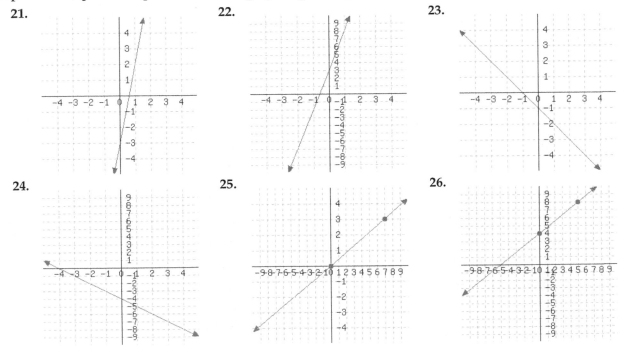

27. **28.**

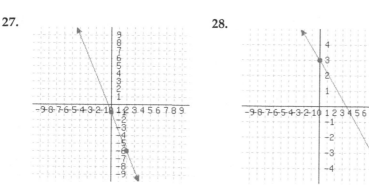

29. Graph the equation $y = 4x$.

30. Graph the equation $y = 5x$.

31. Graph the equation $y = -3x$.

32. Graph the equation $y = -2x$.

33. Graph the equation $y = \frac{5}{2}x$.

34. Graph the equation $y = \frac{1}{4}x$.

35. Graph the equation $y = -\frac{1}{3}x$.

36. Graph the equation $y = -\frac{5}{4}x$.

37. Graph the equation $y = 5x + 2$.

38. Graph the equation $y = 3x + 6$.

39. Graph the equation $y = -4x + 3$.

40. Graph the equation $y = -2x + 5$.

41. Graph the equation $y = x - 4$.

42. Graph the equation $y = x + 2$.

43. Graph the equation $y = -x + 3$.

44. Graph the equation $y = -x - 5$.

45. Graph the equation $y = \frac{2}{3}x + 4$.

46. Graph the equation $y = \frac{3}{2}x - 5$.

47. Graph the equation $y = -\frac{3}{5}x - 1$.

48. Graph the equation $y = -\frac{1}{5}x + 1$.

Writing a Slope-Intercept Equation Given Two Points Find the following line's equation in slope-intercept form.

49. The line passes through the points $(2, 12)$ and $(4, 20)$.

50. The line passes through the points $(4, 21)$ and $(1, 6)$.

51. The line passes through the points $(-5, 13)$ and $(3, -3)$.

52. The line passes through the points $(2, -14)$ and $(-1, 1)$.

53. The line passes through the points $(5, -12)$ and $(4, -11)$.

54. The line passes through the points $(1, -6)$ and $(-2, -3)$.

55. The line passes through the points $(7, 11)$ and $(21, 19)$.

56. The line passes through the points $(-9, -3)$ and $(9, 7)$.

57. The line passes through the points $(-5, 13)$ and $(-10, 19)$.

58. The line passes through the points $(6, -4)$ and $(3, 3)$.

Applications

59. A gym charges members $40 for a registration fee, and then $38 per month. You became a member some time ago, and now you have paid a total of $534 to the gym. How many months have passed since you joined the gym?

☐ months have passed since you joined the gym.

60. Your cell phone company charges a $29 monthly fee, plus $0.15 per minute of talk time. One month your cell phone bill was $98. How many minutes did you spend talking on the phone that month?

   You spent [   ] talking on the phone that month.

61. A school purchased a batch of T-shirts from a company. The company charged $3 per T-shirt, and gave the school a $60 rebate. If the school had a net expense of $960 from the purchase, how many T-shirts did the school buy?

   The school purchased [   ] T-shirts.

62. Laney hired a face-painter for a birthday party. The painter charged a flat fee of $55, and then charged $5.50 per person. In the end, Laney paid a total of $181.50. How many people used the face-painter's service?

   [   ] people used the face-painter's service.

63. A certain country has 277.29 million acres of forest. Every year, the country loses 3.51 million acres of forest mainly due to deforestation for farming purposes. If this situation continues at this pace, how many years later will the country have only 136.89 million acres of forest left? (Use an equation to solve this problem.)

   After [   ] years, this country would have 136.89 million acres of forest left.

64. Irene has $77 in her piggy bank. She plans to purchase some Pokemon cards, which costs $1.45 each. She plans to save $65.40 to purchase another toy. At most how many Pokemon cards can he purchase?

   Write an equation to solve this problem.

   Irene can purchase at most [   ] Pokemon cards.

65. By your cell phone contract, you pay a monthly fee plus $0.05 for each minute you spend on the phone. In one month, you spent 290 minutes over the phone, and had a bill totaling $32.50.

   Let x be the number of minutes you spend on the phone in a month, and let y be your total cell phone bill for that month, in dollars. Use a linear equation to model your monthly bill based on the number of minutes you spend on the phone.

   a. This line's slope-intercept equation is [   ].

   b. If you spend 150 minutes on the phone in a month, you would be billed [   ].

   c. If your bill was $42.50 one month, you must have spent [   ] minutes on the phone in that month.

66. A company set aside a certain amount of money in the year 2000. The company spent exactly $38,000 from that fund each year on perks for its employees. In 2002, there was still $702,000 left in the fund.

   Let x be the number of years since 2000, and let y be the amount of money, in dollars, left in the fund that year. Use a linear equation to model the amount of money left in the fund after so many years.

   a. The linear model's slope-intercept equation is [   ].

   b. In the year 2010, there was [   ] left in the fund.

c. In the year [   ], the fund will be empty.

67. A biologist has been observing a tree's height. This type of tree typically grows by 0.24 feet each month. Fourteen months into the observation, the tree was 15.06 feet tall.

Let x be the number of months passed since the observations started, and let y be the tree's height at that time, in feet. Use a linear equation to model the tree's height as the number of months pass.

   a. This line's slope-intercept equation is [   ].

   b. 27 months after the observations started, the tree would be [   ] feet in height.

   c. [   ] months after the observation started, the tree would be 25.86 feet tall.

68. Scientists are conducting an experiment with a gas in a sealed container. The mass of the gas is measured, and the scientists realize that the gas is leaking over time in a linear way. Each minute, they lose 7.7 grams. Five minutes since the experiment started, the remaining gas had a mass of 331.1 grams.

Let x be the number of minutes that have passed since the experiment started, and let y be the mass of the gas in grams at that moment. Use a linear equation to model the weight of the gas over time.

   a. This line's slope-intercept equation is [   ].

   b. 34 minutes after the experiment started, there would be [   ] grams of gas left.

   c. If a linear model continues to be accurate, [   ] minutes since the experiment started, all gas in the container will be gone.

69. A company set aside a certain amount of money in the year 2000. The company spent exactly the same amount from that fund each year on perks for its employees. In 2003, there was still $617,000 left in the fund. In 2007, there was $425,000 left.

Let x be the number of years since 2000, and let y be the amount of money, in dollars, left in the fund that year. Use a linear equation to model the amount of money left in the fund after so many years.

   a. The linear model's slope-intercept equation is [   ].

   b. In the year 2010, there was [   ] left in the fund.

   c. In the year [   ], the fund will be empty.

70. By your cell phone contract, you pay a monthly fee plus some money for each minute you use the phone during the month. In one month, you spent 300 minutes on the phone, and paid $15.50. In another month, you spent 360 minutes on the phone, and paid $16.40.

Let x be the number of minutes you talk over the phone in a month, and let y be your cell phone bill, in dollars, for that month. Use a linear equation to model your monthly bill based on the number of minutes you talk over the phone.

a. This linear model's slope-intercept equation is [   ].

b. If you spent 150 minutes over the phone in a month, you would pay [   ].

c. If in a month, you paid $17.60 of cell phone bill, you must have spent [   ] minutes on the phone in that month.

71. Scientists are conducting an experiment with a gas in a sealed container. The mass of the gas is measured, and the scientists realize that the gas is leaking over time in a linear way.
    Seven minutes since the experiment started, the gas had a mass of 248.2 grams.
    Thirteen minutes since the experiment started, the gas had a mass of 204.4 grams.
    Let x be the number of minutes that have passed since the experiment started, and let y be the mass of the gas in grams at that moment. Use a linear equation to model the weight of the gas over time.

    a. This line's slope-intercept equation is [   ].

    b. 34 minutes after the experiment started, there would be [   ] grams of gas left.

    c. If a linear model continues to be accurate, [   ] minutes since the experiment started, all gas in the container will be gone.

72. A biologist has been observing a tree's height. 14 months into the observation, the tree was 16 feet tall. 20 months into the observation, the tree was 16.9 feet tall.
    Let x be the number of months passed since the observations started, and let y be the tree's height at that time, in feet. Use a linear equation to model the tree's height as the number of months pass.

    a. This line's slope-intercept equation is [   ].

    b. 27 months after the observations started, the tree would be [   ] feet in height.

    c. [   ] months after the observation started, the tree would be 21.85 feet tall.

Challenge

73. Line S has the equation $y = ax + b$ and Line T has the equation $y = cx + d$. Suppose $a > b > c > d > 0$.

    a. What can you say about Line S and Line T, given that $a > c$? Give as much information about Line S and Line T as possible.

    b. What can you say about Line S and Line T, given that $b > d$? Give as much information about Line S and Line T as possible.

3.6 Point-Slope Form

In Section 3.5, we learned that a linear equation can be written in slope-intercept form, $y = mx + b$. This section covers an alternative that is often more useful depending on the application: point-slope form.

3.6.1 Point-Slope Motivation and Definition

Starting in 1990, the population of the United States has been growing by about 2.865 million people per year. Also, back in 1990, the population was 253 million. Since the rate of growth has been roughly constant, a linear model is appropriate. Let's try to write an equation to model this.

We consider using slope-intercept form (3.5.1), but we would need to know the y-intercept, and nothing in the background tells us that. We'd need to know the population of the United States in the year 0, before there even was a United States.

We could do some side work to calculate the y-intercept, but let's try something else. Here are some things we know:

1. The slope equation is $m = \frac{y_2 - y_1}{x_2 - x_1}$.

2. The slope is $m = 2.865 \frac{\text{million people}}{\text{year}}$, or $m = \frac{2.865 \text{ million people}}{1 \text{ year}}$.

3. One point on the line is $(1990, 253)$, because in *1990*, the population was *253* million.

If we use the generic (x, y) to represent a point *somewhere* on this line, then the rate of change between $(1990, 253)$ and (x, y) has to be 2.865. So

$$\frac{y - 253}{x - 1990} = 2.865.$$

There is good reason[1] to want to isolate y in this equation:

$$\frac{y - 253}{x - 1990} = 2.865$$

$$\frac{y - 253}{x - 1990} \cdot (x - 1990) = 2.865 \cdot (x - 1990)$$

$$y - 253 = 2.865(x - 1990) \qquad \text{(could distribute, but not going to)}$$

$$y = 2.865(x - 1990) + 253$$

This is a good place to stop. We have isolated y, and three *meaningful* numbers appear in the equation: the rate of growth, a certain year, and the population in that year. This is a specific example of *point-slope form*. Before we look deeper at point-slope form, let's continue reducing the line equation into slope-intercept form by distributing and combining like terms.

$$y = 2.865(x - 1990) + 253$$
$$y = 2.865x - 5701.35 + 253 \qquad \text{(distributed the 2.865)}$$
$$y = 2.865x - 5448.35 \qquad \text{combined like terms}$$

One concern with slope-intercept form (3.5.1) is that it uses the y-intercept, which might be somewhat meaningless in the context of an application. For example, here we have found that the y-intercept is at

---

[1] It will help us to see that y (population) *depends* on x (whatever year it is).

(0, −5448.35), but what practical use is that? It's nonsense to say that in the year 0, the population of the United States was −5448.35 million. It doesn't make sense to have a negative population. It doesn't make sense to talk about the United States population before there even was a United States. And it doesn't make sense to use this model for years earlier than 1990 because the background information says clearly that the rate of change we have applies to years 1990 and later.

For all these reasons, we prefer the equation when it was in the form

$$y = 2.865(x − 1990) + 253$$

Definition 3.6.2 Point-Slope Form. When x and y have a linear relationship where m is the slope and (x_0, y_0) is some specific point that the line passes through, one equation for this relationship is

$$y = m(x − x_0) + y_0 \tag{3.6.1}$$

and this equation is called the **point-slope form** of the line. It is called this because the slope and one point on the line are immediately discernible from the numbers in the equation.

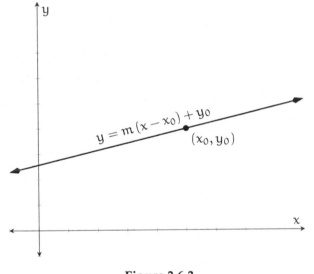

Figure 3.6.3

◊

There is a subtraction sign and an addition sign in point-slope form (3.6.1), and you may have trouble remembering which is which. But remember that that the line is supposed to pass through (x_0, y_0). So substituting x_0 in for x should leave y equal to y_0. And it does. For example, consider our example equation $y = 2.865(x − 1990) + 253$. Here, x_0 is 1990 and y_0 is 253. And:

$$
\begin{aligned}
y &= 2.865(x − 1990) + 253 &&\text{substitute 1990 for } x \dots \\
y &= 2.865(1990 − 1990) + 253 \\
y &= 2.865(0) + 253 \\
y &= 253 &&\dots \text{and } y \text{ works out to be 253}
\end{aligned}
$$

The subtraction is exactly where it needs to be to wipe out $m(x - x_0)$ and leave you with y_0. More generally:

$$y = m(\overset{\overset{x_0}{\downarrow}}{x} - x_0) + \underset{\underset{y_0}{\downarrow}}{y_0}$$

Remark 3.6.4 Alternative Point-Slope Form. It is also common to define point-slope form as

$$y - y_0 = m(x - x_0) \qquad (3.6.2)$$

by subtracting y_0 from each side. If you learn about point-slope form from some other resource, you may come across this. We feel that the $y = m(x - x_0) + y_0$ form will be more helpful with college algebra, statistics, and calculus.

Checkpoint 3.6.5 Consider the line in this graph:

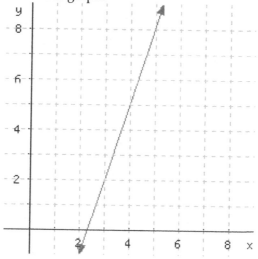

a. Identify a point visible on this line that has integer coordinates, and write it as an ordered pair.

b. What is the slope of the line?

c. Use point-slope form to write an equation for this line, making use of a point with integer coordinates.

Explanation.

a. The visible points with integer coordinates are $(2, -1)$, $(3, 2)$, $(4, 5)$, and $(5, 8)$.

b. Several slope triangles are visible where the "run" is 1 and the "rise" is 3. So the slope is $\frac{3}{1} = 3$.

c. Using $(3, 2)$, the point-slope equation is $y = 3(x - 3) + 2$. (You could use other points, like $(2, -1)$, and get a different-looking equation like $y = 3(x - 2) + (-1)$ which simplifies to $y = 3(x - 2) - 1$.)

In Checkpoint 3.6.5, the solution explains that each of the following are acceptable equations for the same line:

$$y = 3(x - 3) + 2 \qquad\qquad\qquad y = 3(x - 2) - 1$$

The first uses $(3, 2)$ as a point on the line, and the second uses $(2, -1)$. Are those two equations really equivalent? Let's distribute and simplify each of them to get slope-intercept form (3.5.1).

$$y = 3(x - 3) + 2 \qquad\qquad y = 3(x - 2) - 1$$
$$y = 3x - 9 + 2 \qquad\qquad y = 3x - 6 - 1$$
$$y = 3x - 7 \qquad\qquad\qquad y = 3x - 7$$

So, yes. It didn't matter which point we used to write a point-slope equation. We get different-looking equations that still represent the same line.

Point-slope form is preferable when we know a line's slope and a point on it, but we don't know the y-intercept. We recognie that distributing the slope and combining like terms can always be used to find the line's slope-intercept form.

Example 3.6.6 A spa chain has been losing customers at a roughly constant rate since the year 2010. In 2013, it had 2975 customers; in 2016, it had 2585 customers. Management estimated that the company will go out of business once its customer base decreases to 1800. If this trend continues, when will the company close?

The given information tells us two points on the line: $(2013, 2975)$ and $(2016, 2585)$. The slope formula (3.4.3) will give us the slope. After labeling those two points as $(\overset{x_1}{2013}, \overset{y_1}{2975})$ and $(\overset{x_2}{2016}, \overset{y_2}{2585})$, we have:

$$\begin{aligned}
\text{slope} &= \frac{y_2 - y_1}{x_2 - x_1} \\
&= \frac{2585 - 2975}{2016 - 2013} \\
&= \frac{-390}{3} \\
&= -130
\end{aligned}$$

And considering units, this means they are losing 130 customers per year.

Let's note that we could try to make an equation for this line in slope-intercept form, but then we would need to calculate the y-intercept, which in context would correspond to the number of customers in year 0. We could do it, but we'd be working with numbers that have no real-world meaning in this context.

For point-slope form, since we calculated the slope, we know at least this much:

$$y = -130(x - x_0) + y_0.$$

Now we can pick one of those two given points, say $(2013, 2975)$, and get the equation

$$y = -130(x - 2013) + 2975.$$

Note that all three numbers in this equation have meaning in the context of the spa chain. The -130 tells us how many customers are leaving per year, the 2013 represents a year, and the 2975 tells us the number of customers in that year.

We're ready to answer the question about when the chain might go out of business. We need to substitute the given value of 1800 into the appropriate place in our equation. In order to substitute correctly, we must clearly understand what the variable y represents including its units, and what the variable x represents including its units. Write down those definitions first in any question you attempt to answer. It will save you time in the long run, and avoid frustration. Knowing the variable y represents the number of customers in a given year allows one to understand that y must be replaced with 1800 customers. Knowing the variable x represents a year allows one to understand that x will *not* be susbstituted, because we are trying to *solve* for what year something happens.

After substituting y in the equation with 1800, we
will solve for x, and find the answer we seek.

$$y = -130(x - 2013) + 2975$$
$$1800 = -130(x - 2013) + 2975$$
$$1800 - 2975 = -130(x - 2013)$$
$$-1175 = -130(x - 2013)$$
$$\frac{-1175}{-130} = \frac{-130(x - 2013)}{-130}$$
$$9.038 \approx x - 2013$$
$$9.038 + 2013 \approx x$$
$$2022 \approx x$$

We find that at this rate the company is headed toward a collapse in 2022.

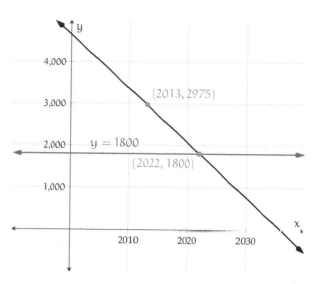

Figure 3.6.7: $y = -130(x - 2013) + 2975$

Figure 3.6.7 illustrates one line representing the spa's customer base, and another line representing the
customer level that would cause the business to close. To make a graph of $y = -130(x - 2013) + 2975$, we
first marked the point $(2013, 2975)$ and from there used the slope of -130.

Checkpoint 3.6.8 If we go state by state and compare the Republican presidential candidate's 2012 vote
share (x) to the Republican presidential candidate's 2016 vote share (y), we get the following graph (called
a "scatterplot", used in statistics) where a trendline has been superimposed.

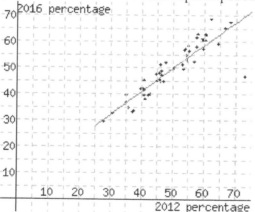

Find a point-slope equation for this line. (Note that a slope-intercept equation would use the y-intercept
coordinate b, and that would not be meaningful in context, since no state had anywhere near zero percent
Republican vote.)

Explanation. We need to calculate slope first. And for that, we need to identify two points on the line.
conveniently, the line appears to pass right through $(50, 50)$. We have to take a second point somewhere,
and $(75, 72)$ seems like a reasonable roughly accurate choice. The slope equation gives us that

$$m = \frac{72 - 50}{75 - 50} = \frac{22}{25} = 0.88.$$

Using $(50, 50)$ as the point, the point-slope equation would then be

$$y = 0.88(x - 50) + 50.$$

3.6.2 Using Two Points to Build a Linear Equation

Since two points can determine a line's location, we can calculate a line's equation using just the coordinates from any two points it passes through.

Example 3.6.9 A line passes through $(-6, 0)$ and $(9, -10)$. Find this line's equation in both point-slope and slope-intercept form.

Explanation.   We will use the slope formula (3.4.3) to find the slope first. After labeling those two points as $(\overset{x_1}{-6}, \overset{y_1}{0})$ and $(\overset{x_2}{9}, \overset{y_2}{-10})$, we have:

$$\text{slope} = \frac{y_2 - y_1}{x_2 - x_1}$$

$$= \frac{-}{-} \qquad \text{(reserving place holders)}$$

$$= \frac{-0}{-(-6)} \qquad \text{(fill in first point, vertically)}$$

$$= \frac{-10 - 0}{9 - (-6)} \qquad \text{(fill in second point, vertically)}$$

$$= \frac{-10}{15}$$

$$= -\frac{2}{3}$$

The point-slope equation is $y = -\frac{2}{3}(x - x_0) + y_0$. Next, we will use $(9, -10)$ and substitute x_0 with 9 and y_0 with -10, and we have:

$$y = -\frac{2}{3}(x - x_0) + y_0$$

$$y = -\frac{2}{3}(x - 9) + (-10)$$

$$y = -\frac{2}{3}(x - 9) - 10$$

Next, we will change the point-slope equation into slope-intercept form:

$$y = -\frac{2}{3}(x - 9) - 10$$

$$y = -\frac{2}{3}x + 6 - 10$$

$$y = -\frac{2}{3}x - 4$$

Checkpoint 3.6.10 A line passes through $(37, 40)$ and $(-11, -60)$. Find equations for this line using both point-slope and slope-intercept form.

An equation for this line in slope-intercept form is $\boxed{}$

Explanation.   First, use the slope formula to find the slope of this line:

$$m = \frac{y_2 - y_1}{x_2 - x_1} = \frac{-60 - 40}{-11 - 37}$$
$$= \frac{-100}{-48}$$
$$= \frac{25}{12}.$$

The generic point-slope equation is $y = m(x - x_0) + y_0$. We have found the slope, m, and we may use $(37, 40)$ for (x_0, y_0). So an equation in point-slope form is $y = \frac{25}{12}(x - 37) + 40$.

To find a slope-intercept form equation, we can take the generic $y = mx + b$ and substitute in the value of m we found. Also, we know that $(x, y) = (-11, -60)$ should make the equation true. So we have

$$y = mx + b$$
$$-60 = \frac{25}{12}(-11) + b \qquad \text{(now we may solve for } b\text{)}$$
$$-60 \cdot 12 = \left(\frac{25}{12}(-11) + b\right) \cdot 12 \quad \text{(clear the denominator)}$$
$$-720 = 25(-11) + 12b \qquad \text{(distribute and multiply)}$$
$$-720 = -275 + 12b$$
$$-720 + 275 = 264 + 12b + 275$$
$$-445 = 12b$$
$$\frac{-445}{12} = \frac{12b}{12}$$
$$b = -\frac{445}{12}.$$

So the slope-intercept equation is $y = \frac{25}{12}x - \frac{445}{12}$. Note that the slope-intercept equation has an unfriendly fraction, and the fact that this can happen is another reason to use the point-slope form whenever it is reasonable to do so.

3.6.3 More on Point-Slope Form

We can tell a lot about a linear equation now that we have learned both slope-intercept form (3.5.1) and point-slope form (3.6.1). For example, we can know that $y = 4x + 2$ is in slope-intercept form because it looks like $y = mx + b$. It will graph as a line with slope 4 and vertical intercept $(0, 2)$. Likewise, we know that the equation $y = -5(x - 3) + 2$ is in point-slope form because it looks like $y = m(x - x_0) + y_0$. It will graph as a line that has slope -5 and will pass through the point $(3, 2)$.

Example 3.6.11 For the equations below, state whether they are in slope-intercept form or point-slope form. Then identify the slope of the line and at least one point that the line will pass through.
  a. $y = -3x + 2$
  b. $y = 9(x + 1) - 6$
  c. $y = 5 - x$
  d. $y = -\frac{12}{5}(x - 9) + 1$

Explanation.

a. The equation $y = -3x + 2$ is in slope-intercept form. The slope is -3 and the vertical intercept is $(0, 2)$.

b. The equation $y = 9(x + 1) - 6$ is in point-slope form. The slope is 9 and the line passes through the point $(-1, -6)$.

c. The equation $y = 5 - x$ is almost in slope-intercept form. If we rearrange the right hand side to be $y = -x + 5$, we can see that the slope is -1 and the vertical intercept is $(0, 5)$.

d. The equation $y = -\frac{12}{5}(x - 9) + 1$ is in point-slope form. The slope is $-\frac{12}{5}$ and the line passes through the point $(9, 1)$.

Example 3.6.12
Consider the graph in Figure 3.6.13.

a. Using the point-slope form of a line, find three different linear equations for the line shown in the graph. Three integer-valued points are shown for convenience.

b. Determine the slope-intercept form of the equation of this line.

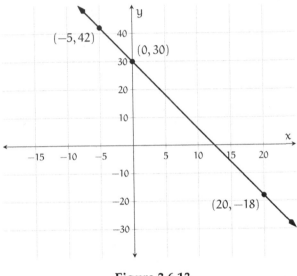

Figure 3.6.13

Explanation.

a. To write *any* of the equations representing this line in point-slope form, we must first find the slope of the line and we can use the slope formula (3.4.3) to do so. We will arbitrarily choose $(0, 30)$ and $(-5, 42)$ as the two points. Inputting these points into the slope formula yields:

$$\begin{aligned}
m &= \frac{y_2 - y_1}{x_2 - x_1} \\
&= \frac{42 - 30}{-5 - 0} \\
&= \frac{12}{-5} \\
&= -\frac{12}{5}
\end{aligned}$$

Thus the slope of the line is $-\frac{12}{5}$.

Next, we need to write an equation in point-slope form based on each point shown. Using the point

(0, 30), we have:

$$y = -\frac{12}{5}(x - 0) + 30$$

(This simplifies to $y = -\frac{12}{5}x + 30$.)

The next point is $(20, -18)$. Using this point, we can write an equation for this line as:

$$y = -\frac{12}{5}(x - 20) - 18$$

Finally, we can also use the point $(-5, 42)$ to write an equation for this line:

$$y = -\frac{12}{5}(x - (-5)) + 42$$

which can also be written as:

$$y = -\frac{12}{5}(x + 5) + 42$$

b. As $(0, 30)$ is the vertical intercept, we can write the equation of this line in slope-intercept form as $y = -\frac{12}{5}x + 30$. It's important to note that each of the equations that were written in point-slope form simplify to this, making all four equations equivalent.

3.6.4 Reading Questions

1. Explain why there are some situations where point-slope form is preferable to slope-intercept form.

2. There are basically two steps to convert a point-slope form line equation into a slope-intercept form line equation. What are they?

3. If a line has equation $y = 2(x + 5) + 6$, we can see that the line passes through a certain point. To find the x-coordinate of that point, you might look at the 5 and have memorized that you should negate that. Instead, you could train yourself to look at the x and realize the important number is -5 because that is what it takes to [   ].

3.6.5 Exercises

Review and Warmup

1. Evaluate $5B + 10A$ for $B = 8$ and $A = 2$.

2. Evaluate $10C - 8b$ for $C = -4$ and $b = 10$.

3. Evaluate

$$\frac{y_2 - y_1}{x_2 - x_1}$$

for $x_1 = -19$, $x_2 = 17$, $y_1 = 9$, and $y_2 = -19$:

4. Evaluate

$$\frac{y_2 - y_1}{x_2 - x_1}$$

for $x_1 = -15$, $x_2 = 3$, $y_1 = -15$, and $y_2 = 11$:

Point-Slope Form

5. A line's equation is given in point-slope form:
$$y = 5(x - 5) + 28$$
This line's slope is ◻.
A point on this line that is apparent from the given equation is ◻.

6. A line's equation is given in point-slope form:
$$y = 2(x - 1) + 5$$
This line's slope is ◻.
A point on this line that is apparent from the given equation is ◻.

7. A line's equation is given in point-slope form:
$$y = -2(x + 2) + 5$$
This line's slope is ◻.
A point on this line that is apparent from the given equation is ◻.

8. A line's equation is given in point-slope form:
$$y = -3(x + 4) + 7$$
This line's slope is ◻.
A point on this line that is apparent from the given equation is ◻.

9. A line's equation is given in point-slope form:
$$y = \left(-\frac{7}{8}\right)(x + 24) + 20$$
This line's slope is ◻.
A point on this line that is apparent from the given equation is ◻.

10. A line's equation is given in point-slope form:
$$y = \frac{8}{5}(x + 15) - 28$$
This line's slope is ◻.
A point on this line that is apparent from the given equation is ◻.

11. A line's equation is given in point-slope form:
$$y = \frac{9}{2}(x - 6) + 24$$
This line's slope is ◻.
A point on this line that is apparent from the given equation is ◻.

12. A line's equation is given in point-slope form:
$$y = \left(-\frac{1}{8}\right)(x - 8) - 4$$
This line's slope is ◻.
A point on this line that is apparent from the given equation is ◻.

13. A line passes through the points $(5, 15)$ and $(2, 9)$. Find this line's equation in point-slope form.
Using the point $(5, 15)$, this line's point-slope form equation is
◻
Using the point $(2, 9)$, this line's point-slope form equation is
◻

14. A line passes through the points $(2, 8)$ and $(5, 17)$. Find this line's equation in point-slope form.
Using the point $(2, 8)$, this line's point-slope form equation is
◻
Using the point $(5, 17)$, this line's point-slope form equation is
◻

15. A line passes through the points $(3, -1)$ and $(2, 2)$. Find this line's equation in point-slope form.

Using the point $(3, -1)$, this line's point-slope form equation is

$$\boxed{}.$$

Using the point $(2, 2)$, this line's point-slope form equation is

$$\boxed{}.$$

16. A line passes through the points $(-4, 17)$ and $(-1, 8)$. Find this line's equation in point-slope form.

Using the point $(-4, 17)$, this line's point-slope form equation is

$$\boxed{}.$$

Using the point $(-1, 8)$, this line's point-slope form equation is

$$\boxed{}.$$

17. A line passes through the points $(0, 9)$ and $(7, 15)$. Find this line's equation in point-slope form.

Using the point $(0, 9)$, this line's point-slope form equation is

$$\boxed{}.$$

Using the point $(7, 15)$, this line's point-slope form equation is

$$\boxed{}.$$

18. A line passes through the points $(-27, -13)$ and $(-18, -6)$. Find this line's equation in point-slope form.

Using the point $(-27, -13)$, this line's point-slope form equation is

$$\boxed{}.$$

Using the point $(-18, -6)$, this line's point-slope form equation is

$$\boxed{}.$$

19. A line's slope is 5. The line passes through the point $(2, 12)$. Find an equation for this line in both point-slope and slope-intercept form.

20. A line's slope is 5. The line passes through the point $(5, 26)$. Find an equation for this line in both point-slope and slope-intercept form.

21. A line's slope is -5. The line passes through the point $(-3, 17)$. Find an equation for this line in both point-slope and slope-intercept form.

22. A line's slope is -5. The line passes through the point $(2, -12)$. Find an equation for this line in both point-slope and slope-intercept form.

23. A line's slope is 1. The line passes through the point $(5, 2)$. Find an equation for this line in both point-slope and slope-intercept form.

24. A line's slope is 1. The line passes through the point $(1, -1)$. Find an equation for this line in both point-slope and slope-intercept form.

25. A line's slope is -1. The line passes through the point $(4, -6)$. Find an equation for this line in both point-slope and slope-intercept form.

26. A line's slope is -1. The line passes through the point $(5, -4)$. Find an equation for this line in both point-slope and slope-intercept form.

27. A line's slope is $\frac{7}{6}$. The line passes through the point $(-6, -4)$. Find an equation for this line in both point-slope and slope-intercept form.

28. A line's slope is $\frac{8}{3}$. The line passes through the point $(-9, -28)$. Find an equation for this line in both point-slope and slope-intercept form.

29. A line's slope is $-\frac{9}{8}$. The line passes through the point $(16, -13)$. Find an equation for this line in both point-slope and slope-intercept form.

30. A line's slope is $-\frac{1}{6}$. The line passes through the point $(18, 2)$. Find an equation for this line in both point-slope and slope-intercept form.

Point-Slope and Slope-Intercept Change this equation from point-slope form to slope-intercept form.

31. $y = 2(x + 1) - 5$

32. $y = 2(x - 3) + 10$

33. $y = -4(x - 2) - 11$

34. $y = -4(x - 2) - 12$

35. $y = \dfrac{6}{7}(x + 7) - 1$

36. $y = \dfrac{7}{5}(x - 15) + 25$

37. $y = -\dfrac{8}{9}(x - 27) - 23$

38. $y = -\dfrac{9}{8}(x + 8) + 7$

Point-Slope Form and Graphs Determine the point-slope form of the linear equation from its graph.

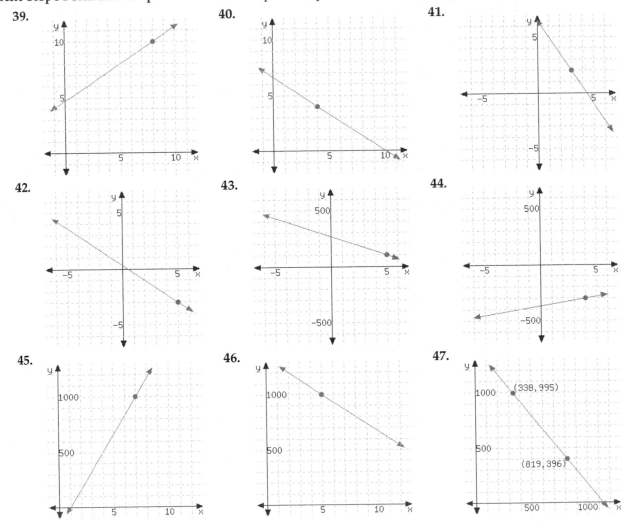

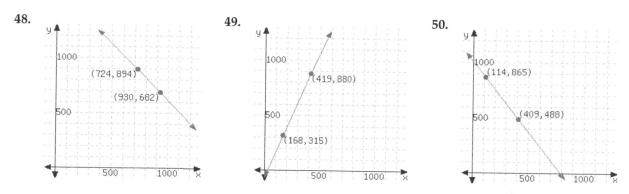

48. (724, 894) (930, 682)

49. (419, 880) (168, 315)

50. (114, 865) (409, 488)

51. Graph the linear equation
$y = -\frac{8}{3}(x - 4) - 5$ by identifying the slope and one point on this line.

52. Graph the linear equation $y = \frac{5}{7}(x + 3) + 2$ by identifying the slope and one point on this line.

53. Graph the linear equation $y = \frac{3}{4}(x + 2) + 1$ by identifying the slope and one point on this line.

54. Graph the linear equation
$y = -\frac{5}{2}(x - 1) - 5$ by identifying the slope and one point on this line.

55. Graph the linear equation $y = -3(x - 9) + 4$ by identifying the slope and one point on this line.

56. Graph the linear equation $y = 7(x + 3) - 10$ by identifying the slope and one point on this line.

57. Graph the linear equation
$y = 8(x + 12) - 20$ by identifying the slope and one point on this line.

58. Graph the linear equation
$y = -5(x - 20) - 70$ by identifying the slope and one point on this line.

Applications

59. By your cell phone contract, you pay a monthly fee plus $0.04 for each minute you spend on the phone. In one month, you spent 280 minutes over the phone, and had a bill totaling $24.20.

Let x be the number of minutes you spend on the phone in a month, and let y be your total cell phone bill for that month, in dollars. Use a linear equation to model your monthly bill based on the number of minutes you spend on the phone.

a. A point-slope equation to model this is [   ].

b. If you spend 170 minutes on the phone in a month, you would be billed [   ].

c. If your bill was $31.80 one month, you must have spent [   ] minutes on the phone in that month.

60. A company set aside a certain amount of money in the year 2000. The company spent exactly $34,000 from that fund each year on perks for its employees. In 2002, there was still $889,000 left in the fund.

Let x be the number of years since 2000, and let y be the amount of money, in dollars, left in the fund that year. Use a linear equation to model the amount of money left in the fund after so many years.

a. A point-slope equation to model this is [   ].

b. In the year 2011, there was [   ] left in the fund.

c. In the year [   ], the fund will be empty.

61. A biologist has been observing a tree's height. This type of tree typically grows by 0.21 feet each month. Thirteen months into the observation, the tree was 18.03 feet tall.

Let x be the number of months passed since the observations started, and let y be the tree's height at that time, in feet. Use a linear equation to model the tree's height as the number of months pass.

   a. A point-slope equation to model this is [   ].

   b. 28 months after the observations started, the tree would be [   ] feet in height.

   c. [   ] months after the observation started, the tree would be 27.27 feet tall.

62. Scientists are conducting an experiment with a gas in a sealed container. The mass of the gas is measured, and the scientists realize that the gas is leaking over time in a linear way. Each minute, they lose 2.8 grams. Ten minutes since the experiment started, the remaining gas had a mass of 103.6 grams.

Let x be the number of minutes that have passed since the experiment started, and let y be the mass of the gas in grams at that moment. Use a linear equation to model the weight of the gas over time.

   a. A point-slope equation to model this is [   ].

   b. 37 minutes after the experiment started, there would be [   ] grams of gas left.

   c. If a linear model continues to be accurate, [   ] minutes since the experiment started, all gas in the container will be gone.

63. A company set aside a certain amount of money in the year 2000. The company spent exactly the same amount from that fund each year on perks for its employees. In 2003, there was still $808,000 left in the fund. In 2006, there was $676,000 left.

Let x be the number of years since 2000, and let y be the amount of money, in dollars, left in the fund that year. Use a linear equation to model the amount of money left in the fund after so many years.

   a. A point-slope equation to model this is [   ].

   b. In the year 2010, there was [   ] left in the fund.

   c. In the year [   ], the fund will be empty.

64. By your cell phone contract, you pay a monthly fee plus some money for each minute you use the phone during the month. In one month, you spent 290 minutes on the phone, and paid $33.85. In another month, you spent 340 minutes on the phone, and paid $37.10.

Let x be the number of minutes you talk over the phone in a month, and let y be your cell phone bill, in dollars, for that month. Use a linear equation to model your monthly bill based on the number of minutes you talk over the phone.

    a. A point-slope equation to model this is [＿＿＿＿＿＿＿＿＿＿].

    b. If you spent 170 minutes over the phone in a month, you would pay [＿＿＿＿＿＿＿＿＿＿].

    c. If in a month, you paid \$42.30 of cell phone bill, you must have spent [＿＿＿＿＿＿＿＿＿＿] minutes on the phone in that month.

65. Scientists are conducting an experiment with a gas in a sealed container. The mass of the gas is measured, and the scientists realize that the gas is leaking over time in a linear way.
    Six minutes since the experiment started, the gas had a mass of 81.6 grams.
    Eleven minutes since the experiment started, the gas had a mass of 69.6 grams.
    Let x be the number of minutes that have passed since the experiment started, and let y be the mass of the gas in grams at that moment. Use a linear equation to model the weight of the gas over time.

    a. A point-slope equation to model this is [＿＿＿＿＿＿＿＿＿＿].

    b. 36 minutes after the experiment started, there would be [＿＿＿＿＿＿＿＿] grams of gas left.

    c. If a linear model continues to be accurate, [＿＿＿＿＿＿＿＿] minutes since the experiment started, all gas in the container will be gone.

66. A biologist has been observing a tree's height. 13 months into the observation, the tree was 19.06 feet tall. 19 months into the observation, the tree was 19.78 feet tall.
    Let x be the number of months passed since the observations started, and let y be the tree's height at that time, in feet. Use a linear equation to model the tree's height as the number of months pass.

    a. A point-slope equation to model this is [＿＿＿＿＿＿＿＿＿＿].

    b. 28 months after the observations started, the tree would be [＿＿＿＿＿＿＿＿] feet in height.

    c. [＿＿＿＿＿＿＿＿] months after the observation started, the tree would be 23.62 feet tall.

3.7 Standard Form

We've seen that a linear relationship can be expressed with an equation in slope-intercept form (3.5.1) or with an equation in point-slope form (3.6.1). There is a third form that you can use to write line equations. It's known as *standard form*.

3.7.1 Standard Form Definition

Imagine trying to gather donations to pay for a $10,000 medical procedure you cannot afford. Oversimplifying the mathematics a bit, suppose that there were only two types of donors in the world: those who will donate $20 and those who will donate $100. How many of each, or what combination, do you need to reach the funding goal? As in, if x people donate $20 and y people donate $100, what numbers could x and y be? The donors of the first type have collectively donated $20x$ dollars, and the donors of the second type have collectively donated $100y$. Reflect on the meaning of $20x$ and $100y$. Make sure you understand their meaning before reading on.

So altogether you'd need

$$20x + 100y = 10000$$

This is an example of a line equation in **standard form**.

Definition 3.7.2 Standard Form. It is always possible to write an equation for a line in the form

$$Ax + By = C \tag{3.7.1}$$

where A, B, and C are three numbers (each of which might be 0, although at least one of A and B must be nonzero). This form of a line equation is called **standard form**. In the context of an application, the meaning of A, B, and C depends on that context. This equation is called **standard form** perhaps because *any* line can be written this way, even vertical lines (which cannot be written using slope-intercept or point-slope form equations). ◊

Checkpoint 3.7.3 For each of the following equations, identify what form they are in.

$2.7x + 3.4y = -82$	(□ slope-intercept	□ point-slope	□ standard	□ other linear	□ not linear)
$y = \frac{2}{7}(x - 3) + \frac{1}{10}$	(□ slope-intercept	□ point-slope	□ standard	□ other linear	□ not linear)
$12x - 3 = y + 2$	(□ slope-intercept	□ point-slope	□ standard	□ other linear	□ not linear)
$y = x^2 + 5$	(□ slope-intercept	□ point-slope	□ standard	□ other linear	□ not linear)
$x - y = 10$	(□ slope-intercept	□ point-slope	□ standard	□ other linear	□ not linear)
$y = 4x + 1$	(□ slope-intercept	□ point-slope	□ standard	□ other linear	□ not linear)

Explanation. $2.7x + 3.4y = -82$ is in standard form, with $A = 2.7$, $B = 3.4$, and $C = -82$.

$y = \frac{2}{7}(x - 3) + \frac{1}{10}$ is in point-slope form, with slope $\frac{2}{7}$, and passing through $\left(3, \frac{1}{10}\right)$.

$12x - 3 = y + 2$ is linear, but not in any of the forms we have studied. Using algebra, you can rearrange it to read $y = 12x - 5$.

$y = x^2 + 5$ is not linear. The exponent on x is a dead giveaway.

$x - y = 10$ is in standard form, with $A = 1$, $B = -1$, and $C = 10$.

$y = 4x + 1$ is in slope-intercept form, with slope 4 and y-intercept at $(0, 1)$.

Returning to the example with donations for the medical procedure, let's examine the equation

$$20x + 100y = 10000.$$

What units are attached to all of the parts of this equation? Both x and y are numbers of people. The 10000 is in dollars. Both the 20 and the 100 are in dollars per person. Note how both sides of the equation are in dollars. On the right, that fact is clear. On the left, $20x$ is in dollars since 20 is in dollars per person, and x is in people. The same is true for $100y$, and the two dollar amounts $20x$ and $100y$ add to a dollar amount.

What is the slope of the linear relationship? It's not immediately visible since m is not part of the standard form equation. But we can use algebra to isolate y:

$$20x + 100y = 10000$$
$$100y = -20x + 10000$$
$$y = \frac{-20x + 10000}{100}$$
$$y = \frac{-20x}{100} + \frac{10000}{100}$$
$$y = -\frac{1}{5}x + 100.$$

And we see that the slope is $-\frac{1}{5}$. OK, what units are on that slope? As always, the units on slope are $\frac{y\text{-unit}}{x\text{-unit}}$. In this case that's $\frac{\text{person}}{\text{person}}$, which sounds a little weird and seems like it should be simplified away to unitless. But this slope of $-\frac{1}{5}\frac{\text{person}}{\text{person}}$ is saying that for every 5 extra people who donate \$20 each, you need 1 fewer person donating \$100 to still reach your goal.

What is the y-intercept? Since we've already converted the equation into slope-intercept form, we can see that it is at $(0, 100)$. This tells us that if 0 people donate \$20, then you will need 100 people to each donate \$100.

What does a graph for this line look like? We've already converted into slope-intercept form, and we could use that to make the graph. But when given a line in standard form, there is another approach that is often used. Returning to

$$20x + 100y = 10000,$$

let's calculate the y-intercept and the x-intercept. Recall that these are *points* where the line crosses the y-axis and x-axis. To be on the y-axis means that $x = 0$, and to be on the x-axis means that $y = 0$. All these zeros make the resulting algebra easy to finish:

$$20x + 100y = 10000 \qquad\qquad 20x + 100y = 10000$$
$$20(0) + 100y = 10000 \qquad\qquad 20x + 100(0) = 10000$$
$$100y = 10000 \qquad\qquad 20x = 10000$$
$$y = \frac{10000}{100} \qquad\qquad x = \frac{10000}{20}$$
$$y = 100 \qquad\qquad x = 500$$

So we have a y-intercept at $(0, 100)$ and an x-intercept at $(500, 0)$. If we plot these, we get to mark especially relevant points given the context, and then drawing a straight line between them gives us Figure 3.7.4.

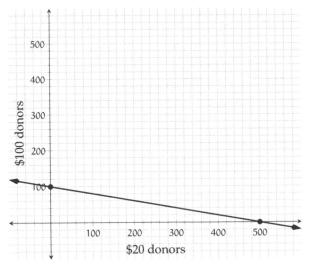

Figure 3.7.4

3.7.2 The x- and y-Intercepts

With a linear relationship (and other types of equations too), we are often interested in the x-intercept and y-intercept because they have special meaning in context. For example, in Figure 3.7.4, the x-intercept implies that if *no one* donates \$100, you need 500 people to donate \$20 to get us to \$10,000. And the y-intercept implies if *no one* donates \$20, you need 100 people to donate \$100. Let's look at another example.

Example 3.7.5 James owns a restaurant that uses about 32 lb of flour every day. He just purchased 1200 lb of flour. Model the amount of flour that remains x days later with a linear equation, and interpret the meaning of its x-intercept and y-intercept.

Since the rate of change is constant (-32 lb every day), and we know the initial value, we can model the amount of flour at the restaurant with a slope-intercept form (3.5.1) equation:

$$y = -32x + 1200$$

where x represents the number of days passed since the initial purchase, and y represents the amount of flour left (in lb.)

A line's x-intercept is in the form of $(x, 0)$, since to be on the x-axis, the y-coordinate must be 0. To find this line's x-intercept, we substitute y in the equation with 0, and solve for x:

$$y = -32x + 1200$$
$$0 = -32x + 1200$$
$$0 - 1200 = -32x$$
$$-1200 = -32x$$
$$\frac{-1200}{-32} = x$$
$$37.5 = x$$

So the line's x-intercept is at $(37.5, 0)$. In context this means the flour would last for 37.5 days.

A line's y-intercept is in the form of $(0, y)$. This line equation is already in slope-intercept form, so we can just see that its y-intercept is at $(0, 1200)$. In general though, we would substitute x in the equation with 0, and we have:

$$y = -32x + 1200$$
$$y = -32(0) + 1200$$
$$y = 1200$$

So yes, the line's y-intercept is at $(0, 1200)$. This means that when the flour was purchased, there was 1200 lb of it. In other words, the y-intercept tells us one of the original pieces of information: in the beginning, James purchased 1200 lb of flour.

If a line is in standard form, it's often easiest to graph it using its two intercepts.

Example 3.7.6 Graph $2x - 3y = -6$ using its intercepts. And then use the intercepts to calculate the line's slope.

Explanation. To graph a line by its x-intercept and y-intercept, it might help to first set up a table like in Figure 3.7.7:

	x-value	y-value	Intercepts
x-intercept		0	
y-intercept	0		

Figure 3.7.7: Intercepts of $2x - 3y = -6$

A table like this might help you stay focused on the fact that we are searching for *two* points. As we've noted earlier, an x-intercept is on the x-axis, and so its y-coordinate must be 0. This is worth taking special note of: to find an x-intercept, y must be 0. This is why we put 0 in the y-value cell of the x-intercept. Similarly, a line's y-intercept has $x = 0$, and we put 0 into the x-value cell of the y-intercept.

Next, we calculate the line's x-intercept by substituting $y = 0$ into the equation

$$2x - 3y = -6$$
$$2x - 3(0) = -6$$
$$2x = -6$$
$$x = -3$$

So the line's x-intercept is $(-3, 0)$.

Now we can complete the table:

Similarly, we substitute $x = 0$ into the equation to calculate the y-intercept:

$$2x - 3y = -6$$
$$2(0) - 3y = -6$$
$$-3y = -6$$
$$y = 2$$

So the line's y-intercept is $(0, 2)$.

	x-value	y-value	Intercepts
x-intercept	−3	0	$(-3, 0)$
y-intercept	0	2	$(0, 2)$

Figure 3.7.8: Intercepts of $2x - 3y = -6$

With both intercepts' coordinates, we can graph the line:

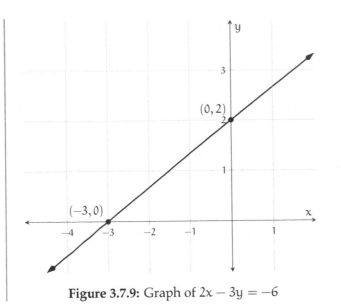

Figure 3.7.9: Graph of $2x - 3y = -6$

There is a slope triangle from the x-intercept to the origin up to the y-intercept. It tells us that the slope is

$$m = \frac{\Delta y}{\Delta x} = \frac{2}{3}.$$

This last example generalizes to a fact worth noting.

Fact 3.7.10 *If a line's x-intercept is at $(r, 0)$ and its y-intercept is at $(0, b)$, then the slope of the line is $-\frac{b}{r}$. (Unless the line passes through the origin, in which case both r and b equal 0, and then this fraction is undefined. And the slope of the line could be anything.)*

Checkpoint 3.7.11 Consider the line with equation $2x + 4.3y = \frac{1000}{99}$.

   a. What is its x-intercept?

   b. What is its y-intercept?

   c. What is its slope?

Explanation.

   a. To find the x-intercept:

$$2x + 4.3y = \frac{1000}{99}$$
$$2x + 4.3(0) = \frac{1000}{99}$$
$$2x = \frac{1000}{99}$$
$$x = \frac{500}{99}$$

So the x-intercept is at $\left(\frac{500}{99}, 0\right)$.

b. To find the y-intercept:

$$2x + 4.3y = \frac{1000}{99}$$

$$2(0) + 4.3y = \frac{1000}{99}$$

$$4.3y = \frac{1000}{99}$$

$$y = \frac{1}{4.3} \cdot \frac{1000}{99}$$

$$y \approx 2.349\ldots$$

So the y-intercept is at about $(0, 2.349)$.

c. Since we have the x- and y-intercepts, we can calculate the slope:

$$m \approx -\frac{2.349}{\frac{500}{99}} = -\frac{2.349 \cdot 99}{500} \approx -0.4561.$$

3.7.3 Transforming between Standard Form and Slope-Intercept Form

Sometimes a linear equation arises in standard form, but it would be useful to see that equation in slope-intercept form (3.5.1). Or perhaps, vice versa.

A linear equation in slope-intercept form (3.5.1) tells us important information about the line: its slope m and y-intercept $(0, b)$. However, a line's standard form does not show those two important values. As a result, we often need to change a line's equation from standard form to slope-intercept form. Let's look at some examples.

Example 3.7.12 Change $2x - 3y = -6$ to slope-intercept form, and then graph it.

Explanation.   Since a line in slope-intercept form looks like $y = \ldots$, we will solve for y in $2x - 3y = -6$:

$$2x - 3y = -6$$
$$-3y = -6 - 2x$$
$$-3y = -2x - 6$$
$$y = \frac{-2x - 6}{-3}$$
$$y = \frac{-2x}{-3} - \frac{6}{-3}$$
$$y = \frac{2}{3}x + 2$$

In the third line, we wrote $-2x - 6$ on the right side, instead of $-6 - 2x$. The only reason we did this is because we are headed to slope-intercept form, where the x-term is traditionally written first.

Now we can see that the slope is $\frac{2}{3}$ and the y-intercept is at $(0, 2)$. With these things found, we can graph the line using slope triangles.

Compare this graphing method with the Graphing by Intercepts method in Example 3.7.6. We have more points in this graph, thus we can graph the line more accurately.

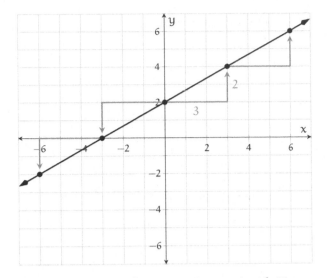

Figure 3.7.13: Graphing $2x - 3y = -6$ with Slope Triangles

Example 3.7.14 Graph $2x - 3y = 0$.

Explanation. First, we will try (and fail) to graph this line using its x- and y-intercepts.
   Trying to find the x-intercept:

$$2x - 3y = 0$$
$$2x - 3(0) = 0$$
$$2x = 0$$
$$x = 0$$

So the line's x-intercept is at $(0, 0)$, at the origin.
   Huh, that is *also* on the y-axis...
   Trying to find the y-intercept:

$$2x - 3y = 0$$
$$2(0) - 3y = 0$$
$$-3y = 0$$
$$y = 0$$

So the line's y-intercept is also at $(0, 0)$.
   Since both intercepts are the same point, there is no way to use the intercepts alone to graph this line. So what can be done?

Several approaches are out there, but one is to convert the line equation into slope-intercept form:

$$2x - 3y = 0$$
$$-3y = 0 - 2x$$
$$-3y = -2x$$
$$y = \frac{-2x}{-3}$$
$$y = \frac{2}{3}x$$

So the line's slope is $\frac{2}{3}$, and we can graph the line using slope triangles and the intercept at $(0, 0)$, as in Figure 3.7.15.

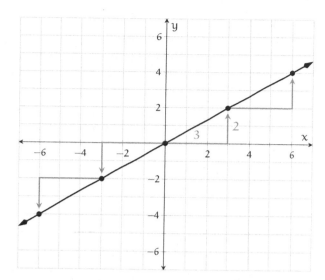

Figure 3.7.15: Graphing $2x - 3y = 0$ with Slope Triangles

In summary, if $C = 0$ in a standard form equation, it's convenient to graph it by first converting the equation to slope-intercept form (3.5.1).

Example 3.7.16 Write the equation $y = \frac{2}{3}x + 2$ in standard form.

Explanation. Once we subtract $\frac{2}{3}x$ on both sides of the equation, we have

$$-\frac{2}{3}x + y = 2$$

Technically, this equation is already in standard form $Ax + By = C$. However, you might like to end up with an equation that has no fractions, so you could multiply each side by 3:

$$3 \cdot \left(-\frac{2}{3}x + y\right) = 3 \cdot 2$$
$$-x + 3y = 6$$

3.7.4 Reading Questions

1. What kind of line can be written in standard form, but cannot be written in slope-intercept or point-slope form?

2. What are some reasons why you might care to find the x- and y-intercepts of a line?

3. What is not immediately apparent from standard form, that *is* immediately apparent from slope-intercept form and point-slope form?

3.7.5 Exercises

Review and Warmup Solve the linear equation for y.

   1. $24x + 3y = 54$ **2.** $12x - 4y = -28$ **3.** $-3x - y = 17$

   4. $-5x - y = -9$ **5.** $6x - 9y = 6$ **6.** $9x - 2y = -1$

Slope and y-intercept Find the line's slope and y-intercept.

   7.   A line has equation $-3x + y = 4$.

   This line's slope is [   ].

   This line's y-intercept is [   ].

   8.   A line has equation $-x - y = -6$.

   This line's slope is [   ].

   This line's y-intercept is [   ].

   9.   A line has equation $15x + 3y = -9$.

   This line's slope is [   ].

   This line's y-intercept is [   ].

   10.   A line has equation $12x - 3y = 6$.

   This line's slope is [   ].

   This line's y-intercept is [   ].

   11.   A line has equation $x + 4y = -8$.

   This line's slope is [   ].

   This line's y-intercept is [   ].

   12.   A line has equation $5x + 6y = 30$.

   This line's slope is [   ].

   This line's y-intercept is [   ].

   13.   A line has equation $6x - 7y = 28$.

   This line's slope is [   ].

   This line's y-intercept is [   ].

   14.   A line has equation $18x + 15y = 15$.

   This line's slope is [   ].

   This line's y-intercept is [   ].

   15.   A line has equation $4x - 24y = 0$.

   This line's slope is [   ].

   This line's y-intercept is [   ].

   16.   A line has equation $2x - 8y = 0$.

   This line's slope is [   ].

   This line's y-intercept is [   ].

   17.   A line has equation $6x + 9y = 4$.

   This line's slope is [   ].

   This line's y-intercept is [   ].

   18.   A line has equation $12x + 8y = 5$.

   This line's slope is [   ].

   This line's y-intercept is [   ].

Converting to Standard Form

   19.   Rewrite $y = 5x - 2$ in standard form.   **20.**   Rewrite $y = 6x - 7$ in standard form.

   21.   Rewrite $y = \frac{7}{8}x - 5$ in standard form.   **22.**   Rewrite $y = -\frac{8}{5}x + 3$ in standard form.

Graphs and Standard Form

   23.   Find the y-intercept and x-intercept of the line given by the equation. If a particular intercept does not exist, enter none into all the answer blanks for that row.

$$7x + 2y = 14$$

	x-value	y-value	Location (as an ordered pair)
y-intercept	_____	_____	_____
x-intercept	_____	_____	_____

24. Find the y-intercept and x-intercept of the line given by the equation. If a particular intercept does not exist, enter none into all the answer blanks for that row.

$$2x + 7y = -28$$

	x-value	y-value	Location (as an ordered pair)
y-intercept	_____	_____	_____
x-intercept	_____	_____	_____

25. Find the y-intercept and x-intercept of the line given by the equation. If a particular intercept does not exist, enter none into all the answer blanks for that row.

$$2x - 5y = -30$$

	x-value	y-value	Location (as an ordered pair)
y-intercept	_____	_____	_____
x-intercept	_____	_____	_____

26. Find the y-intercept and x-intercept of the line given by the equation. If a particular intercept does not exist, enter none into all the answer blanks for that row.

$$x - 3y = -3$$

	x-value	y-value	Location (as an ordered pair)
y-intercept	_____	_____	_____
x-intercept	_____	_____	_____

27. Find the x- and y-intercepts of the line with equation $4x + 6y = 24$. Then find one other point on the line. Use your results to graph the line.

28. Find the x- and y-intercepts of the line with equation $4x + 5y = -40$. Then find one other point on the line. Use your results to graph the line.

29. Find the x- and y-intercepts of the line with equation $5x - 2y = 10$. Then find one other point on the line. Use your results to graph the line.

30. Find the x- and y-intercepts of the line with equation $5x - 6y = -90$. Then find one other point on the line. Use your results to graph the line.

31. Find the x- and y-intercepts of the line with equation $x + 5y = -15$. Then find one other point on the line. Use your results to graph the line.

32. Find the x- and y-intercepts of the line with equation $6x + y = -18$. Then find one other point on the line. Use your results to graph the line.

33. Make a graph of the line $x + y = 2$.

34. Make a graph of the line $-5x - y = -3$.

35. Make a graph of the line $x + 5y = 5$.

36. Make a graph of the line $x - 2y = 2$.

37. Make a graph of the line $20x - 4y = 8$.

38. Make a graph of the line $3x + 5y = 10$.

39. Make a graph of the line $-3x + 2y = 6$.

40. Make a graph of the line $-4x - 5y = 10$.

41. Make a graph of the line $4x - 5y = 0$.

42. Make a graph of the line $5x + 7y = 0$.

Interpreting Intercepts in Context

43. Kara is buying some tea bags and some sugar bags. Each tea bag costs 8 cents, and each sugar bag costs 3 cents. She can spend a total of $3.60.

    Assume Kara will purchase x tea bags and y sugar bags. Use a linear equation to model the number of tea bags and sugar bags she can purchase.

    Find this line's x-intercept, and interpret its meaning in this context.

    ⊙ *A*. The x-intercept is (0, 120). It implies Kara can purchase 120 sugar bags with no tea bags.

    ⊙ *B*. The x-intercept is (0,45). It implies Kara can purchase 45 sugar bags with no tea bags.

    ⊙ *C*. The x-intercept is (45,0). It implies Kara can purchase 45 tea bags with no sugar bags.

    ⊙ *D*. The x-intercept is (120,0). It implies Kara can purchase 120 tea bags with no sugar bags.

44. Corey is buying some tea bags and some sugar bags. Each tea bag costs 6 cents, and each sugar bag costs 5 cents. He can spend a total of $1.50.

    Assume Corey will purchase x tea bags and y sugar bags. Use a linear equation to model the number of tea bags and sugar bags he can purchase.

    Find this line's y-intercept, and interpret its meaning in this context.

    ⊙ *A*. The y-intercept is (0, 30). It implies Corey can purchase 30 sugar bags with no tea bags.

    ⊙ *B*. The y-intercept is (0,25). It implies Corey can purchase 25 sugar bags with no tea bags.

    ⊙ *C*. The y-intercept is (30,0). It implies Corey can purchase 30 tea bags with no sugar bags.

    ⊙ *D*. The y-intercept is (25,0). It implies Corey can purchase 25 tea bags with no sugar bags.

45. An engine's tank can hold 60 gallons of gasoline. It was refilled with a full tank, and has been running without breaks, consuming 3 gallons of gas per hour.

    Assume the engine has been running for x hours since its tank was refilled, and assume there are y gallons of gas left in the tank. Use a linear equation to model the amount of gas in the tank as time passes.

    Find this line's x-intercept, and interpret its meaning in this context.

    ⊙ *A*. The x-intercept is (60,0). It implies the engine will run out of gas 60 hours after its tank was refilled.

    ⊙ *B*. The x-intercept is (20,0). It implies the engine will run out of gas 20 hours after its tank was refilled.

    ⊙ *C*. The x-intercept is (0,20). It implies the engine started with 20 gallons of gas in its tank.

    ⊙ *D*. The x-intercept is (0,60). It implies the engine started with 60 gallons of gas in its tank.

46. An engine's tank can hold 100 gallons of gasoline. It was refilled with a full tank, and has been running without breaks, consuming 2.5 gallons of gas per hour.

    Assume the engine has been running for x hours since its tank was refilled, and assume there are y gallons of gas left in the tank. Use a linear equation to model the amount of gas in the tank as time passes.

Find this line's y-intercept, and interpret its meaning in this context.

⊙ **A.** The y-intercept is (100,0). It implies the engine will run out of gas 100 hours after its tank was refilled.

⊙ **B.** The y-intercept is (0,40). It implies the engine started with 40 gallons of gas in its tank.

⊙ **C.** The y-intercept is (0,100). It implies the engine started with 100 gallons of gas in its tank.

⊙ **D.** The y-intercept is (40,0). It implies the engine will run out of gas 40 hours after its tank was refilled.

47. A new car of a certain model costs \$46,800.00. According to Blue Book, its value decreases by \$2,600.00 every year.

Assume x years since its purchase, the car's value is y dollars. Use a linear equation to model the car's value.

Find this line's x-intercept, and interpret its meaning in this context.

⊙ **A.** The x-intercept is (0,18). It implies the car would have no more value 18 years since its purchase.

⊙ **B.** The x-intercept is (46800,0). It implies the car's initial value was 46800.

⊙ **C.** The x-intercept is (18,0). It implies the car would have no more value 18 years since its purchase.

⊙ **D.** The x-intercept is (0,46800). It implies the car's initial value was 46800.

48. A new car of a certain model costs \$65,000.00. According to Blue Book, its value decreases by \$2,600.00 every year.

Assume x years since its purchase, the car's value is y dollars. Use a linear equation to model the car's value.

Find this line's y-intercept, and interpret its meaning in this context.

⊙ **A.** The y-intercept is (65000,0). It implies the car's initial value was 65000.

⊙ **B.** The y-intercept is (25,0). It implies the car would have no more value 25 years since its purchase.

⊙ **C.** The y-intercept is (0,65000). It implies the car's initial value was 65000.

⊙ **D.** The y-intercept is (0,25). It implies the car would have no more value 25 years since its purchase.

Challenge

49. Fill in the variables A, B, and C in $Ax + By = C$ with the numbers 10, 11 and 14. You may only use each number once.

a. For the steepest possible slope, A must be ⬚, B must be ⬚, and C must be ⬚.

b. For the shallowest possible slope, A must be ⬚, B must be ⬚, and C must be ⬚.

3.8 Horizontal, Vertical, Parallel, and Perpendicular Lines

The equations of horizontal and vertical lines distinguish them from other line equations enough to merit a special investigation. In addition, pairs of lines that are parallel or perpendicular to each other have interesting features and properties. This section examines the geometric features of these types of lines.

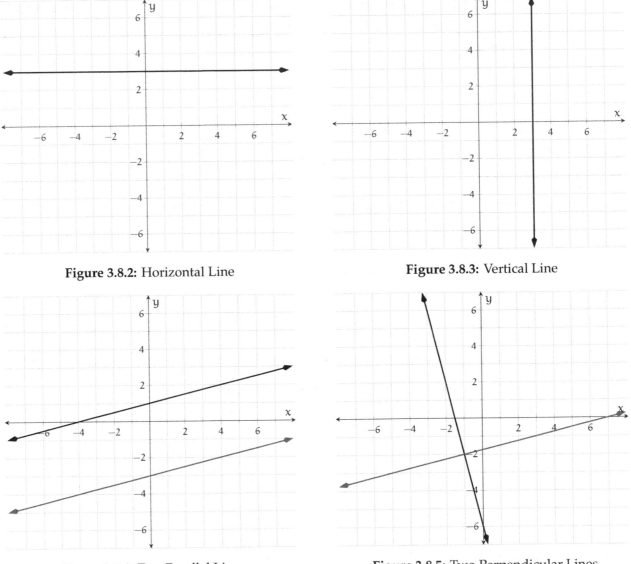

Figure 3.8.2: Horizontal Line

Figure 3.8.3: Vertical Line

Figure 3.8.4: Two Parallel Lines

Figure 3.8.5: Two Perpendicular Lines

3.8.1 Horizontal Lines and Vertical Lines

We learned in Section 3.7 that all lines can be written in standard form (3.7.1). When either A or B equal 0, we end up with a horizontal or vertical line, as we will soon see. Let's take the standard form line equation,

$Ax + Bx = C$, and one at a time let $A = 0$ and $B = 0$ and simplify each equation.

$$Ax + By = C$$
$$0x + By = C$$
$$By = C$$
$$y = \frac{C}{B}$$
$$y = k$$

$$Ax + By = C$$
$$Ax + 0y = C$$
$$Ax = C$$
$$x = \frac{C}{A}$$
$$x = h$$

At the end we just renamed the constant numbers $\frac{C}{B}$ and $\frac{C}{A}$ to k and h because of tradition. What is important, is that you view h and k (as well as A, B, and C) as constants: numbers that have some specific value and don't change in the context of one problem.

Think about one of these equations: $y = k$. It says that the y value is the same no matter where you are on the line. If you wanted to plot points on this line, you are free to move far to the left or far to the right on the x-axis, but then you always move up (or down) to make the y-value equal k. What does such a line look like?

Example 3.8.6
Let's plot the line with equation $y = 3$. (Note that this is the same as $0x + 1y = 3$.) To plot some points, it doesn't matter what x-values we use. All that matters is that y is *always* 3.

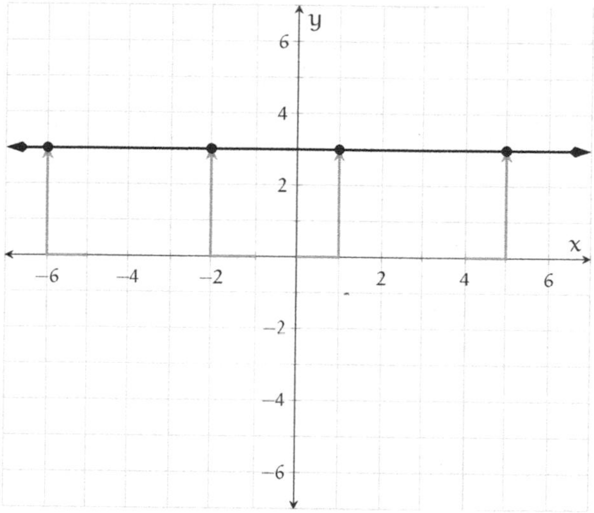

Figure 3.8.7: $y = 3$

A line like this is **horizontal**, parallel to the horizontal axis. All lines with an equation in the form

$$y = k$$

(or, in standard form, $0x + By = C$) are **horizontal**.

Example 3.8.8
Let's plot the line with equation $x = 5$. Points on the line always have $x = 5$, so if we wanted to make a table for plotting points, we are *required* to make all of the x-values be 5. From there, we have complete freedom to let y take any value. Here we take some random y-values.

x	y
5	−6
5	−2
5	1
5	5

These points are plotted in Figure 3.8.9.

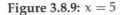

Figure 3.8.9: $x = 5$

Note that the equation for this line is the same as $x + 0y = 5$. An alternative for making a table is to choose our y-values first and substitute them into the equation.

y	$x + 0y = 5 \implies x = 5$	Ordered Pair
−6	$x + 0(−6) = 5 \implies x = 5$	$(5, −6)$
−2	$x + 0(−2) = 5 \implies x = 5$	$(5, −2)$
1	$x + 0(1) = 5 \implies x = 5$	$(5, 1)$
5	$x + 0(5) = 5 \implies x = 5$	$(5, 5)$

In each case no matter what value y is, we find that the equation tells us that $x = 5$.

A line like this is **vertical**, parallel to the vertical axis. All lines with an equation in the form

$$x = h$$

(or, in standard form, $Ax + 0y = C$) are vertical.

Example 3.8.10 Zero Slope. In Checkpoint 3.4.17, we learned that a horizontal line's slope is 0, because the distance doesn't change as time moves on. So the numerator in the slope formula (3.4.3) is 0. Now, if we know a line's slope and its y-intercept, we can use slope-intercept form (3.5.1) to write its equation:

$$y = mx + b$$
$$y = 0x + b$$
$$y = b$$

This provides us with an alternative way to think about equations of horizontal lines. They have a certain y-intercept b, and they have slope 0.

We use horizontal lines to model scenarios where there is no change in y-values, like when Kato stopped for 12 hours (he deserved a rest)!

Checkpoint 3.8.11 Plotting Points. Suppose you need to plot the equation $y = -4.25$. Since the equation is in "$y =$" form, you decide to make a table of points. Fill out some points for this table.

x	y

Explanation. We can use whatever values for x that we like, as long as they are all different. The equation tells us the y-value has to be -4.25 each time.

x	y
-2	-4.25
-1	-4.25
0	-4.25
1	-4.25
2	-4.25

Now that we have a table, we could use its values to assist with plotting the line.

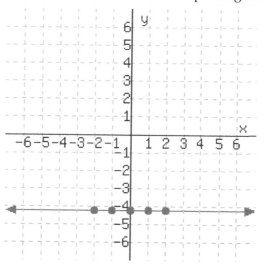

Example 3.8.12 Slope of a Vertical Line. What is the slope of a vertical line? Figure 3.8.13 shows three lines passing through the origin, each steeper than the last. In each graph, you can see a slope triangle that uses a "run" of 1 unit.

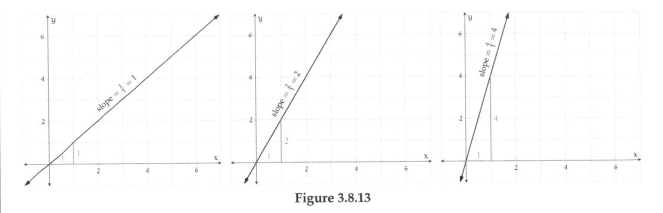

Figure 3.8.13

If we continued making the line steeper and steeper until it was vertical, the slope triangle would still have a "run" of 1, but the "rise" would become larger and larger with no upper limit. The slope would be $m = \frac{\text{very large}}{1}$. Actually if the line is vertical, the "rise" segment we've drawn, will never intercept the line. So the slope of a vertical line can be thought of as "infinitely large." We usually say that the slope of a vertical line is *undefined*. Some people say that a vertical line *has no slope*.

Fact 3.8.14 *The slope of a vertical line is undefined.*

Remark 3.8.15 Be careful not to mix up "no slope" (which means "its slope is undefined") with "has slope 0." If a line has slope 0, it *does* have a slope.

If you are familiar with NBA basketball, some players wear number 0. That's not the same thing as "not having a number". This is similar to the situation with having slope 0 versus not having slope.

Checkpoint 3.8.16 Plotting Points. Suppose you need to plot the equation $x = 3.14$. You decide to try making a table of points. Fill out some points for this table.

x	y
_____	_____
_____	_____
_____	_____
_____	_____
_____	_____

Explanation.   Since the equation says x is always the number 3.14, we have to use this for the x value in all the points. This is different from how we would plot a "$y =$" equation, where we would use several different x-values. We can use whatever values for y that we like, as long as they are all different.

x	y
3.14	−2
3.14	−1
3.14	0
3.14	1
3.14	2

The reason we made a table was to help with plotting the line.

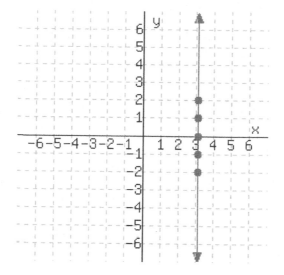

Example 3.8.17 Let x represent the price of a new 60-inch television at Target on Black Friday (which was $650), and let y be the number of hours you will watch something on this TV over its lifetime. What is the relationship between x and y?

Well, there is no getting around the fact that x = 650. As for y, without any extra information about your viewing habits, it could theoretically be as low as 0 or it could be anything larger than that. If we graph this scenario, we have to graph the equation x = 650 which we now know to give a vertical line, and we get Figure 3.8.18.

Figure 3.8.18: New TV: hours watched versus purchase price; negative y-values omitted since they make no sense in context

Horizontal Lines	Vertical Lines
A line is **horizontal** if and only if its equation can be written $$y = k$$ for some constant k.	A line is **vertical** if and only if its equation can be written $$x = h$$ for some constant h.
In standard form (3.7.1), any line with equation $$0x + By = C$$ is horizontal.	In standard form (3.7.1), any line with equation $$Ax + 0y = C$$ is vertical.
If the line with equation $y = k$ is horizontal, it has a y-intercept at $(0, k)$ and has slope 0.	If the line with equation $x = h$ is vertical, it has an x-intercept at $(h, 0)$ and its slope is *undefined*. Some say it has *no* slope, and some say the slope is *infinitely large*.
In the slope-intercept form (3.5.1), any line with equation $$y = 0x + b$$ is horizontal.	It's impossible to write the equation of a vertical line in slope-intercept form (3.5.1), because vertical lines do not have a defined slope.

Figure 3.8.19: Summary of Horizontal and Vertical Line Equations

3.8.2 Parallel Lines

Example 3.8.20

Two trees were planted in the same year, and their growth over time is modeled by the two lines in Figure 3.8.21. Use linear equations to model each tree's growth, and interpret their meanings in this context.

We can see Tree 1's equation is $y = \frac{2}{3}x + 2$, and Tree 2's equation is $y = \frac{2}{3}x + 5$. Tree 1 was 2 feet tall when it was planted, and Tree 2 was 5 feet tall when it was planted. Both trees have been growing at the same rate, $\frac{2}{3}$ feet per year, or 2 feet every 3 years.

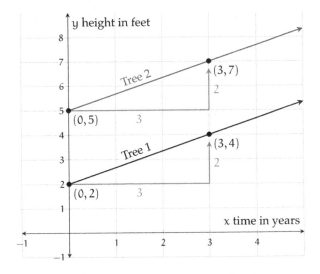

Figure 3.8.21: Two Trees' Growth Chart

An important observation right now is that those two lines are parallel. Why? For lines with positive slopes, the bigger a line's slope, the steeper the line is slanted. As a result, if two lines have the same slope, they are slanted at the same angle, thus they are parallel.

Fact 3.8.22 *Any two vertical lines are parallel to each other. For two non-vertical lines, they are parallel if and only if they have the same slope.*

Checkpoint 3.8.23 A line ℓ is parallel to the line with equation $y = 17.2x - 340.9$, but ℓ has y-intercept at $(0, 128.2)$. What is an equation for ℓ?

Explanation.   Parallel lines have the same slope, and the slope of $y = 17.2x - 340.9$ is 17.2. So ℓ has slope 17.2. And we have been given that ℓ's y-intercept is at $(0, 128.2)$. So we can use slope-intercept form to write its equation as

$$y = 17.2x + 128.2.$$

Checkpoint 3.8.24 A line κ is parallel to the line with equation $y = -3.5x + 17$, but κ passes through the point $(-12, 23)$. What is an equation for κ?

Explanation.   Parallel lines have the same slope, and the slope of $y = -3.5x + 17$ is -3.5. So κ has slope -3.5. And we know a point that κ passes through, so we can use point-slope form to write its equation as

$$y = -3.5(x + 12) + 23.$$

3.8.3 Perpendicular Lines

The slopes of two perpendicular lines have a special relationship too.
    Figure 3.8.25 walks you through an explanation of this relationship.

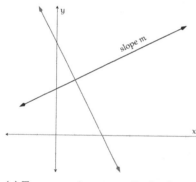 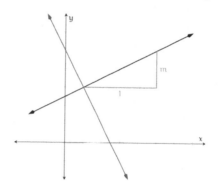 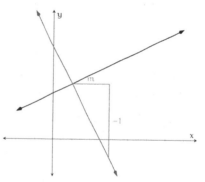

(a) Two generic perpendicular lines, where one has slope m.

(b) Since the one slope is m, we can draw a slope triangle with "run" 1 and "rise" m.

(c) A *congruent* slope triangle can be drawn for the perpendicular line. It's legs have the same lengths, but in different positions, and one is negative.

Figure 3.8.25: The relationship between slopes of perpendicular lines

The second line in Figure 3.8.25 has slope

$$\frac{\Delta y}{\Delta x} = \frac{-1}{m} = -\frac{1}{m}.$$

Fact 3.8.26 *A vertical line and a horizontal line are perpendicular. For two lines that are neither vertical nor horizontal, they are perpendicular if and only if the slope of one is the negative reciprocal of the slope of the other. That is, if one has slope m, the other has slope $-\frac{1}{m}$.*

Another way to say this is that the product of the slopes of two perpendicular lines is -1 (assuming both of the lines have a slope in the first place). That is, if there are two perpendicular lines and we let m_1 and m_2 represent their slopes, then $m_1 \cdot m_2 = -1$.

Not convinced? Here are three pairs of perpendicular lines where we can see if the pattern holds.

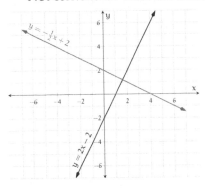
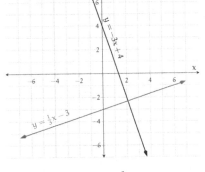
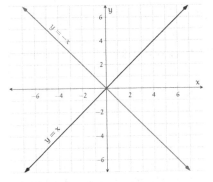

Figure 3.8.27: Graphing $y = 2x - 2$ and $y = -\frac{1}{2}x + 2$. Note the relationship between their slopes: $2 = -\frac{1}{-1/2}$

Figure 3.8.28: Graphing $y = -3x + 4$ and $y = \frac{1}{3}x - 3$. Note the relationship between their slopes: $-3 = -\frac{1}{1/3}$

Figure 3.8.29: Graphing $y = x$ and $y = -x$. Note the relationship between their slopes: $1 = -\frac{1}{-1}$

Example 3.8.30 Line A passes through $(-2, 10)$ and $(3, -10)$. Line B passes through $(-4, -4)$ and $(8, -1)$. Determine whether these two lines are parallel, perpendicular or neither.

Explanation.   We will use the slope formula to find both lines' slopes:

$$
\begin{aligned}
\text{Line A's slope} &= \frac{y_2 - y_1}{x_2 - x_1} & \qquad \text{Line B's slope} &= \frac{y_2 - y_1}{x_2 - x_1} \\
&= \frac{-10 - 10}{3 - (-2)} & &= \frac{-1 - (-4)}{8 - (-4)} \\
&= \frac{-20}{5} & &= \frac{3}{12} \\
&= -4 & &= \frac{1}{4}
\end{aligned}
$$

Their slopes are not the same, so those two lines are not parallel.

The product of their slopes is $(-4) \cdot \frac{1}{4} = -1$, which means the two lines are perpendicular.

Checkpoint 3.8.31 Line A and Line B are perpendicular. Line A's equation is $2x + 3y = 12$. Line B passes through the point $(4, -3)$. Find an equation for Line B.

Explanation. First, we will find Line A's slope by rewriting its equation from standard form to slope-intercept form:

$$2x + 3y = 12$$
$$3y = 12 - 2x$$
$$3y = -2x + 12$$
$$y = \frac{-2x + 12}{3}$$
$$y = -\frac{2}{3}x + 4$$

So Line A's slope is $-\frac{2}{3}$. Since Line B is perpendicular to Line A, its slope is $-\frac{1}{-\frac{2}{3}} = \frac{3}{2}$. It's also given that Line B passes through $(4, -3)$, so we can write Line B's point-slope form equation:

$$y = m(x - x_0) + y_0$$
$$y = \frac{3}{2}(x - 4) - 3$$

3.8.4 Reading Questions

1. Explain the difference between a line that has no slope and a line that has slope 0.

2. If you make a table of x- and y-values for either a horizontal line or a vertical line, what is going to happen in one of the two columns?

3. If you know two points on one line, and you know two points on a second line, what could you do to determine whether or not the two lines are perpendicular?

3.8.5 Exercises

Review and Warmup

1. Evaluate the following expressions. If the answer is undefined, you may answer with DNE (meaning "does not exist").

    a. $\dfrac{7}{0}$

    b. $\dfrac{0}{7}$

2. Evaluate the following expressions. If the answer is undefined, you may answer with DNE (meaning "does not exist").

    a. $\dfrac{0}{8}$

    b. $\dfrac{8}{0}$

3. A line passes through the points $(5, 8)$ and $(-3, 8)$. Find this line's slope.

4. A line passes through the points $(3, 10)$ and $(-1, 10)$. Find this line's slope.

5. A line passes through the points $(-8, -5)$ and $(-8, 3)$. Find this line's slope.

6. A line passes through the points $(-6, -1)$ and $(-6, 5)$. Find this line's slope.

7. Consider the equation:

$$y = 1$$

Which of the following ordered pairs are solutions to the given equation? There may be more than one correct answer.

☐ (4, 1)   ☐ (−4, 1)
☐ (0, 7)   ☐ (1, 4)

8. Consider the equation:

$$y = 1$$

Which of the following ordered pairs are solutions to the given equation? There may be more than one correct answer.

☐ (−6, 1)   ☐ (5, 1)
☐ (0, 9)   ☐ (1, 2)

9. Consider the equation:

$$x + 1 = 0$$

Which of the following ordered pairs are solutions to the given equation? There may be more than one correct answer.

☐ (−1, 0)   ☐ (−1, 3)
☐ (0, −6)   ☐ (1, −1)

10. Consider the equation:

$$x + 1 = 0$$

Which of the following ordered pairs are solutions to the given equation? There may be more than one correct answer.

☐ (1, −1)   ☐ (−1, 0)
☐ (0, −8)   ☐ (−1, 4)

Tables for Horizontal and Vertical Lines

11. Fill out this table for the equation $y = 8$. The first row is an example.

x	y	Points
−3	8	(−3, 8)
−2	___	___
−1	___	___
0	___	___
1	___	___
2	___	___

12. Fill out this table for the equation $y = 9$. The first row is an example.

x	y	Points
−3	9	(−3, 9)
−2	___	___
−1	___	___
0	___	___
1	___	___
2	___	___

13. Fill out this table for the equation $x = -1$. The first row is an example.

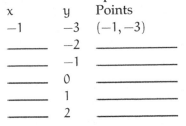

x	y	Points
−1	−3	(−1, −3)
___	−2	___
___	−1	___
___	0	___
___	1	___
___	2	___

14. Fill out this table for the equation $x = -9$. The first row is an example.

x	y	Points
−9	−3	(−9, −3)
___	−2	___
___	−1	___
___	0	___
___	1	___
___	2	___

Line Equations A line's graph is shown. Write an equation for the line.

15.

16.

17.

18.

19. A line passes through the points $(-2, 3)$ and $(-3, 3)$. Find an equation for this line.
An equation for this line is

.

20. A line passes through the points $(5, 6)$ and $(2, 6)$. Find an equation for this line.
An equation for this line is

.

21. A line passes through the points $(8, 1)$ and $(8, -5)$. Find an equation for this line.
An equation for this line is

22. A line passes through the points $(10, -3)$ and $(10, 0)$. Find an equation for this line.
An equation for this line is

.

Intercepts

23. Find the y-intercept and x-intercept of the line given by the equation. If a particular intercept does not exist, enter none into all the answer blanks for that row.

$$x = -8$$

	x-value	y-value	Location
y-intercept	_____	_____	_____
x-intercept	_____	_____	_____

24. Find the y-intercept and x-intercept of the line given by the equation. If a particular intercept does not exist, enter none into all the answer blanks for that row.

$$x = -6$$

	x-value	y-value	Location
y-intercept	_____	_____	_____
x-intercept	_____	_____	_____

25. Find the y-intercept and x-intercept of the line given by the equation. If a particular intercept does not exist, enter none into all the answer blanks for that row.

$$y = -4$$

	x-value	y-value	Location
y-intercept	_____	_____	_____
x-intercept	_____	_____	_____

26. Find the y-intercept and x-intercept of the line given by the equation. If a particular intercept does not exist, enter none into all the answer blanks for that row.

$$y = -1$$

	x-value	y-value	Location
y-intercept	_____	_____	_____
x-intercept	_____	_____	_____

Graphs of Horizontal and Vertical Lines

27. Graph the line $y = 1$.

28. Graph the line $y + 5 = 0$.

29. Graph the line $x = 2$.

30. Graph the line $x - 3 = 0$.

Parallel or Perpendicular?

31. Line m passes points $(1, 3)$ and $(-3, -9)$.
Line n passes points $(5, 20)$ and $(4, 17)$.
These two lines are   ($\square$ parallel
$\square$ perpendicular $\square$ neither parallel nor perpendicular) .

32. Line m passes points $(-21, 28)$ and $(-7, 16)$.
Line n passes points $(-35, 33)$ and $(7, -3)$.
These two linea are   ($\square$ parallel
$\square$ perpendicular $\square$ neither parallel nor perpendicular) .

33. Line m passes points $(-5, 8)$ and $(5, 6)$.
Line n passes points $(-4, -16)$ and $(2, 14)$.
These two lines are   ($\square$ parallel
$\square$ perpendicular $\square$ neither parallel nor perpendicular) .

34. Line m passes points $(-5, 15)$ and $(5, -1)$.
Line n passes points $(-16, 0)$ and $(-24, -5)$.
These two lines are   ($\square$ parallel
$\square$ perpendicular $\square$ neither parallel nor perpendicular) .

35. Line m passes points $(-3, -5)$ and $(-4, -4)$.
Line n passes points $(-2, -9)$ and $(1, 3)$.
These two lines are   ($\square$ parallel
$\square$ perpendicular $\square$ neither parallel nor perpendicular) .

36. Line m passes points $(6, -8)$ and $(4, -8)$.
Line n passes points $(3, 7)$ and $(10, 7)$.
These two lines are   ($\square$ parallel
$\square$ perpendicular $\square$ neither parallel nor perpendicular) .

37. Line m passes points $(-6, -2)$ and $(-6, -9)$.
Line n passes points $(1, 3)$ and $(1, -1)$.
These two lines are   ($\square$ parallel
$\square$ perpendicular $\square$ neither parallel nor perpendicular) .

38. Line m passes points $(-4, -9)$ and $(-4, 0)$.
Line n passes points $(3, 10)$ and $(3, 1)$.
These two lines are   ($\square$ parallel
$\square$ perpendicular $\square$ neither parallel nor perpendicular) .

Parallel and Perpendicular Line Equations

39. A line passes through the point $(9, 5)$, and it's parallel to the line $y = -2$. Find an equation for this line.

40. A line passes through the point $(-3, -2)$, and it's parallel to the line $y = 1$. Find an equation for this line.

41. A line passes through the point $(-10, 5)$, and it's parallel to the line $x = 3$. Find an equation for this line.

42. A line passes through the point $(4, -7)$, and it's parallel to the line $x = 5$. Find an equation for this line.

43. Line k has the equation $y = 4x - 2$.
Line ℓ is parallel to line k, but passes
through the point $(4, 18)$.
Find an equation for line ℓ in both
point-slope form and slope-intercept form.
An equation for ℓ in point-slope form is:

[ ]

An equation for ℓ in slope-intercept form is:

[ ]

44. Line k has the equation $y = 5x + 5$.
Line ℓ is parallel to line k, but passes
through the point $(1, -5)$.
Find an equation for line ℓ in both
point-slope form and slope-intercept form.
An equation for ℓ in point-slope form is:

[ ]

An equation for ℓ in slope-intercept form is:

[ ]

45. Line k has the equation $y = -\frac{1}{7}x - 3$.
Line ℓ is parallel to line k, but passes
through the point $(-2, -\frac{5}{7})$.
Find an equation for line ℓ in both
point-slope form and slope-intercept form.
An equation for ℓ in point-slope form is:

[ ]

An equation for ℓ in slope-intercept form is:

[ ]

46. Line k has the equation $y = -\frac{2}{9}x + 10$.
Line ℓ is parallel to line k, but passes
through the point $(3, -\frac{11}{3})$.
Find an equation for line ℓ in both
point-slope form and slope-intercept form.
An equation for ℓ in point-slope form is:

[ ]

An equation for ℓ in slope-intercept form is:

[ ]

47. Line k has the equation $y = -x + 9$.
Line ℓ is perpendicular to line k, and passes
through the point $(-1, -4)$.
Find an equation for line ℓ.

48. Line k has the equation $y = 4x + 2$.
Line ℓ is perpendicular to line k and passes
through the point $(2, \frac{9}{2})$.
Find an equation for line ℓ in both
point-slope form and slope-intercept form.
An equation for ℓ in point-slope form is:

[ ]

An equation for ℓ in slope-intercept form is:

[ ]

49. Line k's equation is $y = -\frac{6}{5}x - 3$.
Line ℓ is perpendicular to line k and passes
through the point $(2, \frac{14}{3})$.
Find an equation for line ℓ in both
point-slope form and slope-intercept form.
An equation for ℓ in point-slope form is:

[ ]

An equation for ℓ in slope-intercept form is:

[ ]

50. Line k has the equation $x - 9y = -45$.
Line ℓ is perpendicular to line k and passes
through the point $(1, -8)$.
Find an equation for line ℓ in both
point-slope form and slope-intercept form.
An equation for ℓ in point-slope form is:

[ ]

An equation for ℓ in slope-intercept form is:

[ ]

Challenge

51. Prove that a triangle with vertices at the points $(1, 1)$, $(-4, 4)$, and $(-3, 0)$ is a right triangle.

3.9 Summary of Graphing Lines

The previous several sections have demonstrated several methods for plotting a graph of a linear equation. In this section, we review these methods.

We have learned three forms to write a linear equation:

- slope-intercept form

$$y = mx + b$$

- point-slope form

$$y = m(x - x_0) + y_0$$

- standard form

$$Ax + By = C$$

We have studied two special types of line:

- horizontal line

$$y = k$$

- vertical line

$$x = h$$

We have practiced three ways to graph a line:

- building a table of x- and y-values

- plotting *one* point (often the y-intercept) and drawing slope triangles

- plotting its x-intercept and y-intercept

3.9.1 Graphing Lines in Slope-Intercept Form

In the following examples we will graph $y = -2x + 1$, which is in slope-intercept form (3.5.1), with different methods and compare them.

Example 3.9.2 Building a Table of x- and y-values. First, we will graph $y = -2x + 1$ by building a table of values. In theory this method can be used for any type of equation, linear or not.

x-value	y-value	Point
−2	$y = -2(-2) + 1 = 5$	$(-2, 5)$
−1	$y = -2(-1) + 1 = 3$	$(-1, 3)$
0	$y = -2(0) + 1 = 1$	$(0, 1)$
1	$y = -2(1) + 1 = -1$	$(1, -1)$
2	$y = -2(2) + 1 = -3$	$(2, -3)$

Figure 3.9.3: Table for $y = -2x + 1$

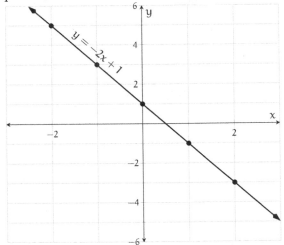

Figure 3.9.4: Graphing $y = -2x + 1$ using a table of values

Example 3.9.5 Using Slope Triangles. Although making a table is straightforward, the slope triangle method is faster and reinforces the true meaning of slope. With the slope triangle method, we first identify some point on the line. Given a line in slope-intercept form (3.5.1), we know the y-intercept. For the line $y = 2x + 1$, the y-intercept is $(0, 1)$. Plot this first, and then we can draw slope triangles in both directions to find more points.

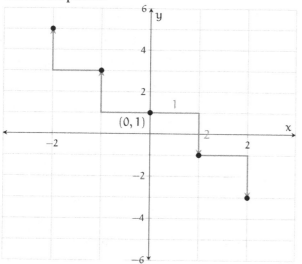

Figure 3.9.6: Marking a point and some slope triangles

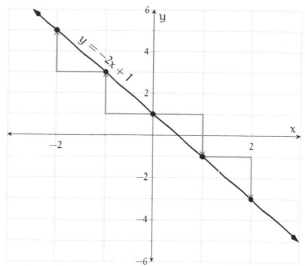

Figure 3.9.7: Graphing $y = -2x + 1$ by slope triangles

Compared to the table method, the slope triangle method:

- is less straightforward;

- doesn't take the time and space to make a table;

- doesn't involve lots of calculations where you might make a human error;

- shows slope triangles, which reinforces the meaning of slope.

Example 3.9.8 Using intercepts. If we use the x- and y-intercepts to plot $y = -2x + 1$, we have some calculation to do. While it is apparent that the y-intercept is at $(0, 1)$, where is the x-intercept?

Set $y = 0$.

$$y = -2x + 1$$
$$0 = -2x + 1$$
$$0 - 1 = -2x$$
$$-1 = -2x$$
$$\frac{-1}{-2} = x$$
$$\frac{1}{2} = x$$

So the x-intercept is at $\left(\frac{1}{2}, 0\right)$. Plotting both intercepts:

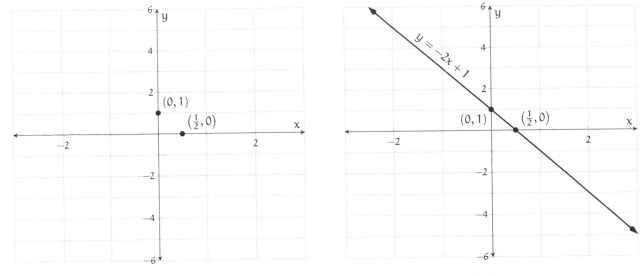

Figure 3.9.9: Marking intercepts   **Figure 3.9.10:** Using slope triangles

This worked, but here are some observations about why this method is not the greatest.

- We had to plot a point with a fraction in its coordinates.

- We only plotted two points and they turned out very close to each other, so even the slightest inaccuracy in our drawing skills could result in a line that is way off.

When a line is presented in slope-intercept form (3.5.1) and b is an integer, our opinion is that the slope triangle method is the best choice for making its graph.

3.9.2 Graphing Lines in Point-Slope Form

When we graph a line in point-slope form (3.6.1) like $y = \frac{2}{3}(x + 1) + 3$, the slope triangle method is the obvious choice. We can see a point on the line, $(-1, 3)$, and the slope is apparent: $\frac{2}{3}$. Here is the graph:

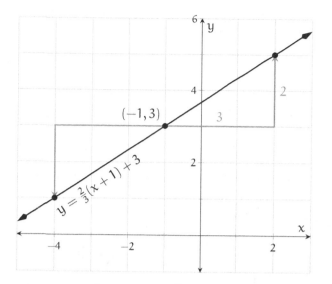

Figure 3.9.11: Graphing $y - 3 = \frac{2}{3}(x + 1)$ using slope triangles

Other graphing methods would take more work and miss the purpose of point-slope form (3.6.1). To graph a line in point-slope form (3.6.1), we recommend always using slope triangles.

3.9.3 Graphing Lines in Standard Form

In the following examples we will graph $3x + 4y = 12$, which is in standard form (3.7.1), with different methods and compare them.

Example 3.9.12 Building a Table of x- and y-values. To make a table, we could substitute x for various numbers and use algebra to find the corresponding y-values. Let's start with $x = -2$, planning to move on to $x = -1, 0, 1, 2$.

$$3x + 4y = 12$$
$$3(-2) + 4y = 12$$
$$-6 + 4y = 12$$
$$4y12 + 6$$
$$4y = 18$$
$$y = \frac{18}{4} = \frac{9}{2}$$

The first point we found is $\left(-2, \frac{9}{2}\right)$. This has been a lot of calculation, and we ended up with a fraction we will have to plot. *And* we have to repeat this process a few more times to get more points for the table. The table method is generally not a preferred way to graph a line in standard form (3.7.1). Let's look at other options.

Example 3.9.13 Using intercepts. Next, we will try graphing $3x + 4y = 12$ using intercepts. We set up a small table to record the two intercepts:

	x-value	y-value	Intercept
x-intercept		0	
y-intercept	0		

We have to calculate the line's x-intercept by substituting $y = 0$ into the equation:

$$3x + 4y = 12$$
$$3x + 4(0) = 12$$
$$3x = 12$$
$$x = \frac{12}{3}$$
$$x = 4$$

And similarly for the y-intercept:

$$3x + 4y = 12$$
$$3(0) + 4y = 12$$
$$4y = 12$$
$$y = \frac{12}{4}$$
$$y = 3$$

So the line's x-intercept is at $(4, 0)$ and its y-intercept is at $(0, 3)$. Now we can complete the table and then graph the line:

	x-value	y-value	Intercepts
x-intercept	4	0	$(4, 0)$
y-intercept	0	3	$(0, 3)$

Figure 3.9.14: Intercepts of $3x + 4y = 12$

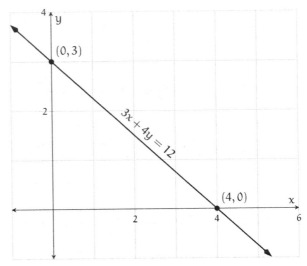

Figure 3.9.15: Graph of $3x + 4y = 12$

Example 3.9.16 With Slope Triangles.
We can always rearrange $3x + 4y = 12$ into slope-intercept form (3.5.1), and then graph it with the slope triangle method:

$$3x + 4y = 12$$
$$4y = 12 - 3x$$
$$4y = -3x + 12$$
$$y = \frac{-3x + 12}{4}$$
$$y = -\frac{3}{4}x + 3$$

With the y-intercept at $(0, 3)$ and slope $-\frac{3}{4}$, we can graph the line using slope triangles:

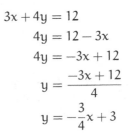

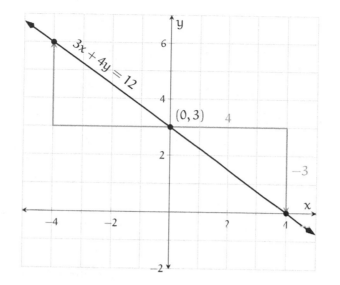

Figure 3.9.17: Graphing $3x + 4y = 12$ using slope triangles

Compared with the intercepts method, the slope triangle method takes more time, but produces points and so makes a more accurate graph. Also sometimes (as with Example 3.7.14) when we graph a standard form equation like $2x - 3y = 0$, the intercepts method doesn't work because both intercepts are actually at the same point (at the origin), and we have to resort to something else like slope triangles anyway.

Here are some observations about graphing a line equation that is in standard form (3.7.1):

- The intercepts method might be the quickest approach.

- The intercepts method only tells us two intercepts of the line. When we need to know more information, like the line's slope, and get a more accurate graph, we should take the time to convert the equation into slope-intercept form.

- When $C = 0$ in a standard form equation (3.7.1) we cannot use the intercepts method to plot the line anyway.

3.9.4 Graphing Horizontal and Vertical Lines

We learned in Section 3.8 that equations in the form $x = h$ and $y = k$ make vertical and horizontal lines. But perhaps you will one day find yourself not remembering which is which. Making a table and plotting points can quickly remind you which type of equation makes which type of line. Let's build a table for $y = 2$ and another one for $x = -3$:

x-value	y-value	Point
0	2	$(0, 2)$
1	2	$(1, 2)$

Figure 3.9.18: Table of values for $y = 2$

x-value	y-value	Point
−3	0	$(-3, 0)$
−3	1	$(-3, 1)$

Figure 3.9.19: Table of values for $x = -3$

With two points on each line, we can graph them:

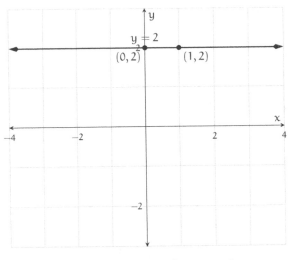

Figure 3.9.20: Graphing $y = 2$

Figure 3.9.21: Graphing $x = -3$

3.9.5 Exercises

Graphing by Table

1. Use a table to make a plot of $y = 4x + 3$.

2. Use a table to make a plot of $y = -5x - 1$.

3. Use a table to make a plot of $y = -\frac{3}{4}x - 1$.

4. Use a table to make a plot of $y = \frac{5}{3}x + 3$.

Graphing Standard Form Equations

5. First find the x- and y-intercepts of the line with equation $6x + 5y = -90$. Then find one other point on the line. Use your results to graph the line.

6. First find the x- and y-intercepts of the line with equation $2x - 3y = -6$. Then find one other point on the line. Use your results to graph the line.

7. First find the x- and y-intercepts of the line with equation $3x + y = -9$. Then find one other point on the line. Use your results to graph the line.

8. First find the x- and y-intercepts of the line with equation $-15x + 3y = -3$. Then find one other point on the line. Use your results to graph the line.

9. First find the x- and y-intercepts of the line with equation $4x + 3y = -3$. Then find one other point on the line. Use your results to graph the line.

10. First find the x- and y-intercepts of the line with equation $-4x - 5y = 5$. Then find one other point on the line. Use your results to graph the line.

11. First find the x- and y-intercepts of the line with equation $5x - 3y = 0$. Then find one other point on the line. Use your results to graph the line.

12. First find the x- and y-intercepts of the line with equation $2x + 9y = 0$. Then find one other point on the line. Use your results to graph the line.

Graphing Slope-Intercept Equations

13. Use the slope and y-intercept from the line $y = -5x$ to plot the line. Use slope triangles.

14. Use the slope and y-intercept from the line $y = 3x - 6$ to plot the line. Use slope triangles.

15. Use the slope and y-intercept from the line $y = -\frac{2}{5}x + 2$ to plot the line. Use slope triangles.

16. Use the slope and y-intercept from the line $y = \frac{10}{3}x - 3$ to plot the line. Use slope triangles.

Graphing Horizontal and Vertical Lines

17. Plot the line $y = 1$.

18. Plot the line $y = -4$.

19. Plot the line $x = -8$.

20. Plot the line $x = 5$.

Choosing the Best Method to Graph Lines

21. Use whatever method you think best to plot $y = 2x + 2$.

22. Use whatever method you think best to plot $y = -3x + 6$.

23. Use whatever method you think best to plot $y = -\frac{3}{4}x - 1$.

24. Use whatever method you think best to plot $y = \frac{5}{3}x - 3$.

25. Use whatever method you think best to plot $y = -\frac{3}{4}(x - 5) + 2$.

26. Use whatever method you think best to plot $y = \frac{2}{5}(x + 1) - 3$.

27. Use whatever method you think best to plot $3x + 2y = 6$.

28. Use whatever method you think best to plot $5x - 4y = 8$.

29. Use whatever method you think best to plot $3x - 4y = 0$.

30. Use whatever method you think best to plot $9x + 6y = 0$.

31. Use whatever method you think best to plot $x = -3$.

32. Use whatever method you think best to plot $x = 2$.

33. Use whatever method you think best to plot $y = -7$.

34. Use whatever method you think best to plot $y = 5$.

3.10 Graphing Lines Chapter Review

3.10.1 Cartesian Coordinates

In Section 3.1 we covered the definition of the Cartesian Coordinate System and how to plot points using the x- and y-axes.

Example 3.10.1 On paper, sketch a Cartesian coordinate system with units, and then plot the following points: $(3, 2), (-5, -1), (0, -3), (4, 0)$.

Explanation.

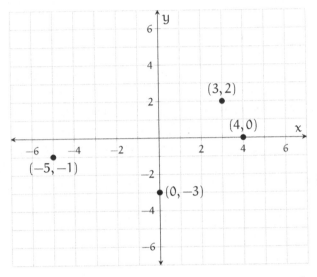

Figure 3.10.2: A Cartesian grid with the four points plotted.

3.10.2 Graphing Equations

In Section 3.2 we covered how to plot solutions to equations to produce a graph of the equation.

Example 3.10.3 Graph the equation $y = -2x + 5$.

Explanation.

x	$y = -2x + 5$	Point
-2		
-1		
0		
1		
2		

(a) Set up the table

x	$y = -2x + 5$	Point
-2	$-2(-2) + 5 = 9$	$(-2, 9)$
-1	$-2(-1) + 5 = 7$	$(-1, 7)$
0	$-2(0) + 5 = 5$	$(0, 5)$
1	$-2(1) + 5 = 3$	$(1, 3)$
2	$-2(2) + 5 = 1$	$(2, 1)$

(b) Complete the table

Figure 3.10.4: Making a table for $y = -2x + 5$

We use points from the table to graph the equation. First, plot each point carefully. Then, connect the points with a smooth curve. Here, the curve is a straight line. Lastly, we can communicate that the graph extends further by sketching arrows on both ends of the line.

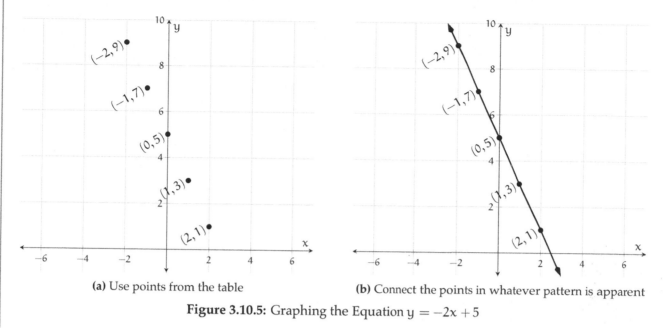

(a) Use points from the table

(b) Connect the points in whatever pattern is apparent

Figure 3.10.5: Graphing the Equation $y = -2x + 5$

3.10.3 Exploring Two-Variable Data and Rate of Change

In Section 3.3 we covered how to find patterns in tables of data and how to calculate the rate of change between points in data.

Example 3.10.6
Write an equation in the form $y = \ldots$ suggested by the pattern in the table.

x	y
0	−4
1	−6
2	−8
3	−10

Figure 3.10.7: A table of linear data.

Explanation.

We consider how the values change from one row to the next. From row to row, the x-value increases by 1. Also, the y-value decreases by 2 from row to row.

	x	y	
	0	−4	
$+1 \rightarrow$	1	−6	$\leftarrow -2$
$+1 \rightarrow$	2	−8	$\leftarrow -2$
$+1 \rightarrow$	3	−10	$\leftarrow -2$

Since row-to-row change is always 1 for x and is always −2 for y, the rate of change from one row to another row is always the same: −2 units of y for every 1 unit of x.

We know that the output for $x = 0$ is $y = -4$. And our observation about the constant rate of change tells us that if we increase the input by x units from 0, the output should decrease by $\overbrace{(-2) + (-2) + \cdots + (-2)}^{x \text{ times}}$, which is $-2x$. So the output would be $-4 - 2x$.

So the equation is $y = -2x - 4$.

3.10.4 Slope

In Section 3.4 we covered the definition of slope and how to use slope triangles to calculate slope. There is also the slope formula (3.4.3) which helps find the slope through any two points.

Example 3.10.8 Find the slope of the line in the following graph.

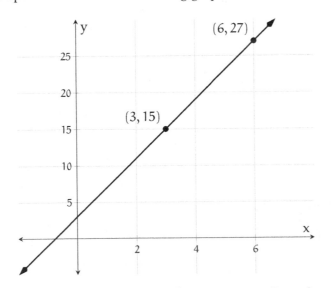

Figure 3.10.9: The line with two points indicated.

Explanation.

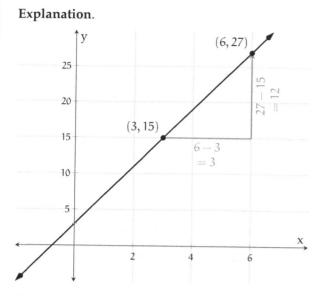

Figure 3.10.10: The line with a slope triangle drawn.

We picked two points on the line, and then drew a slope triangle. Next, we will do:

$$\text{slope} = \frac{12}{3} = 4$$

The line's slope is 4.

Example 3.10.11 Finding a Line's Slope by the Slope Formula. Use the slope formula (3.4.3) to find the slope of the line that passes through the points $(-5, 25)$ and $(4, -2)$.

Explanation.

$$\begin{aligned}
\text{slope} &= \frac{y_2 - y_1}{x_2 - x_1} \\
&= \frac{-2 - (25)}{4 - (-5)} \\
&= \frac{-27}{9} \\
&= -3
\end{aligned}$$

The line's slope is -3.

3.10.5 Slope-Intercept Form

In Section 3.5 we covered the definition of slope intercept-form and both wrote equations in slope-intercept form and graphed lines given in slope-intercept form.

Example 3.10.12 Graph the line $y = -\frac{5}{2}x + 4$.

Explanation.

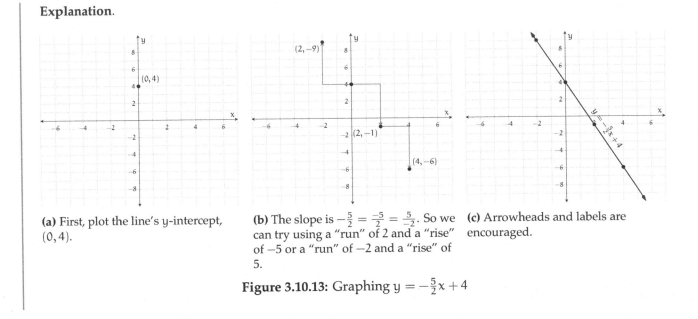

(a) First, plot the line's y-intercept, $(0, 4)$.

(b) The slope is $-\frac{5}{2} = \frac{-5}{2} = \frac{5}{-2}$. So we can try using a "run" of 2 and a "rise" of -5 or a "run" of -2 and a "rise" of 5.

(c) Arrowheads and labels are encouraged.

Figure 3.10.13: Graphing $y = -\frac{5}{2}x + 4$

Writing a Line's Equation in Slope-Intercept Form Based on Graph. Given a line's graph, we can identify its y-intercept, and then find its slope using a slope triangle. With a line's slope and y-intercept, we can write its equation in the form of $y = mx + b$.

Example 3.10.14
Find the equation of the line in the graph.

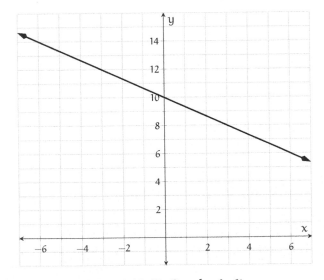

Figure 3.10.15: Graph of a line

Explanation.

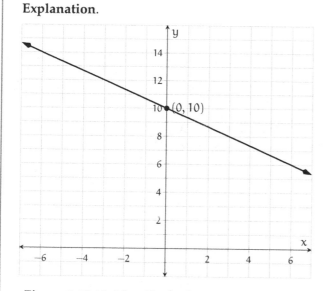

Figure 3.10.16: Identify the line's y-intercept, 10.

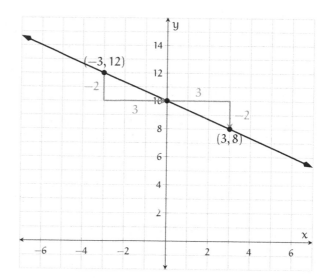

Figure 3.10.17: Identify the line's slope using a slope triangle. Note that we can pick any two points on the line to create a slope triangle. We would get the same slope: $-\frac{2}{3}$

With the line's slope $-\frac{2}{3}$ and y-intercept 10, we can write the line's equation in slope-intercept form: $y = -\frac{2}{3}x + 10$.

3.10.6 Point-Slope Form

In Section 3.6 we covered the definition of point-slope form and both wrote equations in point-slope form and graphed lines given in point-slope form.

Example 3.10.18 A line passes through $(-6, 0)$ and $(9, -10)$. Find this line's equation in point-slope form. .

Explanation. We will use the slope formula (3.4.3) to find the slope first. After labeling those two points as $(\overset{x_1}{-6}, \overset{y_1}{0})$ and $(\overset{x_2}{9}, \overset{y_2}{-10})$, we have:

$$
\begin{aligned}
\text{slope} &= \frac{y_2 - y_1}{x_2 - x_1} \\
&= \frac{-10 - 0}{9 - (-6)} \\
&= \frac{-10}{15} \\
&= -\frac{2}{3}
\end{aligned}
$$

Now the point-slope equation looks like $y = -\frac{2}{3}(x - x_0) + y_0$. Next, we will use $(9, -10)$ and substitute x_0 with 9 and y_0 with -10, and we have:

$$
y = -\frac{2}{3}(x - x_0) + y_0
$$

$$y = -\frac{2}{3}(x - 9) + (-10)$$

$$y = -\frac{2}{3}(x - 9) - 10$$

3.10.7 Standard Form

In Section 3.7 we covered the definition of standard form of a linear equation. We converted equations from standard form to slope-intercept form and vice versa. We also graphed lines from standard form by finding the intercepts of the line.

Example 3.10.19

   a. Convert $2x + 3y = 6$ into slope-intercept form.

   b. Convert $y = -\frac{4}{7}x - 3$ into standard form.

Explanation.

a.
$$2x + 3y = 6$$
$$2x + 3y - 2x = 6 - 2x$$
$$3y = -2x + 6$$
$$\frac{3y}{3} = \frac{-2x + 6}{3}$$
$$y = \frac{-2x}{3} + \frac{6}{3}$$
$$y = -\frac{2}{3}x + 2$$

The line's equation in slope-intercept form is $y = -\frac{2}{3}x + 2$.

b.
$$y = -\frac{4}{7}x - 3$$
$$7 \cdot y = 7 \cdot (-\frac{4}{7}x - 3)$$
$$7y = 7 \cdot (-\frac{4}{7}x) - 7 \cdot 3$$
$$7y = -4x - 21$$
$$7y + 4x = -4x - 21 + 4x$$
$$4x + 7y = -21$$

The line's equation in standard form is $4x + 7y = -21$.

To graph a line in standard form, we could first change it to slope-intercept form, and then graph the line by its y-intercept and slope triangles. A second method is to graph the line by its x-intercept and y-intercept.

Example 3.10.20 Graph $2x - 3y = -6$ using its intercepts. And then use the intercepts to calculate the line's slope.

Explanation. We calculate the line's x-intercept by substituting $y = 0$ into the equation

$$2x - 3y = -6$$
$$2x - 3(0) = -6$$
$$2x = -6$$
$$x = -3$$

So the line's x-intercept is $(-3, 0)$.

Similarly, we substitute $x = 0$ into the equation to calculate the y-intercept:

$$2x - 3y = -6$$
$$2(0) - 3y = -6$$

$$-3y = -6$$
$$y = 2$$

So the line's y-intercept is $(0, 2)$.

With both intercepts' coordinates, we can graph the line:

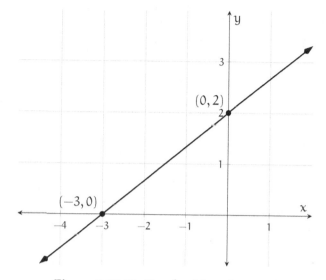

Figure 3.10.21: Graph of $2x - 3y = -6$

Now that we have graphed the line we can read the slope. The rise is 2 units and the run is 3 units so the slope is $\frac{2}{3}$.

3.10.8 Horizontal, Vertical, Parallel, and Perpendicular Lines

In Section 3.8 we studied horizontal and vertical lines. We also covered the relationships between the slopes of parallel and perpendicular lines.

Example 3.10.22 Line m's equation is $y = -2x + 20$. Line n is parallel to m, and line n also passes the point $(4, -3)$. Find an equation for line n in point-slope form.

Explanation. Since parallel lines have the same slope, line n's slope is also -2. Since line n also passes the point $(4, -3)$, we can write line n's equation in point-slope form:

$$y = m(x - x_1) + y_1$$
$$y = -2(x - 4) + (-3)$$
$$y = -2(x - 4) - 3$$

Two lines are perpendicular if and only if the product of their slopes is -1.

Example 3.10.23 Line m's equation is $y = -2x + 20$. Line n is perpendicular to m, and line q also passes the point $(4, -3)$. Find an equation for line q in slope-intercept form.

Explanation. Since line m and q are perpendicular, the product of their slopes is -1. Because line m's slope is given as -2, we can find line q's slope is $\frac{1}{2}$.

Since line q also passes the point $(4, -3)$, we can write line q's equation in point-slope form:

$$y = m(x - x_1) + y_1$$
$$y = \frac{1}{2}(x - 4) + (-3)$$
$$y = \frac{1}{2}(x - 4) - 3$$

We can now convert this equation to slope-intercept form:

$$y = \frac{1}{2}(x - 4) - 3$$
$$y = \frac{1}{2}x - 2 - 3$$
$$y = \frac{1}{2}x - 5$$

3.10.9 Exercises

1. Sketch the points $(8, 2)$, $(5, 5)$, $(-3, 0)$, $\left(0, -\frac{14}{3}\right)$, $(3, -2.5)$, and $(-5, 7)$ on a Cartesian plane.

2. Locate each point in the graph:

Write each point's position as an ordered pair, like $(1, 2)$.

$$A = \underline{\hspace{1cm}} \qquad B = \underline{\hspace{1cm}}$$
$$C = \underline{\hspace{1cm}} \qquad D = \underline{\hspace{1cm}}$$

3. Consider the equation
$y = -\frac{7}{8}x - 4$
Which of the following ordered pairs are solutions to the given equation? There may be more than one correct answer.

☐ $(0, -4)$ ☐ $(-8, 8)$ ☐ $(8, -8)$
☐ $(-24, 17)$

4. Consider the equation
$y = -\frac{3}{2}x - 1$
Which of the following ordered pairs are solutions to the given equation? There may be more than one correct answer.

☐ $(-2, 2)$ ☐ $(10, -13)$
☐ $(0, -1)$ ☐ $(-8, 13)$

5. Write an equation in the form $y = \ldots$ suggested by the pattern in the table.

x	y
0	−4
1	−2
2	0
3	2

6. Write an equation in the form $y = \ldots$ suggested by the pattern in the table.

x	y
0	3
1	−2
?	−7
3	−12

7. Below is a line's graph.

The slope of this line is

8. Below is a line's graph.

The slope of this line is

9. Below is a line's graph.

The slope of this line is

10. Below is a line's graph.

The slope of this line is

11. Below is a line's graph.

The slope of this line is

12. Below is a line's graph.

The slope of this line is

13. A line passes through the points $(-8, 15)$ and $(4, 6)$. Find this line's slope.

14. A line passes through the points $(-6, 6)$ and $(2, -6)$. Find this line's slope.

15. A line passes through the points $(4, -4)$ and $(-2, -4)$. Find this line's slope.

16. A line passes through the points $(2, -2)$ and $(-5, -2)$. Find this line's slope.

17. A line passes through the points $(1, -1)$ and $(1, 3)$. Find this line's slope.

18. A line passes through the points $(3, -2)$ and $(3, 1)$. Find this line's slope.

19. A line's graph is given. What is this line's slope-intercept equation?

20. A line's graph is given. What is this line's slope-intercept equation?

21. Find the line's slope and y-intercept. A line has equation $3x - 8y = -32$.

This line's slope is [ ].

This line's y-intercept is [ ].

22. Find the line's slope and y-intercept. A line has equation $3x - 2y = 4$.

This line's slope is [ ].

This line's y-intercept is [ ].

23. A line passes through the points $(9, -6)$ and $(-18, -12)$. Find this line's equation in point-slope form.
Using the point $(9, -6)$, this line's point-slope form equation is

[ ].

Using the point $(-18, -12)$, this line's point-slope form equation is

[ ].

24. A line passes through the points $(12, 2)$ and $(8, -1)$. Find this line's equation in point-slope form.
Using the point $(12, 2)$, this line's point-slope form equation is

[ ].

Using the point $(8, -1)$, this line's point-slope form equation is

[ ].

25. Scientists are conducting an experiment with a gas in a sealed container. The mass of the gas is measured, and the scientists realize that the gas is leaking over time in a linear way. Each minute, they lose 3 grams. Ten minutes since the experiment started, the remaining gas had a mass of 102 grams.

Let x be the number of minutes that have passed since the experiment started, and let y be the mass of the gas in grams at that moment. Use a linear equation to model the weight of the gas over time.

a. This line's slope-intercept equation is [ ].

b. 31 minutes after the experiment started, there would be [ ] grams of gas left.

c. If a linear model continues to be accurate, [_____] minutes since the experiment started, all gas in the container will be gone.

26. Scientists are conducting an experiment with a gas in a sealed container. The mass of the gas is measured, and the scientists realize that the gas is leaking over time in a linear way. Each minute, they lose 8.8 grams. Seven minutes since the experiment started, the remaining gas had a mass of 334.4 grams. Let x be the number of minutes that have passed since the experiment started, and let y be the mass of the gas in grams at that moment. Use a linear equation to model the weight of the gas over time.

   a. This line's slope-intercept equation is [_____].

   b. 31 minutes after the experiment started, there would be [_____] grams of gas left.

   c. If a linear model continues to be accurate, [_____] minutes since the experiment started, all gas in the container will be gone.

27. Find the y-intercept and x-intercept of the line given by the equation. If a particular intercept does not exist, enter none into all the answer blanks for that row.

$$6x + 5y = -90$$

	x-value	y-value	Location (as an ordered pair)
y-intercept	_____	_____	_____
x-intercept	_____	_____	_____

28. Find the y-intercept and x-intercept of the line given by the equation. If a particular intercept does not exist, enter none into all the answer blanks for that row.

$$6x + 3y = -18$$

	x-value	y-value	Location (as an ordered pair)
y-intercept	_____	_____	_____
x-intercept	_____	_____	_____

29. Find the line's slope and y-intercept. A line has equation $-9x + y = 7$.

   This line's slope is [_____].

   This line's y-intercept is [_____].

30. Find the line's slope and y-intercept. A line has equation $-x - y = 10$.

   This line's slope is [_____].

   This line's y-intercept is [_____].

31. Find the line's slope and y-intercept. A line has equation $3x + 6y = 1$.

   This line's slope is [_____].

   This line's y-intercept is [_____].

32. Find the line's slope and y-intercept. A line has equation $8x + 20y = 1$.

   This line's slope is [_____].

   This line's y-intercept is [_____].

33. Fill out this table for the equation $x = -7$.
The first row is an example.

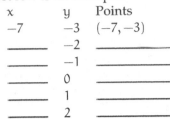

x	y	Points
−7	−3	(−7, −3)
___	−2	_____
___	−1	_____
___	0	_____
___	1	_____
___	2	_____

34. Fill out this table for the equation $x = -6$.
The first row is an example.

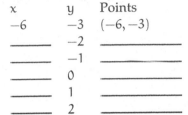

x	y	Points
−6	−3	(−6, −3)
___	−2	_____
___	−1	_____
___	0	_____
___	1	_____
___	2	_____

35. A line's graph is shown. Write an equation for the line.

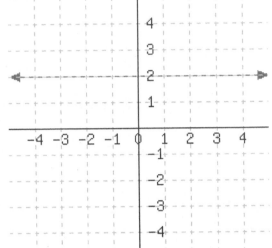

36. A line's graph is shown. Write an equation for the line.

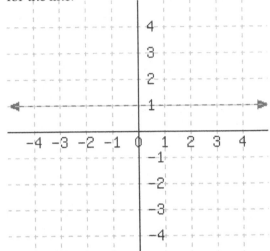

37. Line m passes points $(5, -10)$ and $(5, 9)$.
Line n passes points $(4, 10)$ and $(4, -4)$.
These two lines are   (☐ parallel
☐ perpendicular   ☐ neither parallel nor perpendicular) .

38. Line m passes points $(7, 4)$ and $(7, -3)$.
Line n passes points $(-1, 10)$ and $(-1, 7)$.
These two lines are   (☐ parallel
☐ perpendicular   ☐ neither parallel nor perpendicular) .

39. Line k's equation is $y = \frac{9}{4}x - 4$.
Line ℓ is perpendicular to line k and passes through the point $(-9, 9)$.
Find an equation for line ℓ in both slope-intercept form and point-slope forms.
An equation for ℓ in slope-intercept form is:

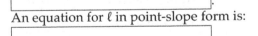

An equation for ℓ in point-slope form is:

40. Line k's equation is $y = -\frac{2}{9}x + 4$.
Line ℓ is perpendicular to line k and passes through the point $(4, 23)$.
Find an equation for line ℓ in both slope-intercept form and point-slope forms.
An equation for ℓ in slope-intercept form is:

An equation for ℓ in point-slope form is:

41. Graph the linear inequality $y > \frac{4}{3}x + 1$.

42. Graph the linear inequality $y \le -\frac{1}{2}x - 3$.

43. Graph the linear inequality $y \ge 3$.

44. Graph the linear inequality $3x + 2y < -6$.

Chapter 4

Systems of Linear Equations

4.1 Solving Systems of Linear Equations by Graphing

We have learned how to graph a line given its equation. In this section, we will learn what a *system* of *two* linear equations is, and how to use graphing to solve such a system.

4.1.1 Solving Systems of Equations by Graphing

Example 4.1.2
Fabiana and David are running at constant speeds in parallel lanes on a track. David starts out ahead of Fabiana, but Fabiana is running faster. We want to determine when Fabiana will catch up with David. Let's start by looking at the graph of each runner's distance over time, in Figure 4.1.3.

Each of the two lines has an equation, as discussed in Chapter 3. The line representing David appears to have y-intercept $(0, 4)$ and slope $\frac{4}{3}$, so its equation is $y = \frac{4}{3}t + 4$. The line representing Fabiana appears to have y-intercept $(0, 0)$ and slope 2, so its equation is $y = 2t$.

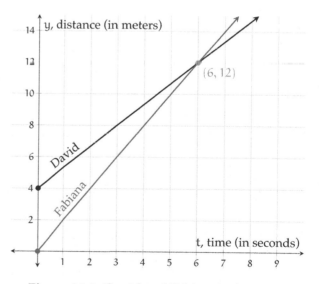

Figure 4.1.3: David and Fabiana's distances.

When these two equations are together as a package, we have what is called a "system of linear equations":

$$\begin{cases} y = \frac{4}{3}t + 4 \\ y = 2t \end{cases}$$

257

The large left brace indicates that this is a collection of two distinct equations, not one equation that was somehow algebraically manipulated into an equivalent equation.

As we can see in Figure 4.1.3, the graphs of the two equations cross at the point $(6, 12)$. We refer to the point $(6, 12)$ as the solution to this system of linear equations. To denote the solution set, we write $\{(6, 12)\}$. It's more valuable to interpret these numbers in context whenever possible: it took 6 seconds for the two runners to meet up, and when they met they were 12 meters up the track.

Definition 4.1.4 System of Linear Equations. A **system of linear equations** is any pairing of two (or more) linear equations. A **solution to a system of linear equations** is any point that is a solution for all of the equations in the system. The **solution set to a system of linear equations** is the collection of all solutions to the system.   ◊

Remark 4.1.5 In Example 4.1.2, we stated that the solution was the point $(6, 12)$. It makes sense to write this as an ordered pair when we're given a graph. In some cases when we have no graph, particularly when our variables are not x and y, it might not be clear which variable "comes first" and we won't be able to write an ordered pair. Nevertheless, given the context we can write meaningful summary statements.

Example 4.1.6 Determine the solution to the system of equations graphed in Figure 4.1.7.

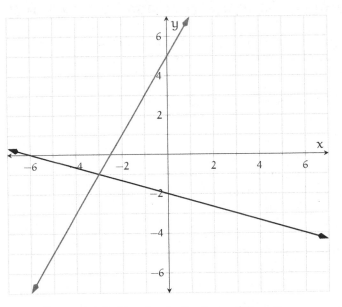

Figure 4.1.7: Graph of a System of Equations

Explanation.   The two lines intersect where $x = -3$ and $y = -1$, so the solution is the point $(-3, -1)$. We write the solution set as $\{(-3, -1)\}$.

Checkpoint 4.1.8 Determine the solution to the system of equations graphed below.

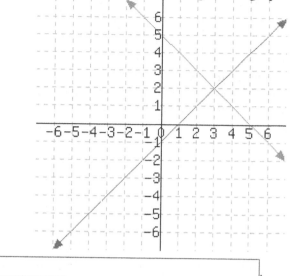

The solution is the point [   ].

Explanation. The two lines intersect where $x = 3$ and $y = 2$, so the solution is the point $(3, 2)$. We write the solution set as $\{(3, 2)\}$.

Now let's look at an example where *we* need to make a graph to find the solution.

Example 4.1.9 Solve the following system of equations by graphing:

$$\begin{cases} y = \frac{1}{2}x + 4 \\ y = -x - 5 \end{cases}$$

Notice that each of these equations is written in slope-intercept form. The first equation, $y = \frac{1}{2}x + 4$, is a linear equation with a slope of $\frac{1}{2}$ and a y-intercept of $(0, 4)$. The second equation, $y = -x - 5$, is a linear equation with a slope of -1 and a y-intercept of $(0, -5)$. We'll use this information to graph both lines.

It appears that the two lines intersect where $x = -6$ and $y = 1$, so the solution of the system of equations would be the point $(-6, 1)$. We should check this with the two original equations.

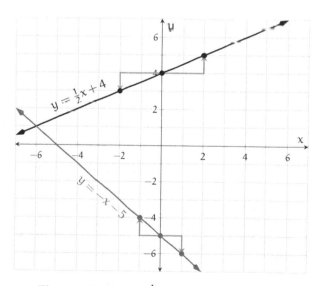

Figure 4.1.10: $y = \frac{1}{2}x + 4$ and $y = -x - 5$.

$$y = \frac{1}{2}x + 4 \qquad\qquad y = -x - 5$$

$$1 \stackrel{?}{=} \frac{1}{2}(-6) + 4 \qquad 1 \stackrel{?}{=} -(-6) - 5$$

$$1 \stackrel{\checkmark}{=} -3 + 4 \qquad\qquad 1 \stackrel{\checkmark}{=} 6 - 5$$

This verifies that $(-6, 1)$ is the solution, and we write the solution set as $\{(-6, 1)\}$.

Example 4.1.11 Solve the following system of equations by graphing:

$$\begin{cases} x - 3y = -12 \\ 2x + 3y = 3 \end{cases}$$

Explanation. Since both line equations are given in standard form, we'll graph each one by finding the intercepts. Recall that to find the x-intercept of each equation, replace y with 0 and solve for x. Similarly, to find the y-intercept of each equation, replace x with 0 and solve for y.

For our first linear equation, we have:

$$x - 3(0) = -12 \qquad 0 - 3y = -12$$
$$x = -12 \qquad -3y = -12$$
$$y = 4.$$

So the intercepts are $(-12, 0)$ and $(0, 4)$.

For our second linear equation, we have:

$$2x + 3(0) = 3 \qquad 2(0) + 3y = 3$$
$$2x = 3 \qquad 3y = 3$$
$$x = \frac{3}{2} \qquad y = 1.$$

So the intercepts are $\left(\frac{3}{2}, 0\right)$ and $(0, 1)$.

Now we can graph each line by plotting the intercepts and connecting these points:

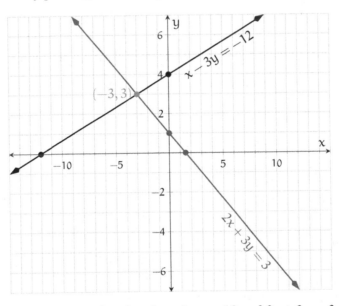

Figure 4.1.12: Graphs of $x - 3y = -12$ and $2x + 3y = 3$

It appears that the solution of the system of equations is the point of intersection of those two lines, which is $(-3, 3)$. It's important to check this is correct, because when making a hand-drawn graph, it would be easy to be off by a little bit. To check, we can substitute the values of x and y from the point $(-3, 3)$ into each equation:

$$x - 3y = -12$$
$$-3 - 3(3) \overset{?}{=} -12$$
$$-3 - 9 \overset{\checkmark}{=} -12$$

$$2x + 3y = 3$$
$$2(-3) + 3(3) \overset{?}{=} 3$$
$$-6 + 9 \overset{\checkmark}{=} 3$$

So we have checked that $(-3, 3)$ is indeed the solution for the system. We write the solution set as $\{(-3, 3)\}$.

Example 4.1.13 A college has a north campus and a south campus. The north campus has 18,000 students, and the south campus has 4,000 students. In the past five years, the north campus lost 4,000 students, and the south campus gained 3,000 students. If these trends continue, in how many years would the two campuses have the same number of students? Write and solve a system of equations modeling this problem.

Explanation. Since all the given student counts are in the thousands, we make the decision to measure student population in thousands. So for instance, the north campus starts with a student population of 18 (thousand students).

The north campus lost 4 thousand students in 5 years. So it is losing students at a rate of $\frac{4\text{ thousand}}{5\text{ year}}$, or $\frac{4}{5}\frac{\text{thousand}}{\text{year}}$. This rate of change should be interpreted as a negative number, because the north campus is losing students over time. So we have a linear model with starting value 18 thousand students, and a slope of $-\frac{4}{5}$ thousand students per year. In other words,

$$y = -\frac{4}{5}t + 18,$$

where y stands for the number of students in thousands, and t stands for the number of years into the future.

Similarly, the number of students at the south campus can be modeled by $y = \frac{3}{5}t + 4$. Now we have a system of equations:

$$\begin{cases} y = -\dfrac{4}{5}t + 18 \\ y = \dfrac{3}{5}t + 4 \end{cases}$$

We will graph both lines using their slopes and y-intercepts.

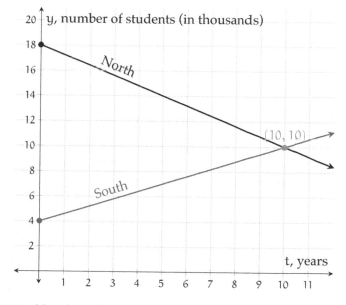

Figure 4.1.14: Number of Students at the South Campus and North Campus

According to the graph, the lines intersect at $(10, 10)$. So if the trends continue, both campuses will have 10,000 students 10 years from now.

Example 4.1.15 Solve the following system of equations by graphing:

$$\begin{cases} y = 3(x-2)+1 \\ y = -\frac{1}{2}(x+1)-1 \end{cases}$$

Explanation.   Since both line equations are given in point-slope form, we can start by graphing the point indicated in each equation and use the slope to determine the rest of the line.

For our first equation, $y = 3(x-2)+1$, the point indicated in the equation is $(2,1)$ and the slope is 3.

For our second equation, $y = -\frac{1}{2}(x+1)-1$, the point indicated in the equation is $(-1,-1)$ and the slope is $-\frac{1}{2}$.

Now we can graph each line by plotting the points and using their slopes.

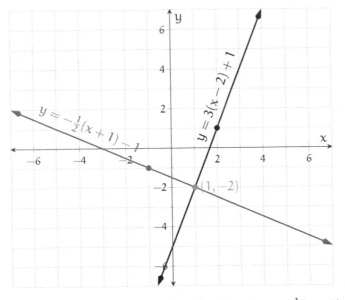

Figure 4.1.16: Graphs of $y = 3(x-2)+1$ and $y = -\frac{1}{2}(x+1)-1$

It appears that the solution of the system of equations is the point of intersection of those two lines, which is $(1,-2)$. It's important to check this is correct, because when making a hand-drawn graph, it would be easy to be off by a little bit. To check, we can substitute the values of x and y from the point $(1,-2)$ into each equation:

$$y = 3(x-2)+1$$
$$-2 \overset{?}{=} 3(1-2)+1$$
$$-2 \overset{?}{=} 3(-1)+1$$
$$-2 \overset{\checkmark}{=} -3+1$$

$$y = -\frac{1}{2}(x+1)-1$$
$$-2 \overset{?}{=} -\frac{1}{2}(1+1)-1$$
$$-2 \overset{?}{=} -\frac{1}{2}(2)-1$$
$$-2 \overset{\checkmark}{=} -1-1$$

So we have checked that $(2,-1)$ is indeed the solution for the system. We write the solution set as $\{(2,-1)\}$.

4.1.2 Special Systems of Equations

Recall that when we solved linear equations in one variable, there were two special cases discussed in detail in Section 2.4. In one special case, like with the equation $x = x + 1$, there is no solution. And in the another case, like with the equation $x = x$, there are infinitely many solutions. When solving systems of equations in two variables, we have similar special cases to consider.

Example 4.1.17 Parallel Lines. Let's look at the graphs of two lines with the same slope, $y = 2x - 4$ and $y = 2x + 1$:

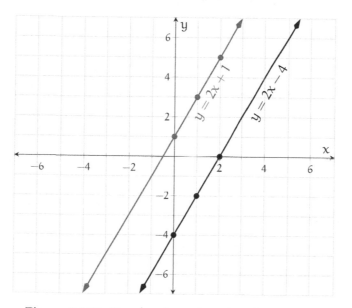

Figure 4.1.18: Graphs of $y = 2x - 4$ and $y = 2x + 1$

For this system of equations, what is the solution? Since the two lines have the same slope they are **parallel lines** and will never intersect. This means that there is *no solution* to this system of equations. We write the solution set as ∅.

The symbol ∅ is a special symbol that represents the **empty set**, a *set* that has no numbers in it which can also be written simply as { }. This symbol is *not* the same thing as the number zero. The *number* of eggs in an empty egg carton is zero whereas the empty carton itself could represent the empty set. The symbols for the empty set and the number zero may look similar depending on how you write the number zero, so try to keep the concepts separate.

Example 4.1.19 Coinciding Lines. Next we'll look at the other special case. Let's start with this system of equations:

$$\begin{cases} y = 2x - 4 \\ 6x - 3y = \quad 12 \end{cases}$$

To solve this system of equations, we want to graph each line. The first equation is in slope-intercept form and can be graphed easily using its slope of 2 and its y-intercept of $(0, -4)$.

The second equation, $6x - 3y = 12$, can either be graphed by solving for y and using the slope-intercept form or by finding the intercepts. If we use the intercept method, we'll find that this line has an x-intercept of $(2, 0)$ and a y-intercept of $(0, -4)$. When we graph both lines we get Figure 4.1.20.

Now we can see these are actually the *same* line, or **coinciding lines**. To determine the solution to this system, we'll note that they overlap everywhere. This means that we have an infinite number of solutions: *all* points that fall on the line. It may be enough to report that there are infinitely many solutions. In order to be more specific, all we can do is say that any ordered pair (x, y) satisfying the line equation is a solution. In set-builder notation, we would write $\{(x, y) \mid y = 2x - 4\}$.

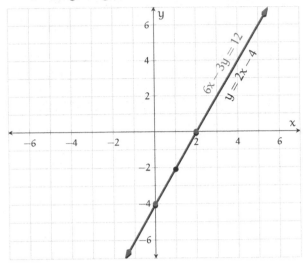

Figure 4.1.20: Graphs of $y = 2x - 4$ and $6x - 3y = 12$

Remark 4.1.21 In Example 4.1.19, what would have happened if we had decided to convert the second line equation into slope-intercept form?

$$6x - 3y = 12$$
$$6x - 3y - 6x = 12 - 6x$$
$$-3y = -6x + 12$$
$$-\frac{1}{3} \cdot (-3y) = -\frac{1}{3} \cdot (-6x + 12)$$
$$y = 2x - 4$$

This is the literally the same as the first equation in our system. This is a different way to show that these two equations are equivalent and represent the same line. Any time we try to solve a system where the equations are equivalent, we'll have an infinite number of solutions.

Warning 4.1.22 Notice that for a system of equations with infinite solutions like Example 4.1.19, we didn't say that *every* point was a solution. Rather, *every point that falls on that line* is a solution. It would be incorrect to state this solution set as "all real numbers" or as "all ordered pairs."

List 4.1.23: A summary of the three types of systems of equations and their solution sets.

Intersecting Lines: If two linear equations make lines with different slopes, the system has one solution.

Parallel Lines: If two linear equations make lines with the same slope but different y-intercepts, the system has no solution.

Coinciding Lines: If two linear equations make lines with the same slope and the same y-intercept (in other words, they make the same line), the system has infinitely many solutions. This solution set consists of all ordered pairs on that line.

4.1.3 Reading Questions

1. What is the purpose of the one big left brace in a system of two equations?

2. When you find a solution to a system of two linear equations in two variables, why should you check the solution? Would it be good enough to only substitute the numbers into *one* of the original two equations?

3. Suppose you have a system of two linear equations, and you know the system has exactly one solution. What can you say about the slopes of the two lines that the two equations define?

4.1.4 Exercises

Warmup and Review Find the line's slope and y-intercept.

1. A line has equation $y = 3x + 5$.
   This line's slope is [ ].
   This line's y-intercept is [ ].

2. A line has equation $y = 4x + 1$.
   This line's slope is [ ].
   This line's y-intercept is [ ].

3. A line has equation $y = -x - 1$.
   This line's slope is [ ].
   This line's y-intercept is [ ].

4. A line has equation $y = -x + 1$.
   This line's slope is [ ].
   This line's y-intercept is [ ].

5. A line has equation $y = -\dfrac{6x}{5} + 7$.
   This line's slope is [ ].
   This line's y-intercept is [ ].

6. A line has equation $y = -\dfrac{8x}{7} + 4$.
   This line's slope is [ ].
   This line's y-intercept is [ ].

7. A line has equation $y = \dfrac{x}{10} - 4$.
   This line's slope is [ ].
   This line's y-intercept is [ ].

8. A line has equation $y = \dfrac{x}{10} + 10$.
   This line's slope is [ ].
   This line's y-intercept is [ ].

9. Graph the equation $y = -3x$.

10. Graph the equation $y = \frac{1}{4}x$.

11. Graph the equation $y = \frac{2}{3}x + 4$.

12. Graph the equation $y = -2x + 5$.

Solve the linear equation for y.

13. $16x + 2y = -8$

14. $6x - 2y = 28$

15. $8x + 4y = 40$

16. $3x + 5y = 45$

Checking Solutions for System of Equations

17. Decide whether $(1, -3)$ is a solution to the system of equations:

$$\begin{cases} x - 2y = 7 \\ 2x + 4y = -10 \end{cases}$$

The point $(1, -3)$ ($\square$ is $\square$ is not)   a solution.

18. Decide whether $(2, 4)$ is a solution to the system of equations:

$$\begin{cases} -5x - 5y = -30 \\ 2x - 2y = -4 \end{cases}$$

The point $(2, 4)$ ($\square$ is $\square$ is not)   a solution.

19. Decide whether $(3, 1)$ is a solution to the system of equations:

$$\begin{cases} -x + 3y = 0 \\ y = -2x + 7 \end{cases}$$

The point $(3, 1)$ ($\square$ is $\square$ is not)   a solution.

20. Decide whether $(4, -3)$ is a solution to the system of equations:

$$\begin{cases} 4x + 2y = 13 \\ y = -4x + 13 \end{cases}$$

The point $(4, -3)$ ($\square$ is $\square$ is not)   a solution.

21. Decide whether $\left(\frac{8}{5}, \frac{4}{5}\right)$ is a solution to the system of equations:

$$\begin{cases} -10x + 5y = -12 \\ 10x + 15y = 28 \end{cases}$$

The point $\left(\frac{8}{5}, \frac{4}{5}\right)$ ($\square$ is $\square$ is not)   a solution.

22. Decide whether $\left(\frac{7}{2}, \frac{9}{2}\right)$ is a solution to the system of equations:

$$\begin{cases} 2x - 2y = -2 \\ -6x - 4y = -39 \end{cases}$$

The point $\left(\frac{7}{2}, \frac{9}{2}\right)$ ($\square$ is $\square$ is not)   a solution.

Using a Graph to Solve a System Use a graph to solve the system of equations.

23. $\begin{cases} y = -\dfrac{5}{2}x - 4 \\ y = 2x + 5 \end{cases}$

24. $\begin{cases} y = \dfrac{2}{3}x + 5 \\ y = -2x - 11 \end{cases}$

25. $\begin{cases} y = 12x + 7 \\ 3x + y = -8 \end{cases}$

26. $\begin{cases} y = -3x + 5 \\ 4x + y = 8 \end{cases}$

27. $\begin{cases} x + y = 0 \\ 3x - y = 8 \end{cases}$

28. $\begin{cases} 4x - 2y = 4 \\ x + 2y = 6 \end{cases}$

29. $\begin{cases} y = 4x - 5 \\ y = -1 \end{cases}$

30. $\begin{cases} 3x - 4y = 12 \\ y = 3 \end{cases}$

31. $\begin{cases} x + y = -1 \\ x = 2 \end{cases}$

32. $\begin{cases} x - 2y = -4 \\ x = -4 \end{cases}$

33. $\begin{cases} y = 2(x + 3) - 5 \\ y = -\dfrac{4}{3}(x - 4) - 1 \end{cases}$

34. $\begin{cases} y = -\dfrac{2}{3}(x - 6) - 2 \\ y = -\dfrac{1}{2}(x - 1) + 2 \end{cases}$

35. $\begin{cases} y = -\dfrac{1}{2}(x - 6) + 4 \\ y = 4(x + 1) - 6 \end{cases}$

36. $\begin{cases} y = \dfrac{5}{6}(x - 6) + 4 \\ y = 2(x + 1) + 4 \end{cases}$

37. $\begin{cases} y = -\dfrac{4}{5}x + 8 \\ 4x + 5y = -35 \end{cases}$

38. $\begin{cases} 2x - 7y = 28 \\ y = \dfrac{2}{7}x - 3 \end{cases}$

39. $\begin{cases} -10x + 15y = 60 \\ 6x - 9y = 36 \end{cases}$

40. $\begin{cases} 6x - 8y = 32 \\ 9x - 12y = 12 \end{cases}$

41. $\begin{cases} y = -\dfrac{3}{5}x + 7 \\ 9x + 15y = 105 \end{cases}$

42. $\begin{cases} 9y - 12x = 18 \\ y = \dfrac{4}{3}x + 2 \end{cases}$

Determining the Number of Solutions in a System of Equations

43. Simply by looking at this system of equations, decide the number of solutions it has.

$$\begin{cases} y = \dfrac{4}{5}x + 2 \\ y = \dfrac{4}{5}x + 4 \end{cases}$$

The system has   (□ no solution   □ one solution   □ infinitely many solutions)   .

44. Simply by looking at this system of equations, decide the number of solutions it has.

$$\begin{cases} y = -2x + 1 \\ y = -2x - 2 \end{cases}$$

The system has   (□ no solution   □ one solution   □ infinitely many solutions)   .

45. Without graphing this system of equations, decide the number of solutions it has.

$$\begin{cases} y = -\dfrac{6}{5}x + 1 \\ 27x - 15y = 30 \end{cases}$$

The system has   (□ no solution   □ one solution   □ infinitely many solutions)   .

46. Without graphing this system of equations, decide the number of solutions it has.

$$\begin{cases} y = \dfrac{5}{2}x + 3 \\ 21x - 6y = 12 \end{cases}$$

The system has   (□ no solution   □ one solution   □ infinitely many solutions)   .

47. Without graphing this system of equations, decide the number of solutions it has.

$$\begin{cases} 3x - 3y = 0 \\ 4x - 2y = -8 \end{cases}$$

The system has   (☐ no solution   ☐ one solution   ☐ infinitely many solutions)   .

48. Without graphing this system of equations, decide the number of solutions it has.

$$\begin{cases} 3x - 12y = 36 \\ 2x - 8y = 24 \end{cases}$$

The system has   (☐ no solution   ☐ one solution   ☐ infinitely many solutions)   .

49. Simply by looking at this system of equations, decide the number of solutions it has.

$$\begin{cases} x = -5 \\ y = 1 \end{cases}$$

The system has   (☐ no solution   ☐ one solution   ☐ infinitely many solutions)   .

50. Simply by looking at this system of equations, decide the number of solutions it has.

$$\begin{cases} x = 2 \\ y = -5 \end{cases}$$

The system has   (☐ no solution   ☐ one solution   ☐ infinitely many solutions)   .

4.2 Substitution

In Section 4.1, we focused on solving systems of equations by graphing. In addition to being time consuming, graphing can be an awkward method to determine the exact solution when the solution has large numbers, fractions, or decimals. There are two symbolic methods for solving systems of linear equations, and in this section we will use one of them: substitution.

4.2.1 Solving Systems of Equations Using Substitution

Example 4.2.2 The Interview. In 2014, the New York Times[1] posted the following about the movie, "The Interview":

> "The Interview" generated roughly $15 million in online sales and rentals during its first four days of availability, Sony Pictures said on Sunday.

> Sony did not say how much of that total represented $6 digital rentals versus $15 sales. The studio said there were about two million transactions overall.

A few days later, Joey Devilla cleverly pointed out in his blog[2], that there is enough information given to find the amount of sales versus rentals. Using algebra, we can write a system of equations and solve it to find the two quantities.[3]

First, we will define variables. We need two variables, because there are two unknown quantities: how many sales there were and how many rentals there were. Let r be the number of rental transactions and let s be the number of sales transactions.

If you are unsure how to write an equation from the background information, use the units to help you. The units of each term in an equation must match because we can only add like quantities. Both r and s are in transactions. The article says that the total number of transactions is 2 million. So our first equation will add the total number of rental and sales transactions and set that equal to 2 million. Our equation is:

$$(r \text{ transactions}) + (s \text{ transactions}) = 2{,}000{,}000 \text{ transactions}$$

Without the units:

$$r + s = 2{,}000{,}000$$

The price of each rental was $6. That means the problem has given us a *rate* of $6 \frac{\text{dollars}}{\text{transaction}}$ to work with. The rate unit suggests this should be multiplied by something measured in transactions. It makes sense to multiply by r, and then the number of dollars generated from rentals was $6r$. Similarly, the price of each sale was $15, so the revenue from sales was $15s$. The total revenue was $15 million, which we can represent with this equation:

$$\left(6 \, \tfrac{\text{dollars}}{\text{transaction}}\right) (r \text{ transactions}) + \left(15 \, \tfrac{\text{dollars}}{\text{transaction}}\right) (s \text{ transactions}) = \$15{,}000{,}000$$

Without the units:

$$6r + 15s = 15{,}000{,}000$$

Here is our system of equations:

$$\begin{cases} r + s = 2{,}000{,}000 \\ 6r + 15s = 15{,}000{,}000 \end{cases}$$

To solve the system, we will use the **substitution** method. The idea is to use *one* equation to find an expression that is equal to r but, cleverly, does not use the variable "r." Then, substitute this for r into the *other* equation. This leaves you with *one* equation that only has *one* variable.

The first equation from the system is an easy one to solve for r:

$$r + s = 2,000,000$$
$$r = 2,000,000 - s$$

This tells us that the expression $2,000,000 - s$ is equal to r, so we can *substitute* it for r in the second equation:

$$6r + 15s = 15,000,000$$
$$6(2,000,000 - s) + 15s = 15,000,000$$

Now we have an equation with only one variable, s, which we will solve for:

$$6(2,000,000 - s) + 15s = 15,000,000$$
$$12,000,000 - 6s + 15s = 15,000,000$$
$$12,000,000 + 9s = 15,000,000$$
$$9s = 3,000,000$$
$$\frac{9s}{9} = \frac{3,000,000}{9}$$
$$s = 333,333.\overline{3}$$

At this point, we know that $s = 333,333.\overline{3}$. This tells us that out of the 2 million transactions, roughly 333,333 were from online sales. Recall that we solved the first equation for r, and found $r = 2,000,000 - s$.

$$r = 2,000,000 - s$$
$$r = 2,000,000 - 333,333.\overline{3}$$
$$r = 1,666,666.\overline{6}$$

To check our answer, we will see if $s = 333,333.\overline{3}$ and $r = 1,666,666.\overline{6}$ make the original equations true:

$$r + s = 2,000,000 \qquad\qquad 6r + 15s = 15,000,000$$
$$1,666,666.\overline{6} + 333,333.\overline{3} \stackrel{?}{=} 2,000,000 \qquad 6\left(1,666,666.\overline{6}\right) + 15\left(333,333.\overline{3}\right) \stackrel{?}{=} 15,000,000$$
$$2,000,000 \stackrel{\checkmark}{=} 2,000,000 \qquad\qquad 10,000,000 + 5,000,000 \stackrel{\checkmark}{=} 15,000,000$$

In summary, there were roughly 333,333 copies sold and roughly 1,666,667 copies rented.

Remark 4.2.3 In Example 4.2.2, we *chose* to solve the equation $r + s = 2,000,000$ for r. We could just as easily have instead solved for s and substituted that result into the second equation instead. The summary conclusion would have been the same.

Remark 4.2.4 In Example 4.2.2, we rounded the solution values because only whole numbers make sense in the context of the problem. It was OK to round, because the original information we had to work with were rounded. In fact, it would be OK to round even more to $s = 330,000$ and $r = 1,700,000$, as long as we

---

[1](nyti.ms/2pupebT)
[2]http://www.joeydevilla.com/2014/12/31/
[3]Although since the given information uses approximate values, the solutions we will find will only be approximations too.

communicate clearly that we rounded and our values are rough.

In other exercises where there is no context and nothing suggests the given numbers are approximations, it is not OK to round and all answers should be communicated with their exact values.

Example 4.2.5 Solve the system of equations using substitution:

$$\begin{cases} x + 2y = 8 \\ 3x - 2y = 8 \end{cases}$$

Explanation. To use substitution, we need to solve for *one* of the variables in *one* of our equations. Looking at both equations, it will be easiest to solve for x in the first equation:

$$x + 2y = 8$$
$$x - 8 - 2y$$

Next, we replace x in the second equation with $8 - 2y$, giving us a linear equation in only one variable, y, that we may solve:

$$3x - 2y = 8$$
$$3(8 - 2y) - 2y = 8$$
$$24 - 6y - 2y = 8$$
$$24 - 8y = 8$$
$$-8y = -16$$
$$y = 2$$

Now that we have the value for y, we need to find the value for x. We have already solved the first equation for x, so that is the easiest equation to use.

$$x = 8 - 2y$$
$$x = 8 - 2(2)$$
$$x = 8 - 4$$
$$x = 4$$

To check this solution, we replace x with 4 and y with 2 in each equation:

$$x + 2y = 8 \qquad\qquad 3x - 2y = 8$$
$$4 + 2(2) \overset{?}{=} 8 \qquad\qquad 3(4) - 2(2) \overset{?}{=} 8$$
$$4 + 4 \overset{\checkmark}{=} 8 \qquad\qquad 12 - 4 \overset{\checkmark}{=} 8$$

We conclude then that this system of equations is true when $x = 4$ and $y = 2$. Our solution is the point $(4, 2)$ and we write the solution set as $\{(4, 2)\}$.

Checkpoint 4.2.6 Solve the following system of equations.

$$\begin{cases} x + 3y = -60 \\ 40 = 5x - 5y \end{cases}$$

Explanation. These equations have no fractions; let's try to keep it that way.

$$\begin{cases} x + 3y = -60 \\ 40 = 5x - 5y \end{cases}$$

Since one of the coefficients of x is 1, it is wise to solve for the x in terms of the other variable and then use substitution to complete the problem.

$$x = -3y - 60 \quad \text{(from the first equation)}$$

which we can substitute in for x into the second equation:

$$40 = 5(-3y - 60) - 5y \quad \text{(from the second equation)}$$
$$40 = -20y - 300$$
$$20y = -340$$
$$y = -17$$

We can substitute this for y back into the first equation to find x.

$$x = -3\,(-17) - 60 \quad \text{(from the first equation, after we had solved for x in terms of$y$)}$$
$$x = 51 - 60$$
$$x = -9$$

So the solution is $x = -9, y = -17$.

Example 4.2.7 Solve this system of equations using substitution:

$$\begin{cases} 3x - 7y = 5 \\ -5x + 2y = 11 \end{cases}$$

Explanation. We need to solve for *one* of the variables in *one* of our equations. Looking at both equations, it will be easiest to solve for y in the second equation. The coefficient of y in that equation is smallest.

$$-5x + 2y = 11$$
$$2y = 11 + 5x$$
$$\frac{2y}{2} = \frac{11 + 5x}{2}$$
$$y = \frac{11}{2} + \frac{5}{2}x$$

Note that in this example, there are fractions once we solve for y. We should take care with the steps that follow that the fraction arithmetic is correct.

Replace y in the first equation with $\frac{11}{2} + \frac{5}{2}x$, giving us a linear equation in only one variable, x, that we may solve:

$$3x - 7y = 5$$
$$3x - 7\left(\frac{11}{2} + \frac{5}{2}x\right) = 5$$
$$3x - 7 \cdot \frac{11}{2} - 7 \cdot \frac{5}{2}x = 5$$
$$3x - \frac{77}{2} - \frac{35}{2}x = 5$$
$$\frac{6}{2}x - \frac{77}{2} - \frac{35}{2}x = 5$$
$$-\frac{29}{2}x - \frac{77}{2} = 5$$
$$-\frac{29}{2}x = \frac{10}{2} + \frac{77}{2}$$
$$-\frac{29}{2}x = \frac{87}{2}$$
$$-\frac{2}{29} \cdot \left(-\frac{29}{2}x\right) = -\frac{2}{29} \cdot \left(\frac{87}{2}\right)$$
$$x = -3$$

Now that we have the value for x, we need to find the value for y. We have already solved the second equation for y, so that is the easiest equation to use.

$$y = \frac{11}{2} + \frac{5}{2}x$$
$$y = \frac{11}{2} + \frac{5}{2}(-3)$$
$$y = \frac{11}{2} - \frac{15}{2}$$
$$y = -\frac{4}{2}$$
$$y = -2$$

To check this solution, we replace x with -3 and y with -2 in each equation:

$$3x - 7y = 5 \qquad\qquad -5x + 2y = 11$$
$$3(-3) - 7(-2) \overset{?}{=} 5 \qquad\qquad -5(-3) + 2(-2) \overset{?}{=} 11$$
$$-9 + 14 \overset{\checkmark}{=} 5 \qquad\qquad 15 - 4 \overset{\checkmark}{=} 11$$

We conclude then that this system of equations is true when $x = -3$ and $y = -2$. Our solution is the point $(-3, -2)$ and we write the solution set as $\{(-3, -2)\}$.

Example 4.2.8 Clearing Fraction Denominators Before Solving. Solve the system of equations using the substitution method:

$$\begin{cases} \dfrac{x}{3} - \dfrac{1}{2}y = \dfrac{5}{6} \\ \dfrac{1}{4}x = \dfrac{y}{2} + 1 \end{cases}$$

Explanation. When a system of equations has fraction coefficients, it can be helpful to take steps that replace the fractions with whole numbers. With each equation, we may multiply each side by the least common multiple of all the denominators.

In the first equation, the least common multiple of the denominators is 6, so:

$$\frac{x}{3} - \frac{1}{2}y = \frac{5}{6}$$
$$6 \cdot \left(\frac{x}{3} - \frac{1}{2}y\right) = 6 \cdot \frac{5}{6}$$
$$6 \cdot \frac{x}{3} - 6 \cdot \frac{1}{2}y = 6 \cdot \frac{5}{6}$$
$$2x - 3y = 5$$

In the second equation, the least common multiple of the denominators is 4, so:

$$\frac{1}{4}x = \frac{y}{2} + 1$$
$$4 \cdot \frac{1}{4}x = 4 \cdot \frac{y}{2} + 4 \cdot 1$$
$$4 \cdot \frac{1}{4}x = 4 \cdot \frac{y}{2} + 4 \cdot 1$$
$$x = 2y + 4$$

Now we have this system that is equivalent to the original system of equations, but there are no fraction coefficients:

$$\begin{cases} 2x - 3y = 5 \\ x = 2y + 4 \end{cases}$$

The second equation is already solved for x, so we will substitute x in the first equation with $2y + 4$, and we have:

$$2x - 3y = 5$$
$$2(2y + 4) - 3y = 5$$
$$4y + 8 - 3y = 5$$
$$y + 8 = 5$$
$$y = -3$$

And we have solved for y. To find x, we know $x = 2y + 4$, so we have:

$$x = 2y + 4$$
$$x = 2(-3) + 4$$
$$x = -6 + 4$$
$$x = -2$$

The solution is $(-2, -3)$. Checking this solution is left as an exercise.

Checkpoint 4.2.9 Try a similar exercise.

Solve the following system of equations.

$$\begin{cases} -3 = -m + \dfrac{1}{2}r \\ -m + \dfrac{4}{3} = -r \end{cases}$$

Explanation. If an equation involves fractions, it is helpful to clear denominators by multiplying both sides of the equation by a common multiple of the denominators.

$$\begin{cases} 2(-3) = 2\left(-m + \dfrac{1}{2}r\right) \\ 3\left(-m + \dfrac{4}{3}\right) = 3(-r) \end{cases}$$

$$\begin{cases} -6 = -2m + r \\ -3m + 4 = -3r \end{cases}$$

Since one of the coefficients of r is 1, it is wise to solve for r in terms of the other variable and then use substitution to complete the problem.

$$2m - 6 = r \quad \text{(from the first equation)}$$

which we can substitute in for r into the second equation:

$$4 - 3m = -3(2m - 6) \quad \text{(from the second equation)}$$
$$4 - 3m = 18 - 6m$$
$$3m = 14$$
$$m = \frac{14}{3}$$

We can substitute this back for m into the first equation to find r.

$$2\left(\frac{14}{3}\right) - 6 = r \quad \text{(from the first equation, after we had solved for r in terms of m)}$$
$$\frac{28}{3} + (-6) = r$$
$$\frac{10}{3} = r$$

So the solution is $m = \frac{14}{3}, r = \frac{10}{3}$.

For summary reference, here is the general procedure.

Process 4.2.10 Solving Systems of Equations by Substitution. *To solve a system of equations by substitution,*

1. *Solve one of the equations for one of the variables.*

2. *Substitute that expression into the* other *equation. There should now only be one variable in that equation.*

3. *Solve that equation for the one remaining variable.*

4. *Substitute that value into an earlier equation and solve for the other variable.*

5. *Verify your solution in the original equations.*

4.2.2 Applications of Systems of Equations

Example 4.2.11 Two Different Interest Rates. Notah made some large purchases with his two credit cards one month and took on a total of $8,400 in debt from the two cards. He didn't make any payments the first month, so the two credit card debts each started to accrue interest. That month, his Visa card charged 2% interest and his Mastercard charged 2.5% interest. Because of this, Notah's total debt grew by $178. How much money did Notah charge to each card?

Explanation.   To start, we will define two variables based on our two unknowns. Let v be the amount charged to the Visa card (in dollars) and let m be the amount charged to the Mastercard (in dollars).

To determine our equations, notice that we are given two different totals. We will use these to form our two equations. The total amount charged is $8,400 so we have:

$$(v \text{ dollars}) + (m \text{ dollars}) = \$8400$$

Or without units:

$$v + m = 8400$$

The other total we were given is the total amount of interest, $178, which is also in dollars. The Visa had v dollars charged to it and accrues 2% interest. So $0.02v$ is the dollar amount of interest that comes from using this card. Similarly, $0.025m$ is the dollar amount of interest from using the Mastercard. Together:

$$0.02(v \text{ dollars}) + 0.025(m \text{ dollars}) = \$178$$

Or without units:

$$0.02v + 0.025m = 178$$

As a system, we write:

$$\begin{cases} v + m = 8400 \\ 0.02v + 0.025m = 178 \end{cases}$$

To solve this system by substitution, notice that it will be easier to solve for one of the variables in the first equation. We'll solve that equation for v:

$$v + m = 8400$$
$$v = 8400 - m$$

Now we will substitute $8400 - m$ for v in the second equation:

$$0.02v + 0.025m = 178$$
$$0.02(8400 - m) + 0.025m = 178$$
$$168 - 0.02m + 0.025m = 178$$
$$168 + 0.005m = 178$$
$$0.005m = 10$$
$$\frac{0.005m}{0.005} = \frac{10}{0.005}$$
$$m = 2000$$

Lastly, we can determine the value of v by using the earlier equation where we isolated v:

$$v = 8400 - m$$
$$v = 8400 - 2000$$
$$v = 6400$$

In summary, Notah charged \$6400 to the Visa and \$2000 to the Mastercard. We should check that these numbers work as solutions to our original system *and* that they make sense in context. (For instance, if one of these numbers were negative, or was something small like \$0.50, they wouldn't make sense as credit card debt.)

The next two examples are called **mixture problems**, because they involve mixing two quantities together to form a combination and we want to find out how much of each quantity to mix.

Example 4.2.12 Mixing Solutions with Two Different Concentrations. La Vonda is a meticulous bartender and she needs to serve 600 milliliters of Rob Roy, an alcoholic cocktail that is 34% alcohol by volume. The main ingredients are scotch that is 42% alcohol and vermouth that is 18% alcohol. How many milliliters of each ingredient should she mix together to make the concentration she needs?

Explanation. The two unknowns are the quantities of each ingredient. Let s be the amount of scotch (in mL) and let v be the amount of vermouth (in mL).

One quantity given to us in the problem is 600 mL. Since this is the total volume of the mixed drink, we must have:

$$(s\,\text{mL}) + (v\,\text{mL}) = 600\,\text{mL}$$

Or without units:

$$s + v = 600$$

To build the second equation, we have to think about the alcohol concentrations for the scotch, vermouth, and Rob Roy. It can be tricky to think about percentages like these correctly. One strategy is to focus on the *amount* (in mL) of *alcohol* being mixed. If we have s milliliters of scotch that is 42% alcohol, then $0.42s$ is the actual *amount* (in mL) of alcohol in that scotch. Similarly, $0.18v$ is the amount of alcohol in the vermouth. And the final cocktail is 600 mL of liquid that is 34% alcohol, so it has $0.34(600) = 204$ milliliters of alcohol. All this means:

$$0.42(s\,\text{mL}) + 0.18(v\,\text{mL}) = 204\,\text{mL}$$

Or without units:

$$0.42s + 0.18v = 204$$

So our system is:

$$\begin{cases} s + \quad v = 600 \\ 0.42s + 0.18v = 204 \end{cases}$$

To solve this system, we'll solve for s in the first equation:

$$s + v = 600$$
$$s = 600 - v$$

And then substitute s in the second equation with $600 - v$:

$$0.42s + 0.18v = 204$$
$$0.42(600 - v) + 0.18v = 204$$
$$252 - 0.42v + 0.18v = 204$$
$$252 - 0.24v = 204$$
$$-0.24v = -48$$
$$\frac{-0.24v}{-0.24} = \frac{-48}{-0.24}$$
$$v = 200$$

As a last step, we will determine s using the equation where we had isolated s:

$$s = 600 - v$$
$$s = 600 - 200$$
$$s = 400$$

In summary, LaVonda needs to combine 400 mL of scotch with 200 mL of vermouth to create 600 mL of Rob Roy that is 34% alcohol by volume.

As a check for Example 4.2.12, we will use **estimation** to see that our solution is reasonable. Since LaVonda is making a 34% solution, she would need to use more of the 42% concentration than the 18% concentration, because 34% is closer to 42% than to 18%. This agrees with our answer because we found that she needed 400 mL of the 42% solution and 200 mL of the 18% solution. This is an added check that we have found reasonable answers.

Example 4.2.13 Mixing a Coffee Blend. Desi owns a coffee shop and they want to mix two different types of coffee beans to make a blend that sells for $12.50 per pound. They have some coffee beans from Columbia that sell for $9.00 per pound and some coffee beans from Honduras that sell for $14.00 per pound. How many pounds of each should they mix to make 30 pounds of the blend?

Explanation.   Before we begin, it may be helpful to try to estimate the solution. Let's compare the three prices. Since $12.50 is between the prices of $9.00 and $14.00, this mixture is possible. Now we need to estimate the amount of each type needed. The price of the blend ($12.50 per pound) is closer to the higher priced beans ($14.00 per pound) than the lower priced beans ($9.00 per pound). So we will need to use more of that type. Keeping in mind that we need a total of 30 pounds, we roughly estimate 20 pounds of the $14.00 Honduran beans and 10 pounds of the $9.00 Columbian beans. How good is our estimate? Next we will solve this exercise exactly.

To set up our system of equations we define variables, letting C be the amount of Columbian coffee beans (in pounds) and H be the amount of Honduran coffee beans (in pounds).

The equations in our system will come from the total amount of beans and the total cost. The equation for the total amount of beans can be written as:

$$(C \text{ lb}) + (H \text{ lb}) = 30 \text{ lb}$$

Or without units:

$$C + H = 30$$

To build the second equation, we have to think about the cost of all these beans. If we have C pounds of Columbian beans that cost $9.00 per pound, then 9C is the cost of those beans in dollars. Similarly, 14H is the cost of the Honduran beans. And the total cost is for 30 pounds of beans priced at $12.50 per pound, totaling $12.5(30) = 37.5$ dollars. All this means:

$$\left(9\ \tfrac{\text{dollars}}{\text{lb}}\right)(C\ \text{lb}) + \left(14\ \tfrac{\text{dollars}}{\text{lb}}\right)(H\ \text{lb}) = \left(12.50\ \tfrac{\text{dollars}}{\text{lb}}\right)(30\ \text{lb})$$

Or without units and carrying out the multiplication on the right:

$$9C + 14H = 37.5$$

Now our system is:

$$\begin{cases} C + H = 30 \\ 9C + 14H = 37.50 \end{cases}$$

To solve the system, we'll solve the first equation for C:

$$C + H = 30$$
$$C = 30 - H$$

Next, we'll substitute C in the second equation with $30 - H$:

$$9C + 14H = 375$$
$$9(30 - H) + 14H = 375$$
$$270 - 9H + 14H = 375$$
$$270 + 5H = 375$$
$$5H = 105$$
$$H = 21$$

Since $H = 21$, we can conclude that $C = 9$.

In summary, Desi needs to mix 21 pounds of the Honduran coffee beans with 9 pounds of the Columbian coffee beans to create this blend. Our estimate at the beginning was pretty close, so we feel this answer is reasonable.

4.2.3 Solving Special Systems of Equations with Substitution

Remember the two special cases we encountered when solving by graphing in Subsection 4.1.2? If the two lines represented by a system of equations have the same slope, then they might be separate lines that never meet, meaning the system has no solutions. Or they might coincide as the same line, in which case there are infinitely many solutions represented by all the points on that line. Let's see what happens when we use the substitution method on each of the special cases.

Example 4.2.14 A System with No Solution. Solve the system of equations using the substitution method:

$$\begin{cases} y = 2x - 1 \\ 4x - 2y = 3 \end{cases}$$

Explanation.   Since the first equation is already solved for y, we will substitute $2x - 1$ for y in the second equation, and we have:

$$4x - 2y = 3$$
$$4x - 2(2x - 1) = 3$$
$$4x - 4x + 2 = 3$$
$$2 = 3$$

Even though we were only intending to substitute away y, we ended up with an equation where there are no variables at all. This will happen whenever the lines have the same slope. This tells us the system represents either parallel or coinciding lines. Since $2 = 3$ is false no matter what values x and y might be, there can be no solution to the system. So the lines are parallel and *distinct*. We write the solution set using the empty set symbol: the solution set is $\emptyset$.

To verify this, re-write the second equation, $4x - 2y = 3$, in slope-intercept form:

$$4x - 2y = 3$$
$$-2y = -4x + 3$$
$$\frac{-2y}{-2} = \frac{-4x + 3}{-2}$$
$$y = \frac{-4x}{-2} + \frac{3}{-2}$$
$$y = 2x - \frac{3}{2}$$

So the system is equivalent to:

$$\begin{cases} y = 2x - 1 \\ y = 2x - \dfrac{3}{2} \end{cases}$$

Now it is easier to see that the two lines have the same slope but different y-intercepts. They are parallel and distinct lines, so the system has no solution.

Example 4.2.15 A System with Infinitely Many Solutions. Solve the system of equations using the substitution method:

$$\begin{cases} y = 2x - 1 \\ 4x - 2y = 2 \end{cases}$$

Explanation.   Since $y = 2x - 1$, we will substitute $2x - 1$ for y in the second equation and we have:

$$4x - 2y = 2$$
$$4x - 2(2x - 1) = 2$$
$$4x - 4x + 2 = 2$$
$$2 = 2$$

Even though we were only intending to substitute away y, we ended up with an equation where there are no variables at all. This will happen whenever the lines have the same slope. This tells us the system represents either parallel or coinciding lines. Since $2 = 2$ is true no matter what values x and y might be, the system equations are true no matter what x is, as long as $y = 2x - 1$. So the lines *coincide*. We write the solution set as $\{(x, y) \mid y = 2x - 1\}$.

To verify this, re-write the second equation, $4x - 2y = 2$, in slope-intercept form:

$$4x - 2y = 2$$
$$-2y = -4x + 2$$
$$\frac{-2y}{-2} = \frac{-4x}{-2} + \frac{2}{-2}$$
$$y = 2x - 1$$

The system looks like:

$$\begin{cases} y = 2x - 1 \\ y = 2x - 1 \end{cases}$$

Now it is easier to see that the two equations represent the same line. Every point on the line is a solution to the system, so the system has infinitely many solutions. The solution set is $\{(x, y) \mid y = 2x - 1\}$.

4.2.4 Reading Questions

1. Give an example of a system of two equations in x and y where it would be nicer to solve the system using substitution than by graphing the two lines that the equations define. Explain why substitution would be nicer than graphing for your example system.

2. What might be a good first step if you have a system of two linear equations in two variables where there are fractions appearing in the equations?

3. In an application problem, thinking about the ☐ can help you understand how to set up equations.

4.2.5 Exercises

Review and Warmup Solve the equation.

1. $\dfrac{5}{8} - 9a = 6$

2. $\dfrac{7}{4} - 7c = 6$

3. $\dfrac{3}{10} - \dfrac{1}{10}A = 4$

4. $\dfrac{7}{8} - \dfrac{1}{8}C = 1$

Solve the linear equation for y.

5. $-40x - 5y = -50$

6. $5y - 15x = -5$

7. $25x + 5y = -60$

8. $12x - 2y = -34$

9. $6x - y = -16$

10. $3x - y = -2$

Solving System of Equations Using Substitution Solve the following system of equations.

11. $\begin{cases} -4 + r = 0 \\ \quad 6 = -2r + 2c \end{cases}$

12. $\begin{cases} 4y = -4x \\ 4 = -x \end{cases}$

13. $\begin{cases} \quad -2y = -8 \\ -8 - 4x = -y \end{cases}$

14. $\begin{cases} -40 - 3y - 4x = 0 \\ \qquad\qquad 0 = -20 - 5y \end{cases}$

15. $\begin{cases} y = -5x + 21 \\ y = 2x + 7 \end{cases}$

16. $\begin{cases} y = -7 - 3x \\ y = 4x + 21 \end{cases}$

17. $\begin{cases} a = -3c + 5 \\ 2a + c = -10 \end{cases}$

18. $\begin{cases} b = -30 + 4m \\ 3b + 3m = -45 \end{cases}$

19. $\begin{cases} m = -20 - 5b \\ -m + 5b = 30 \end{cases}$

20. $\begin{cases} t = 12 - 2B \\ 2B - 5t = -12 \end{cases}$

21. $\begin{cases} x = 2y - 18 \\ 3y + 3x = 18 \end{cases}$

22. $\begin{cases} x = -18 + 5y \\ -3y - 3x = 36 \end{cases}$

23. $\begin{cases} x + y = -15 \\ 15 - 4x = -y \end{cases}$

24. $\begin{cases} 0 = x + 3y \\ y - 5x + 32 = 0 \end{cases}$

25. $\begin{cases} y = x + \dfrac{1}{2} \\ y = x - \dfrac{1}{2} \end{cases}$

26. $\begin{cases} C = 2 - 5q \\ C = 5 - 5q \end{cases}$

27. $\begin{cases} 2y = -8 - B \\ -5B - 2y = -8 \end{cases}$

28. $\begin{cases} -46 + 2a + 5A = 0 \\ \qquad\qquad 5a = -A \end{cases}$

29. $\begin{cases} -5m - 4 = 0 \\ \qquad -3m = -2 + 5A \end{cases}$

30. $\begin{cases} 5y = -3x - 2 \\ 5x = 5 \end{cases}$

31. $\begin{cases} -5x = 3 + y \\ -5x = -3y + 4 \end{cases}$

32. $\begin{cases} 2y + 2 = 3x \\ 5x + y = 3 \end{cases}$

33. $\begin{cases} 0 = 4 - y - 4x \\ -2x = 4y + 2 \end{cases}$

34. $\begin{cases} -x + 3y = -2 \\ -2x + 2y = 1 \end{cases}$

35. $\begin{cases} c = 1 \\ -2p + c = \dfrac{1}{4} \end{cases}$

36. $\begin{cases} -3p - 4A - 5 = 0 \\ \qquad\qquad -1 + A = 0 \end{cases}$

37. $\begin{cases} 0 = -4r - t - \dfrac{5}{2} \\ 0 = -2 + \dfrac{2}{5}r \end{cases}$

38. $\begin{cases} -\dfrac{2}{3} = -n + \dfrac{3}{2}C \\ \qquad 0 = 1 - n \end{cases}$

39. $\begin{cases} x + \dfrac{5}{2} + \dfrac{5}{3}y = 0 \\ \dfrac{3}{4}x - \dfrac{1}{4} = 2y \end{cases}$

40. $\begin{cases} \dfrac{4}{3}x + 2 = y \\ x + 2y = \dfrac{2}{3} \end{cases}$

41. $\begin{cases} 0 = -\dfrac{5}{3}y + \dfrac{5}{2} + x \\ 0 = 3x + \dfrac{4}{3} - y \end{cases}$

42. $\begin{cases} -\dfrac{3}{2}x - y = -\dfrac{1}{5} \\ -y = -\dfrac{3}{5}x + 1 \end{cases}$

43. $\begin{cases} -3y - 5x = -3 \\ 2y + 2x = -2 \end{cases}$

44. $\begin{cases} 5x - 3y = -1 \\ -3y - 4x = -4 \end{cases}$

45. $\begin{cases} x + 4y = \dfrac{49}{10} \\ -2x - y = -\dfrac{77}{40} \end{cases}$

46. $\begin{cases} -5x + y = -\dfrac{71}{12} \\ -4x + 5y = -\dfrac{19}{12} \end{cases}$

47. $\begin{cases} \dfrac{1}{5}x - \dfrac{1}{2}y = -\dfrac{97}{60} \\ \dfrac{1}{5}x + \dfrac{1}{4}y = \dfrac{121}{120} \end{cases}$

48. $\begin{cases} -\dfrac{1}{5}x + \dfrac{1}{2}y = \dfrac{31}{100} \\ -\dfrac{1}{3}x + \dfrac{1}{2}y = \dfrac{3}{20} \end{cases}$

49. $\begin{cases} 2x + 3y = 36 \\ 5x + 4y = 55 \end{cases}$

50. $\begin{cases} 4x + 2y = 26 \\ 5x + y = 28 \end{cases}$

51. $\begin{cases} -x + 6y = -32 \\ 5x + 4y = 24 \end{cases}$

52. $\begin{cases} 4x - 5y = -5 \\ 4x + 3y = 67 \end{cases}$

53. $\begin{cases} -x - 3y = 3 \\ -x - 2y = 5 \end{cases}$

54. $\begin{cases} -4x - 5y = 53 \\ -x - 5y = 32 \end{cases}$

55. $\begin{cases} 3x + 4y = 24 \\ 3x = -12 \end{cases}$

56. $\begin{cases} -3x + y = 7 \\ 3x = -6 \end{cases}$

57. $\begin{cases} 3x + 2y = 6 \\ -9x - 6y = 6 \end{cases}$

58. $\begin{cases} 4x + 5y = 6 \\ -8x - 10y = 6 \end{cases}$

59. $\begin{cases} 4x + 3y = 5 \\ 12x + 9y = 15 \end{cases}$

60. $\begin{cases} 5x + y = 5 \\ 20x + 4y = 20 \end{cases}$

Applications

61. A rectangle's length is 5 feet shorter than five times its width. The rectangle's perimeter is 590 feet. Find the rectangle's length and width.

The rectangle's length is [   ] feet, and its width is [   ] feet.

62. A school fund raising event sold a total of 191 tickets and generated a total revenue of $586.25. There are two types of tickets: adult tickets and child tickets. Each adult ticket costs $6.95, and each child ticket costs $1.50. Write and solve a system of equations to answer the following questions.

[   ] adult tickets and [   ] child tickets were sold.

63. Phone Company A charges a monthly fee of $43.80, and $0.02 for each minute of talk time. Phone Company B charges a monthly fee of $35.00, and $0.06 for each minute of talk time. Write and solve a system equation to answer the following questions.

These two companies would charge the same amount on a monthly bill when the talk time was

[   ] minutes.

64. Company A's revenue this fiscal year is $878,000, but its revenue is decreasing by $17,000 each year. Company B's revenue this fiscal year is $488,000, and its revenue is increasing by $13,000 each year. Write and solve a system of equations to answer the following question.

After [   ] years, Company B will catch up with Company A in revenue.

65. A test has 25 problems, which are worth a total of 100 points. There are two types of problems in the test. Each multiple-choice problem is worth 3 points, and each short-answer problem is worth 8 points. Write and solve a system equation to answer the following questions.

This test has [   ] multiple-choice problems and [   ] short-answer problems.

66. Candi invested a total of $7,500 in two accounts. One account pays 3% interest annually; the other pays 4% interest annually. At the end of the year, Candi earned a total of $255 in interest. Write and solve a system of equations to find how much money Candi invested in each account.

Candi invested [   ] in the 3% account and [   ] in the 4% account.

67. Katherine invested a total of $13,000 in two accounts. After a year, one account lost 8.8%, while the other account gained 4.6%. In total, Katherine lost $608. Write and solve a system of equations to find how much money Katherine invested in each account.

Katherine invested [   ] in the account with 8.8% loss and [   ] in the account with 4.6% gain.

68. Town A and Town B were located close to each other, and recently merged into one city. Town A had a population with 8% Asians. Town B had a population with 10% Asians. After the merge, the new city has a total of 4000 residents, with 9.3% Asians. Write and solve a system of equations to find how many residents Town A and Town B used to have.

Town A used to have [   ] residents, and Town B used to have [   ] residents.

69. You poured some 6% alcohol solution and some 12% alcohol solution into a mixing container. Now you have 600 grams of 10% alcohol solution. How many grams of 6% solution and how many grams of 12% solution did you pour into the mixing container?

Write and solve a system equation to answer the following questions.

You mixed [   ] grams of 6% solution with [   ] grams of 12% solution.

70. Briana invested a total of $10,000 in two accounts. One account pays 7% interest annually; the other pays 2% interest annually. At the end of the year, Briana earned a total of $400 in interest. How much money did Briana invest in each account?

Briana invested [   ] in the 7% account and [   ] in the 2% account.

71. Blake invested a total of $52,000 in two accounts. One account pays 5.5% interest annually; the other pays 4.6% interest annually. At the end of the year, Blake earned a total interest of $2,734. How much money did Blake invest in each account?

Blake invested [   ] in the 5.5% account and [   ] in the 4.6% account.

72. Renee invested a total of $9,000 in two accounts. One account pays 3% interest annually; the other pays 6% interest annually. At the end of the year, Renee earned the same amount of interest from both accounts. How much money did Renee invest in each account?

    Renee invested [   ] in the 3% account and [   ] in the 6% account.

73. Stephen invested a total of $40,000 in two accounts. One account pays 6.6% interest annually; the other pays 3.4% interest annually. At the end of the year, Stephen earned the same amount of interest from both accounts. How much money did Stephen invest in each account?

    Stephen invested [   ] in the 6.6% account [   ] in the 3.4% account.

74. Hannah invested a total of $12,000 in two accounts. After a year, one account had *earned* 11.7%, while the other account had *lost* 7.6%. In total, Hannah had a net gain of $535.50. How much money did Hannah invest in each account?

    Hannah invested [   ] in the account that grew by 11.7% and [   ] in the account that fell by 7.6%.

75. You've poured some 12% (by mass) alcohol solution and some 8% alcohol solution into a large glass mixing container. Now you have 800 grams of 10% alcohol solution. How many grams of 12% solution and how many grams of 8% solution did you pour into the mixing container?

    You poured [   ] grams of 12% solution and [   ] grams of 8% solution into the mixing container.

76. A store has some beans selling for $1.70 per pound, and some vegetables selling for $3.10 per pound. The store plans to use them to produce 14 pounds of mixture and sell for $2.57 per pound. How many pounds of beans and how many pounds of vegetables should be used?

    To produce 14 pounds of mixture, the store should use [   ] pounds of beans and [   ] pounds of vegetables.

77. Town A and Town B were located close to each other, and recently merged into one city. Town A had a population with 6% African Americans. Town B had a population with 10% African Americans. After the merge, the new city has a total of 4000 residents, with 8.8% African Americans. How many residents did Town A and Town B used to have?

    Town A used to have [   ] residents, and Town B used to have [   ] residents.

4.3 Elimination

We learned how to solve a system of linear equations using substitution in Section 4.2. In this section, we will learn a second symbolic method for solving systems of linear equations.

4.3.1 Solving Systems of Equations by Elimination

Example 4.3.2 Alicia has $1000 to give to her two grandchildren for New Year's. She would like to give the older grandchild $120 more than the younger grandchild, because that is the cost of the older grandchild's college textbooks this term. How much money should she give to each grandchild?

To answer this question, we will demonstrate a new technique. You may have a very good way for finding how much money Alicia should give to each grandchild, but right now we will try to see this new method.

Let A be the dollar amount she gives to her older grandchild, and B be the dollar amount she gives to her younger grandchild. (As always, we start solving a word problem like this by defining the variables, including their units.) Since the total she has to give is $1000, we can say that $A + B = 1000$. And since she wants to give $120 more to the older grandchild, we can say that $A - B = 120$. So we have the system of equations:

$$\begin{cases} A + B = 1000 \\ A - B = 120 \end{cases}$$

We could solve this system by substitution as we learned in Section 4.2, but there is an easier method. If we add together the *left* sides from the two equations, it should equal the sum of the *right* sides:

$$\begin{array}{rcr} A + B & & 1000 \\ + A - B & = & + 120 \end{array}$$

So we have:

$$2A = 1120$$

Note that the variable B is eliminated. This happened because the " $+ B$ " and the " $- B$ " perfectly cancel each other out when they are added. With only one variable left, it doesn't take much to finish:

$$2A = 1120$$
$$A = 560$$

To finish solving this system of equations, we need the value of B. For now, an easy way to find B is to substitute in our value of A into one of the original equations:

$$A + B = 1000$$
$$560 + B = 1000$$
$$B = 440$$

To check our work, substitute $A = 560$ and $B = 440$ into the original equations:

$$A + B = 1000 \qquad\qquad A - B = 120$$
$$560 + 440 \overset{?}{=} 1000 \qquad\qquad 560 - 440 \overset{?}{=} 120$$
$$1000 \overset{\checkmark}{=} 1000 \qquad\qquad 120 \overset{\checkmark}{=} 120$$

This confirms that our solution is correct. In summary, Alicia should give \$560 to her older grandchild, and \$440 to her younger grandchild.

This method for solving the system of equations in Example 4.3.2 worked because B and $-B$ add to zero. Once the B-terms were eliminated we were able to solve for A. This method is called the **elimination method**. Some people call it the **addition method**, because we added the corresponding sides from the two equations to eliminate a variable.

If neither variable can be immediately eliminated, we can still use this method but it will require that we first adjust one or both of the equations. Let's look at an example where we need to adjust one of the equations.

Example 4.3.3 Scaling One Equation. Solve the system of equations using the elimination method.

$$\begin{cases} 3x - 4y = 2 \\ 5x + 8y = 18 \end{cases}$$

Explanation. To start, we want to see whether it will be easier to eliminate x or y. We see that the coefficients of x in each equation are 3 and 5, and the coefficients of y are -4 and 8. Because 8 is a multiple of 4 and the coefficients already have opposite signs, the y variable will be easier to eliminate.

To eliminate the y terms, we will multiply each side of the first equation by 2 so that we will have $-8y$. We can call this process scaling the first equation by 2.

$$\begin{cases} 2 \cdot (3x - 4y) = 2 \cdot (2) \\ 5x + 8y = 18 \end{cases}$$
$$\begin{cases} 6x - 8y = 4 \\ 5x + 8y = 18 \end{cases}$$

We now have an equivalent system of equations where the y-terms can be eliminated:

$$\begin{aligned} 6x - 8y &\\ + 5x + 8y &\end{aligned} = \begin{aligned} 4 \\ + 18 \end{aligned}$$

So we have:

$$11x = 22$$
$$x = 2$$

To solve for y, we can substitute 2 for x into either of the original equations or the new one. We use the first original equation, $3x - 4y = 2$:

$$3x - 4y = 2$$
$$3(2) - 4y = 2$$
$$6 - 4y = 2$$
$$-4y = -4$$
$$y = 1$$

Our solution is $x = 2$ and $y = 1$. We will check this in both of the original equations:

$$5x + 8y = 18 \qquad\qquad\qquad 3x - 4y = 2$$
$$5(2) + 8(1) \overset{?}{=} 18 \qquad\qquad 3(2) - 4(1) \overset{?}{=} 2$$
$$10 + 8 \overset{\checkmark}{=} 18 \qquad\qquad\qquad 6 - 4 \overset{\checkmark}{=} 2$$

The solution to this system is $(2, 1)$ and the solution set is $\{(2, 1)\}$.

Checkpoint 4.3.4 Solve the following system of equations.

$$\begin{cases} 5x + 4y = -7 \\ 5x + 2y = -1 \end{cases}$$

Explanation.

1. We subtract the two equations, which will cancel the terms in involving x and give $4y - 2y = -7 - (-1)$.

2. This gives $y = -3$.

3. Now that we have y, we find x using either equation. Let's use the first: $5x - 12 = -7$, so $x = 1$.

4. The solution to the system is $(1, -3)$. It is left as an exercise to check. Please also note that you may have solved this problem a different way.

Here's an example where we have to scale both equations.

Example 4.3.5 Scaling Both Equations. Solve the system of equations using the elimination method.

$$\begin{cases} 2x + 3y = 10 \\ -3x + 5y = -15 \end{cases}$$

Explanation. Considering the coefficients of x (2 and -3) and the coefficients of y (3 and 5) we see that we cannot eliminate the x or the y variable by scaling a single equation. We will need to scale *both*.

The x-terms already have opposite signs, so we choose to eliminate x. The least common multiple of 2 and 3 is 6. We can scale the first equation by 3 and the second equation by 2 so that the equations have terms $6x$ and $-6x$, which will cancel when added.

$$\begin{cases} 3 \cdot (2x + 3y) = 3 \cdot (10) \\ 2 \cdot (-3x + 5y) = 2 \cdot (-15) \end{cases}$$

$$\begin{cases} 6x + 9y = 30 \\ -6x + 10y = -30 \end{cases}$$

At this point we can add the corresponding sides from the two equations and solve for y:

$$\begin{array}{r} 6x + 9y \\ -6x + 10y \end{array} = \begin{array}{r} 30 \\ -30 \end{array}$$

So we have:

$$19y = 0$$
$$y = 0$$

To solve for x, we'll replace y with 0 in $2x + 3y = 10$:

$$2x + 3y = 10$$
$$2x + 3(0) = 10$$
$$2x = 10$$
$$x = 5$$

We'll check the system using $x = 5$ and $y = 0$ in each of the original equations:

$$2x + 3y = 10 \qquad\qquad -3x + 5y = -15$$
$$2(5) + 3(0) \stackrel{?}{=} 10 \qquad\qquad -3(5) + 5(0) \stackrel{?}{=} -15$$
$$10 + 0 \stackrel{\checkmark}{=} 10 \qquad\qquad -15 + 0 \stackrel{\checkmark}{=} -15$$

So the system's solution is $(5, 0)$ and the solution set is $\{(5, 0)\}$.

Checkpoint 4.3.6 Try a similar exercise.

Solve the following system of equations.

$$\begin{cases} 3x + 4y = -26 \\ 5x + 5y = -40 \end{cases}$$

Explanation.

1. Let's multiply the *first* equation by 5 and the *second* equation by 3

$$15x + 20y = -130$$
$$15x + 15y = -120$$

2. Subtracting these two equations gives $20y - 15y = -10$, so $y = -2$.

3. Now that we have y, we can use either equation to find x; let's use the first one:

$$3x + (4) \cdot (-2) = -26$$

so $x = -6$.

4. The solution to the system is $(-6, -2)$. It is left as an exercise to check. Please also note that you may have solved this problem a different way.

Example 4.3.7 Meal Planning. Javed is on a meal plan and needs to consume 600 calories and 20 grams of fat for breakfast. A small avocado contains 300 calories and 30 grams of fat. He has bagels that contain 400 calories and 8 grams of fat. Write and solve a system of equations to determine how much bagel and avocado would combine to make his target calories and fat.

Explanation.   To write this system of equations, we first need to define our variables. Let A be the number of avocados consumed and let B be the number of bagels consumed. Both A and B might be fractions. For our first equation, we will count calories from the avocados and bagels:

$$\left(300 \, \tfrac{\text{calories}}{\text{avocado}}\right) (A \text{ avocados}) + \left(400 \, \tfrac{\text{calories}}{\text{bagel}}\right) (B \text{ bagel}) = 600 \text{ calories}$$

Or, without the units:

$$300A + 400B = 600$$

Similarly, for our second equation, we will count the grams of fat:

$$\left(30 \, \tfrac{\text{g fat}}{\text{avocado}}\right) (A \text{ avocados}) + \left(8 \, \tfrac{\text{g fat}}{\text{bagel}}\right) (B \text{ bagel}) = 20 \text{ g fat}$$

Or, without the units:

$$30A + 8B = 20$$

So the system of equations is:

$$\begin{cases} 300A + 400B = 600 \\ 30A + 8B = 20 \end{cases}$$

Since none of the coefficients are equal to 1, it will be easier to use the elimination method to solve this system. Looking at the terms $300A$ and $30A$, we can eliminate the A variable if we multiply the second equation by -10 to get $-300A$:

$$\begin{cases} 300A + 400B = 600 \\ -10 \cdot (30A + 8B) = -10 \cdot (20) \end{cases}$$

$$\begin{cases} 300A + 400B = 600 \\ -300A + (-80B) = -200 \end{cases}$$

When we add the corresponding sides from the two equations together we have:

$$\frac{300A + 400B}{-300A - 80B} = \frac{600}{-200}$$

So we have:

$$320B = 400$$

$$\frac{320B}{320} = \frac{400}{320}$$

$$B = \frac{5}{4}$$

We now know that Javed should eat $\frac{5}{4}$ bagels (or one and one-quarter bagels). To determine the number of avocados, we will substitute B with $\frac{5}{4}$ in either of our original equations.

$$300A + 400B = 600$$
$$300A + 400\left(\frac{5}{4}\right) = 600$$
$$300A + 500 = 600$$
$$300A = 100$$
$$\frac{300A}{300} = \frac{100}{300}$$
$$A = \frac{1}{3}$$

To check this result, try using $B = \frac{5}{4}$ and $A = \frac{1}{3}$ in each of the original equations:

$$300A + 400B = 600 \qquad\qquad 30A + 8B = 20$$
$$300\left(\frac{1}{3}\right) + 400\left(\frac{5}{4}\right) \overset{?}{=} 600 \qquad\qquad 30\left(\frac{1}{3}\right) + 8\left(\frac{5}{4}\right) \overset{?}{=} 20$$
$$100 + 500 \overset{\checkmark}{=} 600 \qquad\qquad 10 + 10 \overset{\checkmark}{=} 20$$

In summary, Javed can eat $\frac{5}{4}$ of a bagel (so one and one-quarter bagel) and $\frac{1}{3}$ of an avocado in order to consume exactly 600 calories and 20 grams of fat.

For summary reference, here is the general procedure.

Process 4.3.8 Solving Systems of Equations by Elimination. *To solve a system of equations by elimination,*

1. *Algebraically manipulate both equations into standard form, unless the variables are already aligned (e.g. if both equations are in slope intercept form already).*

2. *Scale one or both of the equations to force one of the variables to have equal but opposite sign in the two equations.*

3. *Add the corresponding sides of the two equations together which should have the effect that one variable cancels out entirely.*

4. *Solve the resulting equation for the one remaining variable.*

5. *Substitute that value into either of the original equations to find the other variable.*

6. *Verify your solution.*

4.3.2 Solving Special Systems of Equations with Elimination

Remember the two special cases we encountered when solving by graphing and substitution? Sometimes a system of equations has no solutions at all, and sometimes the solution set is infinite with all of the points on one line satisfying the equations. Let's see what happens when we use the elimination method on each of the special cases.

Example 4.3.9 A System with Infinitely Many Solutions. Solve the system of equations using the elimination method.

$$\begin{cases} 3x + 4y = 5 \\ 6x + 8y = 10 \end{cases}$$

Explanation. To eliminate the x-terms, we multiply each term in the first equation by -2, and we have:

$$\begin{cases} -2 \cdot (3x + 4y) = -2 \cdot 5 \\ 6x + 8y = 10 \end{cases}$$

$$\begin{cases} -6x + -8y = -10 \\ 6x + 8y = 10 \end{cases}$$

We might notice that the equations look very similar. Adding the respective sides of the equation, we have:

$$0 = 0$$

Both of the variables have been eliminated. Since the statement $0 = 0$ is true no matter what x and y are, the solution set is infinite. Specifically, you just need any (x, y) satisfying *one* of the two equations, since the two equations represent the same line. We can write the solution set as $\{(x, y) \mid 3x + 4y = 5\}$.

Example 4.3.10 A System with No Solution. Solve the system of equations using the elimination method.

$$\begin{cases} 10x + 6y = 9 \\ 25x + 15y = 4 \end{cases}$$

Explanation. To eliminate the x-terms, we will scale the first equation by -5 and the second by 2:

$$\begin{cases} -5 \cdot (10x + 6y) = -5 \cdot (9) \\ 2 \cdot (25x + 15y) = 2 \cdot (4) \end{cases}$$

$$\begin{cases} -50x + (-30y) = -45 \\ 50x + 30y = 8 \end{cases}$$

Adding the respective sides of the equation, we have:

$$0 = -37$$

Both of the variables have been eliminated. In this case, the statement $0 = -37$ is just false, no matter what x and y are. So the system has no solution.

4.3.3 Deciding to Use Substitution versus Elimination

In every example so far from this section, both equations were in standard form, $Ax + By = C$. And all of the coefficients were integers . If none of the coefficients are equal to 1 then it is usually easier to use the elimination method, because otherwise you will probably have some fraction arithmetic to do in the middle of the substitution method. If there *is* a coefficient of 1, then it is a matter of preference.

Example 4.3.11 A college used to have a north campus with 6000 students and a south campus with 15,000 students. The percentage of students at the north campus who self-identify as LGBTQ was three times the percentage at the south campus. After the merge, 5.5% of students identify as LGBTQ. What percentage of students on each campus identified as LGBTQ before the merge?

Explanation. We will define N as the percentage (as a decimal) of students at the north campus and S as the percentage (as a decimal) of students at the south campus that identified as LGBTQ. Since the percentage of students at the north campus was three times the percentage at the south campus, we have:

$$N = 3S$$

For our second equation, we will count LGBTQ students at the various campuses. At the north campus, multiply the population, 6000, by the percentage N to get 6000N. This must be the actual number of LGBTQ students. Similarly, the south campus has 15000S LGBTQ students, and the combined school has $21000(0.055) = 1155$. When we combine the two campuses, we have:

$$6000N + 15000S = 1155$$

We write the system as:

$$\begin{cases} N = 3S \\ 6000N + 15000S = 1155 \end{cases}$$

Because the first equation is already solved for N, this is a good time to *not* use the elimination method. Instead we can substitute N in our second equation with 3S and solve for S:

$$6000N + 15000S = 1155$$
$$6000(3S) + 15000S = 1155$$
$$18000S + 15000S = 1155$$
$$33000S = 1155$$
$$\frac{33000S}{33000} = \frac{1155}{33000}$$
$$S = 0.035$$

We can determine N using the first equation:

$$N = 3S$$
$$N = 3(0.035)$$
$$N = 0.105$$

Before the merge, 10.5% of the north campus students self-identified as LGBTQ, and 3.5% of the south campus students self-identified as LGBTQ.

If you need to solve a system, and one of the equations is not in standard form, substitution may be easier. But you also may find it easier to convert the equations into standard form. Additionally, if the system's coefficients are fractions or decimals, you may take an additional step to scale the equations so that they only have integer coefficients.

Example 4.3.12 Solve the system of equations using the method of your choice.

$$\begin{cases} -\dfrac{1}{3}y = \dfrac{1}{15}x + \dfrac{1}{5} \\ \dfrac{5}{2}x - y = 6 \end{cases}$$

Explanation.   First, we can cancel the fractions by using the least common multiple of the denominators in each equation, similarly to the topic of Section 2.3. We have:

$$\begin{cases} 15 \cdot -\dfrac{1}{3}y = 15 \cdot \left(\dfrac{1}{15}x + \dfrac{1}{5}\right) \\ 2 \cdot \left(\dfrac{5}{2}x - y\right) = 2 \cdot (6) \end{cases}$$

$$\begin{cases} -5y = x + 3 \\ 5x - 2y = 12 \end{cases}$$

We could put convert the first equation into standard form by subtracting x from both sides, and then use elimination. However, the x-variable in the first equation has a coefficient of 1, so the substitution method may be faster. Solving for x in the first equation we have:

$$-5y = x + 3$$
$$-5y - 3 = x + 3 - 3$$
$$-5y - 3 = x$$

Substituting $-5y - 3$ for x in the second equation we have:

$$5(-5y - 3) - 2y = 12$$
$$-25y - 15 - 2y = 12$$
$$-27y - 15 = 12$$
$$-27y = 27$$
$$y = -1$$

Using the equation where we isolated x and substituting -1 for y, we have:

$$-5(-1) - 3 = x$$
$$5 - 3 = x$$
$$2 = x$$

The solution is $(2, -1)$. Checking the solution is left as an exercise.

Example 4.3.13 A penny is made by combining copper and zinc. A chemistry reference source says copper has a density of $9 \frac{g}{cm^3}$ and zinc has a density of $7.1 \frac{g}{cm^3}$. A penny's mass is $2.5\,g$ and its volume is $0.35\,cm^3$. How many cm^3 each of copper and zinc go into one penny?

Explanation.   Let c be the volume of copper and z be the volume of zinc in one penny, both measured in cm^3. Since the total volume is 0.35 cm^3, one equation is:

$$\left(c \text{ cm}^3\right) + \left(z \text{ cm}^3\right) = 0.35 \text{ cm}^3$$

Or without units:

$$c + z = 0.35.$$

For the second equation, we will examine the masses of copper and zinc. Since copper has a density of $9 \frac{g}{cm^3}$ and we are using c to represent the volume of copper, the mass of copper is $9c$. Similarly, the mass of zinc is 7.1. Since the total mass is 2.5 g, we have the equation:

$$\left(9 \tfrac{g}{cm^3}\right)\left(c \text{ cm}^3\right) + \left(7.1 \tfrac{g}{cm^3}\right)\left(z \text{ cm}^3\right) = 2.5 \text{ g}$$

Or without units:

$$9c + 7.1z = 2.5.$$

So we have a system of equations:

$$\begin{cases} c + \quad z = 0.35 \\ 9c + 7.1z = \quad 2.5 \end{cases}$$

Since the coefficient of c (or z) in the first equation is 1, we could solve for one of these variables and use substitution to complete the problem. Some decimal arithmetic would be required. Alternatively, we can scale the equations by the right power of 10 to make all the coefficients integers:

$$\begin{cases} 100 \cdot (c + \quad z) = 100 \cdot (0.35) \\ 10 \cdot (9c + 7.1z) = \quad 10 \cdot (2.5) \end{cases}$$

$$\begin{cases} 100c + 100z = 35 \\ 90c + 71z \ = 25 \end{cases}$$

Now to set up elimination, scale each equation again to eliminate c:

$$\begin{cases} 9 \cdot (100c + 100z) = \quad 9 \cdot (35) \\ -10 \cdot (90c + \ 71z) = -10 \cdot (25) \end{cases}$$

$$\begin{cases} 900c + 900z \quad = 315 \\ -900c + (-710z) = -250 \end{cases}$$

Adding the corresponding sides from the two equations gives

$$190z = 65,$$

from which we find $z = \frac{65}{190} \approx 0.342$. So there is about 0.342 cm^3 of zinc in a penny. To solve for c, we can use one of the original equations:

$$c + z = 0.35$$
$$c + 0.342 \approx 0.35$$
$$c \approx 0.008$$

Therefore there is about 0.342 cm^3 of zinc and 0.008 cm^3 of copper in a penny.

To summarize, if a variable is already isolated or has a coefficient of 1, consider using the substitution method. If both equations are in standard form or none of the coefficients are equal to 1, we suggest using the elimination method. Either way, if you have fraction or decimal coefficients, it may help to scale your equations so that only integer coefficients remain.

4.3.4 Reading Questions

1. What is another name that the "elimination method" goes by?

2. To use the elimination method, usually the first step is to ⬚ at least one equation.

3. Describe a good situation to use the substitution method instead of the elimination method for solving a system of two linear equations in two variables.

4.3.5 Exercises

Review and Warmup Solve the equation.

1. $\dfrac{3}{4} - 10x = 6$

2. $\dfrac{7}{10} - 8r = 6$

3. $\dfrac{5}{6} - \dfrac{1}{6}a = 5$

4. $\dfrac{5}{2} - \dfrac{1}{2}b = 2$

5. $\dfrac{8A}{9} - 9 = -\dfrac{89}{9}$

6. $\dfrac{4B}{5} - 7 = -\dfrac{43}{5}$

Solving System of Equations by Elimination Solve the following system of equations.

7. $\begin{cases} 4x + 2y = 4 \\ 3x + y = 7 \end{cases}$

8. $\begin{cases} x + y = 13 \\ 2x + 3y = 32 \end{cases}$

9. $\begin{cases} 4x - 2y = 42 \\ 5x + 2y = 48 \end{cases}$

10. $\begin{cases} -5x + 3y = 18 \\ 4x + 6y = -90 \end{cases}$

11. $\begin{cases} -4x - 4y = 8 \\ -4x - 5y = 3 \end{cases}$

12. $\begin{cases} -2x - y = 10 \\ -4x - 3y = 22 \end{cases}$

13. $\begin{cases} -3x + 2y = -14 \\ -2x = 4 \end{cases}$

14. $\begin{cases} x - y = -4 \\ -2x = 0 \end{cases}$

15. $\begin{cases} 4x + 2y = -4 \\ -8x - 4y = -4 \end{cases}$

16. $\begin{cases} 4x + y = -4 \\ 12x + 3y = -4 \end{cases}$

17. $\begin{cases} 5x + 4y = -5 \\ 20x + 16y = -20 \end{cases}$

18. $\begin{cases} 5x + 2y = -5 \\ -10x - 4y = 10 \end{cases}$

19. $\begin{cases} 6 + C = -2q \\ 6 - 4C = 5q \end{cases}$

20. $\begin{cases} -y = -57 + 4B \\ -5y = B - 38 \end{cases}$

21. $\begin{cases} -5y - x = 2 \\ y + 4x = 4 \end{cases}$

22. $\begin{cases} -4x + 5y = -4 \\ y - 2x = 1 \end{cases}$

23. $\begin{cases} -y = -4x - 30 \\ -30 + 3x + 3y = 0 \end{cases}$

24. $\begin{cases} 2x = 5y + 34 \\ 3x + 51 = -y \end{cases}$

25. $\begin{cases} y + 3 = 4x \\ -1 - 4y - 3x = 0 \end{cases}$

26. $\begin{cases} -3 = 2y + x \\ 3x = -2y \end{cases}$

27. $\begin{cases} 3x - 4y = -3 \\ 1 - x + 4y = 0 \end{cases}$

28. $\begin{cases} -5n + 2c = -2 \\ -n + 5 = 2c \end{cases}$

29. $\begin{cases} -3p + \dfrac{1}{2} - 3c = 0 \\ -\dfrac{4}{5} + p = -\dfrac{1}{3}c \end{cases}$

30. $\begin{cases} q = \dfrac{3}{5} - y \\ 0 = \dfrac{1}{3}q - \dfrac{5}{2} + \dfrac{5}{4}y \end{cases}$

31. $\begin{cases} -C = 5 + 2n \\ \dfrac{1}{2} = -\dfrac{3}{4}C - \dfrac{3}{2}n \end{cases}$

32. $\begin{cases} -y - 4 - \dfrac{3}{4}x = 0 \\ 2y - 2x = \dfrac{4}{5} \end{cases}$

33. $\begin{cases} 3x + 13 = 5y \\ -12x = -20y + 52 \end{cases}$

34. $\begin{cases} 0 = 1 + 4x + 4y \\ x + 1 + y = 0 \end{cases}$

35. $\begin{cases} x + y = \dfrac{17}{6} \\ 2x - 4y = \dfrac{2}{3} \end{cases}$

36. $\begin{cases} -x + y = -\dfrac{13}{12} \\ -3x - 3y = -\dfrac{67}{4} \end{cases}$

37. $\begin{cases} \dfrac{1}{2}x - \dfrac{1}{3}y = -\dfrac{13}{18} \\ \dfrac{1}{5}x - \dfrac{1}{2}y = -\dfrac{217}{180} \end{cases}$

38. $\begin{cases} -\dfrac{1}{5}x + \dfrac{1}{3}y = \dfrac{59}{200} \\ -\dfrac{1}{2}x + \dfrac{1}{4}y = \dfrac{13}{160} \end{cases}$

Applications

39. A test has 17 problems, which are worth a total of 72 points. There are two types of problems in the test. Each multiple-choice problem is worth 3 points, and each short-answer problem is worth 6 points. Write and solve a system of equations to answer the following questions.

This test has [_____] multiple-choice problems and [_____] short-answer problems.

40. Kandace invested a total of $7,000 in two accounts. One account pays 5% interest annually; the other pays 4% interest annually. At the end of the year, Kandace earned a total of $305 in interest. Write and solve a system of equations to find how much money Kandace invested in each account.

Kandace invested [_____] in the 5% account and [_____] in the 4% account.

41. Adrian invested a total of $12,000 in two accounts. After a year, one account lost 6.8%, while the other account gained 6.9%. In total, Adrian lost $473.50. Write and solve a system of equations to find how much money Adrian invested in each.

Adrian invested [   ] in the account with 6.8% loss and [   ] in the account with 6.9% gain.

42. Town A and Town B were located close to each other, and recently merged into one city. Town A had a population with 12% whites. Town B had a population with 10% whites. After the merge, the new city has a total of 4000 residents, with 10.7% whites. Write and solve a system of equations to find how many residents Town A and Town B used to have.

Town A used to have [   ] residents, and Town B used to have [   ] residents.

43. You poured some 6% alcohol solution and some 10% alcohol solution into a mixing container. Now you have 600 grams of 8.8% alcohol solution. Write and solve a system of equations to find how many grams of 6% solution and how many grams of 10% solution you poured into the mixing container.

You mixed [   ] grams of 6% solution with [   ] grams of 10% solution.

44. You will purchase some CDs and DVDs. If you purchase 15 CDs and 14 DVDs, it will cost you $165.60; if you purchase 14 CDs and 15 DVDs, it will cost you $166.45. Write and solve a system of equations to answer the following questions.

Each CD costs [   ] and each DVD costs [   ].

45. A school fund raising event sold a total of 235 tickets and generated a total revenue of $1,085.60. There are two types of tickets: adult tickets and child tickets. Each adult ticket costs $5.80, and each child ticket costs $3.90. Write and solve a system of equations to answer the following questions.

[   ] adult tickets and [   ] child tickets were sold.

46. Phone Company A charges a monthly fee of $42.00, and $0.04 for each minute of talk time. Phone Company B charges a monthly fee of $30.00, and $0.10 for each minute of talk time. Write and solve a system equation to answer the following questions.

These two companies would charge the same amount on a monthly bill when the talk time was [   ] minutes.

47. Company A's revenue this fiscal year is $843,000, but its revenue is decreasing by $8,000 each year. Company B's revenue this fiscal year is $634,000, and its revenue is increasing by $11,000 each year. Write and solve a system of equations to answer the following question.

After [   ] years, Company B will catch up with Company A in revenue.

48. If a boat travels from Town A to Town B, it has to travel 1190 mi along a river. A boat traveled from Town A to Town B along the river's current with its engine running at full speed. This trip took 42.5 hr. Then the boat traveled back from Town B to Town A, again with the engine at full speed, but this time against the river's current. This trip took 119 hr. Write and solve a system of equations to answer the following questions.

The boat's speed in still water with the engine running at full speed is [   ].

The river current's speed was [   ].

49. A small fair charges different admission for adults and children. It charges $2.50 for adults, and $1.50 for children. On a certain day, the total revenue is $3,764 and the fair admits 2000 people. How many adults and children were admitted?

There were [   ] adults and [   ] children at the fair.

Challenge

50. Find the value of b so that the system of equations has an infinite number of solutions.

$$\begin{cases} -16x + 28y = -4 \\ 4x - by = 1 \end{cases}$$

4.4 Systems of Linear Equations Chapter Review

4.4.1 Solving Systems of Linear Equations by Graphing

In Section 4.1 we covered the definition of system of linear equations and how a solution to a system of linear equation is a point where the graphs of the two equations cross. We also considered special systems of equations where the lines they define coincide or never cross.

Example 4.4.1 Solving Systems of Linear Equations by Graphing. Solve the following system of equations by graphing:

$$\begin{cases} y = -\dfrac{2}{3}x - 4 \\ y = -4x - 14 \end{cases}$$

Explanation.

The first equation, $y = -\frac{2}{3}x - 4$, is a linear equation in slope-intercept form with a slope of $-\frac{2}{3}$ and a y-intercept of $(0, -4)$. The second equation, $y = -4x - 14$, is a linear equation in slope-intercept form with a slope of -4 and a y-intercept of $(0, -14)$. We'll use this information to graph both lines in Figure 4.4.2.

The two lines intersect where $x = -3$ and $y = -2$, so the solution of the system of equations is the point $(-3, -2)$. We write the solution set as $\{(-3, -2)\}$.

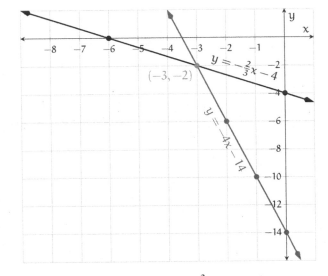

Figure 4.4.2: Graphs of $y = -\frac{2}{3}x - 4$ and $y = -4x - 14$.

Example 4.4.3 Special Systems of Equations. Solve the following system of equations by graphing:

$$\begin{cases} y = \dfrac{3}{2}(x - 1) + 4 \\ 3x - 2y = 4 \end{cases}$$

Explanation. The first equation, $y = \frac{3}{2}(x - 1) + 4$, is a linear equation in point-slope form with a slope of $\frac{3}{2}$ that passes through the point $(1, 4)$. The second equation, $3x - 2y = 4$, is a linear equation in standard form To graph this line, we either need to find the intercepts or put the equation into slope-intercept form. Just for practice, we will put the line in slope-intercept form.

$$3x - 2y = 4$$
$$-2y = -3x + 4$$

$$\frac{-2y}{-2} = \frac{-3x}{-2} + \frac{4}{-2}$$

$$y = \frac{3}{2}x - 2$$

We'll use this information to graph both lines:

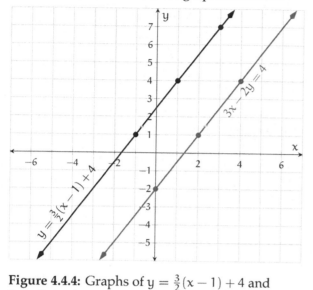

The two lines never intersect: they are parallel. So there are no solutions to the system of equations. We write the solution set as ∅.

Figure 4.4.4: Graphs of $y = \frac{3}{2}(x - 1) + 4$ and $3x - 2y = 4$.

4.4.2 Substitution

In Section 4.2, we covered the substitution method of solving systems of equations. We isolated one variable in one equation and then substituted into the other equation to solve for one variable.

Example 4.4.5 Solving Systems of Equations Using Substitution. Solve this system of equations using substitution:

$$\begin{cases} -5x + 6y = -10 \\ 4x - 3y = -1 \end{cases}$$

Explanation. We need to solve for *one* of the variables in *one* of our equations. Looking at both equations, it will be best to solve for y in the second equation. The coefficient of y in that equation is smallest.

$$4x - 3y = -1$$
$$-3y = -1 - 4x$$
$$\frac{-3y}{-3} = \frac{-1}{-3} - \frac{4x}{-3}$$
$$y = \frac{1}{3} + \frac{4}{3}x$$

Replace y in the first equation with $\frac{1}{3} + \frac{4}{3}x$, giving us a linear equation in only one variable, x, that we may solve:

$$-5x + 6y = -10$$
$$-5x + 6\left(\frac{1}{3} + \frac{4}{3}x\right) = -10$$
$$-5x + 2 + 8x = -10$$
$$3x + 2 = -10$$
$$3x = -12$$
$$x = -4$$

Now that we have the value for x, we need to find the value for y. We have already solved the second equation for y, so that is the easiest equation to use.

$$y = \frac{1}{3} + \frac{4}{3}x$$
$$y = \frac{1}{3} + \frac{4}{3}(-4)$$
$$y = \frac{1}{3} - \frac{16}{3}$$
$$y = -\frac{15}{3}$$
$$y = -5$$

To check this solution, we replace x with -4 and y with -5 in each equation:

$$-5x + 6y = -10$$
$$-5(-4) + 6(-5) \overset{?}{=} -10$$
$$20 - 30 \overset{\checkmark}{=} -10$$

$$4x - 3y = -1$$
$$4(-4) - 3(-4) \overset{?}{=} -1$$
$$-16 + 15 \overset{\checkmark}{=} -1$$

We conclude then that this system of equations is true when $x = -4$ and $y = -5$. Our solution is the point $(-4, -5)$ and we write the solution set as $\{(-4, -5)\}$.

Example 4.4.6 Applications of Systems of Equations. The Rusk Ranch Nature Center[1] in south-western Oregon is a volunteer run nonprofit that exists to promote the wellbeing of the local communities and conserve local nature with an emphasis on native butterflies. They sell admission tickets: $6 for adults and $4 for children. Amanda, who was working at the front desk, counted that one day she sold a total of 79 tickets and had $384 in the register from those ticket sales. She didn't bother to count how many were adult tickets and how many were child tickets because she knew she could use math to figure it out at the end of the day. So, how many of the 79 tickets were adult and how many were child?

Explanation. Let's let a represent the number of adult tickets sold and c represent the number of child tickets sold. We need to build two equations to solve a system for both variables.

The first equation we will build relates to the fact that there were 79 total tickets sold. If we combine both the number of adult tickets and child tickets, the total is 79. This fact becomes:

$$a + c = 79$$

For the second equation we need to use the per-ticket dollar amounts to generate the total cost of $384. The amount of money that was made from adult tickets is found my multiplying the number of adult tickets sold, a, by the price per ticket, $6. Similarly, the amount of money from child tickets is found my multiplying the number of child tickets sold, c, by the price per ticket, $4. These two amounts will add to be $384. This fact becomes:

$$6a + 4c = 384$$

And so, our system is

$$\begin{cases} a + c = 79 \\ 6a + 4c = 384 \end{cases}$$

To solve, we will use the substitution method and solve the first equation for the variable a.

$$a + c = 79$$
$$a = 79 - c$$

Now we will substitute $79 - c$ for a in the second equation.

$$6a + 4c = 384$$
$$6(79 - c) + 4c = 384$$
$$474 - 6c + 4c = 384$$
$$474 - 2c = 384$$
$$-2c = -90$$
$$c = 45$$

Last, we will solve for a by substituting 45 in for c in the equation $a = 79 - c$.

$$a = 79 - c$$
$$a = 79 - 45$$
$$a = 34$$

Our conclusion is that Amanda sold 34 adult tickets and 45 child tickets.

Example 4.4.7 Solving Special Systems of Equations with Substitution. Solve the systems of linear equations using substitution.

a.
$$\begin{cases} 3x - 5y = 9 \\ \quad x = \dfrac{5}{3}y + 3 \end{cases}$$

b.
$$\begin{cases} \quad y + 7 = 4x \\ 2y - 8x = 7 \end{cases}$$

Explanation. To solve the systems using substitution, we first need to solve for one variable in one equation, then substitute into the *other* equation.

a. In this case, x is already solved for in the second equation so we can substitute $\frac{5}{3}y + 3$ everywhere we see x in the first equation. Then simplify and solve for y.

$$3x - 5y = 9$$
$$3\left(\frac{5}{3}y + 3\right) - 5y = 9$$
$$5y + 9 - 5y = 9$$
$$9 = 9$$

We will stop here since we have eliminated all of the variables in the equation and ended with a *true* statement. Since 9 always equals 9, no matter what, then any value of y must make the original equation, $3\left(\frac{5}{3}y + 3\right) - 5y = 9$ true. If you recall from the section on substitution, this means that both lines $3x - 5y = 9$ and $x = \frac{5}{3}y + 3$ are in fact the same line. Since a solution to a system of linear equations is any point where the lines touch, *all* points along both lines are solutions. We can say this

---

[1]ruskranchnaturecenter.org

in English as, "The solutions are all points on the line $3x - 5y = 9$," or in math as, "The solution set is $\{(x, y) \mid 3x - 5y = 9\}$."

b. We will first solve the top equation for y.

$$y + 7 = 4x$$
$$y = 4x - 7$$

Now we can substitute $4x - 7$ wherever we see y in the second equation.

$$2y - 8x = 7$$
$$2(4x - 7) - 8x = 7$$
$$8x - 14 - 8x = 7$$
$$-14 = 7$$

We will stop here since we have eliminated all of the variables in the equation and ended with a *false* statement. Since -14 never equals 7, then no values of x and y can make the original system true. If you recall from the section on substitution, this means that the lines $y + 7 = 4x$ and $2y - 8x = 7$ are parallel. Since a solution to a system of linear equations is any point where the lines touch, and parallel lines never touch, *no* points are solutions. We can say this in English as, "There are no solutions," or in math as, "The solution set is $\emptyset$."

4.4.3 Elimination

In Section 4.3, we explored a third way of solving systems of linear equations called elimination where we add two equations together to cancel a variable.

Example 4.4.8 Solving Systems of Equations by Elimination. Solve the system using elimination.

$$\begin{cases} 4x - 6y = 13 \\ 5x + 4y = -1 \end{cases}$$

Explanation.   To solve the system using elimination, we first need to scale one or both of the equations so that one variable has equal but opposite coefficients in the system. In this case, we will choose to make y have opposite coefficients because the signs are already opposite for that variable in the system.

We need to multiply the first equation by 2 and the second equation by 3.

$$\begin{cases} 4x - 6y = 13 \\ 5x + 4y = -1 \end{cases}$$

$$\begin{cases} 2 \cdot (4x - 6y) = 2 \cdot (13) \\ 3 \cdot (5x + 4y) = 3 \cdot (-1) \end{cases}$$

$$\begin{cases} 8x - 12y = 26 \\ 15x + 12y = -3 \end{cases}$$

We now have an equivalent system of equations where the y-terms can be eliminated:

$$\frac{8x - 12y}{+ \ 15x + 12y} = \frac{26}{+ \ (-3)}$$

So we have:

$$23x = 23$$
$$x = 1$$

To solve for y, we will substitute 1 for x into either of the original equations. We will use the first equation, $4x - 6y = 13$:

$$4x - 6y = 13$$
$$4(1) - 6y = 13$$
$$4 - 6y = 13$$
$$-6y = 9$$
$$\frac{6y}{-6} = \frac{9}{-6}$$
$$y = -\frac{3}{2}$$

To verify this, we substitute the x and y values into both of the original equations.

$$4x - 6y = 13$$
$$4(1) - 6\left(-\frac{3}{2}\right) \stackrel{?}{=} 13$$
$$4 + 9 \stackrel{\checkmark}{=} 13$$

$$5x + 4y = 1$$
$$5(1) + 4\left(-\frac{3}{2}\right) \stackrel{?}{=} -1$$
$$5 - 6 \stackrel{\checkmark}{=} -1$$

So the solution is the point $\left(-\frac{3}{2}, 1\right)$ and the solution set is $\left\{\left(-\frac{3}{2}, 1\right)\right\}$.

Example 4.4.9 Solving Special Systems of Equations with Elimination. Solve the system of equations using the elimination method.

$$\begin{cases} 24x + 6y = 9 \\ 8x + 2y = 2 \end{cases}$$

Explanation. To eliminate the x-terms, we will scale the second equation by -3.

$$\begin{cases} 24x + 6y = 9 \\ -3 \cdot (8x + 2y) = -3 \cdot (2) \end{cases}$$
$$\begin{cases} 24x + 6y = 9 \\ -24x - 6y = -6 \end{cases}$$

Adding the respective sides of the equation, we have:

$$0 = 3$$

Both of the variables have been eliminated. In this case, the statement $0 = 3$ is just false, no matter what x and y are. So the system has no solution. The solution set is $\emptyset$.

Example 4.4.10 Deciding to Use Substitution versus Elimination. Decide which method would be easiest to solve the systems of linear equations: substitution or elimination.

a.
$$\begin{cases} 2x + 3y = -11 \\ 5x - 6y = 13 \end{cases}$$

b.
$$\begin{cases} x - 7y = 10 \\ 9x - 16y = -4 \end{cases}$$

c.
$$\begin{cases} 6x + 30y = 15 \\ 4x + 20y = 10 \end{cases}$$

d.
$$\begin{cases} y = 3x - 2 \\ y = 7x + 6 \end{cases}$$

Explanation.

a. Elimination is probably easiest here. Multiply the first equation by 2 and eliminate the y variables. The solution to this one is $(-1, -3)$ if you want to solve it for practice.

b. Substitution is probably easiest here. Solve the first equation for x and substitute it into the second equation. We *could* use elimination if we multiplied the first equation by -9 and eliminate the x variable, but it's probably a little more work than substitution. The solution to this one is $(-4, -2)$ if you want to solve it for practice.

c. Elimination is probably easiest here. Multiply the first equation by 2 and the second equation by -3. Doing this will eliminate both variables and leave you with $0 = 0$. This should mean that all points on the line are solutions. So the solution set is $\{(x, y) \mid 6x + 30y = 15\}$.

d. Substitution is definitely easiest here. Substituting y from one equation into y in the other equation gives you $3x - 2 = 7x + 6$. Solve this and find then find y and you should get the solution to the system to be $(-2, -8)$ if you want to solve it for practice.

4.4.4 Exercises

Solving Systems of Linear Equations by Graphing Use a graph to solve the system of equations.

1.
$$\begin{cases} x + y = 0 \\ 3x - y = 8 \end{cases}$$

2.
$$\begin{cases} 4x - 2y = 4 \\ x + 2y = 6 \end{cases}$$

3.
$$\begin{cases} x + y = -1 \\ x = 2 \end{cases}$$

4.
$$\begin{cases} x - 2y = -4 \\ x = -4 \end{cases}$$

5.
$$\begin{cases} -10x + 15y = 60 \\ 6x - 9y = 36 \end{cases}$$

6.
$$\begin{cases} 6x - 8y = 32 \\ 9x - 12y = 12 \end{cases}$$

7.
$$\begin{cases} y = -\dfrac{3}{5}x + 7 \\ 9x + 15y = 105 \end{cases}$$

8.
$$\begin{cases} 9y - 12x = 18 \\ y = \dfrac{4}{3}x + 2 \end{cases}$$

Substitution Solve the following system of equations.

9.
$$\begin{cases} y = -2 - 4x \\ 5x + y = 3 \end{cases}$$

10.
$$\begin{cases} y = -4x - 13 \\ 3x + 4y = 0 \end{cases}$$

11.
$$\begin{cases} 5x + 3y = 11 \\ 5x + 5y = -5 \end{cases}$$

12. $\begin{cases} 2x + 2y = 30 \\ 4x + 3y = 54 \end{cases}$ **13.** $\begin{cases} -4x + 5y = 31 \\ 6x + 6y = -60 \end{cases}$ **14.** $\begin{cases} 2x - 4y = 22 \\ 6x + 2y = -60 \end{cases}$

15. $\begin{cases} 2x + 4y = 5 \\ -6x - 12y = -15 \end{cases}$ **16.** $\begin{cases} 2x + 2y = 5 \\ -8x - 8y = -20 \end{cases}$

17. A rectangle's length is 2 feet shorter than twice its width. The rectangle's perimeter is 176 feet. Find the rectangle's length and width.

The rectangle's length is ☐ feet, and its width is ☐ feet.

18. A school fund raising event sold a total of 202 tickets and generated a total revenue of $806.10. There are two types of tickets: adult tickets and child tickets. Each adult ticket costs $6.65, and each child ticket costs $2.70. Write and solve a system of equations to answer the following questions.

☐ adult tickets and ☐ child tickets were sold.

19. A test has 19 problems, which are worth a total of 97 points. There are two types of problems in the test. Each multiple-choice problem is worth 4 points, and each short-answer problem is worth 7 points. Write and solve a system equation to answer the following questions.

This test has ☐ multiple-choice problems and ☐ short-answer problems.

20. A test has 21 problems, which are worth a total of 110 points. There are two types of problems in the test. Each multiple-choice problem is worth 5 points, and each short-answer problem is worth 6 points. Write and solve a system equation to answer the following questions.

This test has ☐ multiple-choice problems and ☐ short-answer problems.

21. Subin invested a total of $10,000 in two accounts. One account pays 5% interest annually; the other pays 2% interest annually. At the end of the year, Subin earned a total of $320 in interest. Write and solve a system of equations to find how much money Subin invested in each account.

Subin invested ☐ in the 5% account and ☐ in the 2% account.

22. Holli invested a total of $10,000 in two accounts. After a year, one account lost 6.5%, while the other account gained 4.6%. In total, Holli lost $483.50. Write and solve a system of equations to find how much money Holli invested in each account.

Holli invested ☐ in the account with 6.5% loss and ☐ in the account with 4.6% gain.

23. Town A and Town B were located close to each other, and recently merged into one city. Town A had a population with 12% African Americans. Town B had a population with 8% African Americans. After the merge, the new city has a total of 5000 residents, with 9.12% African Americans. Write and solve a system of equations to find how many residents Town A and Town B used to have.

Town A used to have ☐ residents, and Town B used to have ☐ residents.

24. You poured some 6% alcohol solution and some 12% alcohol solution into a mixing container. Now you have 600 grams of 10.8% alcohol solution. How many grams of 6% solution and how many grams of 12% solution did you pour into the mixing container?

Write and solve a system equation to answer the following questions.

You mixed [_____] grams of 6% solution with [_____] grams of 12% solution.

Elimination Solve the following system of equations.

25. $\begin{cases} 4x + 4y = -32 \\ 4x + 5y = -37 \end{cases}$

26. $\begin{cases} x + 3y = 27 \\ 4x + 2y = 18 \end{cases}$

27. $\begin{cases} -3x + 4y = 2 \\ 6x + 2y = 16 \end{cases}$

28. $\begin{cases} 6x - 3y = 42 \\ 3x + 5y = -18 \end{cases}$

29. $\begin{cases} 5x + 5y = 1 \\ 15x + 15y = 1 \end{cases}$

30. $\begin{cases} 5x + 3y = 1 \\ -20x - 12y = 1 \end{cases}$

31. $\begin{cases} x + y = 1 \\ -2x - 2y = -2 \end{cases}$

32. $\begin{cases} x + 5y = 1 \\ 3x + 15y = 3 \end{cases}$

33. A test has 17 problems, which are worth a total of 86 points. There are two types of problems in the test. Each multiple-choice problem is worth 3 points, and each short-answer problem is worth 8 points. Write and solve a system of equations to answer the following questions.

This test has [_____] multiple-choice problems and [_____] short-answer problems.

34. Irene invested a total of $7,000 in two accounts. One account pays 3% interest annually; the other pays 4% interest annually. At the end of the year, Irene earned a total of $255 in interest. Write and solve a system of equations to find how much money Irene invested in each account.

Irene invested [_____] in the 3% account and [_____] in the 4% account.

35. Town A and Town B were located close to each other, and recently merged into one city. Town A had a population with 12% whites. Town B had a population with 8% whites. After the merge, the new city has a total of 5000 residents, with 8.96% whites. Write and solve a system of equations to find how many residents Town A and Town B used to have.

Town A used to have [_____] residents, and Town B used to have [_____] residents.

36. You poured some 12% alcohol solution and some 6% alcohol solution into a mixing container. Now you have 640 grams of 9% alcohol solution. Write and solve a system of equations to find how many grams of 12% solution and how many grams of 6% solution you poured into the mixing container.

You mixed [_____] grams of 12% solution with [_____] grams of 6% solution.

37. If a boat travels from Town A to Town B, it has to travel 5002.5 mi along a river. A boat traveled from Town A to Town B along the river's current with its engine running at full speed. This trip took 172.5 hr. Then the boat traveled back from Town B to Town A, again with the engine at full speed, but this time against the river's current. This trip took 217.5 hr. Write and solve a system of equations to answer the following questions.

The boat's speed in still water with the engine running at full speed is [_____].

The river current's speed was [_____].

38. A small fair charges different admission for adults and children. It charges $2.25 for adults, and $0.25 for children. On a certain day, the total revenue is $4,615 and the fair admits 4100 people. How many adults and children were admitted?

There were [_____] adults and [_____] children at the fair.

Appendix A

Basic Math Review

This appendix is *mostly* intended to *review* topics from a basic math course, especially Sections A.1–A.5. These topics are covered differently than they would be covered for a student seeing them for the first time.

A.1 Arithmetic with Negative Numbers

Adding, subtracting, multiplying, dividing, and raising to powers each have peculiarities when using negative numbers. This section reviews arithmetic with signed (both positive and negative) numbers.

A.1.1 Signed Numbers

Is it valid to subtract a large number from a smaller one? It may be hard to imagine what it would mean physically to subtract 8 cars from your garage if you only have 1 car in there in the first place. Nevertheless, mathematics has found a way to give meaning to expressions like $1 - 8$ using **signed numbers**.

In daily life, the signed numbers we might see most often are temperatures. Most people on Earth use the Celsius scale; if you're not familiar with the Celsius temperature scale, think about these examples:

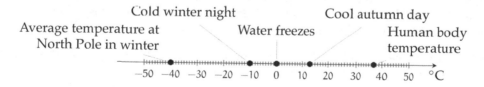

Figure A.1.2: Number line with interesting Celsius temperatures

Figure A.1.2 uses a **number line** to illustrate these positive and negative numbers. A number line is a useful device for visualizing how numbers relate to each other and combine with each other. Values to the right of 0 are called **positive** numbers and values to the left of 0 are called **negative numbers**.

Warning A.1.3 Subtraction Sign versus Negative Sign. Unfortunately, the symbol we use for subtraction looks just like the symbol we use for marking a negative number. It will help to identify when a "minus" sign means "subtract" or means "negative." The key is to see if there is a number to its left, not counting anything farther left than an open parenthesis. Here are some examples.

- -13 has one negative sign and no subtraction sign.

- $20 - 13$ has no negative signs and one subtraction sign.

- $-20 - 13$ has a negative sign and then a subtraction sign.

- $(-20)(-13)$ has two negative signs and no subtraction sign.

Checkpoint A.1.4 Identify "minus" signs.

In each expression, how many negative signs and subtraction signs are there?

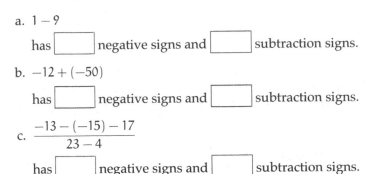

a. $1 - 9$

has ☐ negative signs and ☐ subtraction signs.

b. $-12 + (-50)$

has ☐ negative signs and ☐ subtraction signs.

c. $\dfrac{-13 - (-15) - 17}{23 - 4}$

has ☐ negative signs and ☐ subtraction signs.

Explanation.

a. $1 - 9$ has zero negative signs and one subtraction sign.

b. $-12 + (-50)$ has two negative signs and zero subtraction signs.

c. $\dfrac{-13 - (-15) - 17}{23 - 4}$ has two negative signs and three subtraction signs.

A.1.2 Adding

An easy way to think about adding two numbers with the *same sign* is to simply (at first) ignore the signs, and add the numbers as if they were both positive. Then make sure your result is either positive or negative, depending on what the sign was of the two numbers you started with.

Example A.1.5 Add Two Negative Numbers. If you needed to add -18 and -7, note that both are negative. Maybe you have this expression in front of you:

$$-18 + -7$$

but that "plus minus" is awkward, and in this book you are more likely to have this expression:

$$-18 + (-7)$$

with extra parentheses. (How many subtraction signs do you see? How many negative signs?)

Since *both* our terms are *negative*, we can add 18 and 7 to get 25 and immediately realize that our final result should be negative. So our result is -25:

$$-18 + (-7) = -25$$

This approach works because adding numbers is like having two people tugging on a rope in one direction or the other, with strength indicated by each number. In Example A.1.5 we have two people pulling to the left, one with strength 18, the other with strength 7. Their forces combine to pull *left* with strength 25, giving us our total of −25, as illustrated in Figure A.1.6.

If we are adding two numbers that have *opposite* signs, then the two people tugging the rope are opposing each other. If either of them is using more strength, then the overall effect will be a net pull in that person's direction. And the overall pull on the rope will be the *difference* of the two strengths. This is illustrated in Figure A.1.7.

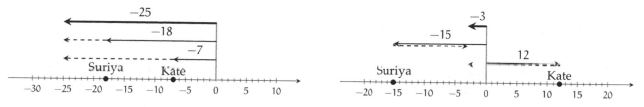

Figure A.1.6: Working together   **Figure A.1.7:** Working in opposition

Example A.1.8 Adding One Number of Each Sign. Here are four examples of addition where one number is positive and the other is negative.

a. $-15 + 12$

We have one number of each sign, with sizes 15 and 12. Their difference is 3. But of the two numbers, the negative number dominated. So the result from adding these is −3.

b. $200 + (-100)$

We have one number of each sign, with sizes 200 and 100. Their difference is 100. But of the two numbers, the positive number dominated. So the result from adding these is 100.

c. $12.8 + (-20)$

We have one number of each sign, with sizes 12.8 and 20. Their difference is 7.2. But of the two numbers, the negative number dominated. So the result from adding these is −7.2.

d. $-87.3 + 87.3$

We have one number of each sign, both with size 87.3. The opposing forces cancel each other, leaving a result of 0.

Checkpoint A.1.9 Take a moment to practice adding when at least one negative number is involved. The expectation is that readers can make these calculations here without a calculator.

a. Add $-1 + 9$.

b. Add $-12 + (-98)$.

c. Add $100 + (-123)$.

d. Find the sum $-2.1 + (-2.1)$.

e. Find the sum $-34.67 + 81.53$.

Explanation.

    a. The two numbers have opposite sign, so we can think to subtract $9 - 1 = 8$. Of the two numbers we added, the positive is larger, so we stick with postive 8 as the answer.

    b. The two numbers are both negative, so we can add $12 + 98 = 110$, and take the negative of that as the answer: -110.

    c. The two numbers have opposite sign, so we can think to subtract $123 - 100 = 23$. Of the two numbers we added, the negative is larger, so we take the negative of 23 as the answer. That is, the answer is -23.

    d. The two numbers are both negative, so we can add $2.1 + 2.1 = 4.2$, and take the negative of that as the answer: -4.2.

    e. The two numbers have opposite sign, so we can think to subtract $81.53 - 34.67 = 46.86$. Of the two numbers we added, the positive is larger, so we stick with postive 46.86 as the answer.

A.1.3 Subtracting

Perhaps you can handle a subtraction such as $18 - 5$, where a small positive number is subtracted from a larger number. There are other instances of subtraction that might leave you scratching your head. In such situations, we recommend that you view each subtraction as *adding* the opposite number.

	Original	Adding the Opposite
Subtracting a larger positive number:	$12 - 30$	$12 + (-30)$
Subtracting from a negative number:	$-8.1 - 17$	$-8.1 + (-17)$
Subtracting a negative number:	$42 - (-23)$	$42 + 23$

The benefit is that perhaps you already mastered addition with positive and negative numbers, and this strategy that you convert subtraction to addition means you don't have all that much more to learn. These examples might be computed as follows:

$$12 - 30 = 12 + (-30) \qquad -8.1 - 17 = -8.1 + (-17) \qquad 42 - (-23) = 42 + 23$$
$$= -18 \qquad\qquad\qquad = -25.1 \qquad\qquad\qquad = 65$$

Checkpoint A.1.10 Take a moment to practice subtracting when at least one negative number is involved. The expectation is that readers can make these calculations here without a calculator.

    a. Subtract -1 from 9.   d. Find the difference $-5.9 - (-3.1)$.

    b. Subtract $32 - 50$.

    c. Subtract $108 - (-108)$.   e. Find the difference $-12.04 - 17.2$.

Explanation.

    a. After writing this as $9 - (-1)$, we can rewrite it as $9 + 1$ and get 10.

    b. Subtrcting in the oppsite order with the larger number first, $50 - 32 = 18$. But since we were asked to subtract the larger number *from* the smaller number, the answer is -18.

    c. After writing this as $108 - (-108)$, we can rewrite it as $108 + 108$ and get 216.

d. After writing this as $-5.9 - (-3.1)$, we can rewrite it as $-5.9 + 3.1$. Now it is the *sum* of two numbers of opposite sign, so we can subtract $5.9 - 3.1$ to get 2.8. But we were adding numbers where the negative number was larger, so the final answer should be -2.8.

e. Since we are subtracting a positive number from a negative number, the result should be an even more negative number. We can add $12.04 + 17.2$ to get 29.24, but our final answer should be the opposite, -29.24.

A.1.4 Multiplying

Making sense of multiplication of negative numbers isn't quite so straightforward, but it's possible. Should the product of 3 and -7 be a positive number or a negative number? Remembering that we can view multiplication as repeated addition, we can see this result on a number line:

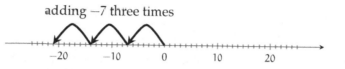

Figure A.1.11: Viewing $3 \cdot (-7)$ as repeated addition

Figure A.1.11 illustrates that $3 \cdot (-7) = -21$, and so it would seem that a positive number times a negative number will always give a negative result. (Note that it would not change things if the negative number came first in the product, since the order of multiplication doesn't affect the result.)

What about the product $-3 \cdot (-7)$, where both factors are negative? Should the product be positive or negative? If $3 \cdot (-7)$ can be seen as adding -7 three times as in Figure A.1.12, then it isn't too crazy to interpret $-3 \cdot (-7)$ as *subtracting* -7 three times, as in Figure A.1.12.

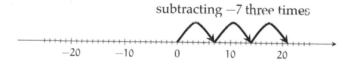

Figure A.1.12: Viewing $-3 \cdot (-7)$ as repeated subtraction

This illustrates that $-3 \cdot (-7) = 21$, and it would seem that a negative number times a negative number always gives a positive result.

Positive and negative numbers are not the whole story. The number 0 is neither positive nor negative. What happens with multiplication by 0? You can choose to view $7 \cdot 0$ as adding the number 0 seven times. And you can choose to view $0 \cdot 7$ as adding the number 7 zero times. Either way, you really added nothing at all, which is the same as adding 0.

Fact A.1.13 Multiplication by 0. *Multiplying any number by 0 results in 0.*

Checkpoint A.1.14 Here are some practice exercises with multiplication and signed numbers. The expectation is that readers can make these calculations here without a calculator.

a. Multiply $-13 \cdot 2$.

b. Find the product of 30 and -50.

c. Compute $-12(-7)$.

d. Find the product $-285(0)$.

Explanation.

    a. Since $13 \cdot 2 = 26$, and we are multiplying numbers of opposite signs, the answer is negative: -26.

    b. Since $30 \cdot 50 = 1500$, and we are multiplying numbers of opposite signs, the answer is negative: -1500.

    c. Since $12 \cdot 7 = 84$, and we are multiplying numbers of the same sign, the answer is positive: 84.

    d. Any number multiplied by 0 is 0.

A.1.5 Powers

For early sections of this book the only exponents you will see will be the **natural numbers** : $\{1, 2, 3, \ldots\}$. But negative numbers can and will arise as the *base* of a power.

    An exponent is a shorthand for how many times to multiply by the base. For example,

$$(-2)^5 \text{ means } \overbrace{(-2) \cdot (-2) \cdot (-2) \cdot (-2) \cdot (-2)}^{5 \text{ instances}}$$

Will the result here be positive or negative? Since we can view $(-2)^5$ as repeated multiplication, and we now understand that multiplying two negatives gives a positive result, this expression can be thought of this way:

$$\underbrace{\underbrace{(-2) \cdot (-2)}_{\text{positive}} \cdot \underbrace{(-2) \cdot (-2)}_{\text{positive}} \cdot (-2)}_{\text{positive}}$$

and that lone last negative number will be responsible for making the final product negative.

    More generally, if the base of a power is negative, then whether or not the result is positive or negative depends on if the exponent is even or odd. It depends on whether or not the factors can all be paired up to "cancel" negative signs, or if there will be a lone factor left by itself.

    Once you understand whether the result is positive or negative, for a moment you may forget about signs. Continuing the example, you may calculate that $2^5 = 32$, and then since we know $(-2)^5$ is negative, you can report

$$(-2)^5 = -32$$

Warning A.1.15 Negative Signs and Exponents. Expressions like -3^4 may not mean what you think they mean. What base do you see here? The correct answer is 3. The exponent 4 *only* applies to the 3, not to -3. So this expression, -3^4, is actually the same as $-(3^4)$, which is -81. Be careful not to treat -3^4 as having base -3. That would make it equivalent to $(-3)^4$, which is *positive* 81.

Checkpoint A.1.16 Here is some practice with natural exponents on negative bases. The expectation is that readers can make these calculations here without a calculator.

    a. Compute $(-8)^2$.

    b. Calculate the power $(-1)^{203}$.

    c. Find $(-3)^3$.

    d. Calculate -5^2.

Explanation.

    a. Since 8^2 is 64 and we are raising a negative number to an *even* power, the answer is positive: 64.

    b. Since 1^{203} is 1 and we are raising a negative number to an *odd* power, the answer is negative: -1.

    c. Since 3^3 is 27 and we are raising a negative number to an *odd* power, the answer is negative: -27.

d. Careful: here we are raising *positive* 5 to the second power to get 25 and *then* negating the result: −25. Since we don't see "$(-5)^2$," the answer is not positive 25.

A.1.6 Summary

Addition Add two negative numbers: add their positive counterparts and make the result negative.

Add a positive with a negative: find their difference using subtraction, and keep the sign of the dominant number.

Subtraction Any subtraction can be converted to addition of the opposite number. For all but the most basic subtractions, this is a useful strategy.

Multiplication Multiply two negative numbers: multiply their positive counterparts and make the result positive.

Multiply a positive with a negative: multiply their positive counterparts and make the result negative.

Multiply any number by 0: the result will be 0.

Division (not discussed in this section) Division by some number is the same as multiplication by its reciprocal. So the multiplication rules can be adopted.

Division of 0 by any nonzero number always results in 0.

Division of any number by 0 is always undefined.

Powers Raise a negative number to an even power: raise the positive counterpart to that power.

Raise a negative number to an odd power: raise the positive counterpart to that power, then make the result negative.

Expressions like -2^4 mean $-(2^4)$, not $(-2)^4$.

A.1.7 Exercises

1. Add the following.
   a. $-9 + (-3)$
   b. $-6 + (-5)$
   c. $-1 + (-7)$

2. Add the following.
   a. $-8 + (-1)$
   b. $-5 + (-6)$
   c. $-1 + (-9)$

3. Add the following.
   a. $5 + (-9)$
   b. $5 + (-1)$
   c. $8 + (-8)$

4. Add the following.
   a. $5 + (-6)$
   b. $8 + (-2)$
   c. $8 + (-8)$

5. Add the following.
   a. $-7 + 1$
   b. $-3 + 10$
   c. $-3 + 3$

6. Add the following.
   a. $-9 + 2$
   b. $-4 + 7$
   c. $-3 + 3$

7. Add the following.
   a. $-71 + (-16)$
   b. $-32 + 87$
   c. $78 + (-23)$

8. Add the following.
   a. $-61 + (-47)$
   b. $-84 + 62$
   c. $77 + (-69)$

9. Subtract the following.

a. $3 - 7$

b. $8 - 2$

c. $5 - 19$

10. Subtract the following.

a. $4 - 10$

b. $5 - 1$

c. $5 - 14$

11. Subtract the following.

a. $-2 - 3$

b. $-8 - 4$

c. $-5 - 5$

12. Subtract the following.

a. $-1 - 2$

b. $-6 - 3$

c. $-5 - 5$

13. Subtract the following.

a. $-5 - (-8)$

b. $-6 - (-1)$

c. $-5 - (-5)$

14. Subtract the following.

a. $-1 - (-7)$

b. $-9 - (-2)$

c. $-5 - (-5)$

15. Perform the given addition and subtraction.

a. $-18 - 2 + (-9)$

b. $7 - (-13) + (-11)$

16. Perform the given addition and subtraction.

a. $-17 - 9 + (-5)$

b. $4 - (-14) + (-17)$

17. Perform the given addition and subtraction.

a. $-16 - 5 + (-1)$

b. $1 - (-14) + (-11)$

18. Perform the given addition and subtraction.

a. $-14 - 2 + (-7)$

b. $9 - (-14) + (-17)$

19. Multiply the following.

a. $(-9) \cdot (-1)$

b. $(-4) \cdot 5$

c. $7 \cdot (-2)$

d. $(-6) \cdot 0$

20. Multiply the following.

a. $(-8) \cdot (-2)$

b. $(-7) \cdot 3$

c. $7 \cdot (-5)$

d. $(-5) \cdot 0$

21. Multiply the following.

a. $(-1) \cdot (-6) \cdot (-3)$

b. $7 \cdot (-7) \cdot (-1)$

c. $(-86) \cdot (-78) \cdot 0$

22. Multiply the following.

a. $(-1) \cdot (-4) \cdot (-5)$

b. $6 \cdot (-7) \cdot (-4)$

c. $(-84) \cdot (-66) \cdot 0$

23. Multiply the following.

a. $(-1)(-2)(-2)(-2)$

b. $(3)(-3)(2)(-3)$

24. Multiply the following.

a. $(-1)(-1)(-3)(-1)$

b. $(1)(-3)(-3)(-1)$

25. Evaluate the following.

a. $\frac{-64}{-8}$

b. $\frac{54}{-6}$

c. $\frac{-63}{7}$

26. Evaluate the following.

a. $\frac{-28}{-7}$

b. $\frac{35}{-5}$

c. $\frac{-28}{7}$

27. Evaluate the following.

a. $\frac{-6}{-1}$

b. $\frac{10}{-1}$

c. $\frac{110}{-110}$

d. $\frac{-17}{-17}$

e. $\frac{11}{0}$

f. $\frac{0}{-3}$

28. Evaluate the following.

a. $\frac{-5}{-1}$

b. $\frac{8}{-1}$

c. $\frac{150}{-150}$

d. $\frac{-20}{-20}$

e. $\frac{10}{0}$

f. $\frac{0}{-8}$

29. Evaluate the following.

a. $(-9)^2$

b. -4^2

30. Evaluate the following.

a. $(\ 7)^2$

b. -6^2

31. Evaluate the following.

a. $(-3)^3$

b. -1^3

32. Evaluate the following.

a. $(-2)^3$

b. -4^3

33. Evaluate the following.

a. 4^2

b. 2^3

c. $(-4)^2$

d. $(-3)^3$

34. Evaluate the following.

a. 5^2

b. 4^3

c. $(-3)^2$

d. $(-5)^3$

35. Evaluate the following.

a. 1^{10}

b. $(-1)^{11}$

c. $(-1)^{12}$

d. 0^{20}

36. Evaluate the following.

a. 1^5

b. $(-1)^{13}$

c. $(-1)^{18}$

d. 0^{18}

Simplify without using a calculator.

37. $-6.53 + (-53.7)$

38. $-7.17 + (-33.3)$

39. $9.8 - 1.93$

40. $9.5 - 5.73$

41. $-4.43 + 5.2$

42. $-2.13 + 6.7$

43. $-4.83 - (-6.4)$

44. $-2.63 - (-7.1)$

45. $57 - 6.33$

46. $63 - 1.03$

47. $-70 + 4.73$

48. $-76 + 8.42$

49. It's given that $94 \cdot 32 = 3008$. Use this fact to calculate the following without using a calculator.
$9.4(-0.032) =$

50. It's given that $19 \cdot 79 = 1501$. Use this fact to calculate the following without using a calculator.
$1.9(-7.9) =$

51. It's given that $26 \cdot 16 = 416$. Use this fact to calculate the following without using a calculator.
$(-2.6)(-0.016)$

52. It's given that $33 \cdot 54 = 1782$. Use this fact to calculate the following without using a calculator.
$(-3.3)(-5.4)$

Applications

53. Consider the following situation in which you borrow money from your cousin:

  - On June 1st, you borrowed 1200 dollars from your cousin.

  - On July 1st, you borrowed 490 more dollars from your cousin.

  - On August 1st, you paid back 690 dollars to your cousin.

  - On September 1st, you borrowed another 820 dollars from your cousin.

How much money do you owe your cousin now?

54. Consider the following scenario in which you study your bank account.

  - On Jan. 1, you had a balance of -310 dollars in your bank account.

  - On Jan. 2, your bank charged 40 dollar overdraft fee.

  - On Jan. 3, you deposited 870 dollars.

  - On Jan. 10, you withdrew 750 dollars.

What is your balance on Jan. 11?

55. A mountain is 1100 feet *above* sea level. A trench is 360 feet *below* sea level. What is the difference in elevation between the mountain top and the bottom of the trench?

56. A mountain is 1200 feet *above* sea level. A trench is 420 feet *below* sea level. What is the difference in elevation between the mountain top and the bottom of the trench?

Challenge

57. Select the correct word to make each statement true.

  a. A positive number minus a positive number is   (☐ sometimes   ☐ always   ☐ never)   negative.

  b. A negative number plus a negative number is   (☐ sometimes   ☐ always   ☐ never)   negative.

  c. A positive number minus a negative number is   (☐ sometimes   ☐ always   ☐ never)   positive.

  d. A negative number multiplied by a negative number is   (☐ sometimes   ☐ always   ☐ never)   negative.

A.2 Fractions and Fraction Arithmetic

The word "fraction" comes from the Latin word *fractio*, which means "break into pieces." For thousands of years, cultures from all over the world have used fractions to understand parts of a whole.

A.2.1 Visualizing Fractions

Parts of a Whole.   One approach to understanding fractions is to think of them as parts of a whole.

In Figure A.2.2, we see 1 whole divided into 7 parts. Since 3 parts are shaded, we have an illustration of the fraction $\frac{3}{7}$. The **denominator** 7 tells us how many parts to cut up the whole; since we have 7 parts, they're called "sevenths." The **numerator** 3 tells us how many sevenths to consider.

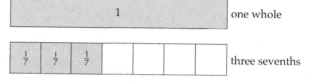

Figure A.2.2: Representing $\frac{3}{7}$ as parts of a whole.

Checkpoint A.2.3 A Fraction as Parts of a Whole. To visualize the fraction $\frac{14}{35}$, you might cut a rectangle into ☐ equal parts, and then count up ☐ of them.

Explanation.   You could cut a rectangle into 35 equal pieces, and then 14 of them would represent $\frac{14}{35}$.

We can also locate fractions on number lines. When ticks are equally spread apart, as in Figure A.2.4, each tick represents a fraction.

Figure A.2.4: Representing $\frac{3}{7}$ on a number line.

Checkpoint A.2.5 A Fraction on a Number Line. In the given number line, what fraction is marked?

Explanation.   There are 8 subdivisions between 0 and 1, and the mark is at the fifth subdivision. So the mark is $\frac{5}{8}$ of the way from 0 to 1 and therefore represents the fraction $\frac{5}{8}$.

Division.   Fractions can also be understood through division.

For example, we can view the fraction $\frac{3}{7}$ as 3 divided into 7 equal parts, as in Figure A.2.6. Just one of those parts represents $\frac{3}{7}$.

Figure A.2.6: Representing $\frac{3}{7}$ on a number line.

Checkpoint A.2.7 Seeing a Fraction as Division Arithmetic. The fraction $\frac{21}{40}$ can be thought of as dividing the whole number ☐ into ☐ equal-sized parts.

Explanation.   Since $\frac{21}{40}$ means the same as $21 \div 40$, it can be thought of as dividing 21 into 40 equal parts.

A.2.2 Equivalent Fractions

It's common to have two fractions that represent the same amount. Consider $\frac{2}{5}$ and $\frac{6}{15}$ represented in various ways in Figures A.2.8–A.2.10.

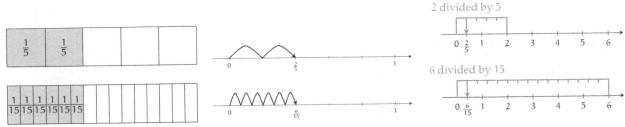

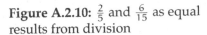

Figure A.2.8: $\frac{2}{5}$ and $\frac{6}{15}$ as equal parts of a whole

Figure A.2.9: $\frac{2}{5}$ and $\frac{6}{15}$ as equal on a number line

Figure A.2.10: $\frac{2}{5}$ and $\frac{6}{15}$ as equal results from division

Those two fractions, $\frac{2}{5}$ and $\frac{6}{15}$ are equal, as those figures demonstrate. In addition, both fractions are equal to 0.4 as a decimal. If we must work with this number, the fraction that uses smaller numbers, $\frac{2}{5}$, is preferable. Working with smaller numbers decreases the likelihood of making a human arithmetic error and it also increases the chances that you might make useful observations about the nature of that number.

So if you are handed a fraction like $\frac{6}{15}$, it is important to try to **reduce** it to "lowest terms." The most important skill you can have to help you do this is to know the multiplication table well. If you know it well, you know that $6 = 2 \cdot 3$ and $15 = 3 \cdot 5$, so you can break down the numerator and denominator that way. Both the numerator and denominator are divisible by 3, so they can be "factored out" and then as factors, cancel out.

$$\frac{6}{15} = \frac{2 \cdot 3}{3 \cdot 5}$$
$$= \frac{2 \cdot \cancel{3}}{\cancel{3} \cdot 5}$$
$$= \frac{2 \cdot 1}{1 \cdot 5}$$
$$= \frac{2}{5}$$

Checkpoint A.2.11 Reduce these fractions into lowest terms.

a. $\dfrac{14}{42}$ b. $\dfrac{8}{30}$ c. $\dfrac{70}{90}$

Explanation.

  a. With $\frac{14}{42}$, we have $\frac{2 \cdot 7}{2 \cdot 3 \cdot 7}$, which reduces to $\frac{1}{3}$.   c. With $\frac{70}{90}$, we have $\frac{7 \cdot 10}{9 \cdot 10}$, which reduces to $\frac{7}{9}$.

  b. With $\frac{8}{30}$, we have $\frac{2 \cdot 2 \cdot 2}{2 \cdot 3 \cdot 5}$, which reduces to $\frac{4}{15}$.

Sometimes it is useful to do the opposite of reducing a fraction, and **build up** the fraction to use larger numbers.

Checkpoint A.2.12 Sayid scored $\frac{21}{25}$ on a recent exam. Build up this fraction so that the denominator is 100, so that Sayid can understand what percent score he earned.

Explanation. To change the denominator from 25 to 100, it needs to be multiplied by 4. So we calculate

$$\frac{21}{25} = \frac{21 \cdot 4}{25 \cdot 4}$$
$$= \frac{84}{100}$$

So the fraction $\frac{21}{25}$ is equivalent to $\frac{84}{100}$. (This means Sayid scored an 84%.)

A.2.3 Multiplying with Fractions

Example A.2.13 Suppose a recipe calls for $\frac{2}{3}$ cup of milk, but we'd like to quadruple the recipe (make it four times as big). We'll need four times as much milk, and one way to measure this out is to fill a measuring cup to $\frac{2}{3}$ full, four times:

When you count up the shaded thirds, there are eight of them. So multiplying $\frac{2}{3}$ by the whole number 4, the result is $\frac{8}{3}$. Mathematically:

$$4 \cdot \frac{2}{3} = \frac{4 \cdot 2}{3}$$
$$= \frac{8}{3}$$

Fact A.2.14 Multiplying a Fraction and a Whole Number. *When you multiply a whole number by a fraction, you may just multiply the whole number by the numerator and leave the denominator alone. In other words, as long as d is not 0, then a whole number and a fraction multiply this way:*

$$a \cdot \frac{c}{d} = \frac{a \cdot c}{d}$$

Example A.2.15 We could also use multiplication to decrease amounts. Suppose we needed to cut the recipe down to just one fifth. Instead of *four* of the $\frac{2}{3}$ cup milk, we need *one fifth* of the $\frac{2}{3}$ cup milk. So instead of multiplying by 4, we multiply by $\frac{1}{5}$. But how much is $\frac{1}{5}$ of $\frac{2}{3}$ cup?
If we cut the measuring cup into five equal vertical strips along with the three equal horizontal strips, then in total there are $3 \cdot 5 = 15$ subdivisions of the cup. Two of those sections represent $\frac{1}{5}$ of the $\frac{2}{3}$ cup.

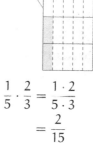

In the end, we have $\frac{2}{15}$ of a cup. The denominator 15 came from multiplying 5 and 3, the denominators of the fractions we had to multiply. The numerator 2 came from multiplying 1 and 2, the numerators of the fractions we had to multiply.

$$\frac{1}{5} \cdot \frac{2}{3} = \frac{1 \cdot 2}{5 \cdot 3}$$
$$= \frac{2}{15}$$

Fact A.2.16 Multiplication with Fractions. *As long as b and d are not 0, then fractions multiply this way:*

$$\frac{a}{b} \cdot \frac{c}{d} = \frac{a \cdot c}{b \cdot d}$$

Checkpoint A.2.17 Simplify these fraction products.

a. $\frac{1}{3} \cdot \frac{10}{7}$

b. $\frac{12}{3} \cdot \frac{15}{3}$

c. $-\frac{14}{5} \cdot \frac{2}{3}$

d. $\frac{70}{27} \cdot \frac{12}{-20}$

Explanation.

a. Multiplying numerators gives 10, and multiplying denominators gives 21. The answer is $\frac{10}{21}$.

b. Before we multiply fractions, note that $\frac{12}{3}$ reduces to 4, and $\frac{15}{3}$ reduces to 5. So we just have $4 \cdot 5 = 20$.

c. Multiplying numerators gives 28, and multiplying denominators gives 15. The result should be negative, so the answer is $-\frac{28}{15}$.

d. Before we multiply fractions, note that $\frac{12}{-20}$ reduces to $\frac{-3}{5}$. So we have $\frac{70}{27} \cdot \frac{-3}{5}$. Both the numerator of the first fraction and denominator of the second fraction are divisible by 5, so it helps to reduce both fractions accordingly and get $\frac{14}{27} \cdot \frac{-3}{1}$. Both the denominator of the first fraction and numerator of the second fraction are divisible by 3, so it helps to reduce both fractions accordingly and get $\frac{14}{9} \cdot \frac{-1}{1}$. Now we are just multiplying $\frac{14}{9}$ by -1, so the result is $\frac{-14}{9}$.

A.2.4 Division with Fractions

How does division with fractions work? Are we able to compute/simplify each of these examples?

a. $3 \div \frac{2}{7}$ 　　　　b. $\frac{18}{19} \div 5$ 　　　　c. $\frac{14}{3} \div \frac{8}{9}$ 　　　　d. $\frac{\frac{2}{5}}{\frac{5}{2}}$

We know that when we divide something by 2, this is the same as multiplying it by $\frac{1}{2}$. Conversely, dividing a number or expression by $\frac{1}{2}$ is the same as multiplying by $\frac{2}{1}$, or just 2. The more general property is that when we divide a number or expression by $\frac{a}{b}$, this is equivalent to multiplying by the reciprocal $\frac{b}{a}$.

Fact A.2.18 Division with Fractions. *As long as* b, c *and* d *are not 0, then division with fractions works this way:*

$$\frac{a}{b} \div \frac{c}{d} = \frac{a}{b} \cdot \frac{d}{c}$$

Example A.2.19 With our examples from the beginning of this subsection:

a. $3 \div \frac{2}{7} = 3 \cdot \frac{7}{2}$

$\quad = \frac{3}{1} \cdot \frac{7}{2}$

$\quad = \frac{21}{2}$

b. $\frac{18}{19} \div 5 = \frac{18}{19} \div \frac{5}{1}$

$\quad = \frac{18}{19} \cdot \frac{1}{5}$

$\quad = \frac{18}{95}$

c. $\frac{14}{3} \div \frac{8}{9} = \frac{14}{3} \cdot \frac{9}{8}$

$\quad = \frac{14}{1} \cdot \frac{3}{8}$

$\quad = \frac{7}{1} \cdot \frac{3}{4}$

$\quad = \frac{21}{4}$

d. $\frac{\frac{2}{5}}{\frac{5}{2}} = \frac{2}{5} \div \frac{5}{2}$

$\quad = \frac{2}{5} \cdot \frac{2}{5}$

$\quad = \frac{4}{25}$

Checkpoint A.2.20 Simplify these fraction division expressions.

   a. $\dfrac{1}{3} \div \dfrac{10}{7}$
      b. $\dfrac{12}{5} \div 5$
      c. $-14 \div \dfrac{3}{2}$
      d. $\dfrac{70}{9} \div \dfrac{11}{-20}$

Explanation.

a. $\begin{aligned}\dfrac{1}{3} \div \dfrac{10}{7} &= \dfrac{1}{3} \cdot \dfrac{7}{10} \\ &= \dfrac{7}{30}\end{aligned}$

c. $\begin{aligned}-14 \div \dfrac{3}{2} &= -14 \cdot \dfrac{2}{3} \\ &= -\dfrac{14}{1} \cdot \dfrac{2}{3} \\ &= -\dfrac{28}{3}\end{aligned}$

b. $\begin{aligned}\dfrac{12}{5} \div 5 &= \dfrac{12}{5} \cdot \dfrac{1}{5} \\ &= \dfrac{12}{25}\end{aligned}$

d. $\begin{aligned}\dfrac{70}{9} \div \dfrac{11}{-20} &= -\dfrac{70}{9} \cdot \dfrac{20}{11} \\ &= -\dfrac{1400}{99}\end{aligned}$

A.2.5 Adding and Subtracting Fractions

With whole numbers and integers, operations of addition and subtraction are relatively straightforward. The situation is almost as straightforward with fractions *if the two fractions have the same denominator.* Consider

$$\frac{7}{2} + \frac{3}{2} = 7 \text{ halves} + 3 \text{ halves}$$

In the same way that 7 tacos and 3 tacos make 10 tacos, we have:

$$\begin{array}{ccccc} 7 \text{ halves} & + & 3 \text{ halves} & - & 10 \text{ halves} \\ \frac{7}{2} & + & \frac{3}{2} & = & \frac{10}{2} \\ & & & = & 5 \end{array}$$

Fact A.2.21 Adding/Subtracting with Fractions Having the Same Denominator. *To add or subtract two fractions having the same denominator,* keep *that denominator, and add or subtract the numerators.*

$$\frac{a}{b} + \frac{c}{b} = \frac{a+c}{b} \qquad\qquad \frac{a}{b} - \frac{c}{b} = \frac{a-c}{b}$$

If it's possible, useful, or required of you, simplify the result by reducing to lowest terms.

Checkpoint A.2.22 Add or subtract these fractions.

   a. $\frac{1}{3} + \frac{10}{3}$
                    b. $\frac{13}{6} - \frac{5}{6}$

Explanation.

a. Since the denominators are both 3, we can add the numerators: $1 + 10 = 11$. The answer is $\frac{11}{3}$.

b. Since the denominators are both 6, we can subtract the numerators: $13 - 5 = 8$. The answer is $\frac{8}{6}$, but that reduces to $\frac{4}{3}$.

Whenever we'd like to combine fractional amounts that don't represent the same number of parts of a whole (that is, when the denominators are different), finding sums and differences is more complicated.

Example A.2.23 Quarters and Dimes. Find the sum $\frac{3}{4} + \frac{2}{10}$. Does this seem intimidating? Consider this:

- $\frac{1}{4}$ of a dollar is a quarter, and so $\frac{3}{4}$ of a dollar is 75 cents.

- $\frac{1}{10}$ of a dollar is a dime, and so $\frac{2}{10}$ of a dollar is 20 cents.

So if you know what to look for, the expression $\frac{3}{4} + \frac{2}{10}$ is like adding 75 cents and 20 cents, which gives you 95 cents. As a fraction of one dollar, that is $\frac{95}{100}$. So we can report

$$\frac{3}{4} + \frac{2}{10} = \frac{95}{100}.$$

(Although we should probably reduce that last fraction to $\frac{19}{20}$.)

This example was not something you can apply to other fraction addition situations, because the denominators here worked especially well with money amounts. But there is something we can learn here. The fraction $\frac{3}{4}$ was equivalent to $\frac{75}{100}$, and the other fraction $\frac{2}{10}$ was equivalent to $\frac{20}{100}$. These *equivalent* fractions have the same denominator and are therefore "easy" to add. What we saw happen was:

$$\frac{3}{4} + \frac{2}{10} = \frac{75}{100} + \frac{20}{100}$$
$$= \frac{95}{100}$$

This realization gives us a strategy for adding (or subtracting) fractions.

Fact A.2.24 Adding/Subtracting Fractions with Different Denominators. *To add (or subtract) generic fractions together, use their denominators to find a **common denominator**. This means some whole number that is a whole multiple of both of the original denominators. Then rewrite the two fractions as equivalent fractions that use this common denominator. Write the result keeping that denominator and adding (or subtracting) the numerators. Reduce the fraction if that is useful or required.*

Example A.2.25 Let's add $\frac{2}{3} + \frac{2}{5}$. The denominators are 3 and 5, so the number 15 would be a good common denominator.

$$\frac{2}{3} + \frac{2}{5} = \frac{2 \cdot 5}{3 \cdot 5} + \frac{2 \cdot 3}{5 \cdot 3}$$
$$= \frac{10}{15} + \frac{6}{15}$$
$$= \frac{16}{15}$$

Checkpoint A.2.26 A chef had $\frac{2}{3}$ cups of flour and needed to use $\frac{1}{8}$ cup to thicken a sauce. How much flour is left? [   ]

Explanation. We need to compute $\frac{2}{3} - \frac{1}{8}$. The denominators are 3 and 8. One common denominator is 24, so we move to rewrite each fraction using 24 as the denominator:

$$\frac{2}{3} - \frac{1}{8} = \frac{2 \cdot 8}{3 \cdot 8} - \frac{1 \cdot 3}{8 \cdot 3}$$
$$= \frac{16}{24} - \frac{3}{24}$$
$$= \frac{13}{24}$$

The numerical result is $\frac{13}{24}$, but a pure number does not answer this question. The amount of flour remaining is $\frac{13}{24}$ *cups*.

A.2.6 Mixed Numbers and Improper Fractions

A simple recipe for bread contains only a few ingredients:

1 1/2 tablespoons yeast
1 1/2 tablespoons kosher salt
6 1/2 cups unbleached, all-purpose flour (more for dusting)

Each ingredient is listed as a **mixed number** that quickly communicates how many whole amounts and how many parts are needed. It's useful for quickly communicating a practical amount of something you are cooking with, measuring on a ruler, purchasing at the grocery store, etc. But it causes trouble in an algebra class. The number 1 1/2 means "one *and* one half." So really,

$$1\frac{1}{2} = 1 + \frac{1}{2}$$

The trouble is that with 1 1/2, you have two numbers written right next to each other. Normally with two math expressions written right next to each other, they should be *multiplied*, not *added*. But with a mixed number, they *should* be added.

Fortunately we just reviewed how to add fractions. If we need to do any arithmetic with a mixed number like 1 1/2, we can treat it as $1 + \frac{1}{2}$ and simplify to get a "nice" fraction instead: $\frac{3}{2}$. A fraction like $\frac{3}{2}$ is called an **improper fraction** because it's actually larger than 1. And a "proper" fraction would be something small that is only *part* of a whole instead of *more* than a whole.

$$1\frac{1}{2} = 1 + \frac{1}{2}$$
$$= \frac{1}{1} + \frac{1}{2}$$
$$= \frac{2}{2} + \frac{1}{2}$$
$$= \frac{3}{2}$$

A.2.7 Exercises

Review and Warmup

1. Which letter is [`[$a]`] on the number line?

2. Which letter is [`[$a]`] on the number line?

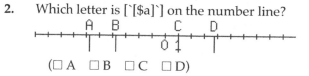

(□ A □ B □ C □ D) (□ A □ B □ C □ D)

3. The dot in the graph can be represented by what fraction?

4. The dot in the graph can be represented by what fraction?

5. The dot in the graph can be represented by what fraction?

6. The dot in the graph can be represented by what fraction?

Reducing Fractions

7. Reduce the fraction $\frac{7}{56}$.

8. Reduce the fraction $\frac{20}{45}$.

9. Reduce the fraction $\frac{70}{84}$.

10. Reduce the fraction $\frac{14}{15}$.

11. Reduce the fraction $\frac{168}{105}$.

12. Reduce the fraction $\frac{30}{6}$.

Building Fractions

13. Find an equivalent fraction to $\frac{3}{4}$ with denominator 20.

14. Find an equivalent fraction to $\frac{3}{5}$ with denominator 10.

15. Find an equivalent fraction to $\frac{3}{11}$ with denominator 44.

16. Find an equivalent fraction to $\frac{11}{13}$ with denominator 26.

Multiplying/Dividing Fractions

17. Multiply: $\frac{4}{9} \cdot \frac{4}{9}$

18. Multiply: $\frac{5}{6} \cdot \frac{5}{8}$

19. Multiply: $\frac{15}{7} \cdot \frac{2}{5}$

20. Multiply: $\frac{3}{7} \cdot \frac{8}{15}$

21. Multiply: $8 \cdot \frac{1}{3}$

22. Multiply: $5 \cdot \frac{2}{9}$

23. Multiply: $-\frac{20}{11} \cdot \frac{7}{5}$

24. Multiply: $-\frac{8}{7} \cdot \frac{11}{26}$

25. Multiply: $28 \cdot \left(-\frac{6}{7}\right)$

26. Multiply: $10 \cdot \left(-\frac{7}{5}\right)$

27. Multiply: $\frac{6}{49} \cdot \frac{5}{4} \cdot \frac{7}{25}$

28. Multiply: $\frac{5}{49} \cdot \frac{2}{25} \cdot \frac{21}{4}$

29. Multiply: $\frac{35}{2} \cdot \frac{1}{25} \cdot 6$

30. Multiply: $\frac{21}{2} \cdot \frac{1}{49} \cdot 10$

31. Divide: $\frac{2}{5} \div \frac{7}{4}$

32. Divide: $\frac{3}{8} \div \frac{5}{3}$

33. Divide: $\frac{1}{12} \div \left(-\frac{10}{9}\right)$

34. Divide: $\frac{7}{20} \div \left(-\frac{9}{25}\right)$

35. Divide: $-\frac{16}{9} \div (-20)$

36. Divide: $-\frac{25}{6} \div (-20)$

37. Divide: $28 \div \frac{7}{5}$

38. Divide: $6 \div \frac{3}{2}$

39. Multiply: $2\frac{1}{10} \cdot 1\frac{4}{21}$

40. Multiply: $2\frac{2}{9} \cdot 1\frac{7}{8}$

Adding/Subtracting Fractions

41. Add: $\frac{3}{32} + \frac{1}{32}$

42. Add: $\frac{17}{32} + \frac{3}{32}$

43. Add: $\frac{4}{7} + \frac{15}{28}$

44. Add: $\frac{4}{9} + \frac{11}{27}$

45. Add: $\frac{4}{9} + \frac{13}{18}$

46. Add: $\frac{1}{10} + \frac{21}{40}$

47. Add: $\dfrac{2}{7} + \dfrac{3}{10}$

48. Add: $\dfrac{1}{6} + \dfrac{1}{7}$

49. Add: $\dfrac{1}{6} + \dfrac{1}{10}$

50. Add: $\dfrac{3}{10} + \dfrac{1}{6}$

51. Add: $\dfrac{5}{6} + \dfrac{9}{10}$

52. Add: $\dfrac{4}{5} + \dfrac{7}{10}$

53. Add: $-\dfrac{1}{11} + \dfrac{6}{11}$

54. Add: $-\dfrac{4}{13} + \dfrac{12}{13}$

55. Add: $-\dfrac{5}{7} + \dfrac{11}{21}$

56. Add: $-\dfrac{4}{7} + \dfrac{3}{14}$

57. Add: $-\dfrac{1}{6} + \dfrac{2}{9}$

58. Add: $-\dfrac{7}{8} + \dfrac{6}{7}$

59. Add: $-1 + \dfrac{9}{10}$

60. Add: $1 + \dfrac{4}{5}$

61. Add: $\dfrac{1}{10} + \dfrac{1}{6} + \dfrac{1}{5}$

62. Add: $\dfrac{3}{10} + \dfrac{2}{9} + \dfrac{1}{6}$

63. Add: $\dfrac{1}{5} + \dfrac{3}{10} + \dfrac{5}{6}$

64. Add: $\dfrac{7}{9} + \dfrac{3}{10} + \dfrac{1}{6}$

65. Subtract: $\dfrac{17}{12} - \dfrac{7}{12}$

66. Subtract: $\dfrac{29}{12} - \dfrac{19}{12}$

67. Subtract: $\dfrac{3}{7} - \dfrac{11}{14}$

68. Subtract: $\dfrac{5}{9} - \dfrac{5}{54}$

69. Subtract: $\dfrac{31}{35} - \dfrac{2}{7}$

70. Subtract: $\dfrac{44}{45} - \dfrac{4}{9}$

71. Subtract: $-\dfrac{1}{6} - \dfrac{9}{10}$

72. Subtract: $-\dfrac{3}{10} - \dfrac{5}{6}$

73. Subtract: $-\dfrac{3}{10} - \left(-\dfrac{5}{6}\right)$

74. Subtract: $-\dfrac{5}{6} - \left(-\dfrac{3}{10}\right)$

75. Subtract: $-4 - \dfrac{18}{5}$

76. Subtract: $-2 - \dfrac{3}{2}$

Applications

77. Kandace walked $\frac{2}{7}$ of a mile in the morning, and then walked $\frac{1}{8}$ of a mile in the afternoon. How far did Kandace walk altogether?

    Kandace walked a total of [⎯⎯⎯⎯⎯⎯⎯⎯⎯⎯⎯] of a mile.

78. Tracei walked $\frac{1}{8}$ of a mile in the morning, and then walked $\frac{4}{11}$ of a mile in the afternoon. How far did Tracei walk altogether?

    Tracei walked a total of [⎯⎯⎯⎯⎯⎯⎯⎯⎯⎯⎯] of a mile.

79. Jessica and Carl are sharing a pizza. Jessica ate $\frac{3}{8}$ of the pizza, and Carl ate $\frac{1}{6}$ of the pizza. How much of the pizza was eaten in total?

    They ate [⎯⎯⎯⎯⎯⎯⎯⎯⎯⎯⎯] of the pizza.

80. A trail's total length is $\frac{32}{63}$ of a mile. It has two legs. The first leg is $\frac{2}{7}$ of a mile long. How long is the second leg?

    The second leg is [⎯⎯⎯⎯⎯⎯⎯⎯⎯⎯⎯] of a mile in length.

81. A trail's total length is $\frac{14}{45}$ of a mile. It has two legs. The first leg is $\frac{1}{5}$ of a mile long. How long is the second leg?

    The second leg is [⎯⎯⎯⎯⎯⎯⎯⎯⎯⎯⎯] of a mile in length.

82. James is participating in a running event. In the first hour, he completed $\frac{2}{9}$ of the total distance. After another hour, in total he had completed $\frac{47}{90}$ of the total distance.

    What fraction of the total distance did James complete during the second hour?

    James completed [   ] of the distance during the second hour.

83. The pie chart represents a school's student population.

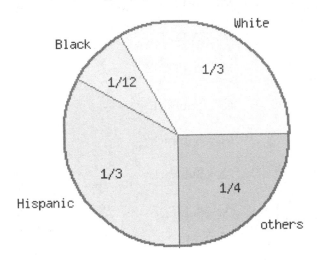

Together, white and black students make up [   ] of the school's population.

84. Each page of a book is $6\frac{3}{4}$ inches in height, and consists of a header (a top margin), a footer (a bottom margin), and the middle part (the body). The header is $\frac{5}{6}$ of an inch thick and the middle part is $5\frac{5}{6}$ inches from top to bottom.

    What is the thickness of the footer?

    The footer is [   ] of an inch thick.

85. Priscilla and Adrian are sharing a pizza. Priscilla ate $\frac{1}{6}$ of the pizza, and Adrian ate $\frac{1}{10}$ of the pizza. How much more pizza did Priscilla eat than Adrian?

    Priscilla ate [   ] more of the pizza than Adrian ate.

86. Emiliano and Maria are sharing a pizza. Emiliano ate $\frac{2}{7}$ of the pizza, and Maria ate $\frac{1}{6}$ of the pizza. How much more pizza did Emiliano eat than Maria?

    Emiliano ate [   ] more of the pizza than Maria ate.

87. A school had a fund-raising event. The revenue came from three resources: ticket sales, auction sales, and donations. Ticket sales account for $\frac{3}{4}$ of the total revenue; auction sales account for $\frac{1}{8}$ of the total revenue. What fraction of the revenue came from donations?

    [   ] of the revenue came from donations.

88. A few years back, a car was purchased for \$23,500. Today it is worth $\frac{1}{5}$ of its original value. What is the car's current value?

    The car's current value is [   ].

89. A few years back, a car was purchased for $20,000. Today it is worth $\frac{1}{5}$ of its original value. What is the car's current value?

   The car's current value is [   ].

90. The pie chart represents a school's student population.

School Population Breakdown by Race

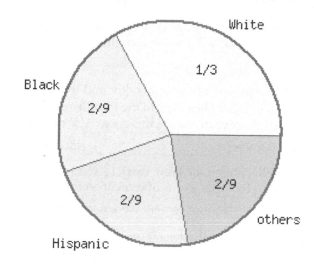

[   ] more of the school is white students than black students.

91. A town has 300 residents in total, of which $\frac{5}{6}$ are Asian Americans. How many Asian Americans reside in this town?

   There are [   ] Asian Americans residing in this town.

92. A company received a grant, and decided to spend $\frac{1}{8}$ of this grant in research and development next year. Out of the money set aside for research and development, $\frac{4}{9}$ will be used to buy new equipment. What fraction of the grant will be used to buy new equipment?

   [   ] of the grant will be used to buy new equipment.

93. A food bank just received 14 kilograms of emergency food. Each family in need is to receive $\frac{2}{5}$ kilograms of food. How many families can be served with the 14 kilograms of food?

   [   ] families can be served with the 14 kilograms of food.

94. A construction team maintains a 52-mile-long sewage pipe. Each day, the team can cover $\frac{4}{5}$ of a mile. How many days will it take the team to complete the maintenance of the entire sewage pipe?

   It will take the team [   ] days to complete maintaining the entire sewage pipe.

95. A child is stacking up tiles. Each tile's height is $\frac{2}{3}$ of a centimeter. How many layers of tiles are needed to reach 12 centimeters in total height?

   To reach the total height of 12 centimeters, [   ] layers of tiles are needed.

96. A restaurant made 300 cups of pudding for a festival.
   Customers at the festival will be served $\frac{1}{5}$ of a cup of pudding per serving. How many cus-

tomers can the restaurant serve at the festival with the 300 cups of pudding?

The restaurant can serve [ ] customers at the festival with the 300 cups of pudding.

97. A 2×4 piece of lumber in your garage is $62\frac{11}{16}$ inches long. A second 2×4 is $55\frac{7}{16}$ inches long. If you lay them end to end, what will the total length be?

The total length will be [ ] inches.

98. A 2×4 piece of lumber in your garage is $38\frac{11}{16}$ inches long. A second 2×4 is $44\frac{7}{8}$ inches long. If you lay them end to end, what will the total length be?

The total length will be [ ] inches.

99. Each page of a book consists of a header, a footer and the middle part. The header is $\frac{1}{9}$ inches in height; the footer is $\frac{11}{18}$ inches in height; and the middle part is $3\frac{4}{9}$ inches in height.
What is the total height of each page in this book? Use mixed number in your answer if needed.

Each page in this book is [ ] inches in height.

100. To pave the road on Ellis Street, the crew used $4\frac{5}{8}$ tons of cement on the first day, and used $4\frac{9}{10}$ tons on the second day. How many tons of cement were used in all?

[ ] tons of cement were used in all.

101. When driving on a high way, noticed a sign saying exit to Johnstown is $1\frac{3}{4}$ miles away, while exit to Jerrystown is $3\frac{1}{2}$ miles away. How far is Johnstown from Jerrystown?

Johnstown and Jerrystown are [ ] miles apart.

102. A cake recipe needs $3\frac{1}{2}$ cups of flour. Using this recipe, to bake 9 cakes, how many cups of flour are needed?

To bake 9 cakes, [ ] cups of flour are needed.

Sketching Fractions

103. Sketch a number line showing each fraction. (Be sure to carefully indicate the correct number of equal parts of the whole.)

(a) $\frac{2}{3}$ (b) $\frac{6}{8}$ (c) $\frac{5}{4}$ (d) $-\frac{4}{5}$

104. Sketch a number line showing each fraction. (Be sure to carefully indicate the correct number of equal parts of the whole.)

(a) $\frac{1}{6}$ (b) $\frac{3}{9}$ (c) $\frac{7}{6}$ (d) $-\frac{8}{5}$

105. Sketch a picture of the product $\frac{3}{5} \cdot \frac{1}{2}$, using a number line or rectangles.

106. Sketch a picture of the sum $\frac{2}{3} + \frac{1}{8}$, using a number line or rectangles.

Challenge

107. Given that $a \neq 0$, simplify $\frac{3}{a} + \frac{6}{a}$.

108. Given that $a \neq 0$, simplify $\frac{4}{a} + \frac{3}{2a}$.

109. Given that $a \neq 0$, simplify $\frac{5}{a} - \frac{9}{5a}$.

A.3 Absolute Value and Square Root

In this section, we will learn the basics of **absolute value** and **square root**. These are actions you can *do* to a given number, often changing the number into something else.

A.3.1 Introduction to Absolute Value

Definition A.3.2 The **absolute value** of a number is the distance between that number and 0 on a number line. For the absolute value of x, we write |x|.   ◇

Let's look at |2| and |−2|, the absolute value of 2 and the absolute value of −2.

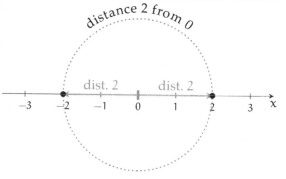

Figure A.3.3: |2| and |−2|

Since the distance between 2 and 0 on the number line is 2 units, the absolute value of 2 is 2. We write |2| = 2.

Since the distance between −2 and 0 on the number line is also 2 units, the absolute value of −2 is also 2. We write |−2| = 2.

Fact A.3.4 Absolute Value. *Taking the absolute value of a number results in whatever the "positive version" of that number is. This is because the real meaning of absolute value is its* distance *from zero.*

Checkpoint A.3.5 Calculating Absolute Value. Try calculating some absolute values.

a. |57| b. |−43| c. $\left|\frac{2}{-5}\right|$

Explanation.

a. 57 is 57 units away from 0 on a number line, so |57| = 57. Another way to think about this is that the "positive version" of 57 is 57.

b. −43 is 43 units away from 0 on a number line, so |−43| = 43. Another way to think about this is that the "positive version" of −43 is 43.

c. $\frac{2}{-5}$ is $\frac{2}{5}$ units away from 0 on a number line, so $\left|\frac{2}{-5}\right| = \frac{2}{5}$. Another way to think about this is that the "positive version" of $\frac{2}{-5}$ is $\frac{2}{5}$.

Warning A.3.6 Absolute Value Does Not Exactly "Make Everything Positive". Students may see an expression like |2 − 5| and incorrectly think it is OK to "make everything positive" and write 2 + 5. This is incorrect since |2 − 5| works out to be 3, not 7, as we are actually taking the absolute value of −3 (the equivalent number inside the absolute value).

A.3.2 Square Root Facts

If you have learned your basic multiplication table, you know:

×	1	2	3	4	5	6	7	8	9
1	1	2	3	4	5	6	7	8	9
2	2	4	6	8	10	12	14	16	18
3	3	6	9	12	15	18	21	24	27
4	4	8	12	16	20	24	28	32	36
5	5	10	15	20	25	30	35	40	45
6	6	12	18	24	30	36	42	48	54
7	7	14	21	28	35	42	49	56	63
8	8	16	24	32	40	48	56	64	72
9	9	18	27	36	45	54	63	72	81

Figure A.3.7: Multiplication table with squares

The numbers along the diagonal are special; they are known as **perfect squares**. And for working with square roots, it will be helpful if you can memorize these first few perfect square numbers.

"Taking a square root" is the opposite action of squaring a number. For example, when you square 3, the result is 9. So when you take the square root of 9, the result is 3. Just knowing that 9 comes about as 3^2 lets us realize that 3 is the square root of 9. This is why memorizing the perfect squares from the multiplication table can be so helpful.

The notation we use for taking a square root is the **radical**, $\sqrt{\ }$. For example, "the square root of 9" is denoted $\sqrt{9}$. And now we know enough to be able to write $\sqrt{9} = 3$.

Tossing in a few extra special square roots, it's advisable to memorize the following:

$$\sqrt{0} = 0 \qquad \sqrt{1} = 1 \qquad \sqrt{4} = 2 \qquad \sqrt{9} = 3$$
$$\sqrt{16} = 4 \qquad \sqrt{25} = 5 \qquad \sqrt{36} = 6 \qquad \sqrt{49} = 7$$
$$\sqrt{64} = 8 \qquad \sqrt{81} = 9 \qquad \sqrt{100} = 10 \qquad \sqrt{121} = 11$$
$$\sqrt{144} = 12 \qquad \sqrt{169} = 13 \qquad \sqrt{196} = 14 \qquad \sqrt{225} = 15$$

A.3.3 Calculating Square Roots with a Calculator

Most square roots are actually numbers with decimal places that go on forever. Take $\sqrt{5}$ as an example:

$$\sqrt{4} = 2 \qquad\qquad \sqrt{5} = ? \qquad\qquad \sqrt{9} = 3$$

Since 5 is between 4 and 9, then $\sqrt{5}$ must be somewhere between 2 and 3. There are no whole numbers between 2 and 3, so $\sqrt{5}$ must be some number with decimal places. If the decimal places eventually stopped, then squaring it would give you another number with decimal places that stop further out. But squaring it gives you 5 with no decimal places. So the only possibility is that $\sqrt{5}$ is a decimal between 2 and 3 that goes on forever. With a calculator, we can see:

$$\sqrt{5} \approx 2.236$$

Actually the decimal will not terminate, and that is why we used the $\approx$ symbol instead of an equals sign. To get 2.236 we rounded down slightly from the true value of $\sqrt{5}$. With a calculator, we can check that $2.236^2 = 4.999696$, a little shy of 5.

A.3.4 Square Roots of Fractions

We can calculate the square root of some fractions by hand, such as $\sqrt{\frac{1}{4}}$. The idea is the same: can you think of a number that you would square to get $\frac{1}{4}$? Being familiar with fraction multiplication, we know that $\frac{1}{2} \cdot \frac{1}{2} = \frac{1}{4}$ and so $\sqrt{\frac{1}{4}} = \frac{1}{2}$.

Checkpoint A.3.8 Square Roots of Fractions. Try calculating some absolute values.

a. $\sqrt{\dfrac{1}{25}}$
   b. $\sqrt{\dfrac{4}{9}}$
   c. $\sqrt{\dfrac{81}{121}}$

Explanation.

a. Since $\sqrt{1} = 1$ and $\sqrt{25} = 5$, then $\sqrt{\dfrac{1}{25}} = \dfrac{1}{5}$.

b. Since $\sqrt{4} = 2$ and $\sqrt{9} = 3$, then $\sqrt{\dfrac{4}{9}} = \dfrac{2}{3}$.

c. Since $\sqrt{81} = 9$ and $\sqrt{121} = 11$, then $\sqrt{\dfrac{81}{121}} = \dfrac{9}{11}$.

A.3.5 Square Root of Negative Numbers

Can we find the square root of a negative number, such as $\sqrt{-25}$? That would mean that there is some number out there that multiplies by itself to make -25. Would $\sqrt{-25}$ be positive or negative? Either way, once you square it (multiply it by itself) the result would be positive. So it couldn't possibly square to -25. So there is no square root of -25 or of any negative number for that matter.

Imaginary Numbers. Mathematicians imagined a new type of number, neither positive nor negative, that would square to a negative result. But that is beyond the scope of this chapter.

If you are confronted with an expression like $\sqrt{-25}$, or any other square root of a negative number, you can state that "there is no real square root" or that the result "does not exist" (as a real number).

A.3.6 Exercises

Review and Warmup

1. Evaluate the expressions.
   a. 1^2
   b. 3^2
   c. 5^2
   d. 7^2
   e. 9^2
   f. 11^2

2. Evaluate the expressions.
   a. 2^2
   b. 4^2
   c. 6^2
   d. 8^2
   e. 10^2
   f. 12^2

Absolute Value Evaluate the following.

3. $|-10|$

4. $|-7|$

5. $|-48.89|$

6. $|-15.76|$

7. $\left|-\dfrac{3}{59}\right|$

8. $\left|-\dfrac{19}{11}\right|$

9. a. $-|1-9|$
    b. $|-1-9|$
    c. $-2|9-1|$

10. a. $-|4-6|$
    b. $|-4-6|$
    c. $-2|6-4|$

11. a. $|10|$

    b. $|-10|$

    c. $-|10|$

    d. $-|-10|$

12. a. $|2|$

    b. $|-2|$

    c. $-|2|$

    d. $-|-2|$

13. a. $|2|$

    b. $|-3|$

    c. $|0|$

    d. $|14 + (-8)|$

    e. $|-8 - (-1)|$

14. a. $|3|$

    b. $|-7|$

    c. $|0|$

    d. $|18 + (-1)|$

    e. $|-8 - (-3)|$

15. Which of the following are square numbers? There may be more than one correct answer.

    ☐ 101   ☐ 80   ☐ 56   ☐ 1   ☐ 16   ☐ 25

16. Which of the following are square numbers? There may be more than one correct answer.

    ☐ 36   ☐ 81   ☐ 55   ☐ 64   ☐ 50   ☐ 62

Square Roots Evaluate the following.

17. a. $\sqrt{64}$

    b. $\sqrt{16}$

    c. $\sqrt{1}$

18. a. $\sqrt{81}$

    b. $\sqrt{144}$

    c. $\sqrt{25}$

19. a. $\sqrt{\dfrac{100}{49}}$

    b. $\sqrt{-\dfrac{121}{36}}$

20. a. $\sqrt{\dfrac{144}{121}}$

    b. $\sqrt{-\dfrac{100}{81}}$

Evaluate the following.

21. Do not use a calculator.

    a. $\sqrt{4}$

    b. $\sqrt{0.04}$

    c. $\sqrt{400}$

22. Do not use a calculator.

    a. $\sqrt{9}$

    b. $\sqrt{0.09}$

    c. $\sqrt{900}$

23. Do not use a calculator.

    a. $\sqrt{16}$

    b. $\sqrt{1600}$

    c. $\sqrt{160000}$

24. Do not use a calculator.

    a. $\sqrt{25}$

    b. $\sqrt{2500}$

    c. $\sqrt{250000}$

25. Do not use a calculator.

    a. $\sqrt{36}$

    b. $\sqrt{0.36}$

    c. $\sqrt{0.0036}$

26. Do not use a calculator.

    a. $\sqrt{64}$

    b. $\sqrt{0.64}$

    c. $\sqrt{0.0064}$

Evaluate the following.

27. Use a calculator to approximate with a decimal.

    $\sqrt{61}$

28. Use a calculator to approximate with a decimal.

    $\sqrt{83}$

Evaluate the following.

29. $\sqrt{\dfrac{121}{144}}$

30. $\sqrt{\dfrac{1}{100}}$

31. $-\sqrt{9}$

32. $-\sqrt{16}$

33. $\sqrt{-25}$

34. $\sqrt{-49}$

35. $\sqrt{-\dfrac{49}{100}}$

36. $\sqrt{-\dfrac{64}{81}}$

37. $-\sqrt{\dfrac{81}{100}}$

38. $-\sqrt{\dfrac{121}{144}}$

39. a. $\sqrt{25} - \sqrt{9}$

b. $\sqrt{25 - 9}$

40. a. $\sqrt{25} - \sqrt{9}$

b. $\sqrt{25 - 9}$

41. $\dfrac{3}{\sqrt{100}}$

42. $\dfrac{3}{\sqrt{49}}$

A.4 Percentages

Percent-related problems arise in everyday life. This section reviews some basic calculations that can be made with percentages.

A.4.1 Converting Percents, Decimals, and English

In many situations when translating from English to math, the word "of" translates as multiplication. Also the word "is" (and many similar words related to "to be") translates to an equals sign. For example:

One third of thirty is ten.

$$\frac{1}{3} \cdot 30 = 10$$

Here is another example, this time involving a percentage. We know that "2 is 50% of 4," so we can say:

2 is 50% of 4

$$2 = 0.5 \cdot 4$$

Example A.4.2 Translate each statement involving percents below into an equation. Define any variables used. (Solving these equations is an exercise).

a. How much is 30% of $24.00?

b. $7.20 is what percent of $24.00?

c. $7.20 is 30% of how much money?

Explanation.   Each question can be translated from English into a math equation by reading it slowly and looking for the right signals.

a. The word "is" means about the same thing as the equals sign. "How much" is a question phrase, and we can let x be the unknown amount (in dollars). The word "of" translates to multiplication, as discussed earlier. So we have:

$$\underset{x}{\text{how much}} \quad \underset{=}{\text{is}} \quad \underset{0.30}{\text{30\%}} \quad \underset{\cdot}{\text{of}} \quad \underset{24}{\text{\$24}}$$

b. Let P be the unknown value. We have:

$$\underset{7.2}{\text{\$7.20}} \quad \underset{=}{\text{is}} \quad \underset{P}{\text{what percent}} \quad \underset{\cdot}{\text{of}} \quad \underset{24}{\text{\$24}}$$

With this setup, P is going to be a decimal value (0.30) that you would translate into a percentage (30%).

c. Let x be the unknown amount (in dollars). We have:

$$\underset{7.2}{\text{\$7.20}} \quad \underset{=}{\text{is}} \quad \underset{0.30}{\text{30\%}} \quad \underset{\cdot}{\text{of}} \quad \underset{x}{\text{how much}}$$

Checkpoint A.4.3 Solve each equation from Example A.4.2.

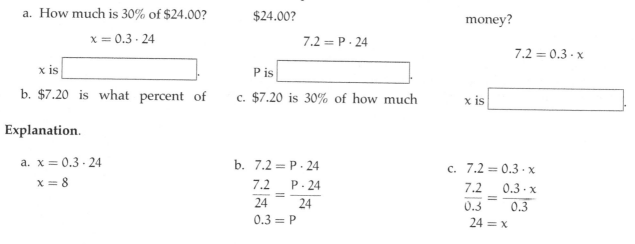

a. How much is 30% of $24.00?

$$x = 0.3 \cdot 24$$

x is [＿＿＿＿＿].

b. $7.20 is what percent of $24.00?

$$7.2 = P \cdot 24$$

P is [＿＿＿＿＿].

c. $7.20 is 30% of how much money?

$$7.2 = 0.3 \cdot x$$

x is [＿＿＿＿＿].

Explanation.

a. $x = 0.3 \cdot 24$
$x = 8$

b. $7.2 = P \cdot 24$
$\dfrac{7.2}{24} = \dfrac{P \cdot 24}{24}$
$0.3 = P$

c. $7.2 = 0.3 \cdot x$
$\dfrac{7.2}{0.3} = \dfrac{0.3 \cdot x}{0.3}$
$24 = x$

A.4.2 Setting up and Solving Percent Equations

An important skill for solving percent-related problems is to boil down a complicated word problem into a simple form like "2 is 50% of 4." Let's look at some further examples.

Example A.4.4
In Fall 2016, Portland Community College had 89,900 enrolled students. According to Figure A.4.5, how many black students were enrolled at PCC in Fall 2016?

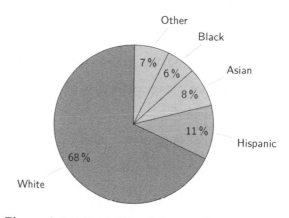

Figure A.4.5: Racial breakdown of PCC students in Fall 2016

Explanation. After reading this word problem and the chart, we can translate the problem into "what is 6% of 89,900?" Let x be the number of black students enrolled at PCC in Fall 2016. We can set up and solve the equation:

$$\underset{x}{\text{what}} \; \underset{=}{\text{is}} \; \underset{0.06}{\text{6\%}} \; \underset{\cdot}{\text{of}} \; \underset{89900}{\text{89,900}}$$

$$x = 5394$$

There was not much "solving" to do, since the variable we wanted to isolate was already isolated.

As of Fall 2016, Portland Community College had 5394 black students. Note: this is not likely to be perfectly accurate, because the numbers we started with (89,900 enrolled students and 6%) appear to be rounded.

Example A.4.6
The bar graph in Figure A.4.7 displays how many students are in each class at a local high school. According to the bar graph, what percentage of the school's student population is freshman?

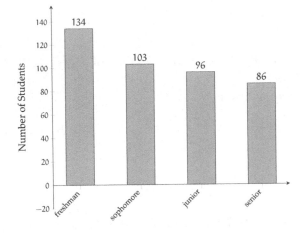

Figure A.4.7: Number of students at a high school by class

Explanation.   The school's total number of students is:

$$134 + 103 + 96 + 86 = 419$$

With that calculated, we can translate the main question:

"What percentage of the school's student population is freshman?"

into:

"What percent of 419 is 134?"

Using P to represent the unknown quantity, we write and solve the equation:

$$
\begin{array}{ccccc}
\text{what percent} & \text{of} & 419 & \text{is} & 134 \\
\big| & \big| & \big| & \big| & \big| \\
P & \cdot & 419 & = & 134
\end{array}
$$

$$\frac{P \cdot 419}{419} = \frac{134}{419}$$

$$P \approx 0.3198$$

$$P \approx 31.98\%$$

Approximately 31.98% of the school's student population is freshman.

Remark A.4.8 When solving equations that do *not* have context we state the solution set. However, when solving an equation or inequality that arises in an application problem (such as the context of the high school in Example A.4.6), it makes more sense to summarize our result with a sentence, using the context of the application. This allows us to communicate the full result, including appropriate units.

Example A.4.9 Carlos just received his monthly paycheck. His gross pay (the amount before taxes and related things are deducted) was $2,346.19, and his total tax and other deductions was $350.21. The rest was deposited directly into his checking account. What percent of his gross pay went into his checking account?

Explanation. Train yourself to read the word problem and not try to pick out numbers to substitute into formulas. You may find it helps to read the problem over to yourself three or more times before you attempt to solve it. There are *three* dollar amounts to discuss in this problem, and many students fall into a trap of using the wrong values in the wrong places. There is the gross pay, the amount that was deducted, and the amount that was deposited. Only two of these have been explicitly written down. We need to use subtraction to find the dollar amount that was deposited:

$$2346.19 - 350.21 = 1995.98$$

Now, we can translate the main question:

"What percent of his gross pay went into his checking account?"

into:

"What percent of $2346.19 is $1995.98?"

Using P to represent the unknown quantity, we write and solve the equation:

$$\underset{\text{what percent}}{P} \quad \underset{\text{of}}{\cdot} \quad \underset{\$2346.19}{2346.19} \quad \underset{\text{is}}{=} \quad \underset{\$1995.98}{1995.98}$$

$$\frac{P \cdot 2346.19}{2346.19} = \frac{1995.98}{2346.19}$$

$$P \approx 0.8507$$

$$P \approx 85.07\%$$

Approximately 85.07% of his gross pay went into his checking account.

Checkpoint A.4.10 Alexis sells cars for a living, and earns 28% of the dealership's sales profit as commission. In a certain month, she plans to earn $2200 in commissions. How much total sales profit does she need to bring in for the dealership?

Alexis needs to bring in [_____] in sales profit.

Explanation. Be careful that you do not calculate 28% of $2200. That might be what a student would do who doesn't thoroughly read the question. If you have ever trained yourself to quickly find numbers in word problems and substitute them into formulas, you must *unlearn* this. The issue is that $2200 is not the dealership's sales profit, and if you mistakenly multiply $0.28 \cdot 2200 = 616$, then $616 makes no sense as an answer to this question. How could Alexis bring in only $616 of sales profit, and earn $2200 in commission?

We can translate the problem into "$2200 is 28% of what?" Letting x be the sales profit for the dealership (in dollars), we can write and solve the equation:

$$\overset{\overset{\displaystyle\$2200 \;\; \text{is} \;\; 28\% \;\; \text{of} \;\; \text{what}}{|\quad|\quad|\quad|\quad|}}{2200} = 0.28 \cdot x$$

$$\frac{2200}{0.28} = \frac{0.28x}{0.28}$$

$$7857.14 \approx x$$

$$x \approx 7857.14$$

To earn $2200 in commission, Alexis needs to bring in approximately $7857.14 of sales profit for the dealership.

Example A.4.11
According to e-Literate, the average cost of a new college textbook has been increasing. Find the percentage of increase from 2009 to 2013.

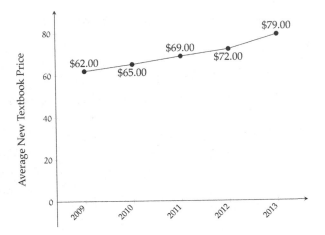

Figure A.4.12: Average New Textbook Price from 2009 to 2013

Explanation. The actual amount of increase from 2009 to 2013 was $79 - 62 = 17$, dollars. We need to answer the question "$17 is what percent of $62?" Note that we are comparing the 17 to 62, not to 79. In these situations where one amount is the earlier amount, the earlier original amount is the one that represents 100%. Let P represent the percent of increase. We can set up and solve the equation:

$$\overset{\overset{\displaystyle\$17 \;\; \text{is} \;\; \text{what percent} \;\; \text{of} \;\; \$62}{|\quad|\qquad|\qquad\quad|\quad|}}{17} = \quad P \quad \cdot 62$$

$$17 = 62P$$

$$\frac{17}{62} = \frac{62P}{62}$$

$$0.2742 \approx P$$

From 2009 to 2013, the average cost of a new textbook increased by approximately 27.42%.

Checkpoint A.4.13 Last month, a full tank of gas for a car you drive cost you $40.00. You hear on the news that gas prices have risen by 12%. By how much, in dollars, has the cost of a full tank gone up?

A full tank of gas now costs ⬚ more than it did last month.

Explanation. Let x represent the amount of increase. We can set up and solve the equation:

$$\underset{0.12}{\overset{12\%}{|}} \cdot \underset{40}{\overset{\text{of old cost}}{|}} \underset{=}{\overset{\text{is}}{|}} \underset{x}{\overset{\text{how much}}{|}}$$

$$4.8 = x$$

A full tank now costs $4.80 more than it did last month.

Example A.4.14 Enrollment at your neighborhood's elementary school two years ago was 417 children. After a 15% increase last year and a 15% decrease this year, what's the new enrollment?

Explanation. It is tempting to think that increasing by 15% and then decreasing by 15% would bring the enrollment right back to where it started. But the 15% decrease applies to the enrollment *after* it had already increased. So that 15% decrease is going to translate to *more* students lost than were gained.

Using 100% as corresponding to the enrollment from two years ago, the enrollment last year was 100% + 15% = 115% of that. But then using 100% as corresponding to the enrollment from last year, the enrollment this year was 100% − 15% = 85% of that. So we can set up and solve the equation

$$\underset{x}{\overset{\text{this year's enrollment}}{|}} \underset{=0.85}{\overset{\text{is}}{|}} \cdot \underset{1.15}{\overset{85\% \text{ of } 115\% \text{ of}}{|}} \cdot \underset{417}{\overset{\text{enrollment two years ago}}{|}}$$

$$x = 0.85 \cdot 1.15 \cdot 417$$

$$x = 407.6175$$

We would round and report that enrollment is now 408 students. (The percentage rise and fall of 15% were probably rounded in the first place, which is why we did not end up with a whole number.)

A.4.3 Exercises

Review and Warmup Write the following percentages as decimals.

1. a. 18%
    b. 53%

2. a. 19%
    b. 58%

3. a. 0.21
    b. 0.65

4. a. 0.22
    b. 0.62

5. a. 3%
    b. 30%
    c. 100%
    d. 300%

6. a. 4%
    b. 40%
    c. 100%
    d. 400%

Write the following decimals as percentages.

7. a. 0.05
    b. 0.5
    c. 5
    d. 1

8. a. 0.06
    b. 0.6
    c. 6
    d. 1

9. a. 7.45
    b. 0.745
    c. 0.0745

10.   a. 8.19

     b. 0.819

     c. 0.0819

11.   a. 973%

     b. 97.3%

     c. 9.73%

12.   a. 147%

     b. 14.7%

     c. 1.47%

Basic Percentage Calculation

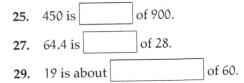

13. 2% of 220 is ____.

14. 7% of 320 is ____.

15. 40% of 420 is ____.

16. 20% of 520 is ____.

17. 670% of 620 is ____.

18. 430% of 710 is ____.

19. 97% of ____ is 785.7.

20. 66% of ____ is 600.6.

21. 4% of ____ is 4.8.

22. 9% of ____ is 19.8.

23. 390% of ____ is 1248.

24. 220% of ____ is 924.

Answer with a percent.

25. 450 is ____ of 900.

26. 354 is ____ of 590.

27. 64.4 is ____ of 28.

28. 223.6 is ____ of 86.

29. 19 is about ____ of 60.

30. 2 is about ____ of 17.

Applications

31. A town has 1500 registered residents. Among them, 38% were Democrats, 34% were Republicans. The rest were Independents. How many registered Independents live in this town?

    There are ____ registered Independent residents in this town.

32. A town has 1900 registered residents. Among them, 35% were Democrats, 22% were Republicans. The rest were Independents. How many registered Independents live in this town?

    There are ____ registered Independent residents in this town.

33. Dave is paying a dinner bill of $30.00. Dave plans to pay 11% in tips. How much tip will Dave pay?

    Dave will pay ____ in tip.

34. Tracei is paying a dinner bill of $34.00. Tracei plans to pay 18% in tips. How much tip will Tracei pay?

    Tracei will pay ____ in tip.

35. Michael is paying a dinner bill of $37.00. Michael plans to pay 14% in tips. How much in total (including bill and tip) will Michael pay?

    Michael will pay ____ in total (including bill and tip).

36. Jessica is paying a dinner bill of $41.00. Jessica plans to pay 10% in tips. How much in total (including bill and tip) will Jessica pay?

    Jessica will pay ____ in total (including bill and tip).

37. A watch's wholesale price was $440.00. The retailer marked up the price by 35%. What's the watch's new price (markup price)?

    The watch's markup price is ____.

38. A watch's wholesale price was $480.00. The retailer marked up the price by 25%. What's the watch's new price (markup price)?

    The watch's markup price is ____.

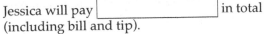

39. In the past few seasons' basketball games, Lindsay attempted 110 free throws, and made 22 of them. What percent of free throws did Lindsay make?

Lindsay made [   ] of free throws in the past few seasons.

40. In the past few seasons' basketball games, Douglas attempted 370 free throws, and made 74 of them. What percent of free throws did Douglas make?

Douglas made [   ] of free throws in the past few seasons.

41. A painting is on sale at $425.00. Its original price was $500.00. What percentage is this off its original price?

The painting was [   ] off its original price.

42. A painting is on sale at $385.00. Its original price was $550.00. What percentage is this off its original price?

The painting was [   ] off its original price.

43. The pie chart represents a collector's collection of signatures from various artists.

Collection of Signatures from Different Artists

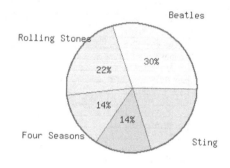

If the collector has a total of 1050 signatures, there are [   ] signatures by Sting.

44. The pie chart represents a collector's collection of signatures from various artists.

Collection of Signatures from Different Artists

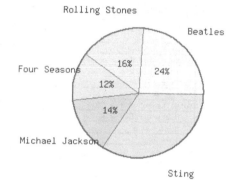

If the collector has a total of 1250 signatures, there are [   ] signatures by Sting.

45. In the last election, 67% of a county's residents, or 24790 people, turned out to vote. How many residents live in this county?

This county has [   ] residents.

46. In the last election, 54% of a county's residents, or 22356 people, turned out to vote. How many residents live in this county?

This county has [   ] residents.

47. 58.14 grams of pure alcohol was used to produce a bottle of 15.3% alcohol solution. What is the weight of the solution in grams?

The alcohol solution weighs [   ].

48. 57.4 grams of pure alcohol was used to produce a bottle of 28.7% alcohol solution. What is the weight of the solution in grams?

The alcohol solution weighs [   ].

49. Ravi paid a dinner and left 16%, or $3.68, in tips. How much was the original bill (without counting the tip)?
The original bill (not including the tip) was
[   ].

50. Laney paid a dinner and left 12%, or $3.24, in tips. How much was the original bill (without counting the tip)?
The original bill (not including the tip) was
[   ].

51. Parnell sells cars for a living. Each month, he earns $1,300.00 of base pay, plus a certain percentage of commission from his sales. One month, Parnell made $53,500.00 in sales, and earned a total of $4,472.55 in that month (including base pay and commission). What percent commission did Parnell earn?

Parnell earned [   ] in commission.

52. Selena sells cars for a living. Each month, she earns $1,300.00 of base pay, plus a certain percentage of commission from her sales.

One month, Selena made $58,000.00 in sales, and earned a total of $3,904.20 in that month (including base pay and commission). What percent commission did Selena earn?

Selena earned [   ] in commission.

53. The following is a nutrition fact label from a certain macaroni and cheese box.

Nutrition Facts		
Serving Size 1 cup		
Servings Per Container 2		
Amount Per Serving		
Calories 300	Calories from Fat 110	
		% Daily Value
Total Fat 6.5 g		10%
Saturated Fat 2 g		15%
Trans Fat 2 g		
Cholesterol 30 mg		10%
Sodium 400 mg		20%
Total Carbohydrate 30 g		11%
Dietary Fiber 0 g		0%
Sugars 5 g		
Protein 5 g		
Vitamin A 2 mg		3%
Vitamin C 2 mg		2.5%
Calcium 2 mg		20%
Iron 3 mg		4%

The highlighted row means each serving of macaroni and cheese in this box contains 6.5 g of fat, which is 10% of an average person's daily intake of fat. What's the recommended daily intake of fat for an average person?

The recommended daily intake of fat for an average person is [   ].

54. The following is a nutrition fact label from a certain macaroni and cheese box.

Nutrition Facts		
Serving Size 1 cup		
Servings Per Container 2		
Amount Per Serving		
Calories 300	Calories from Fat 110	
		% Daily Value
Total Fat 12.6 g		18%
Saturated Fat 2 g		15%
Trans Fat 2 g		
Cholesterol 30 mg		10%
Sodium 400 mg		20%
Total Carbohydrate 30 g		11%
Dietary Fiber 0 g		0%
Sugars 5 g		
Protein 5 g		
Vitamin A 2 mg		3%
Vitamin C 2 mg		2.5%
Calcium 2 mg		20%
Iron 3 mg		4%

The highlighted row means each serving of macaroni and cheese in this box contains 12.6 g of fat, which is 18% of an average person's daily intake of fat. What's the recommended daily intake of fat for an average person?

The recommended daily intake of fat for an average person is [   ].

55. A community college conducted a survey about the number of students riding each bus line available. The following bar graph is the result of the survey.

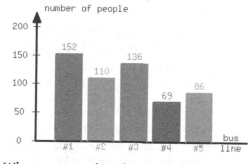

What percent of students ride Bus #1?

Approximately [　　　　　] of students ride Bus #1.

56. A community college conducted a survey about the number of students riding each bus line available. The following bar graph is the result of the survey.

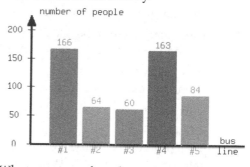

What percent of students ride Bus #1?

Approximately [　　　　　] of students ride Bus #1.

57. Donna earned $75.75 of interest from a mutual fund, which was 0.75% of his total investment. How much money did Donna invest into this <u>mutual fund</u>?

Donna invested [　　　　　] in this mutual fund.

58. Dave earned $71.05 of interest from a mutual fund, which was 0.49% of his total investment. How much money did Dave invest into this <u>mutual fund</u>?

Dave invested [　　　　　] in this mutual fund.

59. A town has 1900 registered residents. Among them, there are 589 Democrats and 513 Republicans. The rest are Independents. What percentage of registered voters in this town are Independents?

In this town, [　　　　　] of all registered voters are Independents.

60. A town has 2300 registered residents. Among them, there are 851 Democrats and 805 Republicans. The rest are Independents. What percentage of registered voters in this town are Independents?

In this town, [　　　　　] of all registered voters are Independents.

Percent Increase/Decrease

61. The population of cats in a shelter decreased from 100 to 80. What is the percentage decrease of the shelter's cat population?

The percentage decrease is [　　　　　].

62. The population of cats in a shelter decreased from 120 to 114. What is the percentage decrease of the shelter's cat population?

The percentage decrease is [　　　　　].

63. The population of cats in a shelter increased from 57 to 72. What is the percentage increase of the shelter's cat population? The percentage increase is approximately

[　　　　　].

64. The population of cats in a shelter increased from 65 to 75. What is the percentage increase of the shelter's cat population? The percentage increase is approximately

[　　　　　].

65. Last year, a small town's population was 770. This year, the population decreased to 769. What is the percentage decrease? The percentage decrease of the town's population was approximately [   ].

66. Last year, a small town's population was 800. This year, the population decreased to 797. What is the percentage decrease? The percentage decrease of the town's population was approximately [   ].

67. Your salary used to be $36,000 per year. You had to take a 2% pay cut. After the cut, your salary was [   ] per year. Then, you earned a 2% raise. After the raise, your salary was [   ] per year.

68. Your salary used to be $49,000 per year. You had to take a 2% pay cut. After the cut, your salary was [   ] per year. Then, you earned a 2% raise. After the raise, your salary was [   ] per year.

69. A house was bought two years ago at the price of $340,000. Each year, the house's value decreased by 4%. What's the house's value this year?
The house's value this year is
[   ].

70. A house was bought two years ago at the price of $200,000. Each year, the house's value decreased by 5%. What's the house's value this year?
The house's value this year is
[   ].

71. This line graph shows a certain stock's price change over a few days.

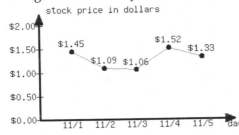

From 11/1 to 11/5, what is the stock price's percentage change?
From 11/1 to 11/5, the stock price's percentage change was approximately
[   ].

72. This line graph shows a certain stock's price change over a few days.

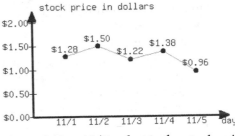

From 11/1 to 11/5, what is the stock price's percentage change?
From 11/1 to 11/5, the stock price's percentage change was approximately
[   ].

A.5 Order of Operations

Mathematical symbols are a means of communication, and it's important that when you write something, everyone else knows exactly what you intended. For example, if we say in English, "two times three squared," do we mean that:

- 2 is multiplied by 3, and then the result is squared?

- or that 2 is multiplied by the result of squaring 3?

English is allowed to have ambiguities like this. But mathematical language needs to be precise and mean the same thing to everyone reading it. For this reason, a standard **order of operations** has been adopted, which we review here.

A.5.1 Grouping Symbols

Consider the math expression $2 \cdot 3^2$. There are two mathematical operations here: a multiplication and an exponentiation. The result of this expression will change depending on which operation you decide to execute first: the multiplication or the exponentiation. If you multiply $2 \cdot 3$, and then square the result, you have 36. If you square 3, and then multiply 2 by the result, you have 18. If we want all people everywhere to interpret $2 \cdot 3^2$ in the same way, then only *one* of these can be correct.

The first tools that we have to tell readers what operations to execute first are grouping symbols, like parentheses and brackets. If you *intend* to execute the multiplication first, then writing

$$(2 \cdot 3)^2$$

clearly tells your reader to do that. And if you *intend* to execute the power first, then writing

$$2 \cdot (3^2)$$

clearly tells your reader to do that.

To visualize the difference between $2 \cdot (3^2)$ or $(2 \cdot 3)^2$, consider these garden plots:

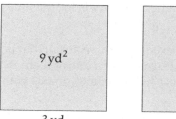

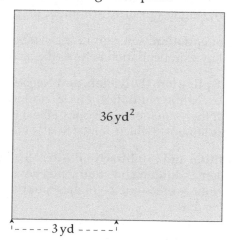

Figure A.5.2: 3 yd is squared, then doubled: $2 \cdot (3^2)$

Figure A.5.3: 3 yd is doubled, then squared: $(2 \cdot 3)^2$

If we calculate 3^2, we have the area of one of the small square garden plots on the left. If we then double that, we have $2 \cdot (3^2)$, the area of the left garden plot.

But if we calculate $(2 \cdot 3)^2$, then first we are doubling 3. So we are calculating the area of a square garden plot whose sides are twice as long. We end up with the area of the garden plot on the right.

The point is that these amounts are different.

Checkpoint A.5.4 Calculate the value of $30 - ((2 + 3) \cdot 2)$, respecting the order that the grouping symbols are telling you to execute the arithmetic operations.

Explanation. The grouping symbols tell us what to work on first. In this exercise, we have grouping symbols within grouping symbols, so any operation in there (the addition) should be executed first:

$$\begin{aligned} 30 - ((2 + 3) \cdot 2) &= 30 - (5 \cdot 2) \\ &= 30 - 10 \\ &= 20 \end{aligned}$$

A.5.2 Beyond Grouping Symbols

If all math expressions used grouping symbols for each and every arithmetic operation, we wouldn't need to say anything more here. In fact, some computer systems work that way, *requiring* the use of grouping symbols all the time. But it is much more common to permit math expressions with no grouping symbols at all, like $5 + 3 \cdot 2$. Should the addition $5 + 3$ be executed first, or should the multiplication $3 \cdot 2$? We need what's known formally as the **order of operations** to tell us what to do.

The **order of operations** is nothing more than an agreement that we all have made to prioritize the arithmetic operations in a certain order.

List A.5.5: Order of Operations

(P)arentheses and other grouping symbols Grouping symbols should always direct you to the highest priority arithmetic first.

(E)xponentiation After grouping symbols, exponentiation has the highest priority. Execute any exponentiation before other arithmetic operations.

(M)ultiplication, (D)ivision, and Negation After all exponentiation has been executed, start executing multiplications, divisions, and negations. These things all have equal priority. If there are more than one of them in your expression, the highest priority is the one that is leftmost (which comes first as you read it).

(A)ddition and (S)ubtraction After all other arithmetic has been executed, these are all that is left. Addition and subtraction have equal priority. If there are more than one of them in your expression, the highest priority is the one that is leftmost (which comes first as you read it).

A common acronym to help you remember this order of operations is PEMDAS. There are a handful of mnemonic devices for remembering this ordering (such as Please Excuse My Dear Aunt Sally, People Eat More Donuts After School, etc.).

We'll start with a few examples that only invoke a few operations each.

Example A.5.6 Use the order of operations to simplify the following expressions.

a. $10 + 2 \cdot 3$. With this expression, we have the operations of addition and multiplication. The order of operations says the multiplication has higher priority, so execute that first:

$$10 + 2 \cdot 3 = 10 + \boxed{2 \cdot 3}$$
$$= 10 + 6$$
$$= 16$$

b. $4 + 10 \div 2 - 1$. With this expression, we have addition, division, and subtraction. According to the order of operations, the first thing we need to do is divide. After that, we'll apply the addition and subtraction, working left to right:

$$4 + 10 \div 2 - 1 = 4 + \boxed{10 \div 2} - 1$$
$$= \boxed{4 + 5} - 1$$
$$= 9 - 1$$
$$= 8$$

c. $7 - 10 + 4$. This example *only* has subtraction and addition. While the acronym PEMDAS may mislead you to do addition before subtraction, remember that these operations have the same priority, and so we work left to right when executing them:

$$7 - 10 + 4 = \boxed{7 - 10} + 4$$
$$= -3 + 4$$
$$= 1$$

d. $20 \div 4 \cdot 7$. This expression has only division and multiplication. Again, remember that although PEMDAS shows "MD," the operations of multiplication and division have the same priority, so we'll apply them left to right:

$$20 \div 4 \cdot 5 = \boxed{20 \div 4} \cdot 5$$
$$= 5 \cdot 5$$
$$= 25$$

e. $(6 + 7)^2$. With this expression, we have addition inside a set of parentheses, and an exponent of 2 outside of that. We must compute the operation inside the parentheses first, and after that we'll apply the exponent:

$$(6 + 7)^2 = (\boxed{6 + 7})^2$$
$$= 13^2$$
$$= 169$$

f. $4(2)^3$. This expression has multiplication and an exponent. There are parentheses too, but no operation inside them. Parentheses used in this manner make it clear that the 4 and 2 are separate numbers, not to be confused with 42. In other words, $4(2)^3$ and 42^3 mean very different things. Exponentiation has the higher priority, so we'll apply the exponent first, and then we'll multiply:

$$4(2)^3 = 4\boxed{(2)^3}$$
$$= 4(8)$$
$$= 32$$

Remark A.5.7 There are many different ways that we write multiplication. We can use the symbols $\cdot$, $\times$, and $*$ to denote multiplication. We can also use parentheses to denote multiplication, as we've seen in Example A.5.6, Item f. Once we start working with variables, there is even another way. No matter how multiplication is written, it does not change the priority that multiplication has in the order of operations.

Checkpoint A.5.8 Practice with order of operations. Simplify this expression one step at a time, using the order of operations.
$$5 - 3(7 - 4)^2$$

Explanation.

$$5 - 3(\boxed{7-4})^2 = 5 - 3\boxed{(3)^2}$$
$$= 5 - \boxed{3(9)}$$
$$= 5 - 27$$
$$= -22$$

A.5.3 Absolute Value Bars, Radicals, and Fraction Bars are Grouping Symbols

When we first discussed grouping symbols, we only mentioned parentheses and brackets. Each of the following operations has an *implied* grouping symbol aside from parentheses and brackets.

Absolute Value Bars The absolute value bars, as in $|2 - 5|$, group the expression inside it just like a set of parentheses would.

Radicals The same is true of the radical symbol—everything inside the radical is grouped, as with $\sqrt{12 - 3}$.

Fraction Bars With a horizontal division bar, the numerator is treated as one group and the denominator as another, as with $\frac{2+3}{5-2}$.

We don't *need* parentheses for these three things since the absolute value bars, radical, and horizontal division bar each denote this grouping on their own. As far as priority in the order of operations goes, it's important to remember that these work just like our most familiar grouping symbols, parentheses.

With absolute value bars and radicals, these grouping symbols also *do* something to what's inside (but only *after* the operations inside have been executed). For example, $|-2| = 2$, and $\sqrt{9} = 3$.

Example A.5.9 Use the order of operations to simplify the following expressions.

a. $4 - 3|5 - 7|$. For this expression, we'll treat the absolute value bars just like we treat parentheses. This implies we'll simplify what's inside the bars first, and then compute the absolute value. After that, we'll multiply and then finally subtract:

$$4 - 3|5 - 7| = 4 - 3\boxed{|5 - 7|}$$
$$= 4 - 3\boxed{|-2|}$$
$$= 4 - \boxed{3(2)}$$
$$= 4 - 6$$
$$= -2$$

We may not do $4 - 3 = 1$ first, because 3 is connected to the absolute value bars by multiplication (although implicitly), which has a higher order than subtraction.

b. $8 - \sqrt{5^2 - 8 \cdot 2}$. This expression has an expression inside the radical of $5^2 - 8 \cdot 2$. We'll treat this radical like we would a set of parentheses, and simplify that internal expression first. We'll then apply the square root, and then our last step will be to subtract that expression from 8:

$$8 - \sqrt{5^2 - 8 \cdot 2} = 8 - \sqrt{\boxed{5^2} - 8 \cdot 2}$$
$$= 8 - \sqrt{25 - \boxed{8 \cdot 2}}$$
$$= 8 - \sqrt{\boxed{25 - 16}}$$
$$= 8 - \boxed{\sqrt{9}}$$
$$= 8 - 3$$
$$= 5$$

c. $\dfrac{2^4 + 3 \cdot 6}{5 - 18 \div 2}$. For this expression, the first thing we want to do is to recognize that the main fraction bar serves as a separator that groups the numerator and groups the denominator. Another way this expression could be written is $(2^4 + 3 \cdot 6) \div (15 - 18 \div 2)$. This implies we'll simplify the numerator and denominator separately according to the order of operations (since there are implicit parentheses around each of these). As a final step we'll simplify the resulting fraction (which is division).

$$\frac{2^4 + 3 \cdot 6}{5 - 18 \div 2} = \frac{\boxed{2^4} + 3 \cdot 6}{5 - \boxed{18 \div 2}}$$
$$= \frac{16 + \boxed{3 \cdot 6}}{\boxed{5 - 9}}$$
$$= \frac{\boxed{16 + 18}}{-4}$$
$$= \frac{34}{-4}$$
$$= -\frac{17}{2}$$

Checkpoint A.5.10 More Practice with Order of Operations. Use the order of operations to evaluate

$$\frac{6 + 3|9 - 10|}{\sqrt{3 + 18 \div 3}}.$$

Explanation. We start by identifying the innermost, highest priority operations:

$$\frac{6 + 3|9 - 10|}{\sqrt{3 + 18 \div 3}} = \frac{6 + 3\left|\boxed{9 - 10}\right|}{\sqrt{3 + \boxed{18 \div 3}}}$$

$$= \frac{6 + 3\boxed{|-1|}}{\sqrt{\boxed{3 + 6}}}$$

$$= \frac{6 + \boxed{3(1)}}{\boxed{\sqrt{9}}}$$

$$= \frac{\boxed{6 + 3}}{3}$$

$$= \frac{9}{3} = 3$$

A.5.4 Negation and Distinguishing $(-a)^m$ from $-a^m$

We noted in the order of operations that using the negative sign to negate a number has the same priority as multiplication and division. To understand why this is, observe that $-1 \cdot 23 = -23$, just for one example. So negating 23 gives the same result as multiplying 23 by -1. For this reason, negation has the same priority in the order of operations as multiplication. This can be a source of misunderstandings.

How would you write a math expression that takes the number -4 and squares it?

$$-4^2? \qquad (-4)^2? \qquad \text{it doesn't matter?}$$

It *does* matter. The second option, $(-4)^2$ is squaring the number -4. The parentheses emphasize this.

But the expression -4^2 is different. There are two actions in this expression: a negation and and exponentiation. According to the order of operations, the exponentiation has higher priority than the negation, so the exponent of 2 in -4^2 applies to the 4 *before* the negative sign (multiplication by -1) is taken into account.

$$-4^2 = -\boxed{4^2}$$
$$= -16$$

and this is not the same as $(-4)^2$, which is *positive* 16.

Warning A.5.11 Negative Numbers Raised to Powers. You may find yourself needing to raise a negative number to a power, and using a calculator to do the work for you. If you do not understand the issue described here, then you may get incorrect results.

- For example, entering -4^2 into a calculator will result in -16, the negative of 4^2.

- But entering (-4)^2 into a calculator will result in 16, the square of -4.

Go ahead and try entering these into your own calculator.

Checkpoint A.5.12 Negating and Raising to Powers. Compute the following:

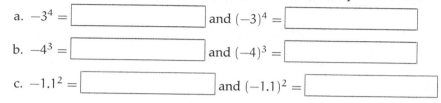

a. $-3^4 = \boxed{}$ and $(-3)^4 = \boxed{}$

b. $-4^3 = \boxed{}$ and $(-4)^3 = \boxed{}$

c. $-1.1^2 = \boxed{}$ and $(-1.1)^2 = \boxed{}$

Explanation. In each part, the first expression asks you to exponentiate and then negate the result. The second expression has a negative number raised to a power. So the answers are:

a. $-3^4 = -81$ and $(-3)^4 = 81$

b. $-4^3 = -64$ and $(-4)^3 = -64$

c. $-1.1^2 = -1.21$ and $(-1.1)^2 = 1.21$

Remark A.5.13 You might observe in the previous example that there is no difference between -4^3 and $(-4)^3$. It's true that the results are the same, -64, but the two expressions still do say different things. With -4^3, you raise to a power first, then negate. With $(-4)^3$, you negate first, then raise to a power.

As was discussed in Subsection A.1.5, if the base of a power is negative, then whether or not the result is positive or negative depends on if the exponent is even or odd. It depends on whether or not the factors can all be paired up to "cancel" negative signs, or if there will be a lone factor left by itself.

A.5.5 More Examples

Here are some example exercises that involve applying the order of operations to more complicated expressions. Try these exercises and read the steps given in each solution.

Example A.5.14 Simplify $10 - 4(5 - 7)^3$.

Explanation. For the expression $10 - 4(5 - 7)^3$, we have simplify what's inside parentheses first, then we'll apply the exponent, then multiply, and finally subtract:

$$10 - 4(5 - 7)^3 = 10 - 4(\boxed{5 - 7})^3$$
$$= 10 - 4\boxed{(-2)^3}$$
$$= 10 - \boxed{4(-8)}$$
$$= 10 - (-32)$$
$$= 10 + 32$$
$$= 42$$

Checkpoint A.5.15 Simplify $24 \div (15 \div 3 + 1) + 2$.

Explanation.   With the expression $24 \div (15 \div 3 + 1) + 2$, we'll simplify what's inside the parentheses according to the order of operations, and then take 24 divided by that expression as our last step:

$$
\begin{aligned}
24 \div (15 \div 3 + 1) + 2 &= 24 \div (\boxed{15 \div 3} + 1) + 2 \\
&= 24 \div (\boxed{5 + 1}) + 2 \\
&= \boxed{24 \div 6} + 2 \\
&= 4 + 2 \\
&= 6
\end{aligned}
$$

Example A.5.16 Simplify $6 - (-8)^2 \div 4 + 1$.

Explanation.   To simplify $6 - (-8)^2 \div 4 + 1$, we'll first apply the exponent of 2 to -8, making sure to recall that $(-8)^2 = 64$. After this, we'll apply division. As a final step, we'll be have subtraction and addition, which we'll apply working left-to-right:

$$
\begin{aligned}
6 - (-8)^2 \div 4 + 1 &= 6 - \boxed{(-8)^2} \div 4 + 1 \\
&= 6 - \boxed{(64) \div 4} + 1 \\
&= \boxed{6 - 16} + 1 \\
&= -10 + 1 \\
&= -9
\end{aligned}
$$

Checkpoint A.5.17 Simplify $(20 - 4^2) \div (4 - 6)^3$.

Explanation.   The expression $(20 - 4^2) \div (4 - 6)^3$ has two sets of parentheses, so our first step will be to simplify what's inside each of those first according to the order of operations. Once we've done that, we'll apply the exponent and then finally divide:

$$
\begin{aligned}
(20 - 4^2) \div (4 - 6)^3 &= (20 - \boxed{4^2}) \div (4 - 6)^3 \\
&= (\boxed{20 - 16}) \div (4 - 6)^3 \\
&= 4 \div (\boxed{4 - 6})^3 \\
&= 4 \div \boxed{(-2)^3} \\
&= 4 \div (-8) \\
&= \frac{4}{-8} \\
&= \frac{1}{-2} \\
&= -\frac{1}{2}
\end{aligned}
$$

Checkpoint A.5.18 Simplify $\dfrac{2|9 - 15| + 1}{\sqrt{(-5)^2 + 12^2}}$.

Explanation. To simplify this expression, the first thing we want to recognize is the role of the main fraction bar, which groups the numerator and denominator. This implies we'll simplify the numerator and denominator separately according to the order of operations, and then reduce the fraction that results:

$$\frac{2|9-15|+1}{\sqrt{(-5)^2+12^2}} = \frac{2\boxed{|9-15|}+1}{\sqrt{\boxed{(-5)^2}+12^2}}$$

$$= \frac{2\boxed{|-6|}+1}{\sqrt{25+\boxed{12^2}}}$$

$$= \frac{\boxed{2(6)}+1}{\sqrt{\boxed{25+144}}}$$

$$= \frac{\boxed{12+1}}{\boxed{\sqrt{169}}}$$

$$= \frac{13}{13}$$

$$= 1$$

A.5.6 Exercises

Review and Warmup

1. Multiply the following.
   a. $(-9) \cdot (-1)$
   b. $(-7) \cdot 3$
   c. $9 \cdot (-4)$
   d. $(-8) \cdot 0$

2. Multiply the following.
   a. $(-9) \cdot (-2)$
   b. $(-5) \cdot 7$
   c. $9 \cdot (-7)$
   d. $(-7) \cdot 0$

3. Multiply the following.
   a. $(-1) \cdot (-6) \cdot (-2)$
   b. $5 \cdot (-6) \cdot (-3)$
   c. $(-90) \cdot (-68) \cdot 0$

4. Multiply the following.
   a. $(-1) \cdot (-4) \cdot (-4)$
   b. $4 \cdot (-6) \cdot (-5)$
   c. $(-88) \cdot (-56) \cdot 0$

5.
   a. Compute -8^2.
   b. Calculate the power -3^2.
   c. Find -6^2.
   d. Calculate $(-1)^{19}$.

6.
   a. Compute -1^{40}.
   b. Calculate the power $(-2)^4$.
   c. Find -4^4.
   d. Calculate -8^2.

Order of Operations Skills Evaluate the following.

7. $6 + 7(3)$

8. $2 + 4(4)$

9. $5(3 + 3)$

10. $4(4 + 5)$

11. $(3 \cdot 2)^2$

12. $(4 \cdot 4)^2$

13. $5 \cdot 3^2$

14. $5 \cdot 2^3$

15. $(12 - 2) \cdot 5$

16. $(8 - 2) \cdot 3$

17. $14 - 3 \cdot 2$

18. $17 - 3 \cdot 5$

19. $6 + 4 \cdot 8$

20. $7 + 2 \cdot 6$

21. $4 - 5 \cdot 8$

22. $5 - 3 \cdot 10$

23. $5 - 2(-7)$

24. $1 - 5(-9)$

25. $-[1 - (2 - 5)^2]$

26. $-[10 - (2 - 7)^2]$

27. $7 - 5[10 - (1 + 4 \cdot 3)]$

28. $7 - 3[4 - (8 + 4 \cdot 5)]$

29. $6 + 3(59 - 2 \cdot 3^3)$

30. $6 + 2(110 - 4 \cdot 3^3)$

31. $-5[4 - (5 - 2 \cdot 5)^2]$

32. $-5[10 - (3 - 4 \cdot 2)^2]$

33. $42 - 3[4^2 - (5 - 1)]$

34. $74 - 2[6^2 - (4 - 2)]$

35. $(9 - 2)^2 + 3(9 - 2^2)$

36. $(13 - 3)^2 + 4(13 - 3^2)$

37. $(4 \cdot 3)^2 - 4 \cdot 3^2$

38. $(4 \cdot 5)^2 - 4 \cdot 5^2$

39. $8 \cdot 4^2 - 125 \div 5^2 \cdot 4 + 5$

40. $9 \cdot 2^2 - 36 \div 3^2 \cdot 4 + 9$

41. $5(9 - 4)^2 - 5(9 - 4^2)$

42. $6(6 - 2)^2 - 6(6 - 2^2)$

43. $\dfrac{5 + 1}{3 - 2}$

44. $\dfrac{4 + 6}{7 - 2}$

45. $\dfrac{8^2 - 3^2}{3 + 8}$

46. $\dfrac{8^2 - 2^2}{7 + 3}$

47. $\dfrac{27 - (-4)^3}{3 - 10}$

48. $\dfrac{27 - (-2)^3}{7 - 12}$

49. $\dfrac{(-2) \cdot (-9) - (-10) \cdot 9}{(-6)^2 + (-38)}$

50. $\dfrac{(-2) \cdot (-3) - (-6) \cdot 7}{(-6)^2 + (-38)}$

51. $-|1 - 5|$

52. $-|1 - 2|$

53. $2 - 7|4 - 9| + 3$

54. $3 - 6|1 - 6| + 3$

55. $-5^2 - |8 \cdot (-5)|$

56. $-4^2 - |6 \cdot (-9)|$

57. $8 - 4\left|-5 + (4 - 5)^3\right|$

58. $9 - 8\left|-1 + (3 - 5)^3\right|$

59. $\dfrac{\left|27 + (-4)^3\right|}{-1}$

60. $\dfrac{\left|1 + (-2)^3\right|}{-1}$

61. $\left|\dfrac{1 + (-4)^3}{-3}\right|$

62. $\left|\dfrac{1 + (-4)^3}{-3}\right|$

63. $\dfrac{-3|5 - 12|}{6 - (-3)^2}$

64. $\dfrac{-3|1 - 7|}{7 - (-1)^2}$

65. $\dfrac{8}{7} + 8 \cdot \dfrac{3}{7}$

66. $\dfrac{8}{3} + 2 \cdot \dfrac{2}{3}$

67. $\left(\dfrac{9}{10} - \dfrac{7}{50}\right) - 2\left(\dfrac{7}{50} - \dfrac{9}{10}\right)$

68. $\left(\dfrac{3}{2} - \dfrac{1}{8}\right) - 2\left(\dfrac{1}{8} - \dfrac{3}{2}\right)$

69. $\left|\dfrac{3}{2} - \dfrac{5}{6}\right| - 2\left|\dfrac{5}{6} - \dfrac{3}{2}\right|$

70. $\left|\dfrac{3}{8} - \dfrac{9}{16}\right| - 2\left|\dfrac{9}{16} - \dfrac{3}{8}\right|$

71. $\dfrac{1}{5} + 4\left(\dfrac{3}{5}\right)^2$

72. $\dfrac{3}{5} + 8\left(\dfrac{2}{5}\right)^2$

73. $\dfrac{3}{4} + \dfrac{1}{3} \div \dfrac{1}{3} - \dfrac{4}{5}$

74. $\dfrac{4}{3} + \dfrac{3}{5} \div \dfrac{1}{5} - \dfrac{5}{2}$

75. $4\sqrt{94 - 93}$

76. $5\sqrt{36 + 28}$

77. $5\sqrt{-8 + 8 \cdot 3}$

78. $2\sqrt{73 + 3 \cdot 9}$

79. $7 - 2\sqrt{61 - 25}$

80. $4 - 3\sqrt{2 + 7}$

81. $\sqrt{36} - 3\sqrt{-9 + 130}$

82. $\sqrt{49} - 5\sqrt{6 + 58}$

83. $\sqrt{33 + 4^2}$

84. $\sqrt{-36 + 10^2}$

85. $\sqrt{8^2 + 6^2}$

86. $\sqrt{9^2 + 12^2}$

87. $\dfrac{\sqrt{81} + 3}{\sqrt{81} - 3}$

88. $\dfrac{\sqrt{4} + 6}{\sqrt{4} - 6}$

89. $\dfrac{\sqrt{-8 + 6 \cdot 4} + |-16 - 7|}{-67 - (-4)^3}$

90. $\dfrac{\sqrt{1 + 8 \cdot 3} + |-18 - 7|}{-2 - (-2)^3}$

91. $4[17 - 5(3 + 8)]$

92. $4[15 - 3(1 + 8)]$

93. $-8^2 - 9[5 - (6 - 4^3)]$

94. $-10^2 - 5[9 - (4 - 4^3)]$

Challenge

95. In this challenge, your job is to create expressions, using addition, subtraction, multiplication, and parentheses. You may use the numbers, $1, 2, 3,$ and 4 in your expression, using each number only once. For example, you could make the expression: $1 + 2 \cdot 3 - 4$.

   a. The greatest value that it is possible to create under these conditions is [   ].

   b. The least value that it is possible to create under these conditions is [   ].

A.6 Set Notation and Types of Numbers

When we talk about *how many* or *how much* of something we have, it often makes sense to use different types of numbers. For example, if we are counting dogs in a shelter, the possibilities are only $0, 1, 2, \ldots$. (It would be difficult to have $\frac{1}{2}$ of a dog.) On the other hand if you were weighing a dog in pounds, it doesn't make sense to only allow yourself to work with whole numbers. The dog might weigh something like 28.35 pounds. These examples highlight how certain kinds of numbers are appropriate for certain situations. We'll classify various types of numbers in this section.

A.6.1 Set Notation

What is the mathematical difference between these three "lists?"

$$28, 31, 30 \qquad \{28, 31, 30\} \qquad (28, 31, 30)$$

To a mathematician, the last one, $(28, 31, 30)$ is an *ordered* triple. What matters is not merely the three numbers, but *also* the order in which they come. The ordered triple $(28, 31, 30)$ is not the same as $(30, 31, 28)$; they have the same numbers in them, but the order has changed. For some context, February has 28 days; *then* March has 31 days; *then* April has 30 days. The order of the three numbers is meaningful in that context.

With curly braces and $\{28, 31, 30\}$, a mathematician sees a collection of numbers and does not particularly care in which order they are written. Such a collection is called a **set**. All that matters is that these numbers are part of a collection. They've been *written* in some particular order because that's necessary to write them down. But you might as well have put the three numbers in a bag and shaken up the bag. For some context, maybe your favorite three NBA players have jersey numbers 30, 31, and 28, and you like them all equally well. It doesn't really matter what order you use to list them.

So we can say:

$$\{28, 31, 30\} = \{30, 31, 28\} \qquad\qquad (28, 31, 30) \neq (30, 31, 28)$$

What about just writing $28, 31, 30$? This list of three numbers is ambiguous. Without the curly braces or parentheses, it's unclear to a reader if the order is important. **Set notation** is the use of curly braces to surround a list/collection of numbers, and we will use set notation frequently in this section.

Checkpoint A.6.2 Set Notation. Practice using (and not using) set notation.

According to Google, the three most common error codes from visiting a web site are 403, 404, and 500.

a. Without knowing which error code is most common, express this set mathematically.

b. Error code 500 is the most common. Error code 403 is the least common of these three. And that leaves 404 in the middle. Express the error codes in a mathematical way that appreciates how frequently they happen, from most often to least often.

Explanation.

a. Since we only have to describe a collection of three numbers and their order doesn't matter, we can write {403,404,500}.

b. Now we must describe the same three numbers and we want readers to know that the order we are writing the numbers matters. We can write (500,404,403).

A.6.2 Different Number Sets

In the introduction, we mentioned how different sets of numbers are appropriate for different situations. Here are the basic sets of numbers that are used in basic algebra.

Natural Numbers When we count, we begin: $1, 2, 3, \ldots$ and continue on in that pattern. These numbers are known as **natural numbers**.

$$\mathbb{N} = \{1, 2, 3, \ldots\}$$

Whole Numbers If we include zero, then we have the set of **whole numbers**.

$\{0, 1, 2, 3, \ldots\}$ has no standard symbol, but some options are $\mathbb{N}_0$, $\mathbb{N} \cup \{0\}$, and $\mathbb{Z}_{\geq 0}$.

Integers If we include the negatives of whole numbers, then we have the set of **integers**.

$$\mathbb{Z} = \{\ldots, -3, -2, -1, 0, 1, 2, 3, \ldots\}.$$

A $\mathbb{Z}$ is used because one word in German for "numbers" is "Zahlen."

Rational Numbers A **rational number** is any number that *can* be written as a fraction of integers, where the denominator is nonzero. Alternatively, a **rational number** is any number that *can* be written with a decimal that terminates or that repeats.

$$\mathbb{Q} = \left\{0, 1, -1, 2, \tfrac{1}{2}, -\tfrac{1}{2}, -2, 3, \tfrac{1}{3}, -\tfrac{1}{3}, -3, \tfrac{3}{2}, \tfrac{2}{3} \ldots\right\}$$

$$\mathbb{Q} = \left\{0, 1, -1, 2, 0.5, -0.5, -2, 3, 0.\overline{3}, -0.\overline{3}, -3, 1.5, 0.\overline{6} \ldots\right\}$$

A $\mathbb{Q}$ is used because fractions are *quotients* of integers.

Irrational Numbers Any number that *cannot* be written as a fraction of integers belongs to the set of **irrational numbers**. Another way to say this is that any number whose decimal places goes on forever without repeating is an **irrational number**. Some examples include $\pi \approx 3.1415926\ldots$, $\sqrt{15} \approx 3.87298\ldots$, $e \approx 2.71828\ldots$

There is no standard symbol for the set of irrational numbers.

Real Numbers Any number that can be marked somewhere on a number line is a **real number**. Real numbers might be the only numbers you are familiar with. For a number to *not* be real, you have to start considering things called *complex numbers*, which are not our concern right now.

The set of real numbers can be denoted with $\mathbb{R}$ for short.

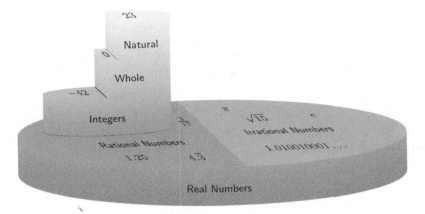

Figure A.6.3: Types of Numbers

Warning A.6.4 Rational Numbers in Other Forms. Any number that *can* be written as a ratio of integers is rational, even if it's not written that way at first. For example, these numbers might not look rational to you at first glance: -4, $\sqrt{9}$, 0π, and $\sqrt[3]{\sqrt{5}+2}-\sqrt[3]{\sqrt{5}-2}$. But they are all rational, because they can respectively be written as $\frac{-4}{1}$, $\frac{3}{1}$, $\frac{0}{1}$, and $\frac{1}{1}$.

Example A.6.5 Determine If Numbers Are This Type or That Type. Determine which numbers from the set $\left\{-102, -7.25, 0, \frac{\pi}{4}, 2, \frac{10}{3}, \sqrt{19}, \sqrt{25}, 10.\overline{7}\right\}$ are natural numbers, whole numbers, integers, rational numbers, irrational numbers, and real numbers.

Explanation.   All of these numbers are real numbers, because all of these numbers can be positioned on the real number line.

Each real number is either rational or irrational, and not both. -102, -7.25, 0, and 2 are rational because we can see directly that their decimal expressions terminate. $10.\overline{7}$ is also rational, because its decimal expression repeats. $\frac{10}{3}$ is rational because it is a ratio of integers. And last but not least, $\sqrt{25}$ is rational, because that's the same thing as 5.

This leaves only $\frac{\pi}{4}$ and $\sqrt{19}$ as irrational numbers. Their decimal expressions go on forever without entering a repetitive cycle.

Only -102, 0, 2, and $\sqrt{25}$ (which is really 5) are integers.

Of these, only 0, 2, and $\sqrt{25}$ are whole numbers, because whole numbers excludes the negative integers.

Of these, only 2 and $\sqrt{25}$ are natural numbers, because the natural numbers exclude 0.

Checkpoint A.6.6

   a. Give an example of a whole number that is not an integer.

   b. Give an example of an integer that is not a whole number.

   c. Give an example of a rational number that is not an integer.

   d. Give an example of a irrational number.

   e. Give an example of a irrational number that is also an integer.

Explanation.

   a. Since all whole numbers belong to integers, we cannot write any whole number which is not an integer.

Type DNE (does not exist) for this question.

b. Any negative integer, like -1, is not a whole number, but is an integer.

c. Any terminating decimal, like 1.2, is a rational number, but is not an integer.

d. π is the easiest number to remember as an irrational number. Another constant worth knowing is $e \approx 2.718$. Finally, the square root of most integers are irrational, like $\sqrt{2}$ and $\sqrt{3}$.

e. All irrational numbers are non-repeating and non-terminating decimals. No irrational numbers are integers.

Checkpoint A.6.7 In the introduction, we mentioned that the different types of numbers are appropriate in different situation. Which number set do you think is most appropriate in each of the following situations?

a. The number of people in a math class that play the ukulele.

This number is best considered as a (☐ natural number ☐ whole number ☐ integer ☐ rational number ☐ irrational number ☐ real number) .

b. The hypotenuse's length in a given right triangle.

This number is best considered as a (☐ natural number ☐ whole number ☐ integer ☐ rational number ☐ irrational number ☐ real number) .

c. The proportion of people in a math class that have a cat.

This number is best considered as a (☐ natural number ☐ whole number ☐ integer ☐ rational number ☐ irrational number ☐ real number) .

d. The number of people in the room with you who have the same birthday as you.

This number is best considered as a (☐ natural number ☐ whole number ☐ integer ☐ rational number ☐ irrational number ☐ real number) .

e. The total revenue (in dollars) generated for ticket sales at a Timbers soccer game.

This number is best considered as a (☐ natural number ☐ whole number ☐ integer ☐ rational number ☐ irrational number ☐ real number) .

Explanation.

a. The number of people who play the ukulele could be $0, 1, 2, \ldots$, so the whole numbers are the appropriate set.

b. A hypotenuse's length could be 1, 1.2, $\sqrt{2}$ (which is irrational), or any other positive number. So the real numbers are the appropriate set.

c. This proportion will be a ratio of integers, as both the total number of people in the class and the number of people who have a cat are integers. So the rational numbers are the appropriate set.

d. We know that the number of people must be a counting number, and since *you* are in the room with yourself, there is at least one person in that room with your birthday. So the natural numbers are the appropriate set.

e. The total revenue will be some number of dollars and cents, such as $631,897.15, which is a terminating decimal and thus a rational number. So the rational numbers are the appropriate set.

A.6.3 Converting Repeating Decimals to Fractions

We have learned that a terminating decimal number is a rational number. It's easy to convert a terminating decimal number into a fraction of integers: you just need to multiply and divide by one of the numbers in the set $\{10, 100, 1000, \ldots\}$. For example, when we say the number 0.123 out loud, we say "one hundred and twenty-three thousandths." While that's a lot to say, it makes it obvious that this number can be written as a ratio:

$$0.123 = \frac{123}{1000}.$$

Similarly,

$$21.28 = \frac{2128}{100} = \frac{532 \cdot 4}{25 \cdot 4} = \frac{532}{25},$$

demonstrating how *any* terminating decimal can be written as a fraction.

Repeating decimals can also be written as a fraction. To understand how, use a calculator to find the decimal for, say, $\frac{73}{99}$ and $\frac{189}{999}$ You will find that

$$\frac{73}{99} = 0.73737373\ldots = 0.\overline{73} \qquad \frac{189}{999} = 0.189189189\ldots = 0.\overline{189}.$$

The pattern is that dividing a number by a number from $\{9, 99, 999, \ldots\}$ with the same number of digits will create a repeating decimal that starts as "0." and then repeats the numerator. We can use this observation to reverse engineer some fractions from repeating decimals.

Checkpoint A.6.8

a. Write the rational number $0.772772772\ldots$ as a fraction.

b. Write the rational number $0.69696969\ldots$ as a fraction.

Explanation.

a. The *three*-digit number 772 repeats after the decimal. So we will make use of the *three*-digit denominator 999. And we have $\frac{772}{999}$.

b. The *two*-digit number 69 repeats after the decimal. So we will make use of the *two*-digit denominator 99. And we have $\frac{69}{99}$. But this fraction can be reduced to $\frac{23}{33}$.

Converting a repeating decimal to a fraction is not always quite this straightforward. There are complications if the number takes a few digits before it begins repeating. For your interest, here is one example on how to do that.

Example A.6.9 Can we convert the repeating decimal $9.134343434\ldots = 9.1\overline{34}$ to a fraction? The trick is to separate its terminating part from its repeating part, like this:

$$9.1 + 0.034343434\ldots.$$

Now note that the terminating part is $\frac{91}{10}$, and the repeating part is almost like our earlier examples, except it has an extra 0 right after the decimal. So we have:

$$\frac{91}{10} + \frac{1}{10} \cdot 0.34343434\ldots.$$

With what we learned in the earlier examples and basic fraction arithmetic, we can continue:

$$9.134343434\ldots = \frac{91}{10} + \frac{1}{10} \cdot 0.34343434\ldots$$

$$= \frac{91}{10} + \frac{1}{10} \cdot \frac{34}{99}$$

$$= \frac{91}{10} + \frac{34}{990}$$

$$= \frac{91 \cdot 99}{10 \cdot 99} + \frac{34}{990}$$

$$= \frac{9009}{990} + \frac{34}{990} = \frac{9043}{990}$$

Check that this is right by entering $\frac{9043}{990}$ into a calculator and seeing if it returns the decimal we started with, $9.134343434\ldots$.

A.6.4 Exercises

Review and Warmup Write the decimal number as a fraction.

1. 0.55
2. 0.65
3. 7.65
4. 8.35
5. 0.992
6. 0.164

Write the fraction as a decimal number.

7. a. $\frac{1}{5}$

    b. $\frac{18}{25}$

8. a. $\frac{2}{5}$

    b. $\frac{21}{25}$

Write the mixed number as a decimal number.

9. a. $6\frac{5}{8} = $ [   ]

    b. $7\frac{9}{16} = $ [   ]

10. a. $3\frac{5}{16} = $ [   ]

    b. $9\frac{3}{5} = $ [   ]

Set Notation

11. There are two numbers that you can square to get 36. Express this collection of two numbers using set notation.

12. There are four positive, even, one-digit numbers. Express this collection of four numbers using set notation.

13. There are six two-digit perfect square numbers. Express this collection of six numbers using set notation.

14. There is a set of three small positive integers where you can square all three numbers, then add the results, and get 77. Express this collection of three numbers using set notation.

Types of Numbers Which of the following are whole numbers? There may be more than one correct answer.

15.
  ☐ -3 ☐ $\sqrt{4}$ ☐ $\frac{8}{29}$
  ☐ $-9.101001000100001\ldots$ ☐ $2.2\overline{39}$
  ☐ 48 ☐ $\sqrt{6}$ ☐ -61751

16.
  ☐ 3.419 ☐ -8 ☐ $\sqrt{6}$
  ☐ 60991 ☐ $6.8\overline{16}$ ☐ -52858
  ☐ 14 ☐ π

Which of the following are integers? There may be more than one correct answer.

17.
- ☐ 79
- ☐ −71143
- ☐ −5.101001000100001...
- ☐ 1.8$\overline{37}$
- ☐ −4
- ☐ $\frac{7}{73}$
- ☐ $\sqrt{10}$
- ☐ 2738

18.
- ☐ −8
- ☐ −35072
- ☐ π
- ☐ $-\frac{10}{79}$
- ☐ 44
- ☐ 3.101001000100001...
- ☐ 0
- ☐ −3.877

Which of the following are rational numbers? There may be more than one correct answer.

19.
- ☐ −3
- ☐ π
- ☐ 10
- ☐ $\sqrt{10}$
- ☐ $\frac{7}{82}$
- ☐ $\sqrt{25}$
- ☐ −26179
- ☐ −6.897

20.
- ☐ π
- ☐ $\sqrt{11}$
- ☐ −8
- ☐ $\frac{6}{73}$
- ☐ 74
- ☐ 27783
- ☐ −17285
- ☐ 6.5$\overline{40}$

Which of the following are irrational numbers? There may be more than one correct answer.

21.
- ☐ −7.955
- ☐ $\frac{4}{77}$
- ☐ −3
- ☐ 0
- ☐ $\sqrt{13}$
- ☐ −8392
- ☐ 40
- ☐ π

22.
- ☐ −8
- ☐ −9.315
- ☐ π
- ☐ $\sqrt{49}$
- ☐ 5
- ☐ $\sqrt{11}$
- ☐ −99499
- ☐ 8.2$\overline{60}$

Which of the following are real numbers? There may be more than one correct answer.

23.
- ☐ 52827
- ☐ $\sqrt{6}$
- ☐ 70
- ☐ π
- ☐ −1.861
- ☐ −90606
- ☐ −5.3$\overline{95}$
- ☐ −3

24.
- ☐ 0
- ☐ −5.939
- ☐ 7.2$\overline{96}$
- ☐ 36
- ☐ $\sqrt{2}$
- ☐ 7.101001000100001...
- ☐ −86767
- ☐ −8

Determine the validity of each statement by selecting True or False.

25.

(a) The number $\sqrt{3}$ is rational

(b) The number $\frac{-\sqrt{11}}{37\sqrt{11}}$ is irrational

(c) The number 0 is a natural number

(d) The number 0 is an integer

(e) The number 5 is an integer, but not a whole number

26.

(a) The number $\sqrt{4}$ is a real number, but not a rational number

(b) The number 0.783144040040004000004... is rational

(c) The number $\sqrt{2^2}$ is a real number, but not a rational number

(d) The number 0.900900900900900... is rational

(e) The number $\frac{23}{17}$ is rational, but not a natural number

27. In each situation, which number set do you think is most appropriate?

a. The number of dogs a student has owned throughout their lifetime.

This number is best considered as a   (□ natural number   □ whole number   □ integer   □ rational number   □ irrational number   □ real number) .

b. The difference between the projected annual expenditures and the actual annual expenditures for a given company.

This number is best considered as a   (□ natural number   □ whole number   □ integer   □ rational number   □ irrational number   □ real number) .

c. The length around swimming pool in the shape of a half circle with radius 10 ft.

This number is best considered as a   (□ natural number   □ whole number   □ integer   □ rational number   □ irrational number   □ real number) .

d. The proportion of students at a college who own a car.

This number is best considered as a   (□ natural number   □ whole number   □ integer   □ rational number   □ irrational number   □ real number) .

e. The width of a sheet of paper, in inches.

This number is best considered as a   (□ natural number   □ whole number   □ integer   □ rational number   □ irrational number   □ real number) .

f. The number of people eating in a non-empty restaurant.

This number is best considered as a   (□ natural number   □ whole number   □ integer   □ rational number   □ irrational number   □ real number) .

28.

a. Give an example of a whole number that is not an integer.

b. Give an example of an integer that is not a whole number.

c. Give an example of a rational number that is not an integer.

d. Give an example of a irrational number.

e. Give an example of a irrational number that is also an integer.

Writing Decimals as Fractions

29. Write the rational number 6.16 as a fraction.

30. Write the rational number 74.973 as a fraction.

31. Write the rational number $0.\overline{79} = 0.7979\ldots$ as a fraction.

32. Write the rational number $0.\overline{936} = 0.936936\ldots$ as a fraction.

33. Write the rational number $7.9\overline{13} = 7.91313\ldots$ as a fraction.

34. Write the rational number $2.6\overline{218} = 2.6218218\ldots$ as a fraction.

Challenge

35. Imagine making up a number with the following pattern. After the decimal point, write the natural numbers 1, 2, 3, 4, 5, etc. The decimal digits will extend forever with this pattern: $0.12345\ldots$.

Is the number a rational number or an irrational number?   (□ rational   □ irrational)

Appendix B

Unit Conversions

Units of Length in the US/Imperial System	Units of Length in the Metric System	System to System Length Conversions
1 foot (ft) = 12 inches (in)	1 meter (m) = 1000 millimeters (mm)	1 inch (in) = 2.54 centimeters (cm)
1 yard (yd) = 3 feet (ft)	1 meter (m) = 100 centimeters (cm)	1 meter (m) ≈ 3.281 feet (ft)
1 yard (yd) = 36 inches (in)	1 meter (m) = 10 decimeters (dm)	1 meter (m) ≈ 1.094 yard (yd)
1 mile (mi) = 5280 feet (ft)	1 dekameter (dam) = 10 meters (m)	1 mile (mi) ≈ 1.609 kilometer (km)
	1 hectometer (hm) = 100 meters (m)	
	1 kilometer (km) = 1000 meters (m)	

Table B.0.1: Length Unit Conversion Factors

Units of Area in the US/Imperial System	Units of Area in the Metric System	System to System Area Conversions
1 acre = 43560 square feet (ft^2)	1 hectare (ha) = 10000 square meters (m^2)	1 hectare (ha) ≈ 2.471 acres
640 acres = 1 square mile (mi^2)	100 hectares (ha) = 1 square kilometer (km^2)	

Table B.0.2: Area Unit Conversion Factors

Units of Volume in the US/Imperial System	Units of Volume in the Metric System	System to System Volume Conversions
1 tablespoon (tbsp) = 3 teaspoon (tsp)	1 cubic centimeter (cc) = 1 cubic centimeter (cm^3)	1 cubic inch (in^3) ≈ 16.39 milliliters (mL)
1 fluid ounce (fl oz) = 2 tablespoons (tbsp)	1 milliliter (mL) = 1 cubic centimeter (cm^3)	1 fluid ounce (fl oz) ≈ 29.57 milliliters (mL)
1 cup (c) = 8 fluid ounces (fl oz)	1 liter (L) = 1000 milliliters (mL)	1 liter (L) ≈ 1.057 quarts (qt)
1 pint (pt) = 2 cups (c)	1 liter (L) = 1000 cubic centimeters (cm^3)	1 gallon (gal) ≈ 3.785 liters (L)
1 quart (qt) = 2 pints (pt)		
1 gallon (gal) = 4 quarts (qt)		
1 gallon (gal) = 231 cubic inches (in^3)		

Table B.0.3: Volume Unit Conversion Factors

Units of Mass/Weight in the US/Imperial System	Units of Mass/Weight in the Metric System	System to System Mass/Weight Conversions
1 pound (lb) = 16 ounces (oz)	1 gram (g) = 1000 milligrams (mg)	1 ounce (oz) ≈ 28.35 grams (g)
1 ton (T) = 2000 pounds (lb)	1 gram (g) = 1000 kilograms (kg)	1 kilogram (kg) ≈ 2.205 pounds (lb)
	1 metric ton (t) = 1000 kilograms (kg)	

Table B.0.4: Weight/Mass Unit Conversion Factors

Precise Units of Time	Imprecise Units of Time	Units of Time in the Metric System
1 week (wk) = 7 days (d)	1 year (yr) ≈ 12 months (mo)	1 second (s) = 1000 milliseconds (ms)
1 day (d) = 24 hours (h)	1 year (yr) ≈ 52 weeks (wk)	1 second (s) = 10^6 microseconds (μs)
1 hour (h) = 60 minutes (min)	1 year (yr) ≈ 365 days (d)	1 second (s) = 10^9 nanoseconds (ns)
1 minute (min) = 60 seconds (s)	1 month (mo) ≈ 30 days (d)	

Table B.0.5: Time Unit Conversion Factors

1 byte (B) = 8 bits (b)	1 kilobit (kb) = 1024 bits (b)
1 kilobyte (kB) = 1024 bytes (B)	1 megabit (Mb) = 1024 kilobits (kb)
1 megabyte (MB) = 1024 kilobytes (kB)	
1 gigabyte (GB) = 1024 megabytes (MB)	
1 terabyte (TB) = 1024 gigabytes (GB)	

Table B.0.6: Computer Storage/Memory Conversion Factors

Index

Made in the USA
Middletown, DE
23 August 2019